Book of Literary
Anecdotes

The Wordsworth
Book of Literary Anecdotes

–

Robert Hendrickson

Wordsworth Reference

First published 1990 by Facts on File, Inc, New York.

This edition published 1997 by Wordsworth Editions Ltd.
Cumberland House, Crib Street, Ware, Hertfordshire SG12 9ET.

Copyright © 1990 by Robert Hendrickson.

ISBN 1-85326-387-7

Printed and bound in Great Britain by Mackays of Chatham PLC.

For my grandson, Brian

CONTENTS

INTRODUCTION

INTRODUCTION

No nation has rivalled Great Britain in the quantity and quality of her literary wits. After reading over the past decade or so thousands of ripostes and drolleries, I'd have to say that Richard Brinsley Sheridan is my favourite among them - and my nomination for the world's greatest literary wit - but the supply of wit is so plentiful that, had the British Empire depended on it for survival, the sun would never have set on that institution. Wilde, Shaw, Dr. Johnson, Goldsmith, Wilkes, Swift, Pope, Foote, Rogers, Disraeli, Jerrold, Sydney Smith, Churchill, Margot Asquith, Beerbohm, Coward, Waugh, Connolly - these are only a few of the great ones who come randomly to mind. Indeed, although I believe this is the most wide-ranging book on the subject so far, I could have doubled its present size. But though this book records at great length the words and deeds of all those so quick with a quip that they make tremble those of us who conceive our best ripostes while going down the stairs, it is not devoted entirely to great wits and their *bon mots*. Our subject is also the touching, even (horror of horrors!) the sentimental story, and of course the literary curiosity that British readers in particular have found amusing since long before Disraeli's father devoted a book to them. There are thousands of these here, too, and I think the reader will be as diverted by them as by the stiletto wit and droll humour of the great British wits who could murder with a few words.

I have included in these few pages writers from several countries belonging to the Commonwealth of Nations, including Canada, Australia and New Zealand, because of their traditional association with Great Britain; similarly, though I am open to criticism here, too, I have included Irish authors who wrote before the creation of the Republic of Ireland. Otherwise British citizenship has been the price of admission, which leaves out Auden and Whistler but lets in James and T.S. Eliot (the only exception here being P.G. Wodehouse, an American citizen in his late years, who, along with his butler Jeeves, is so quintessentially British that my conscience wouldn't permit me to put him anywhere else). I should note that in a few instances anecdotes about people not known primarily as writers have been included, if the anecdotes have literary merit. I'd also like to request readers to send along anecdotes, especially unpublished stories, for possible inclusion in future editions.

The basic ground rules for this collection, gleaned from hundreds of books and hundreds of millions of words, are, first, I've scrupulously tried to exclude anecdotes of living writers and anecdotes of deceased writers that could hurt anyone remaining behind. Writers and their relatives have trouble enough, and John Aubrey is generally right, I think, when he says of his marvellous "rude and hastie collection," *Brief Lives*, that before literary anecdotes are "fitt to lett flie abroad" the "author and the Persons ...ought to be rotten first." Second, I should say that my collection too is "rude and hastie," though I hope hastier than rude; in any case, I tried to be as brief as possible with each entry so that there would be room for more entries. This meant sometimes condensing or paraphrasing what I would have preferred to quote at length, but I hope that in most cases I've managed to get the essence of the author and anecdote. Third, I've tried to indicate when a story is doubtful, or when it has been told about several writers, though I doubtless missed some anecdotes I should have labelled apocryphal (despite checking one or more biographies for most stories). Finally, I've tried to include stories and very brief sketches of all the major British literary figures and represent all the noted literary wits among these with an ample selection of their *bon mots*, but I haven't hesitated to include authors remembered just for their last words or epitaphs. I hope in this last case that the stories may lead readers to the forgotten work of some very deserving writers.

It should be added that this book, which ranges from prehistoric to present times, is arranged alphabetically by author, but has a name and place index, which includes writers mentioned in the text but who haven't an entry themselves. There is also a topic index enabling readers to find one or more anecdotes about certain subjects, such as accidentally destroyed manuscripts, literary hoaxes, love affairs, hard-drinking authors, strange deaths etc etc.

My thanks to my editor, Gerry Helferich, and copy editor Gloria McDarrah, both of whom made valuable contributions to this work. I would also like to thank the people, too numerous to mention here, who suggested anecdotes to me through the years, particularly those correspondents who wrote them from all over the world (including one from Saudi Arabia, whose address I've lost and to whom I can't write to thank) providing me with more literary hors-d'oeuvres after my *Literary Life and Other Curiosities* was published in 1980. But, of course, all the errors herein are my responsibility. I can't even blame them on my wife, Marilyn, who worked as hard on this book as I did but who would be "she who hung the moon and the stars" to me if she neither worked upon nor even read a word of my deathless prose.

Robert Hendrickson

Lascelles Abercrombie (1881–1938)

Ezra Pound once formally challenged the poet and critic to a duel because his alleged "stupidity" (Abercrombie didn't like Pound's work) was "a public menace." The small, slight Abercrombie could hardly see even with his thick glasses and knew he was no match for Pound, a fencing master. But this time his wit proved a better rapier than his opponent's. The fight to the death never materialized because Abercrombie insisted that he had the choice of weapons and chose to have a real "literary duel," to have the duelists "bombard each other with unsold copies of our own books."

∇ ∇ ∇

Joseph Addison (1672–1719)

The author lent a large sum to his friend Temple Stangan but found that ever since Stangan had gone into his debt he meekly agreed with everything Addison said, never arguing as he frequently had in the past. This went on week after week, much to Addison's displeasure, until one day he could stand it no longer and exploded: "Damn it, either contradict me, sir, or pay me my money!"

Addison, founder of *The Spectator*, was a total loss as a public speaker. He once attempted a speech in the House of Commons, beginning: "Mr. Speaker, I conceive—I conceive, sire—sir, I conceive..." He was at this point interrupted by a member who quipped: "The right honorable secretary of state has conceived thrice, and brought forth nothing."

Addison liked to end sentences with prepositions—at least he wrote a good many of them that way—and sentences ending with prepositions are therefore said to have "Addisonian terminations." Interestingly, Richard Hurd, the testy critic who invented "Addisonian termination," is heard of no more today, while Addison's work, dangling prepositions and all, still survives.

His last words were spoken to his stepson, Lord Warwick: "See in what peace a Christian can die."

∇ ∇ ∇

Æ (George William Russell; 1867–1935)

Russell's unusual pen name was a contraction of the word "aeon" (or eon), which he had for some reason once used as a signature. At a literary gathering in Hamburg Æ was offered a drink. "No, thank you, "the Irish poet said, "I was born intoxicated."

Robert Ainsworth (1660–1743)

This determined lexicographer believed that Latin and other foreign languages could best be taught through speech and so published a Latin-English dictionary, *Thesaurus Linguae Latinae Compendiarius* (1736), which long remained a standard work. The book took him over 22 years to write, largely because he had to rewrite a major part of it that his wife maliciously set on fire while they were arguing about some household matter.

∇ ∇ ∇

Richard Aldington (1892–1962)

The poet, novelist and literary critic reviewed a dadaist book containing a poem that in its entirety went:

```
A B C D E F
G H I J K L
M N O P Q R
S T U V W X
    Y Z
```

His unprinted review of the book (the *Times* rejected it) was:

```
1 2 3 4 5
6 7 8 9 10
```

In 1919 Aldington was asked by an American magazine to write an article choosing five writers who would become world famous in the future. Aldington chose James Joyce, T.S. Eliot, D.H. Lawrence, Aldous Huxley and Marcel Proust, but his article was rejected by the editor, who wrote him, "For God's sake, Richard, can't you think of somebody who has been heard of or is even likely to be heard of?"

∇ ∇ ∇

Alfred the Great (848–899?)

The king of England, or the West Saxons, was a precocious child who was sent to Rome to be confirmed at the age of five and was "hallowed...as king" by the much impressed pope. Alfred is heralded as the originator of prose translations from Latin into idiomatic English and as the reviver of learning in his kingdom. His motto was "My will was to live worthily as long as I lived, and after my life to leave to them that should come after, my memory in good works." Early in his life the future king displayed a love of books he would never lose. One day his mother showed him and his brothers an illuminated volume of Saxon poetry. "Whichever of you can soonest learn this volume," she said, "to him will I give it." Alfred responded long before his older brothers. "Will you really give that book to that one of us who can first understand and repeat it to you?" he asked. "Yes," his mother said, "that I will," and, in the words of a historian of the day, he "took the book out of her hand, and went to his master and learned it by heart, whereupon he brought it back to his mother and recited it."

Noted for the restoration of letters in England, Alfred is also remembered by the group of learned men called Alfred's Scholars that he gathered around him. According to legend, he once took refuge in a peasant's hut where the housewife, not recognizing him in his disguise of rags, instructed him to watch some cakes by the fire. When he drifted off and allowed the cakes to burn, she scolded him as an idle and useless wretch.

∇ ∇ ∇

John André (1751–1780)
Major André fancied himself a poet. On the same day that the fabled British Revolutionary War spy was captured, while he was carrying Benedict Arnold's documents for the plan to surrender West Point, the following jingle that André had written appeared in the Loyalist *Royal Gazette* in New York City.

And now I've closed my epic strain
 I tremble as I show it
Lest the same warrior drover, Wayne
 Should ever catch the poet.

Earlier that day, before the poem appeared, Anthony Wayne had been charged with André's execution.

∇ ∇ ∇

Anonymous
A popular admonition to authors in college English composition classes is the anonymous "Avoid Latin derivatives; use brief, terse Anglo-Saxon monosyllables." The only Anglo-Saxon word in the admonition is "Anglo-Saxon."

The name of its author has been lost, but this book dedication, which is about as abject, servile and groveling as a book dedication can get, has survived him:

To the Right Honorable the Earl of Breadalbane. May it please your lordship, with overpowering sentiments of the most profound humility, I prostrate myself at your noble feet, while I offer to your lordship's high consideration these very feeble attempts to describe the indescribable and ineffable beauties of your lordship's delicious estate of Edinample. With tumid emotions of heart-distending pride, and with fervescent feelings of gratitude, I beg leave to acknowledge the honor I have to serve so noble a master, and the many advantages which I, in common with your lordship's other menials, enjoy from the exuberance of your princely liberality. That your lordship may long shine with refulgent brilliancy in the exalted station to which Providence has raised you, and that your noble family, like a bright constellation, may diffuse a splendor and glory through the high sphere of their attraction, is the fervent prayer of your lordship's most humble and most devoted servant.

Notorious as the judge who held the "Bloody Assizes" after Monmouth's Rebellion was put down, George Jeffreys himself was arrested three years later and died in the Tower of London. A number of anecdotes, possibly apocryphal, circulated about him. One time he was supposed to have pointed his cane at an unknown poet about to be tried. "There is a rogue at the end of my cane," he said. "At which end, my Lord?" the poet asked.

This epitaph for an editor can be found in an English churchyard:

Here lies an editor!
Snooks if you will;
In mercy, Kind Providence,
Let him lie still!
He lied for his living: so
He lived while he lied:
When he could not lie longer,
He lied down and died.

Perhaps the best rule for literary punctuation is the old, anonymous maxim of typesetters: "Set type as long as you can hold your breath without getting blue in the face, then put in a comma; when you yawn, put in a semicolon; and when you want to sneeze, that's the time for a paragraph."

No one really knows who wrote Great Britain's national anthem, "God Save the King," which was first sung in public in 1745. Its melody has since been appropriated for patriotic songs by 19 other countries, including Germany and the United States.

News is conveyed by letter, word or mouth
And comes to us from North, East, West and South.

Contrary to the old anonymous rhyme above, which helped popularize the myth, the word *news* wasn't coined from the first letters of the major points of the compass. The word was originally spelled *newes* and derives from the Old English word *niwes*, meaning "new." The legend possibly originated because old newspapers printed a replica of the globe with compass points on their masthead. But the word is much older than the earliest newspapers.

Christopher Anstey (1724–1805)

This poet, creator of the adventures of Squire Blunderhead, was a distinguished student at King's College, Cambridge. He was refused the degree of master of arts that he earned, however, because he made a speech to his fellow students about his teachers, beginning: "Doctors without doctrine, masters of art without arts, and bachelors more powerful with the rod than worthy of the laurel..."

▽ ▽ ▽

Eugene Aram (1704–1759)

A self-taught philologist who was the first to identify the Celtic language as Indo-European, Aram had been at work on a comparative dictionary of all European tongues when he was accused of murder. A skeleton was unearthed in his hometown of Knaresborough and a man named Thomas Houseman confessed that he had been present when Aram murdered his close friend Daniel Clark, as well as another man named Terry, and buried them at St. Robert's Cave. A second skeleton was dug up near the cave and the scholar soon confessed his guilt, claiming that Clark had cuckolded him. Aram tried to commit suicide on the night before his execution by opening the veins in his arm, but he was saved for the hangman. His story was romanticized by Thomas Hood in his poem "The Dream of Eugene Aram" and became the basis for several novels.

▽ ▽ ▽

William Archer (1856–1924)

The Scottish author, who spent a large part of his childhood in Norway and became an authority on Ibsen as well as a dramatist in his own right, believed for a short time that he might join the company of Coleridge and Stevenson (q.q.v.), to whom masterpieces had come in their dreams. Waking from a deep sleep, he thought he had dreamed a perfect drama complete with compelling plot and characters. All he had to do was remember his dream and write it down. Soon he fell back into a peaceful sleep, awakening the next morning with the play clear in his mind. One examining it, however, he found that he had dreamed *Hedda Gabler*.

▽ ▽ ▽

Matthew Arnold (1822–1888)

A cold, reserved man with uncompromisingly severe standards, the poet and critic wrote part of his devastatingly pessimistic "Dover Beach" on his honeymoon. One time a child asked Arnold, also a government education official, to read to her. "It surprises me very much that a little girl of six should not know how to read, and expects to be read to," he said, putting on his most serious tone. "It is disgraceful, and you must promise me to learn at once. If you don't, I shall have to put your father and mother in prison." The child did learn to read in a few weeks.

Remarked Robert Louis Stevenson when Arnold died: "Poor Matt. He's gone to heaven, no doubt—but he won't like God."

▽ ▽ ▽

Oscar Asche (1872–1936)
Australian Oscar Asche, a musical comedy star and writer who made a tidy fortune on the stage, lived to see his name become Australian rhyming slang for cash. "Oscar Asche" for "cash" was eventually shortened to "Oscar," making him probably the only writer whose forename means money in a generic sense.

The Australian dramatist wasn't playing well on a difficult Scottish golf course. "But I guess you've seen worse players," he told his old caddy. Thinking the man didn't hear him when no reply came forth, he repeated himself: "I said 'I guess you've seen worse players.'"

"I heard ye afore," the caddy said. "I was just considerin'."

▽ ▽ ▽

John Ash (1727–1779)
Dr. Johnson included in his *Dictionary* as the derivation of the word "curmudgeon," the French *coeur méchant*, or wicked heart. Since the derivation came from an anonymous letter he attributed it to an "unknown correspondent." When John Ash published his *New and Complete Dictionary of the English Language* 20 years later in 1775, he included Johnson's derivation, but he gave it as: "curmudgeon," derived from *coeur*, "unknown," and *méchant*, "correspondent."

▽ ▽ ▽

Daisy Ashford (1881–1972)
An English girl who was a favorite of playwright James Barrie, Daisy Ashford wrote a humorous novel in 1890 at the age of nine. *The Young Visitors*, not published until 1919, sold over 200,000 copies, and critics called the book a deft portrayal of Victorian society, offering penetrating commentary on the era's shortcomings, and that her characters compared favorably with those of Dickens. Although Daisy was renowned in her time, she never wrote another book, publishing only a few stories—written before her novel.

Margot Asquith (Countess of Oxford and Asquith; 1864–1945)

The countess of Oxford, a noted wit and author, was obsessed with writing obituaries and constantly practiced the art. Once she was staying with Arthur James Balfour. After she left, the British statesman found in the guest room a sheet of paper written in her hand with the lead: "So Arthur Balfour is dead…"

Once Margot Asquith was introduced to American movie star Jean Harlow, who in addressing her mispronounced her name to rhyme with *marplot.* "The *t,*" advised an acid Lady Asquith, "is silent, as in Harlow."

∇ ∇ ∇

Nancy Witcher Astor (Viscountess Astor; 1879–1964)

"Lady Astor, I must tell you that I do not approve of female politicians," Field Marshall Montgomery told her. "That's all right," the political leader and patron of the arts replied. "The only General I approve of is Evangeline Booth."

While running for a parliamentary seat from Plymouth (she became the first woman to sit in Parliament), Lady Astor made a house-to-house appeal for votes in the company of a naval officer. Knocking at one door she asked a little girl who answered if her mother was at home. "No," the child replied, "but she said if a lady comes with a sailor they're to use the upstairs room and leave ten bob."

∇ ∇ ∇

W.H. (Wystan Hugh) Auden (1907–1973)

The British-born Auden became a U.S. citizen in 1946 and is therefore covered at length in *American Literary Anecdotes,* but he deserves here at least one anecdote from the early years in England. It seems that he was first inspired to become a poet, quite suddenly, while walking in a ploughed field with a friend when he was 15. "Tell me, do you write poetry?" the friend asked. "I never had, and said so," Auden later remembered, "but I knew from that very moment what I wished to do."

∇ ∇ ∇

Jane Austen (1775–1817)

Jane Austen's *Sense and Sensibility* wasn't published until 1811, its composition attributed to "a Lady." But the novel was written in 1797 as the revision of a sketch called *Elinor and Marianne* written when the author was 20. Jane Austen wrote her first work, *Love and Friendship*, when only 14. Very shy about her writing, she wrote on small pieces of paper that could easily be slipped under the desk blotter if anyone came into the room.

She confided to her niece, Anna Austen, that for a novel "3 or 4 families in a Country Village is the very thing to work on." To her nephew J. Edward Austen she wrote of "the little bit (two Inches wide) of Ivory on which I work with so fine a brush, as produces little effect after much labour."

An official suggested that she write "an historical romance, illustrative of the history of the House of Coburg..." She replied:

> ...I am fully sensible that an historical romance, founded on the House of Saxe Coburg, might be much more to the purpose of profit or popularity than such pictures of domestic life in country villages as I deal in. But I could no more write a romance than an epic poem. I could not seriously sit down to write a serious romance under any other motive than to save my life; and if it were indispensable for me to keep it up and never relax into laughing at myself or other people, I am sure I would be hung before I had finished the first chapter. No, I must keep to my own style and go on in my own way...

Sir Walter Scott wrote of her in his journal of March 14, 1826: "[Miss Austen] had a talent for describing the involvements and feelings and characters of ordinary life which is to me the most wonderful I have ever met with. The Big Bow-Wow strain I can do myself like any now going; but the exquisite touch, which renders ordinary commonplace things and characters interesting, from the truth of the description and the sentiment, is denied to me."

English author Mary Russell Mitford mentioned her in an 1815 letter to a friend: "I have discovered that our great favourite, Miss Austen, is my country-woman...with whom mamma before her marriage was acquainted. Mamma says that she was then the prettiest, silliest, most affected, husband-hunting butterfly she ever remembers."

A merchant is said to have rented the Winchester house where Jane Austen lived and converted it into a shop. After a few months he asked his landlord, the trustees of Winchester College, to put a commemorative plaque on the premises. "American tourists keep coming into my shop to ask if it's the Jane Austen house," he complained. "They take up my time and it's a great nuisance." Soon the trustees complied, providing a plaque that read: Home of Jane Austen 1775–1817. But two weeks later the man was back demanding that they take down the plaque. "Didn't it help?" the trustees asked. "Twice as many people are bothering me now," the shopkeeper replied. "Only now they are Englishmen. They keep coming in to ask, 'Who was Jane Austen?'"

∇ ∇ ∇

Alfred Austin (1835–1913)

The waspish Austin's appointment as poet laureate in 1896 met with widespread criticism, for his 20 or so volumes of poetry had been much derided and parodied. Things did not change when "Jameson's Ride," his first ode as poet laureate, was published in *The Times* on January 11, 1896, two weeks after the abortive Jameson Raid on Johannesburg. It began:

> Let lawyers and statesmen
>   addle
> Their pates over points of
>   law:
> If sound be our sword, and
>   saddle,
> And gun-gear, who cares one
>   straw? ...

Lord Salisbury's explanation of why Austin was chosen poet laureate in 1896 hardly constituted a good recommendation: "I gave it to him because no one else applied."

"I dare not alter these things," Austin explained when criticized for the grammatical errors in his poems, "they come to me from above."

∇ ∇ ∇ ∇ ∇ ∇ ∇ ∇ ∇

Francis Bacon (First Baron Verulam, Viscount St. Albans; 1561–1626)

A witty murderer was brought before Bacon when he served as England's lord chancellor in 1618. "Your honor should let me go," the man said. "We're kin. My name is Hogg, and Hogg is kin to bacon."

"Not until it's hung," Bacon replied.

Hearing the prophecy "When hemp is spun, England's done," Bacon, despite his scientific training, gave the following interpretation of it, which he had heard as a child. *Hempe*, he explained, is an acrostic, a word formed from the first letters of the names of five of England's rulers: Henry, Edward, Mary with Philips, and Elizabeth. When the last one of them, Elizabeth, died in 1603—when Hempe was spun, or finished—England was done, for the new king, James, was not called king of England, but the king of Great Britain and Ireland.

The making of long words was a popular game in Elizabethan England and *honorificabilitudinity*, meaning "honorableness," was one of the most absurd ones made. Shakespeare made fun of this word by stretching it out still longer in *Love's Labour's Lost*, using its original Latin ablative plural when he has Costard the clown say to the servant Moth: "I marvel thy master hath not eaten thee for a word, for thou art not so long by the head as *honorificabilitudinitatibus.*" This is the word that to some "prove" Bacon was the author of all plays attributed to Shakespeare. For it rearranged letters from the Latin sentence *Hi ludi F. Baconis nati tuiti orbi*, which says, translated: "These plays born of F. Bacon are preserved for the world."

When he was lord chancellor, Bacon had words in the Exchequer court with the great jurist Attorney General Sir Edward Coke.
Said Coke: "Mr. Bacon, if you have any tooth against me, pluck it out, or it will do you more hurt than all the teeth in your head will do you good."
Bacon answered coolly: "Mr. Attorney, I respect you; I fear you not; and the less you speak fo your own greatness, the more I shall think of it."

Heyward's *The Life of Henry IV* enraged Queen Elizabeth and she asked Bacon if there was not treason in the book.
"No, madam, I cannot answer for there being treason in it," Bacon said, "but I am certain it contains much felony."
"How? How and wherein?" Elizabeth demanded.
"In many passages which he has stolen from Tacitus," Bacon replied.

In 1621 Lord Chancellor Bacon was charged before the House of Lords with bribery and confessed that he had been guilty of "corruption and neglect" but had never perverted justice. When a committee of the House of Lords asked him if he stood by his confession, he replied: "It is my act, my hand, my heart: I beseech your lordships to be merciful to a broken reed."

John le Carré did not originate the term *mole*, for "an undercover agent in the enemy camp," says retired intelligence officer Walter L. Pforzheimer. According to a news feature in the *New York Times* (February 7, 1984), Mr. Pforzheimer's extensive library of spy literature contains a rare Elizabethan manuscript that proves the term was coined by Bacon. The sense behind the term, of course, is that a mole burrows underground and sleeps there for long periods.

Bacon once wrote that he had "taken all knowledge to be [his] province." *Chambers Cyclopaedia of English Literature*...gives the following account of his death:

> His devotion to science appears to have been the immediate cause of his death. Travelling his his carriage when there was snow on the ground, he began to consider whether flesh might not be preserved by snow as well as by salt. In order to make the experiment he alighted at a cottage near Highgate, bought a hen, and stuffed it with snow. This so chilled him that he was unable to return home, but went to the Earl of Arundel's house in the neighborhood, where his illness was so much increased by the dampness of the bed into which he was put that he died in a few days...In a letter to the earl, the last which he wrote, after comparing himself to the elder Pliny, "who lost his life by trying an experiment about the burning of Mount Vesuvius," he does not forget to mention his own experiment, which, says he, "succeeded admirably."

▽ ▽ ▽

Enid Bagnold (1889–1981)

The author of *National Velvet* (1935) and *The Chalk Garden* (1955) wrote in her *Autobiography* (1969) that she lost her virginity to the legendary lecher Frank Harris (of whom Oscar Wilde said, "He has no feelings. It is the secret of his success") when they were colleagues on an English magazine. Wrote Miss Bagnold: "'Sex,' said Frank Harris, 'is the gateway to life.' So I went through the gateway in an upper room of the Cafe-Royal."

▽ ▽ ▽

Matthew Baillie (1761–1823)

The noted physician, who wrote the first systematic text on postmortems, was physician to George III and was the brother of Scottish poet and playwright Joanna Baillie (Sir Walter Scott's "immortal Joanna"). Baillie could conduct literary dissections as cutting as his medical ones. "Doctor," prolific dramatist Frederick Reynolds asked him one time, "don't you think I write too much for my nervous system?"

"No, I don't," Baillie replied, "but I think you write too much for your reputation."

William Baldwin (d. 1563)

A poet, printer and preacher, Baldwin wrote what some consider the first English novel, a religious satire called *Beware the Cat* that was completed in 1553 but not published until 1570. Baldwin, who died of the black plague that swept England, in 1556 wrote a verse play featuring 62 characters, each of whose names began with the letter *L*. (See JOHN HEYWOOD.)

▽ ▽ ▽

Peter Bales (1547–c. 1610)

One of the inventors of shorthand writing and the author of several books on the subject, Bales was also a noted calligraphist. Diarist John Evelyn tells us that the dexterous author wrote "the Lord's Prayer, The Creed, Decalogue, with two short prayers in Latin, his own name, motto, day of the month, year of the Lord, and reign of the queen, to whom he presented it at Hampton Court, all of it written within the circle of a single penny, incased in a ring and borders of gold, and covered with a crystal, so accurately wrought as to be very plainly legible, to the great admiration of her majesty…"

▽ ▽ ▽

William Banting (1797–1878)

Banting might have made a fortune had he published his book on dieting a century later, in our weight-conscious era. As it turned out, he merely amused Londoners in the mid 1860s, although his name did become a word. Banting was an enormously overweight cabinetmaker and undertaker who couldn't bend to tie his shoelaces and had to walk downstairs backward to relieve the pressure on his legs. Convinced by his own discomfort, and perhaps from his undertaking activities, that many deaths resulted from overeating, he went on a strict diet, losing 46 pounds and taking 12 inches off his waist. As so many dieters do, he then wrote a book about his experience, setting forth his method of reducing. *Bantingism* called for a meat diet and abstention from practically everything else—beer, butter, sugar, farinaceous foods and even vegetables. Needless to say, it wasn't popular very long, but Londoners humorously took too calling dieting *banting* and to diet *to bant*. Anyway, *banting* didn't hurt Banting, for he lived to the ripe old age of 81 before another undertaker got his business.

▽ ▽ ▽

Robert Barker (fl. 1632)

Barker and his partner Martin Lucas, the king's printers in London in 1632, printed 1,000 copies of what is known as the Wicked Bible, so called because they omitted the word *not* in the seventh commandment, making it read "Thou shalt commit adultery." The printers were prosecuted for their mistake and fined

£3,000. The Wicked Bible is also called the Adulterous Bible and the Unrighteous Bible.

∇ ∇ ∇

Barnabe Barnes (1569?–1609)

Elizabethan dramatists may have killed more people (in their plays) than anyone up to the politicians and generals of World War I. Though the son of the bishop of Durham, Barnes was a particularly violent example, his play *The Divil's Charter*, for instance, showing us Lucrezia Borgia murdered with something called "poison face wash." A violent streak ran through Barnes's personal life. In 1598 he tried to kill the recorder of Berwick with poisoned wine, and was prosecuted by the Star Chamber, but he somehow managed to evade sentencing, escaping to the North. It has been suggested that he might be the "rival poet" of Shakespeare's sonnets.

∇ ∇ ∇

Sir James Matthew Barrie (1860–1937)

Peter Pan, the boy who refused to grow up, has been familiar to readers and theatergoers for several generations, and we now use his name to describe a person who retains in mature years the naturalness of spirit and charm associated with childhood, or one who absolutely refuses to escape from the comfortable irresponsibility of childhood. Barrie introduced his immortal character on the stage in the play *Peter Pan* (1904), although the fantastic world of Peter Pan had previously been presented in his *The Little White Bird* (1902). *Peter Pan*, a poetical pantomime, as it has been called, charmed audiences from the night it first appeared. Peter has since been played by many great stars, ranging from Maude Adams to Mary Martin, and a statue of him stands in Kensington Gardens, London. Barrie, who described his business as "playing hide and seek with angels," named Peter for one of his nephews, for whom he wrote the story, giving the character his last name from the god Pan, "goat-footed," god of forests, meadows, flocks and shepherds. Wendy, Peter's girl friend, also borrowed her name from a real person. This was Barrie's own nickname, bestowed upon him by the daughter of his friend, poet W.E. Henley. Little Margaret Henley called him Friendly, then Friendly-Wendy, and this ultimately became Wendy, the name he dubbed his character.

Barrie was present when the young son of a friend was told that he would be sick the next day if he ate any more cake. "I shall be sick *tonight*," the boy replied laconically and helped himself to another piece. Delighted with the epigram, Barrie decided to use it as the basis for lines spoken in *Peter Pan* (1904). As a reward he gave his friend's son a royalty of a half penny a performance for the life of the copyright.

"For several days after my first book was published," Barrie recalled, "I carried it about in my pocket, and took surreptitious peeps at it to make sure the ink had not faded."

"Sir James," an editor asked the famous author of *Peter Pan*, "I suppose some of your plays do better than others. They are not all successes, I imagine?"
"No," the playwright confided, smiling, "some Peter out and some Pan out."

"It is all very well to be able to write books," he once said to H.G. Wells, "but can you waggle your ears?" Wells, to his dismay, found that he didn't share his friend's peculiar talent.

An arrogant young understudy sent Barrie a telegram advising him that the star in one of his plays had taken sick and that he would be playing the leading role that night. Barrie didn't attend but sent a telegram that the young actor received just after his performance. It read: "Thanks for the warning."

A persistant reporter tried to enter Barrie's flat.
"Sir James Barrie, I presume?" he said when Barrie answered the bell.
"You do," Barrie replied and slammed the door in his face.

A friend noticed that he ordered Brussels sprouts every day and asked him why. "I cannot resist ordering them," he explained. "The words are so lovely to say."

Barrie was sitting next to George Bernard Shaw at a dinner party when Shaw was served his usual vegetarian fare of a large green salad and salad oils. Barrie bent over, stared at the salad, then at Shaw, and asked confidentially, "Tell me one thing, Shaw, have you eaten that or are you going to?"

It is said that when Barrie visited London's staid Athenaeum Club for the first time he asked an octogenarian biologist which way it was to the dining room. The old man immediately burst out crying. He had belonged to the honorary club for over half a century and no one had ever spoken to him before.

Barrie's Kailyard School stories and other works drew heavily on his mother's memories of life in her Scottish village, and his portrait of Wendy in *Peter Pan* owes much to his mother (born Margaret Ogilvy), an orphaned "little mother" old before her time who had to raise her younger brother. So attached was Barrie to his mother that he published a biography of her, *Margaret Ogilvy*, in 1896. This biography was so frankly adoring that one critic found it "a positive act of indecency."

The author told the following story in a speech at the Alpine club in 1896:

"Times have changed since a certain author was executed for murdering his publisher. They say that when the author was on the scaffold he said goodbye to the minister and to the reporters, and then he saw some publishers sitting in the front row below, and to them he did not say goodbye. He said instead, 'I'll see you again.'"

∇ ∇ ∇

Maurice Baring (1874–1945)

"If you would know what the Lord God thinks of money," the prolific Roman Catholic author and journalist remarked to a friend at a high society function, "you have only to look at those to whom he gives it."

∇ ∇ ∇

George Barrington (1755–1804)

After robbing his Dublin schoolmaster when a boy of 15, Barrington ran away from home and joined a gang of pickpockets; they travelled to London, where he was caught picking pockets several times and was finally sentenced to seven years' transportation to Australia. There he mended his ways, becoming a noted author and law officer. He is mainly remembered for the very first thing he wrote, the prologue to a 1796 play performed by himself and other convicts in a Sydney theater. The prologue contained the famous lines:

True patriots we; for be it
    understood,
We left our country for our
    country's good.

∇ ∇ ∇

Isaac Barrow (1630–1677)

This famous preacher and author was noted for his eloquent, well-reasoned sermons, which were even better known for their great length. One time he preached a celebrated Sunday sermon tht lasted a full 3 1/2 hours and he complained that he felt tired from *standing* so long.

Barrow was Newton's teacher and he later resigned his post as professor of mathematics at Cambridge in favor of his pupil. He was a scholar who admired poets and couldn't resist rhyming in Latin. "Poetry is a kind of ingenious nonsense," he once told Newton.

Francis Beaumont (1584–1616) and John Fletcher (1579–1625)

John Dryden wrote that Beaumont was "so accurate a judge of plays that Ben Jonson, while he lived, submitted all his writings to his censure, and 'tis thought used his judgement in correcting if not contriving all his plots." Fletcher is thought to have collaborated with Shakespeare on *Henry VIII*, among other plays. Beaumont and Fletcher collaborated on about 15 plays from 1606 to 1616, when Beaumont died of the plague. Of their partnership John Aubrey said: "There was a wonderful consimility of fancy. They lived together not far from the playhouse, had one wench in the house between them, the same clothes and cloak, & C."

The "twin stars of our stage," as Swinburne called them, were sitting in a tavern appropriating the work involved in a tragedy they were writing. Fletcher wanted to work on one scene, Beaumont another and they finally divided the work equally. During their conversation, however, one of them was overheard saying, "I'll kill the king." Both men were accused of treason, arrested, and held until the authorities were satisfied they were not assassins.

In his classic evaluation of Beaumont and Fletcher the poet Algernon Swinburne claims that Fletcher's father, Bishop Richard Fletcher, died "of overmuch tobacco and the displeasure of Queen Elizabeth at his second marriage...with a lady of such character as figures something too frequently on the stage of his illustrious son."

On a blank page of his copy of Beaumont and Fletcher's (or more likely Fletcher and Massinger's) *Fair Maid of the Inn*, Keats wrote two centuries later:

Bards of Passion and of Mirth,
Ye have left your souls on earth!
Have ye souls in heaven too?

∇ ∇ ∇

Baron Beaverbrook (William Maxwell Aitken; 1879–1964)

The powerful newspaper publisher and author was called upon by David Lloyd George.

"Is the lord at home?" Lloyd George asked the butler.

"No, sir, the lord is out walking."

"Ah," replied Lloyd George. "On the water, I presume."

∇ ∇ ∇

William Beckford (1759–1844)

A man of immense wealth, the former lord mayor of London became a recluse in his middle years, living in mysterious seclusion in his extravagant Fonthill mansion. Beckford's strangest book is his *Biographical Memoirs of Extraordinary*

Painters (1824), in which he included biographies of imaginary artists such as Og of Bason. (Similarly, *Appleton's Cyclopedia of American Biography*, first published in 1886, for many years contained 84 biographies of nonexistent persons sent in by an unknown correspondent; it wasn't until 1936 that they were all weeded out.)

∇ ∇ ∇

Thomas Lovell Beddoes (1803–1849)

Beddoes once hired a theater for a night so that his homosexual lover, a baker named Degen, could play Hotspur in *Henry IV*. Thinking himself the last of the Elizabethans, he tried to grow a beard and dress like Shakespeare. The poet tried to kill himself after an argument with his lover. He cut an artery in his leg, but only succeeded in losing the leg, which had to be amputated after infection set in. Six months later he made another attempt, with curare, and succeeded.

∇ ∇ ∇

Sir Max Beerbohm (1872–1956)

In many ways "the incomparable Max," as Shaw called him, was a quintessential Englishman. Though in 1910 he settled in Italy, for the remaining 45 years of his life (excepting the two World Wars), he never learned to speak Italian.

Beerbohm wasn't universally well regarded. Wrote Vita Sackville-West to her husband: "It always makes me cross when Max is called 'The Incomparable Max.' He is not incomparable at all."

So accurately did he parody Henry James that the Master tried not to read him anywhere near the time he would be working. After reading a Beerbohm parody of himself James found it difficult to write, out of fear that he might be parodying himself.

Beerbohm reviewed French actress Sarah Bernhardt's portrayal of Hamlet in 1899, when she was 65. Wrote the critic: "Her friends ought to have restrained her. The native critics ought not to have encouraged her. The customhouse officials at Charing Cross ought to have confiscated her sable doublet and hose...the only compliment one can conscientiously pay her is that her Hamlet was, from first to last, *très grande dame.*"

An aged Beerbohm and his aged wife attended a party at which England's most beautiful women were present. Looking gravely at the actresses and models eager for attention, he turned to his wife and said, "My dear, you are looking so charming tonight that I simply must talk to you."

Brendan Behan (1923–1964)

Arrested for involvement with the I.R.A. as a boy, the Irish playwright spent time in prison and on his release worked as a housepainter while writing his early plays and books. He had little use for drama critics. "Critics are like eunuchs in a harem," he once remarked. "They're there every night, they see it done every night, they see how it should be done very night, but they can't do it themselves."

∇ ∇ ∇

Aphra Behn (1640?–1689)

"The Incomparable Astraea," as she was known, is said to have been "the first woman to make a living writing," but her life remains a mystery. No one knows who her parents were, what year she was born, or even the right spelling of her first name. She served as a spy for England's Charles II in the Netherlands, during the Dutch War, but wasn't paid and was soon after imprisoned as a debtor. Her debts forced her to write for a living and she produced a great number of popular plays, poems and novels, including such tales of love and adventure as *The Fair Jilt*, *The Rover* and *The Amours of Philander and Sylvia*. She was ridiculed by Pope as Astraea, a name she chose for herself. Mrs. Behn's *Oroonoko* may have suggested the "noble savage" philosophy to Rousseau and was the first novel to express sympathy for oppressed blacks. She is buried in the east cloister of Westminster Abbey.

∇ ∇ ∇

Hilaire Belloc (1870–1953)

Writers don't usually make very good politicians, and it is hard to name one who succeeded in gaining public office. Jack London, H.G. Wells, Henry George, Upton Sinclair and many others were soundly defeated in their election bids. Belloc, who ran for the House of Commons in 1906, had to overcome religious prejudice and made his first campaign speech with a rosary in his hands. "Gentlemen," he announced, "I am a Catholic. As far as possible I go to mass every day...As far as possible, I kneel down and tell these beads every day. If you reject me on account of my religion, I shall thank God that He has spared me the indignity of being your representative." He was elected.

Late in life the author somewhat regretted that he had not specialized instead of writing on a variety of subjects. "My advice to a young writer who is merely thinking of fame," he said half-jokingly, "is to concentrate on one subject. Let him, when he is twenty, write about the earthworm. Let him continue for forty years to write of nothing but the earthworm. When he is sixty, pilgrims wil make a hollow path with their feet to the door of the world's great authority on the earthworm. They will knock at his door and humbly beg to be allowed to see the Master of the Earthworm."

Like many writers Belloc wrote too much in order to make a living, and his work suffered for it. A possibly apocryphal story has him encountering a stranger on a train who was reading one of his least distinguished books. Belloc counted out the price of the volume, handed the money to the man, grabbed the book, and threw it out the train window.

∇ ∇ ∇

(Enoch) Arnold Bennett (1867–1931)

The novelist once bragged that Darius Clayhanger's lingering death scene in his *Clayhanger* trilogy couldn't be bettered, "because I took infinite pains over it. All the time my father was dying, I was at the bedside making copious notes."

Bennett was among the most prolific of writers. His journal entry of January , 1901, reviews his accomplishments for the preceding year:

> Last year I wrote 3 plays.
> *The Postmistress* (1 act)
> *Children of the Mist* (4 acts—in collaboration with Eden Phillpotts)
> *The Chancellor* (4 acts—in collaboration with Arthur Hooley).
> Also a serial, *The Grand Babylon Hotel*, of 70,000 words.
> Also a draft of my Staffordshire novel, *Anna Tellwright*, 80,000 words, and part of the final writing.
> Also a half dozen short stories.
> I also wrote and published 196 articles of various length.
> I also collected, revised, and wrote a preface for a series of my articles from the *Academy*, to be called *Fame and Fiction, an Inquiry into Certain Popularities*.
> I also edited *Woman* till 30th Sept.—when I resigned, and came to live in the country...
> I also advised Pearsons on 50 MS. books...

"I have written between seventy and eighty books," he once remarked. "But I have also written only four: *The Old Wives' Tales, The Card, Clayhanger*, and *Riceyman Steps*."

Ezra Pound called him "Nickel cash-register Bennett." Wrote the American expatriate poet: "The mistake of my life was in beginning in London as if publishers were any different from bucket shops...Arnold Bennett knew his eggs. Whatever his interest in good writing, he never showed the public anything but his AVARICE. Consequently, they adored him."

Bennett was eccentric, even neurotic, about things being done to his exact specifications. When his housekeeper began to brew his tea he would pull out his watch at the instant she poured boiling water into the pot. Exactly four minutes later he would signal her to pour the tea.

His end was infinitely more ironic than the ending of any novel he wrote. The author died of typhoid fever, which he contracted from a glass of water he drank in Paris to demonstrate that the water there was perfectly safe.

∇ ∇ ∇

Jeremy Bentham (1748–1832)

The eminent philosopher and author thought that dead people should all be embalmed and used as their own monuments. He called these auto-icons. "If a country gentleman have rows of trees leading to his dwelling," he wrote, "the auto-icons of his family might alternate with the trees; copal varnish would protect the face from the effects of rain—caoutchouc the habiliments." But then Bentham also had an unusual pet—a teapot.

His utilitarianism was not popular among most authors, given his open hostility to creative literature, especially his aphorism, "Quantity of pleasure being equal, push-pin is as good as poetry."

By the time he was three, his wealthy attorney father had Bentham studying Latin; he had already read in its entirety Paul de Rapin's eight-volume *History of England*. From there he slowed down a bit and only took his Oxford degree by the time he was 15.

Bentham left a large sum to London's University College on the condition that his own preserved body—which was fitted with a wax head made by a French artist and "enclosed in a mahogany case with folding glass doors, seated in his armchair and holding in his hand his favorite walking stick"—be displayed every year at the annual board of directors meeting. This was done for 92 years, until the body was finally made a permanent exhibit at the college.

British classicist C. K. Ogden had a strange condition for giving the 1935 Jeremy Bentham Centennial Lecture. He would not deliver the lecture, he advised all concerned, unless the underclothes on Jeremy Bentham's mummy (see above) were changed. They were and he gave the lecture.

Edmund Clerihew Bentley (1875–1956)

> Sir Humphrey Davy
> Abominated gravy.
> He lived in the odium
> Of having discovered sodium.

This was the first clerihew written by Edmund Clerihew Bentley. The detective-story writer composed it while only a schoolboy, according to his schoolmate G. K. Chesterton, "when he sat listening to a chemical exposition, with his rather bored air and a blank sheet of blotting paper before him." Bentley, one of the few men to have a word honoring his middle name, could in Chesterton's words "write clear and unadulterated nonsense with...serious simplicity." Chesterton called his friend's a "severe and stately form of Free Verse." In any case, the satirical, often biographical verse has seldom been imitated. Bentley's favorite clerihew:

> It was a weakness of Voltaire's
> To forget to say his prayers,
> And which, to his shame,
> He never overcame.

▽ ▽ ▽

Baron Berners (Gerald Hugh Tyrwhitt-Wilson; 1883–1950)

When it was widely rumored that the novelist, artist and composer was to wed Violet Trefusis, well known for her lesbian relationships, Berners had the following item put in several newspaper travel columns: "Lord Berners has left Lesbos for the Isle of Man."

The composer William Walton got an injunction to stop Lord Berners from caricaturing him in his novel *Count Omega.* Berners retaliated with an injunction of his own ordering Walton to stop trying to get into his novels.

▽ ▽ ▽

Charles Bertram (1723–1765)

Another of the great English literary forgers, Bertram produced a manuscript on Roman antiquities that he claimed was written by Richard of Winchester. A teacher of English at a naval academy in Copenhagen, he even published a full book-length commentary on his "discovery." His forgery wasn't exposed until 100 years after his death.

Sir Walter Besant (1836–1901)

A best-selling author with a deep sympathy for the poor, Besant wrote a number of muckraking novels in an attempt to stir public opinion against abysmal working and living conditions in London, as well as critical and biographical books. In 1884 he founded England's first labor union for writers, The Society of Authors, to promote the business interests of authors and help them fight for their rights.

∇ ∇ ∇

John Betjeman (1906–1984)

"Well, Betjeman," Field Marshal Lord Chetwode instructed the poet laureate before his marriage, "If you're going to be my son-in-law you needn't go on calling me 'Sir.' Call me 'Field Marshal.'"

∇ ∇ ∇

Thomas Betterton (c. 1635–1710)

The greatest English actor of his day, playing some 200 roles over his long career, Betterton was also a playwright of some distinction. He was a fair man of exemplary character. One time Colley Cibber, who would become famous as a dramatist, had a bit part in a Betterton play and was so terrified that he ruined the scene. Angrily, Betterton asked who it was that had blundered so badly. "Master Colley," he was told.

"Master Colley! then forfeit [fine] him!" Betterton said.

"Why sir, he has no salary," he was advised.

"No?" Betterton said. "Why then, put him down for ten shillings a week, and forfeit him five shillings."

∇ ∇ ∇

The Bible

Printers have made disastrous mistakes in various Bibles printed over the years. Here are seven of the most outrageous:

- The Sin On Bible, printed in 1716: John 5:14 contains the printer's error "sin on more," instead of "sin no more."
- The Bug Bible, 1535, reads: "Thou shalt not nede to be afrayed for eny bugges [instead of "terror"] by night" in Psalms 91:5.
- The Fool Bible, printed in the reign of Charles I, reads: "The fool hath said in his heart there is a God" in Psalms 14; for this mistake the printers were fined 3,000 pounds.
- The Idle Bible, 1809: The "idole shepherd" (Zechariah 11:17) is printed "the idle shepherd."

- The Large Family Bible, 1820: Isaiah 66:9 reads, "Shall I bring to the birth and not cease [instead of "cause"] to bring forth."
- The Unrighteous Bible, 1653: I Corinthians 6:9 reads, "Know ye not that the unrighteous shall inherit [for "shall not inherit"] the Kingdom of God."
- The Wicked Bible, 1632: The word "not" in the seventh commandment is omitted, making it read: "Thou shalt commit adultery."

∇ ∇ ∇

Augustine Birrell (1850–1933)

Both the charm and unobtrusive scholarship displayed by Birrell in his *Obiter Dicta* and other works led to the formation of the word *birrellism* for shrewd cursory comments on humankind and life in general. Birrell, a barrister elected to Parliament in 1889, became president of the national board of education and chief secretary for Ireland. It is said that he once buried a 19-volume set by the bluestocking author Hannah More in his garden. "The books take up too much room on my shelves," he explained, "and they are just as likely to be dug up from the garden as to be picked out for reading up here."

∇ ∇ ∇

William Blake (1757–1827)

The mystic poet once told a friend: "I write when commanded by the spirits, and the moment I have written I see the words fly about the room in all directions. It is then published and the spirits can read. My manuscripts are of no further use. I have been tempted to burn my manuscripts, but my wife won't let me."

One bright afternoon Blake and his wife and amanuensis sat nude in their English garden reciting passages from *Paradise Lost* as if they were sitting in the Garden of Eden. When a visitor called, the poet cried out to him: "Come in! It's only Adam and Eve, you know!"

"Money flies from me," Blake wrote to poet William Hayley in 1804. "Profit never ventures upon my threshold."

Blake had illustrated his friend Hayley's *Life of Cowper* (1803) and *Ballads Founded on Anecdotes of Animals* (1805), but secretly resented what he considered Hayley's pandering to this gentle man who had been offered and refused the laureateship and about whom Robert Southey had remarked, "Everything is good about him except his poetry." In any case, Blake found relief by writing scurrilous epigrams and doggerel in his notebooks. Finally, he realized that he had to leave Hayley's house if he was to develop as an artist. His final epigram on Hayley is about all that lives on of his employer:

> Thy friendship oft has made my heart to ache:
> So be my enemy—for friendship's sake.

When his consumptive younger brother Robert died in 1787, Blake, who had been very close to him, insisted that he had seen Robert's soul rise up through the ceiling at the moment of death, "clapping its hands for joy."

Worth a fortune today, the 22 plates Blake engraved from 1823–1825 illustrating the Book of Job earned him barely £2 a week.

Perhaps the only case in literature of a preface to a book physically harming a reader occurred in 1814, when Blake read his fellow poet William Wordsworth's preface to his long philosophical poem *The Excursion*. In a letter to Wordsworth's sister Dorothy years later, English journalist Henry Crabb Robinson related that Blake told him that reading the preface, which he violently disagreed with, "caused him a bowel complaint that nearly killed him."

His art and poetry were so little appreciated in his late years that Blake was reduced to engraving advertisements for Wedgwood pottery to help make a living.

Just three days before he died Blake finished his "Ancient of Days," finally exclaiming, "There, that will do! I cannot mend it!" Seeing his wife in tears, he cried, "Stay, Kate! Keep just as you are—I will draw your portrait—for you have ever been an angel to me." The drawing was his last.

∇ ∇ ∇

Frederick S. Boas (1862–1957)

The literary historian was among the longest-lived of authors. Boas published a book when 93, and his last review in the *Times Literary Supplement* appeared a week or so before his death at 95.

∇ ∇ ∇

James Bone (b. 1872)

In his farewell speech on Fleet Street in 1945, the British journalist commented on the phrase "ocean greyhound," words coined by his father, the Glasgow journalist David Drummond Bone, to describe the *Alaska*, which in 1881 became the first ship to cross the Atlantic in less than a week. "To make a cliché," James Bone ventured, "is to make a classic."

James Boswell (1740–1795)

Boswell's *The Life of Samuel Johnson* (1791) is of course the prototype of biographies. Born in Scotland, he met Dr. Johnson only after numerous rebuffs but became both friend and admirer of the great biographer and man of letters. Over a relatively short period, he recorded in detail Johnson's words and activities. "That Boswell was a vain, intemperate man of dubious morals is of no matter to history," writes one biographer. "He shines in the reflected glory of his great portrait." "Bozzy," as he was called, once wrote the following poem about himself, said to be remarkable for its self-perception:

> Boswell is pleasant and gay,
>   For frolic by nature designed;
> He heedlessly rattles away
>   When company is to his mind.
> "This maxim," he says, "you may see,
>   We never can have corn without
>   chaff";
> So not a bent sixpence cares he,
>   Whether with him or at him you
>   laugh.

Macaulay called Boswell's worship of Dr. Johnson "*Lues Boswelliana,* or disease of admiration."

Boswell's amorous activities were revealed in his journals and in letters to his university friends William Johnson Temple and John Johnston. Even allowing for bragging, his exploits exceed the merely promiscuous. He tells, for example, of his preference for sex with prostitutes in London's St. James Park and even records making love one day above the Thames on Westminster Bridge.

Boswell seemed intent on making a reputation as a great lover. He would tell anyone who would listen that he had once made love five times in a single evening. But though he unabashedly broadcast his seed, he wasn't so eager to broadcast the fact that he had contracted gonorrhea 17 times over a period of 30 years.

When the often obsequious Boswell brought Dr. Johnson to meet his wife she didn't like the big, awkward man's manners, but said nothing. When Johnson left, however, she told her husband: "I have seen many a bear led by a man, but I never before saw a man led by a bear."

The first governor-general of British India, Warren Hastings (1732–1818), later impeached for corruption in his administration, was asked what he thought of Boswell's *Life of Johnson*:

"Sir," Hastings replied, "it's the dirtiest book in my library. I knew Boswell intimately; and I well remember when his book first made its appearance, Boswell was so full of it that he could neither think nor talk of anything else; so much so, that meeting Lord Thurlow hurrying through Parliament Street to get to the House of Lords, where an important debate was expected, for which he was already too late, Boswell had the temerity to stop and accost him with: 'Have you read my book?'

"'Yes, damn you!' replied Lord Thurlow, 'every word of it; I could not help myself.'"

∇ ∇ ∇

Horatio William Bottomley (1860–1933)
The noted journalist and wit served as a member of Parliament, but his shady financial scheming led to a long term in prison, where a visitor once found him at work stitching torn mail bags. "Ah, Bottomley," he observed, "sewing?"

"No," replied Bottomley, "reaping."

∇ ∇ ∇

Thomas Bowdler (1754–1825)
His inability to stand the sight of human blood and suffering forced Dr. Thomas Bowdler to abandon his medical practice in London, but this weakness apparently did not apply where vendors of words were concerned. Bowdler so thoroughly purged both Shakespeare and Gibbon that they would have screamed in pain from the bloodletting had they been alive, and to *bowdlerize* soon became a synonym for to radically expurgate or prudishly censor. Bowdler's *Family Shakespeare* was published in 1818. In justifying this 10-volume edition, he explained on the title page that "nothing is added to the text; but those expressions are omitted which cannot with propriety be read aloud in a family," adding later that he had also expunged "Whatever is unfit to be read by a gentleman in a company of ladies." What this really meant was that Bowdler had completely altered the characters of Hamlet, Macbeth, Falstaff and others and totally eliminated "objectionable" characters like Doll Tearsheet. But *The Family Shakespeare* was a best seller and even won some critical acclaim. Bowdler went on to expurgate Edward Gibbon's *The History of the Decline and Fall of the Roman Empire*. He firmly believed that both Shakespeare and Gibbon would have "desired nothing more ardently" than his literary vandalism and he would probably have turned his scalpel to other great authors if death had not excised him from the literary life in 1825.

William Lisle Bowles (1762–1850)

Though Byron mercilessly ridiculed his poems, calling him "the maudlin prince of mournful sonneteers," Bowles's work was championed by Hazlitt, Lamb, Coleridge and many other poets. The clergyman was a very absentminded man who once paid a toll for his horse at a turnpike though he was walking, not riding, that day. Another time he wrote "From the author" in a Bible that poet Tom Moore's wife asked him to inscribe.

∇ ∇ ∇

Maurice C. Bowra (1898–1971)

The classical scholar and wit was swimming with a group of dons in a section of the Thames at Oxford marked "Men Only" when a boatload of women appeared. The naked dons scurried from the water, hastily covering their genitals with towels and clothing, but Bowra draped his towel over his head. "I believe, gentlemen, that I am recognized by my face," he later explained.

∇ ∇ ∇

Samuel Boyse (1708–1749)

Victor Hugo, Edmond Rostand and Ben Franklin liked to write in the nude (the last two in the bathtub), but poet Samuel Boyse had to. Boyse was so poor that he "had not a shirt, a coat, or any kind of apparel to put on," according to Cibber in *The Lives of the Poets*. In the winter of 1740 Boyse had been forced to pawn all his clothes, and his bed sheets as well, and he stayed in bed day and night, writing with a ragged blanket wrapped around him "through which he had cut a hole large enough to admit his arm." For a full six weeks he wrote like this until a kind visitor paid to get his clothes out of pawn. When he found himself in the same situation in later years, he would tie slips of white paper around his neck and wrists to simulate a shirt and go out into the streets like that. Boyse was run over and killed by a hackney coach one day when he stumbled drunkenly into the road.

∇ ∇ ∇

John Bradford (1510?–1555)

On seeing several criminals being led to the scaffold, the Protestant martyr John Bradford remarked: "There, but for the grace of God, goes John Bradford." The religious author's words, without his name, are still very common ones today for expressing one's blessings compared to the fate of another. Bradford was later burned at the stake as a heretic.

Henry Bradley (1845–1923)

The noted philologist and the editor of the *Oxford English Dictionary* learned to read when he was not much more than three years old. What's more he learned to read upside down at this time and could later read just as well that way as he could in the conventional manner. It seems that as a child he taught himself to read during family prayers, following the words upside down as his father read from the great Bible on his knees.

∇ ∇ ∇

Nicholas Breakspear (1100–1159)

Breakspear, a monk, scholar and humanist, was elevated to the Papal See in 1154, becoming Adrian IV, the only Englishman ever to become pope. Also called Hadrian IV, it was he who donated all of Ireland as a papal fief to Henry II of England.

∇ ∇ ∇

Robert Bridges (1844–1930)

When the publicity-shy poet laureate landed in America in 1914 he managed to evade the newspaper interviewers waiting for his ship. The next day one paper headlined: "The King's Canary Refuses to Sing!"

∇ ∇ ∇

John Bright (1811–1889)

Bright was told that Prime Minister and author Benjamin Disraeli was a self-made man. "And he adores his maker," the great orator replied. Another time Bright made a great speech and Disraeli told him, "I would give all I ever had to have made that speech you just made now." Replied Bright: "Well, you might have made it, if you had been honest."

∇ ∇ ∇

Alexander Brome (1620–1666)

The poet's gaiety, wit and hearty drinking songs earned him the title of "the English Anacreon." Brome wrote many pro-Royalist satires, including a ballad in pamphlet form attacking the Rump Parliament whose subject and title are among the most unusual in literature: *Bumm-foder: or Wastepaper Proper to Wipe the Nation's Rump With* (c. 1660).

Richard Brome (c. 1590–1652)

The prolific dramatist worked as a servant in Ben Jonson's household before becoming a playwright. Jonson came to regard him as a friend and pupil, and wrote a sonnet to him that he attached to his first play—which made Brome's reputation. One duty Jonson expected of Brome as his servant was to read nightly "a piece of Virgil, Tacitus, Livy or some better book" to all who came for supper.

∇ ∇ ∇

The Brontë Sisters

The only English authors, and perhaps the only English family, with an umlaut in their surname are the Brontë sisters—Charlotte (1816–55), Emily (1818–48), and Anne (1820–49). Their father, Patrick Brunty, a poor Irishman trying to distinguish himself at Cambridge, changed the family name to Brontë soon after Lord Nelson was created duke of Bronte, adding the German umlaut to give himself more éclat. In German the umlaut is used to indicate an internal vowel change in a word or to show that a letter is pronounced differently than it ordinarily would be. It is also called a diaeresis in English, when it is used above the second of two coupled vowels to show separate pronunciation, as in coöperate.

∇ ∇ ∇

Anne Brontë (1820–1849)

The youngest and most melancholy of the Brontë sisters and the closest to their brother Branwell (q.v.), Anne invented with her sister Emily the kingdom of Gondal, which provided the setting for many of the sisters' poems. All the Brontë children had been playing a game set in an imaginary Glass Town Confederacy in Africa, using a box of wooden soldiers their father had bought them in 1826. After a few years Anne and Emily broke away to invent Gondal. Then, in 1834, Charlotte and Branwell invented their magic kingdom of Angria, about which Charlotte wrote many tales that foreshadowed her later novels.

∇ ∇ ∇

Branwell Brontë (1817–1848)

The brother of Charlotte, Emily and Anne Brontë claimed to have written parts of Emily's *Wuthering Heights*, a boast that is no longer taken seriously. Branwell, who had great promise, squandered his father's money in his attempts to become an artist, took to drink and opium and became a violent drunkard. Discharged from his railway job for culpable negligence, he was employed as a tutor by the Robinson family at Thorp Green Hill, near York, where his sister Anne was governness. Justly charged with making love to his employer's wife, he was fired and spent the last years of his life as a barroom loafer, finally dying in delirium tremens. Anne Brontë used him as a model for her character Arthur Huntingdon in *The Tenant of Wildfell Hall* (1848).

▽ ▽ ▽

Charlotte Brontë (1816–1855)

A frail little woman, only 4 feet 9 inches tall, Charlotte Brontë did not marry until she was 38 and soon after became pregnant. While waking on the moors with her husband, Arthur Nicholls, her father's curate, she developed a severe cold that she was uanble to shake, but it is generally agreed today that the cause of her death was morning sickness (a severe form reportedly called *hyperemesis gravidarum* that can be effectively treated today). The physician in later years said that he regretted losing Charlotte Brontë's child more than any baby he had ever lost.

Charlotte's shyness was doubtless much due to her father, a strange, unsocial widower who loved his six children but had little to do with them, even taking his meals alone in his study. Except for their walks over the moors most of Charlotte's time and that of her younger sisters Emily and Anne was spent alone reading and writing in the bleak rectory where they lived. Both her precocity and terrible loneliness are illustrated by the fact that young Charlotte wrote in the course of 15 months, beginning when she was only 13 years old, at least 23 "novels," which were all completed, though not of any value.

Charlotte Brontë dedicated *Jane Eyre* to William Makepeace Thackeray, and he later invited her to his home, where several of his friends also came to see her. But Miss Brontë proved so shy and uncommunicative ("Do you like London, Miss Brontë?" "Yes and no.") that most of the guests found it one of the dullest evenings they had ever spent. Thackeray agreed. Halfway into the evening he quietly got his hat, "put his fingers to his lips, walked out into the darkness" and went off to his club.

▽ ▽ ▽

Emily Brontë (1818–1848)

There was a strong streak of violence in the little author of *Wuthering Heights*, as is reflected in a story about her subduing the fierce dog Keeper with her bare hands and iron will, but her predominant trait was her quiet stoicism. It was, for example, only two hours before her death of consumption, after she had struggled from her bed and dressed herself, that she finally allowed a doctor to be called. (See her famous poem "Old Stoic.")

Henry Brooke (1703–1783)

In his *The Fool of Quality* (1765–70), the Irish novelist wrote of a publisher he knew who said of his authors: "I can get one of these gentlemen...on whose education more money has been spent...than would maintain a decent family to the end of the world—I can get one of them to labor like a hackney horse from morning to night at less a wage than I could hire...a porter or shoeboy for three hours."

∇ ∇ ∇

Baron Broughton (John Cam Hobhouse; 1786–1869)

The politician and man of letters was a close friend of Lord Byron, whose remains he arranged to have lie in state in London and whose memoirs he ensured were burned soon after the poet died. Hobhouse invented the much-used political phrase "His Majesty's Opposition" and once recalled, "When I invented [it] Canning paid me a compliment on the fortunate hit."

∇ ∇ ∇

Rhoda Broughton (1840–1920)

The novelist had a reputation for audacity when she began writing, but prevailing tastes prevented her from displaying it in her stories. "I began my career as Zola, I finish it as Miss Yonge [a popular romantic novelist]," she once said of herself. When she was a young woman, a good friend of Broughton was jilted by a man because his mother objected to the young lady. Rhoda Broughton sent him a mug inscribed "For a Good Boy."

∇ ∇ ∇

Thomas Brown (1663–1704)

Dr. John Fell's classes at Oxford must have been something to see. The much-respected English divine and originator of Fell types, which he created for the Oxford University Press, was quite a permissive teacher for his day, even allowing classroom debates, which often ended in fistfights. Yet his name came to symbolize someone disliked for no apparent reason. Fell owes his unjust fate to Thomas Brown, once his student at Christ Church and later an author and translator. Dr. Fell had threatened to expel Brown for some classroom offense if he could not translate a couplet of Martial. The resulting jingle bore little resemblance to the 32nd epigram, but Dr. Fell, to his credit, good-naturedly accepted the paraphrase:

> I do not love thee, Dr. Fell
> The reason why I cannot tell;
> But this alone I know full well,
> I do not love thee, Dr. Fell.

Martial's epigram goes:

> I do not love you, Sabidus, the reason I cannot tell;
> This only I can say—I dislike you very well.

∇ ∇ ∇

Thomas Edward Brown (1830–1897)

The author and scholar, a Johnsonian type who came from the Isle of Man, was said to be so fastidious about his prose style that before he answered an invitation he had passages of an English classic read to him.

∇ ∇ ∇

Elizabeth Barrett Browning (1806–1861)

Sonnets from the Portuguese was written for Robert Browning and published, reportedly, only because Browning felt: "I dared not keep to myself the finest Sonnets written in any language since Shakespeare's." There is, of course, no Portuguese model for the sonnets and they were probably called *Sonnets from the Portuguese* because Browning's pet name for his wife was "my little Portuguese."

Through her poem "To Flush, My Dog" the poet's cocker spaniel Flush became perhaps the most famous dog in literary history, though Byron's Boatswain, Pope's Bounce, Lamb's Dash, Newton's Diamond and Matthew Arnold's Geist (see his poem "Geist's Grave"), among others, were well known in their day. Flush appears to have been a one-woman dog, however, with a rather nasty, jealous disposition. Flush, who slept on his mistress's bed, nipped Robert Browning several times when Browning was courting the poet, and might have nipped their great love affair in the butt if Browning hadn't learned to bring along dog biscuits for him.

∇ ∇ ∇

Robert Browning (1812–1889)

Browning pilloried the American medium Daniel Douglas Home as Mr. Sludge in his poem "The Medium." Home, however, retaliated by publicly claiming that Browning was simply angry because when a laurel wreath rose from the table during a Home seance it hovered in the air and landed on Mrs. Browning's head and not his own, despite the fact that he scurried to get himself in good position behind his wife's chair! True or not, Home's story is better than the poem.

He escaped an after-dinner bore who had buttonholed him by breaking away while apologizing: "But my dear fellow, this is too bad. I am monopolizing you."

Browning seemed so unlike a poet to Henry James in his social life that he inspired James's short story "The Private Life," in which the main character, a playwright based on Browning, has a double. The double remains at home writing the plays while the very plain, ordinary Clare Vawdrey attends all the social functions.

Reading the *Life and Letters of Edward FitzGerald*, Browning came upon the following passage in a letter that the translator of the *Rubaiyat* had written to a friend:

> Mrs. [Elizabeth Barrett] Browning's death is rather a relief to me, I must say. No more *Aurora Leighs*, thank God. A woman of real genius, I know, but what is the upshot of it all! She and her sex had better mind the kitchen and her children, and perhaps the poor. Except in such things as little novels, they only devote themselves to what men do much better, leaving that which men do worse or not at all.

FitzGerald was dead and Browning's wife had died 28 years before, but the poet's fury at the words he read inspired him to write one of his last and most memorable poems.

> I chanced upon a new book yesterday;
> I opened it; and where my finger lay,
> 'Twixt page and uncut page, these words I read—
> Some six or seven at most—and learned thereby
> That you, FitzGerald, whom by ear and eye
> She never knew, thanked God my wife was dead.
> Aye dead, and were yourself alive, good Fitz,
> How to return you thanks would task my wits.
> Kicking you seems the common lot of curs,
> While more appropriate greeting lends you grace;
> Surely, to spit there glorifies your face—
> Spitting from lips once sanctified by hers.

The Brownings had planned to be buried together. But when he died Robert Browning could not be interred in the same cemetery as his wife, the cemetery having been closed to burial since her death. He was laid to rest in Westminster Abbey.

▽ ▽ ▽

William Buckland (1784–1856)

Buckland was the first writer to note in England the action of glacial ice on rocks, and his work helped bring geology into high repute. The divine, scientist and author had odder eating habits than the most dissolute Roman emperor; he would try anything, including roast mouse, mole and bluebottle flies. A possibly apocryphal story has him gulping down the preserved heart of France's Louis XIV, after remarking, "I have eaten some strange things, but never the heart of a king."

∇ ∇ ∇

Eustace Budgell (1686–1737)

A prolific man of letters who contributed to the *Spectator, Tatler* and *Guardian* and later published his own weekly, the *Bee*, Eustace Budgell was a confidant of Joseph Addison, his mother's cousin, and other English notables. Budgell, however, was an extravagant eccentric who lost over £20,000 in the infamous South Sea stock scheme and spent huge amounts of money to get elected to Parliament. When his friend and fellow deist Dr. Matthew Tindal died, it seemed that Budgell's financial worries were over, for a legacy of some £2,000 was left him in Tindal's will. But Tindal's nephew charged that Budgell had inserted the bequest in the will, and the courts agreed with him. Budgell was ridiculed in Pope's satire *Epistle to Dr. Arbuthnot* (1735): "Let Budgell charge low Grub Street on his quill, and write whate'er he pleased—except his will." Scandal plagued him for two years as he vainly tried to prove his innocence in various lawsuits. Finally, on May 4, 1737, after filling his pockets with rocks from the beach, he hired a boat at Somerset-Stairs and while the waterman rowed them under the bridge there, threw himself overboard. He had tried to persuade his natural daughter, the actress Anne Eustace, to kill herself with him, but she had refused. Found on his desk was a slip of paper on which he had written of his act of suicide: "What Cato did, and Addison approved, cannot be wrong."

∇ ∇ ∇

Edward George Bulwer-Lytton (First Baron Lytton; 1803–1873)

The well-known author had many enemies besides his wife, Rosina (*q.v.*). The greatest of them was Tennyson. In an anonymous poem Bulwer-Lytton satirized the poet laureate as "School-Miss Alfred." An enraged Tennyson won the day, however, retaliating with a number of verses mocking Lytton as a rouged fop who padded his clothing.

It is said that the fashion of men dressing in formal black evening wear derives from a novel written by Bulwer-Lytton. Baron Lytton, a dandy himself, had the eponymous hero of his novel *Pelham* wear black instead of the bright colors then worn by English gentlemen in the evening. The popular novel created a fashion that still hasn't died.

Lady Rosina Bulwer-Lytton (1802–1882)

When her husband, Baron Bulwer-Lytton, ran for political office Lady Bulwer-Lytton followed him around England viciously heckling his speeches. So much did she hate him that she wrote a letter telling Wilkie Collins that Fosco, the arch villain in his novel *The Woman in White*, was a feeble fiend, indeed. "I know a villain, and have one in my eye at this moment that would far eclipse anything that I have read of in books," she wrote. "Don't think that I am drawing upon my imagination. The man is alive and constantly under my gaze. In fact he is my own husband." Finally, after their separation, Rosina wrote a novel *Cheveley, or The Man of Honour* (1839), in which her husband was the villain. She was certified insane in 1858 and was briefly in the care of a physician, but outlived the baron by nine years.

∇ ∇ ∇

John Bunyan (1628–1688)

Arrested in 1660 for preaching without a license, the nonconformist author was sent to jail, where he began work on *The Pilgrim's Progress*. In 1672, while he was still imprisoned, a Quaker called upon him, trying to convert him. "Friend John," he said, "I come to thee with a message from the Lord; and after having searched for thee in all the prisons of England, I am glad I have found thee at last."

"If the Lord has sent you," Bunyan replied, "you need not have had so much pains to find me out, for the Lord knows I have been here for twelve years."

As a boy he was haunted by dreams of fiends trying to fly away with him. Such terrors plagued him all his life—a price he paid for his powerful imagination and sensibility. He was also governed by strange impulses that prompted him to command puddles to be dry, to pray to trees, to a broomstrick, to the parish bull. At one point in his life he cried, "None knows the terror of these days but myself."

∇ ∇ ∇

Edmund Burke (1729–1797)

Convinced that democracy was but the rule of the mob, the statesman and author supported a government of the aristocracy, to the displeasure of the liberal friends with whom he usually sided. When an acquaintance noted that the democrats in Parliament always had trouble keeping a united front, Burke observed, "Birds of prey are not gregarious."

Always more interested in literature than politics, the great statesman was a prolific writer and member of Dr. Johnson's circle. When he was at the height of his power Burke befriended the impoverished poet George Crabbe after many prominent people refused him help. One time Crabbe arrived at the house too early for dinner and the butler refused to serve any food, "as the company had not come." Replied Burke's wife: "What, is not Mr. Crabbe here? Let it be brought up immediately!"

∇ ∇ ∇

Frances Hodgson Burnett (1849–1924)

The prolific novelist based the velvet-suited lord in her *Little Lord Fauntleroy* (1886) on her second son, Vivian. Her husband Dr. Stephen Townesend was a surgeon, novelist and crusading animal lover. He died from pneumonia after rising from his sick bed and rushing outside to help a fox being chased by hunters across his property.

∇ ∇ ∇

James Burnett (Lord Monboddo; 1714–1799)

A Scottish judge and pioneer in anthropology, Lord Monboddo wrote but two careful, scholarly books over his lifetime, distrusting facility. "Have you read my books?" another, much published, author once asked him. "I have not," Burnett replied. "You write a good deal faster than I am able to read."

∇ ∇ ∇

Robert Burns (1759–1796)

Few authors have matched the abusive invective Burns wrote to a critic in 1791: "Thou eunuch of language: thou butcher, imbruing thy hands in the bowels of orthography: thou arch-heretic in pronunciation: thou pitch-pipe of affected emphasis: thou carpenter, mortising the awkward joints of jarring sentence: thou squeaking dissonance of cadence: thou pimp of gender: thou scape-gallows from the land of syntax: thou scavenger of mood and tense: thou murderous accoucheur of infant learnings: thou *ignis fatuus*, misleading the steps of benighted ignorance: thou pickle-herring in the puppet-show of nonsense."

A man nicknamed The Marquis, who ran a public house in Dumfries, made the mistake of asking Burns to write his epitaph. The poet turned out the following:

Here lies a mock Marquis whose titles were shammed.
If ever he rise, it will be to be damned.

In an autobiographical letter to John Moore, Burns wrote:

My ancient but ignoble blood
has crept through scoundrels since the flood.

There was no doubt about his opinion of sex. "When I was fourteen," he said, "a bonnie, sweet, sonsy [jolly] lass initiated me into a certain delicious passion, which, in spite of acid disappointment, ginhouse prudence, and bookworm philosophy, I hold to be the finest of human joys." Another time he called himself "a fornicator by profession."

Burns "seduced women without compunction," according to our biographer. He fathered not less than 14 children, nine of them illegitimately. And his wife put up with it. Says another biographer: "His daughter Elizabeth, by Anna Park, and his legitimate daughter of the same name were born within a month of each other, and Jean Armour, his wife, suckled them both as uncomplainingly as though they were her own third set of twins."

In his own words, Burns was often in his life "left, like a true poet, without a sixpence." The first edition of his first collection of poems, containing some of his most famous songs, including "To a Mouse" and "The Two Dogs," brought him only £20. His contribution of 100 songs to Thomson's Scottish collection brought him a shawl for his wife, a picture, and £5. By April of 1796 Burns knew he was dying of rheumatic heart disease worsened by his hard life. Hand shaking, he wrote to a friend: "I fear it will be some time before I tune my lyre again. By Babel's streams I have sat and wept. I have only known existence by the pressure of sickness and counted time by the repercussions of pain. I close my eyes in misery and open them without hope..." His last two letters begged for money from his cousin and estranged father-in-law to keep him out of jail and pleaded with his estranged father-in-law to care for his wife, Jean, pregnant with their sixth child, after he died. While he was being buried on July 25th Jean gave birth to their son Maxwell, who died in infancy.

▽ ▽ ▽

Sir Richard Burton (1821–1890)
Burton, translator of the *Arabian Nights* and intrepid explorer of Muslim lands, is buried with his wife in the Mortlake Catholic Cemetery, Mortlake, England. They are interred beneath a concrete, lifesize Arab tent decorated with Christian and Muslim symbols.

When in 1860 a member of the British Royal Society sent Burton a letter ridiculing some of his claims about his travels in Central Africa, Burton did not waste words on him. He simply sent the man a reply consisting of a sketch of himself thumbing his nose at his critic.

"For thirty years I served her Majesty at home and abroad without acknowledgment or reward," Burton said shortly after the triumphal publication of his unexpurgated translation of the *Arabian Nights*. "Then I publish a pornographic book, and at once earn £10,000 and fame. I begin at last to understand the public and what it wants."

"To the pure all things are pure," Sir Richard wrote in the introduction of his translation of the *Arabian Nights*, but his wife, Isabel, thought that the papers the translator of the *Kama Sutra* left behind when he died in 1890 were obscene. She burned them all, including at least one completed book in manuscript.

∇ ∇ ∇

Robert Burton (1577–1640)
The clergyman and author wrote his famous medical masterpiece *The Anatomy of Melancholy* (1621) to try to escape his own melancholy, as he indeed tells us in the preface. Though his later portrait shows a contemplative, humorous face, it is said that his tactic never fully succeeded. While his melancholy nature improved, Burton could laugh only when he went down to the river in Oxford and listened to the bargemen scolding and cursing one another. Much preoccupied with when he would die, he predicted the year of his death many years before it came.

∇ ∇ ∇

Richard de Bury (1287–1345)
Tutor to the Prince of Wales and later bishop of Durham, de Bury was the foremost book collector of his time. His autobiographical *Philobiblon* describes his experiences as a book collector. Writing of his books therein he complained of "that two-legged beast called woman" mistreating them and trading them for silk, fine linen and other luxuries.

∇ ∇ ∇

Richard Busby (1605–1695)
Over his long career—he worked till his death at 90—Dr. Busby helped fashion English literature with his learning and rod. The noted schoolmaster and disciplinarian, headmaster of Westminster School, had among his pupils such greats as Dryden, Smith, Locke and Prior. He once boasted that he at one time or another birched 16 of the bishops then in office with his "little rod."

Dr. Busby, a very short man, was rudely pushed aside in a coffeehouse by a huge Irish baronet who quipped, "May I pass to my seat, O Giant?" The doctor replied "Pass, O Pigmy!" and then the baronet apologized, saying, "I'm sorry, my expression alluded to the size of your intellect."

"And my expression to the size of yours," Busby replied.

▽ ▽ ▽

Samuel Butler (1835–1902)

The six large notebooks the novelist left behind give many insights into his life. One entry recounts his uncomforting words to a very ill woman. "Promise me solemnly," he said to her as she lay on what he believed to be her deathbed, "if you find in the world beyond the grave that you can communicate with me—that there in some way in which you can make me aware of your continued existence—promise me solemnly that you will never, never avail yourself of it."

He adds that the woman recovered "and never, never forgave me."

Butler's famous poem "A Psalm of Montreal" (1878) with the refrain "O God! O Montreal!" was an attack on philistinism, inspired by a visit Butler made to Canada in 1874. There at the Natural History Museum he found to his dismay that a beautiful Greek statue of a Discobolus had been relegated to a basement taxidermy room. It had been stored there, the taxidermist explained, because it was "vulgar," the statue "having neither vest nor pants to cover his lower limbs."

▽ ▽ ▽

George Gordon Byron (Sixth Baron Byron; 1788–1824)

The great romantic poet's ancestors rivaled him in adventures and amorous escapades. Bryon's great uncle, the handsome William, was called the "Wicked Lord" because of his wild life, rakish ways and reckless spending. The poet's grandfather, John Byron, who circumnavigated the globe, earned the nickname "the Nautical Lover" for his wife or mistress in every port. As for Byron's father, Captain John Byron, his devilish ways inspired people to call him "Mad Jack" Byron.

Byron was only 5 feet 8 1/2 inches tall, and his widely varying weight ranged from as little as 137 pounds to 202 pounds. Very sensitive about the club foot he was born with, he was a vain man who is even said to have put up his hair in curlers at night. He excelled at dieting, in part because he hadn't the taste for food that he had for words. Wrote his friend Trelawney:

> [His] terror of getting fat was so great that he reduced his diet to the point of absolute starvation. When he added to his weight, even standing was painful, so he resolved to keep down to eleven stone or shoot himself. He said everything he swallowed was instantly converted to tallow and deposited on his ribs. He was the only human being I ever met with who had sufficient self-restraint and resolution

to resist his proneness to fatten. As he was always hungry, his merit was the greater. Occasionally he relaxed his vigilance, when he swelled apace. I remember one of his old friends saying, "Byron, how well you are looking!" If he had stopped there it had been well, but when he added, "You are getting fat," Byron's brow reddened, and his eye flashed—"Do you call getting fat looking well, as if I were a hog?" and turning to me he muttered, "The beast, I can hardly keep my hands off him." I don't think he had much appetite for his dinner that day, or for many days, and he never forgave the man. He would exist on biscuits and soda water for days together, then, to allay the eternal hunger gnawing at his vitals, he would make up a horrid mess of cold potatoes, rice, fish, or greens, deluged in vinegar, and gobble it up like a famished dog. Either of these unsavoury dishes, with a glass or two of Rhine wine, he cared not how sour, he called feasting sumptuously. Upon my observing he might as well have fresh fish and vegetable instead of stale, he laughed and answered: "I have an advantage over you—I have no palate; one thing is as good as another to me."

A very handsome man, he was the devil incarnate to some proper English ladies. One woman, traveling in Geneva, fainted of fear when Byron unexpectedly came into Madame de Staël's salon. His mistress, Lady Caroline Lamb, remarked of him in her diary: "Mad, bad, and dangerous to know."

While staying in Ravenna, Italy, he lived on the third floor of Count Guiccioli's palace, sharing the count's wife with him and sharing his quarters with a monkey, two cats, six dogs, a crow, a falcon, a badger, and a fox. (While at Trinity College, Cambridge, he kept a dog and a bear in his quarters.)

Living in his own Venetian palace, complete with its 14 servants, a mistress, and assorted pets, including two monkeys, he wrote to a friend that "in the evenings I go out sometimes, and indulge in coition always." He proudly claimed he had different women on 200 consecutive evenings.

Observing Byron in an opera box at La Scala in 1816, another genius, Stendhal, later recalled: "I was struck by his eyes...I have never in my life seen anything more beautiful or more expressive. Even today, if I come to think of the expression which a great painter should give to a genius, this sublime head at once appears before me...I shall never forget the divine expression of his face; it was the serene air of power and genius."

Boxing gloves had been introduced to England by champion Jack Broughton in the 18th century, and the father of British boxing also drew up the first boxing rules, under which gentlemen like Byron learned to box scientifically from teachers like "Gentleman" John Jackson. Wrote the poet of his teacher: "And men unpracticed in exchanging knocks / Must go to Jackson ere they dare to box."

Lord Byron was perhaps the greatest of literary swimmers, whose ranks have included Poe (who once swam 7 1/2 miles from Richmond to Warwick, Virginia, against a tide running two to three miles an hour); Ben Franklin (who taught swimming and invented swim fins); Swinburne (who dipped in the English Channel one Christmas); and Eugene O'Neill (a polar bear swimmer who swam every day throughout the winter). Byron swam the Hellespont (an ancient name for the Dardanelles Strait) in the breast stroke fashion of his day. The poet wanted to emulate the legendary Greek Leander, who fell in love with Hero, the priestess of Venus, and swam the Hellespont every night to visit her; Leander drowned one evening, and Hero, mourning him, drowned herself in the same waters. Byron, who made the swim with a Lieutenant Ekenhead of the Royal Navy, did the four miles (allowing for drifting) in 65 minutes, which is a good enough time for the modern freestyle, as anyone who has done four miles will attest. The poet, who finished five minutes ahead of Ekenhead, alludes to his swim in *Don Juan*:

> A better swimmer you could scarce see ever,
> He could, perhaps, have pass'd the Hellespont
> As once (a feat on which ourselves we prided)
> Leander, Mr. Ekenhead, and I did.

Another time Byron visited a lady in Venice and swam home in the Grand Canal, carrying a torch in one hand to light his way and protect himself from the oars of the *gondolieri*.

Contrary to Dr. Johnson's dictum that only a blockhead wrote for anything but money, Byron often wrote for the exhilaration and glory of writing, sometimes refusing payment for his poems. Even at the height of his fame, when his poems were selling 6,000 copies and more a month, he proudly refused to take payment for any of his work. It was only toward the end of his writing career, in late 1817, that he agreed to accept payment for his poems.

After the publication of the first two cantos of *Childe Harold's Pilgrimage* in 1812 he noted in his diary: "I awoke one morning and found myself famous." From then on publishers couldn't get enough of his work. His long poem *The Corsair*, published by Murray in 1814, sold 10,000 copies on the first day of publication.

The poet was a great admirer of the brilliant wit of playwright Richard Brinsley Sheridan and once recalled a night "When *he* talked and we listened, without one yawn, from six till one in the morning." Another time Byron told a group of friends: "Whatever Sheridan has done or chosen to do has been par excellence the best of its kind. He has written the best comedy *(The School for Scandal)*, the best opera *(The Duenna)*, the best farce *(The Critic)*...the best address (the

Monologue on Garrick) and to crown all delivered the best Oration (the famous Begum speech in Parliament) ever conceived in this country."

The next day word got back to Sheridan of this extravagant compliment and he burst into tears.

"Poor Brinsley," Byron said on hearing this. "If they were tears of pleasure, I would rather have said these few, but most sincere words than have written the *Iliad* or made his own celebrated *Philippic*."

Byron feuded with England's Poet Laureate Robert Southey, not only because he had attacked Byron in print but because Byron felt that in renouncing his youthful revolutionary ideals and accepting the laureateship the poet had betrayed his principles. He would attack the prolific Southey a number of times but his most enduring riposte was the lines:

> He had written much blank verse, and
>   blanker prose,
> And more of both than anybody knows.

The line "Now Barabbas was a publisher" is often attributed to Lord Byron. Byron supposedly received a lavish copy of the Bible from publisher John Murray in gratitude for a favor, only to return it after changing the sentence "Now Barabbas was a robber," in John 18:40, to "Now Barabbas was a publisher." (See also THOMAS CAMPBELL.)

Byron wrote the epitaph for his Newfoundland dog Boatswain, buried in his Newstead Abbey garden vault:

> To mark a friend's remains there stones arise;
> I never had but one—and here he lies.

In his will he directed that he be buried in the same place and further specified "It is my will that my faithful dog not be removed from the said vault."

He wrote in his diary on January 21, 1821, the day before his 33rd birthday:

> Through life's road, so dim and dirty,
> I have dragg'd to three and thirty.
> What have these years left to me?
> Nothing—except, thirty-three.

In an 1819 letter to publisher John Murray, Byron wrote, "I am sure my bones would not rest in an English grave, or my clay mix with the earth of that country. I believe the thought would drive me mad on my deathbed, could I suppose that

any of my friends would be base enough to convey my carcass back to your soil."
After his death in Greece of fever (he had told Lady Blessington the year before
that he would die there) his body was shipped back to England and refused
burial by both Westminster and St. Paul's. He was eventually interred in his
family vault near Newstead, as he had requested long before he went to Greece.

Few literary men, perhaps not another, were such legends in their lifetime. Late
in his life Tennyson recalled the day when as a boy of 15 he heard that Byron had
died: "Byron was dead! I thought the whole word was at an end. I thought
everything was over and finished for everyone—that nothing else mattered. I
remember I walked out alone, and carved 'Byron is dead' into the sandstone."

∇ ∇ ∇ ∇ ∇ ∇ ∇ ∇

Caedmon (fl. 670)

Caedmon, his name apparently Celtic, is the first English poet whose name is
known. He is said by the Venerable Bede in his *Ecclesiastical History* to have been
an old, uneducated herdsman who knew no songs and would leave when his
friends gathered at a feast to sing songs in turn. One evening he left early and
fell asleep tending his cattle. He dreamed that a stranger appeared who ordered
him to sing of "the beginning of created things." Despite his protests that he was
unable to sing, Caedmon was compelled to obey and found himself uttering
"verses which he had never heard before in praise of God the Creator." When
he awoke, he remembered the poem (the first that can be attributed to an
individual in English), of which Bede gives a Latin prose paraphrase that
translates: "Now we must praise the Maker of the heavenly kingdom, the power
of the Creator and his counsel, the deeds of the Father of glory, and how He,
since He is the eternal God, was the Author of all marvels and first created the
heavens as a roof for the children of men, and then, the Almighty Guardian of
the human race, created the earth."

That morning Caedmon told his employer of his dream and was taken to the
monastery at what is now Whitby, where he was tested and found able to
compose religious poetry in excellent metrical form from sacred history that the
monks explained to him. he became a lay brother himself and spent the rest of
his life composing his poems. "He learned all he could by listening to them [the

learned brothers]," Bede tells us, "and then, memorizing it and ruminating over it, like some clean animal chewing the cud, he turned it into the most melodious verse: and it sounded so sweet as he recited it that his teachers became in turn his audience."

Only his first brief dream poem (called "Hymn of Creation") of all Caedmon's work is definitely known to survive. He is not only the first known English poet and the first known English Christian poet, but the first English poet said to be divinely inspired and the first to whom a poem came in a dream. A similar dream story, however, is told of the Icelandic poet Halebjorn Hali. (See also SAMUEL TAYLOR COLERIDGE.)

∇ ∇ ∇

Giraldus Cambrensis (1146?–1220?)

This early English churchman and author, son of the Welsh Princess Nesta, had a sharp tongue that got him in trouble throughout his stormy but fruitful career. He may well have been the first in a long line of sardonic English literary critics, judging by his story about Geoffrey of Monmouth's Latin *History of the Briton* (c. 1136), a book that greatly contributed to the popularity of the Arthurian legends in England but that some writers of the day called pure invention. In his story Giraldus tells of a Welshman who "has the knowledge of occult events" but one night finds "a hairy, rough and hideous creature" in his arms in place of the beautiful damsel he is making love to. He goes mad, but is restored to health "through the merits of the saints," yet still has occult powers because of his familiarity with the evil spirits. Among other powers, Giraldus says, the Welshman "If he looked on a book faultily or falsely written or containing a false passage, although wholly illiterate he would point out the place with his finger...[being] directed by the demon's finger at the place." Giraldus ends his fantastic tale with the following anecdote: "If the spirits oppressed him [the Welshman] too much, the Gospel of St. John was placed on his bosom [and] like birds, they immediately vanished; but when the book was removed, and the *History of the Britons* by Geoffrey [of Monmouth] was substituted in its place, they instantly reappeared in greater numbers, and remained a longer time than usual on his body and on the book."

∇ ∇ ∇

John Campbell (1708–1775)

High up on the list of most absentminded authors, the Scottish writer once became engrossed in a book in a bookstore, purchased it, and didn't realize that he had *written* the book "until he had read it half-way through."

Roy Campbell (1901–1957)

Campbell is probably the only acclaimed poet who was also well known as a bullfighter. After surviving World War II, the swashbuckling South African poet, who lived in England for long period, was killed in an automobile crash.

∇ ∇ ∇

Thomas Campbell (1777–1844)

The lines "Now Barabbas was a publisher" are often attributed to Lord Byron (q.v.), but they may have their origin in the words of Scottish poet Thomas Campbell. Napoleon had had German publisher Johann Palm put to death for printing subversive pamphlets. Later, at an authors' dinner, Campbell proposed this toast: "To Napoleon. [Voices of protest] I agree with you that Napoleon is a tyrant, a monster, the sworn foe of our nation. But, gentlemen—he once shot a publisher!"

Campbell, son of a Glasgow merchant, frequently protested his inevitable association with his most famous work, the long poem *The Pleasures of Hope*, which he wrote when only 22. "When I was young," he confided to a friend, "I was always greeted among my friends as Mr. Campbell, author of *The Pleasure of Hope*. When I married, I was married as the author of *The Pleasures of Hope*, and when I became a father, my son was the son of the author of *The Pleasures of Hope*. Nevertheless, years later at his funeral, his friends could not help but notice the inscription on the poet's coffin, which read: "Thomas Campbell LLD, author of *The Pleasures of Hope*, died, June 15, 1844, aged 67."

∇ ∇ ∇

George Canning (1770–1827)

The Tory prime minister was a poet and witty parodist as well. He is responsible for the verse:

Give me the avowed, the erect, the manly foe;
Bold I can meet—perhaps turn his blow;
But of all plagues, good heaven, thy wrath can send,
Save, save, oh! save me from the Candid Friend!

"How did you like my sermon?" a clergyman asked the statesman and author.

"It was very short," Canning said.

"Yes," said the clergyman, "you know I avoid being tedious."

"Ah, but you were tedious," Canning replied.

Henry Carey (1687?–1743)

"Aldiborontiphoscophornio! Where left you Chrononhotonthologos?" begins Carey's farce *Chrononhotonthologos, The Most Tragical Tragedy That Ever Was Tragedized by Any Company of Tragedians* (1743). These are the longest words ever delivered by an actor on stage. Chrononhotonthologos was the King of Queerummania, and his name is now used, if used at all, for any bombastic person delivering an inflated address. Aldiborontiphoscophornio was a courier in the play. Carey, who wrote the popular song "Sally in My Alley," may have written the words and music to the British anthem "God Save the King."

▽ ▽ ▽

William Carleton (1794–1869)

Black Prophet (1847), a novel about the potato famine, is among this prolific Irish author's best-regarded works. Potatoes were in one way responsible for Carleton becoming a writer. As a bookish young man setting out for Dublin from County Tyrone, he had failed at everything else he tried, including the military, when he applied in Latin to enlist! Finally he sought a job as an apprentice bird taxidermist, but was turned down when he suggested to his prospective employer that the birds be stuffed with potatoes. There was nothing left to do but write.

▽ ▽ ▽

Jane Baillie Welsh Carlyle (1801–1866)

Thomas Carlyle's wife and one of the most remarkable letter-writers of her day, Jane Carlyle was in precarious mental health for many years and only her husband's constant care kept her from a complete breakdown. She died suddenly while out riding, as the immediate result of the shock caused by an accident to her dog running alongside the carriage, but she had been very ill for a year before this. Her will instructed that several wax candles her mother had given her be used to light her "chamber of death"—she had once hurt her mother's feelings by refusing to use the candles and had saved them for years for this purpose. When she died, Carlyle's life became more and more secluded. It has been suggested that their marriage was an unhappy one because of sexual inadequacy on his part, but that remains largely conjecture. It is certain that Jane's death, in his words, "shattered my whole existence into immeasurable ruin" and that he wrote very little else of importance without her.

▽ ▽ ▽

Thomas Carlyle (1795–1881)

Carlyle, who began his literary career in Edinburgh and moved on to London, was a left-handed scribbler with the worst penmanship of any author of his day.

A printer who had recently come to England for employment said on being handed one of his manuscripts: "What! have you got that man here! I fled Scotland to get away from him!"

The author had to rewrite the entire first volume of his *History of the French Revolution* when John Stuart Mill borrowed the manuscript to read and loaned it to his lover (and future wife), whose maid burned it, mistaking it for waste paper. This happened at a time when Carlyle "had not only forgotten the structure of it, but the spirit it was written with was past..." He wrote to his brother that he felt like a man who had "nearly killed himself accomplishing zero." Nevertheless, he accepted half of a £200 check Mill sent him to help make up for the loss and supported himself on it while rewriting his masterpiece. The rewritten work established his reputation.

Carlyle was listening to poet and man of letters (Richard) Monckton Milnes express his disappointment in not being offered a post in Sir Robert Peel's new administration. "No, no," Carlyle interrupted. "Peel knows what he is about; there is only one post fit for you, and that is the office of perpetual president of the Heaven and Hell Amalgamation Society."

Carlyle was never a healthy man; all his life he suffered from stomach pains that he said made him feel as though a rat were gnawing at his insides. Insomnia often plagued him and he hated the noise of London, particularly the crowing of "demon-fowls" in his neighborhood. He stayed in London only to humor his wife, Jane, who loved the city. Finally, the only way he could work in his London house was to build a "sound-proof room" on the top of the house where he would shut himself up with his books.

It was Carlyle's practice in his soundproof room to paste above his desk engraved pictures of the people he was writing about, believing as he did that if he could not accurately visualize his subject he would never be able to make his readers do so.

Carlyle was often criticized for his antidemocratic views, as demonstrated in his "Occasional Discourse on the Nigger Question" (1849). He thought his lifelong friend Emerson, who visited him in England, hopelessly optimistic. One time he explained the U.S. Civil War to a friend this way: "There they are cutting each other's throats, because one-half of them prefer hiring their servants for life, and the other by the hour."

The author was asked by a mutual friend if he wanted to meet with the celebrated but controversial poet Algernon Swinburne, whose work reflected a free spirit and his outspoken repudiation of conventions. Replied the straitlaced Carlyle: "I have no wish to know anyone sitting on a sewer and adding to it."

▽ ▽ ▽

Queen Caroline (1683–1737)

A woman of letters, the queen knew most of the literary figures of her day, helped many young artists get started and saved several from poverty. "She is an amiable philosopher sitting on a throne," Voltaire said of her. As she lay dying, she told George II that he should marry after her death. "No, I will have mistresses," he replied sincerely. "Ah, my God," she said, "that will not interfere!"

▽ ▽ ▽

Lewis Carroll (Charles Lutwidge Dodgson; 1832–1898)

For over a century Carroll's *Alice in Wonderland* (1865) has been the most famous and possibly the most widely read children's book. That there is an *Alice* cult even among adults is witnessed by the numerous works of criticism devoted to the book, which has even been translated into Latin. The model for the fictional Alice was Alice Liddell, daughter of Dean Henry George Liddell, noted coauthor of *Liddell & Scott's Greek Lexicon*, still the standard Greek-English dictionary. Carroll wrote *Alice* for his friend's daughter, who later became Mrs. Reginald Hargreaves. The author apparently made up the story while on a picnic with Alice and her sisters, actually improvising the classic tale as the group rowed about a lake. Incidentally, Carroll is regarded as the greatest 19th-century photographer of children and his best pictures were of Alice Liddell. At first entitled *Alice's Adventures Underground*, his classic book was only published, in expanded form, at the urging of novelist Henry Kingsley, who read the manuscript at the Liddell home.

He was a chronic complainer. While teaching at Christ College, Oxford, he wrote at least 48 letters to the steward complaining about everything from odors in the common room to the meat served for dinner.

▽ ▽ ▽

William Cartwright (1611–1643)

One of Ben Jonson's "sons," the poet, dramatist and preacher was among the most highly regarded authors of his day. King Charles cried when Cartwright died at the age of 33 after contracting typhus. Asked why he wore black on the day of Cartwright's funeral, the monarch replied that "since the Muses had so much mourned for the loss of such a son, it would be a shame for him not to appear in mourning for the loss of such a subject."

Lucius Cary (Viscount Falkland; 1610–1643)

The poet and theological writer, a man of great learning, was an aristocrat but wanted his work to reach everybody. Whenever he thought that a word wasn't perfectly clear, he tried it out on his wife's chambermaid. If she didn't understand it, he didn't use it.

∇ ∇ ∇

James Catnach (1792–1841)

In 1824 London printer James Catnach sold at one penny each the "last speech by the condemned murderers of a merchant named Weare." When the sheet sold out in a day, Catnach decided to capitalize on the murder, headlining another penny paper "We Are Alive Again," but running the first two words together so that the banner read "Weare Alive Again." Gulled buyers of the Catnach penny paper punned on his name after discovering the cheap trick, referring to his paper as *catchpenny*, which soon came to mean any low-priced, fraudulent item. A good story, this is one of the best and earliest examples of folk etymology. But the fault in this ingenious yarn lies in the fact that *catchpenny* was used in the same sense, "any flimflam that might catch a penny," 65 years before the Catnach ploy. Nevertheless, Catnach's paper did give the word catchpenny greater currency.

∇ ∇ ∇

Charles Cavendish (1591–1654)

The mathematician collected a large library of rare mathematical books in manuscript while traveling on the continent. After he died, his wife, ignorant of their worth, sold his valuable collection "by weight to the paste-board makers for Waste-paper." (See also ISAAC NEWTON.)

∇ ∇ ∇

Robert Cecil (Marquess of Salisbury; 1830–1903)

The statesman and author was asked what he thought of Viscount Northcliff's popular newspaper the *Daily Mail*. Replied Lord Salisbury: "By office boys for office boys."

∇ ∇ ∇

James Chalmers (1841–1901)

This Scottish missionary and author, a friend of Robert Louis Stevenson, was studying the cannibals on Goaribari Island off New Guinea with an eye toward their conversion. Unfortunately for Chalmers, the cannibals were also studying him and, liking what they saw, roasted him for a repast.

Thomas Chatterton (1752–1770)

This tale of literary ratiocination involves the little word *its*. Before the 17th century *its* wasn't used to indicate the possessive case; *it* and *his* served this purpose (as in, "For love and devotion toward God also hath its infancie" or, "learning hath his infancy"). From age 12 to 16, the poet Thomas Chatterton wrote, among other forgeries, a number of poems purporting to be the work of an imaginary 15th-century monk, Thomas Rowley. These poems were published after the destitute, despairing Chatterton tore up most of his work and committed suicide by drinking arsenic. They were soon hailed as works of poetic genius. But eight years later critic Thomas Tyrwhitt revealed that the poems were forgeries, finding, among other errors, that one of Chatterton's lines read: "Life and its good I scorn." Chatterton's tragic death at the age of 18 inspired Keats to dedicate "Endymion" to him, while Ruggiero Leoncavallo composed an opera about him and Alfred de Vigny wrote a play called *Chatterton*.

A few days before his suicide Chatterton was walking with a friend in a graveyard when he fell into an open grave. His companion helped him out, delighted, he said, "to be present at the resurrection of a genius." To Chatterton, however, it seemed a premonition of death. "I have been at war with the grave for sometime," he said, "and I find it not so easy to vanquish as I imagined. We can find an asylum to hide from every creditor but that."

As his last poem he wrote:

> Farewell, Bristolia's dingy piles of brick,
> Lovers of Mammon, worshippers of trick!
> Ye spurned the boy who gave you antique lays,
> And paid for learning with your empty praise.
> Farewell, ye quizzling aldermanic fools,
> By nature fitted for corruption's tools!...
>
> Farewell, my mother!— cease, my anguish'd soul,
> Nor let distraction's billows o'er me roll!
> Have merry, heaven! when here I cease to live,
> And this last act of wretchedness forgive.

▽ ▽ ▽

Geoffrey Chaucer (c. 1343–1400)

Chaucer's name is of French origin and was probably pronounced *show-sayr*. Though his own father was a vintner his name meant shoemaker in French.

Chaucer was so valued as a skilled professional soldier that when he was captured by the French at the siege of Rheims in 1360 King Edward III of England paid £16 ($3,840, then a tidy sum) to ransom him.

During the time that he served as "controller of the customs and subsidies" Chaucer was charged with rape. His guilt or innocence has never been determined. It is only known that in 1380 he paid one Cecile Champaigne an unstated sum for withdrawing the suit she had filed against him.

∇ ∇ ∇

G.K. (Gilbert Keith) Chesterton (1874–1936)

Chesterton was obese (see the George Bernard Shaw anecdote) from the time he was a child and it at first seemed that he was stupid, too. He did not learn to read until he was over eight and one of his teachers told him, "If we opened your head, we should not find any brain but only a lump of white fat." He remained at the very bottom of his class until he was about 15. (See also DARWIN.)

Though corpulent he was a jolly man who often made jokes at his own expense. One time he remarked, "Just the other day in the Underground I enjoyed the pleasure of offering my seat to three ladies."

Monsignor John O'Connor, the Catholic cleric who was the model for G.K. Chesterton's celebrated detective Father Brown, frequently had church ushers give white slips of paper to all latecomers to mass without telling them why. When he reached the Notices in the service, he would ask all worshippers who had been given white slips of paper to hold them up. Then he'd comment dryly: "You were all late."

Chesterton gave the classic answer to the old question "What book would you most like to have with you on a desert island?" "Thomas's Guide to Practical Shipbuilding," he replied.

He liked to tell the story of a Victorian editor's complaint about a serial novel his sister-in-law, Mrs. Cecil Chesterton, had written: "You have left your hero and heroine tied up in a cavern for a week, and they are not married!"

Chesterton was told that it was possible to obtain a divorce in the United States on the grounds of incompatibility. "If that is true," he observed, "I find it remarkable that there are any marriages left in the United States."

Like J.M. Barrie (*q.v.*) he had an unusual talent. According to our writer, not least among his multiplicity of talents was "the almost invariable capacity, when throwing buns in the air, to catch them in his mouth."

Observed Chesterton on seeing for the first time the sparkling bright lights of Broadway: "How beautiful it would be for someone who could not read."

In his book *Platitudes in the Making* Holbrook Jackson made disparaging remarks about theology. Reading the entry, Chesterton penciled under it: "Theology is the part of religion that requires brains."

∇ ∇ ∇

William Chillingworth (1602–1644)

The author of the controversial *The Religion of the Protestants a Safe Way to Salvation* (1637) died of syphilis and was buried at Chichester. His enemy Dr. Francis Cheynell threw his book into the grave with him, crying, "Rot with the rotten; let the dead bury the dead."

∇ ∇ ∇

Agatha Christie (1891–1976)

Probably the most remarkable mysterious disappearance in literary history occurred on December 3, 1926, when Agatha Christie, at the height of her fame as a mystery writer, disappeared from her home in Berkshire. After finding her car, police began a 10-day investigation employing over 15,000 volunteers before she was finally found registered under another name at a Yorkshire health spa. Guests testified that she seemed to act like the South African she claimed to be and even followed the Christie story in the papers. Agatha Christie always claimed that she had amnesia, but there has been speculation that she ran away to get even with her first husband, who was visiting his mistress the day she left.

According to a 1977 news story: "Agatha Christie's 16-year-old detective story, *The Pale Horse*, recently saved the life of a 19-month-old girl dying of a condition that baffled London doctors...The Arab baby, flown from the Persian Gulf for treatment, was semiconscious when admitted to Hammersmith Hospital in London. Despite intensive care, her breathing became increasingly difficult and she appeared on the brink of death. The doctors could not diagnose the illness. Then, on morning rounds, nurse Marsha Maitland suggested that the infant might have thallium poisoning. (Thallium is a bluish-white metal with poisonous salts.) The nurse, who had been reading *The Pale Horse*, said the baby's symptoms were remarkably similar to those of a thallium case in the book...Tests confirmed thallium poisoning. Given proper treatment, the baby gradually recovered."

Of her marriage to her second husband, archaeologist Max Mallowan, the writer told reporters: "An archaeologist is the best husband any woman can have. The older she gets, the more interested he is in her."

∇ ∇ ∇

Charles Churchill (1731–1764)

A minister who was forced to resign from his post when his parishioners protested his dandy dressing and loose living, the poet and satirist led a dissolute life, becoming a member of the infamous Hellfire Club with his friends John Wilkes and Sir Francis Dashwood. When his poem "Night" appeared in December 1761, a critic remarked, "This Night, like many others at this time of the year, is very cold, long, dark and dirty."

The poet made many satiric attacks on powerful targets, but one of his best was a poem about Dr. Johnson that he circulated among their mutual friends. It concerned Johnson's never-published edition of Shakespeare, for which his many friends had contributed great sums of money:

He for subscribers baits his hook,
And takes your cash, but where's the book?
No matter where; wise fear, you know,
Forbids the robbing of a foe;
But what, to serve our private ends,
Forbids the cheating of our friends?

Churchill was one of the fattest of the English poets, elephantine in figure, and wrote of himself:

Vast were his bones, his muscles twisted strong;
His face was short, but broader than 'twas long;
His features, though by nature they were large,
Contentment had contrived to overcharge,
And bury meaning, save that we might spy
Sense lowering in the penthouse of his eye;
His arms were two twin oaks; his legs so stout
That they might bear a Mansion House about;
Nor were they, look but at his body there,
Designed by fate a much less weight to bear.

He died young, having led a dissipated life after abandoning the church. Dying as a result of drunkenness, his last words are said to have been: "What a fool I've been!"

▽ ▽ ▽

Lord Randolph Churchill (1849–1895)
Lord Randolph Churchill, Sir Winston's father, didn't quite share his son's passion for literature. He is said to have hired a man to read boring books for him and to sit in his place listening to the club bore tell dull stories.

▽ ▽ ▽

Sir Winston Churchill (1874–1965)
Churchill's parents despaired of his ever making a living, so poorly did he do in school. Mainly because he refused to study what he didn't like, he was always at the bottom of his class up until he entered Sandhurst. He had failed the entrance exam to the military academy twice, but passed on his third attempt after studying with a "crammer." (See also CHESTERTON and DARWIN.)

Soon after he returned to London after covering the Boer War, Churchill was strolling through Hyde Park listening to its famed soapbox speakers. One man kept vociferously denouncing Queen Victoria. "Why don't you do something?" Churchill demanded of an English bobby nearby. "Why don't you arrest the man?"

"Well, you see, it's this way, sir," the policeman explained. "It don't 'urt 'er, and it might 'elp 'im."

While Churchill was first lord of the Admiralty (1911–15), he remarked acidly, in answer to a protest about British naval traditions being violated, that the traditions of the navy were "rum, sodomy, and the lash."

Quipped British Prime Minister David Lloyd George of him: "He has spoilt himself by reading about Napoleon."

Another time Lloyd George told a friend: "Winston would go up to his creator and say that he would very much like to see His Son, about whom he had heard a great deal and, if possible, would like to call on the Holy Ghost. Winston *loves* meeting people."

Shortly after Churchill had switched from the Conservative side of the House of Commons to the Liberal side, a brazen young woman approached him in one of England's corridors of power.

"There are two things I don't like about you, Mr. Churchill," she said.

"And what are they?" he asked.

"Your new politics and your new mustache."

"My dear madam," Churchill replied, "pray do not disturb yourself. You are not likely to come in contact with either."

Noticing the pompous Sir Stafford Cripps pass by, Churchill turned to a friend and observed: "There, but for the grace of God, goes God."

Churchill was more than capable of obfuscating speech. Once, in a parliamentary debate with Joseph Chamberlain, he admitted that he might have been guilty of a "terminological inexactitude."

Replied Chamberlain, "I prefer the ugly little English three-letter word: l-i-e."

Said another British politician of Churchill: "Winston has devoted the best years of his life to preparing his impromptu speeches."

"Writing is an adventure," Churchill said in explaining his avocation. "To begin with, it is a toy and an amusement. Then it becomes a mistress, then it becomes a master, then it becomes a tyrant. The last phase is that just as you are about to be reconciled to your servitude, you kill the monster and fling him to the public."

"There is a good saying to the effect that when a new book appears one should read an old one," Churchill remarked. "As an author I would not recommend too strict an adherence to this saying."

"Well, I hope he doesn't have feet of clay, too," Churchill said of Greek Prime Minister Plasteras.

Churchill found it difficult to tolerate the pomposity of Charles de Gaulle, leader of the Free French during World War II. "Of all the crosses I have to bear," he once told a friend, "the heaviest is the Cross of Lorraine."

A press worker "corrected" in the printer's proof of his memoirs a sentence that ended with a preposition. Churchill reportedly changed it back, noting in the margin of the proofs: "This is the sort of impertinence [or nonsense] up with which I will not put."

Churchill was accosted by a voter after winning an election to Parliament. "I presume we may expect you to continue to be humbly subservient to the powerful interests that control your vote," the man said. "I'll thank you to keep my wife's name out of this," Churchill replied.

"Have you read my recent book?" Churchill's cousin and political opponent Lord Londonberry asked.

"No," Churchill replied. "I only read for pleasure or profit."

Churchill wasn't very impressed with Clement Atlee, his successor as prime minister. He once told a friend Atlee was "A sheep in sheep's clothing." Another time he made this observation: "He [Atlee] has the gift of compressing the largest amount of words into the smallest amount of thought."

"May I have some breast?" Churchill asked his American hostess at a buffet luncheon.

"In this country, Mr. Churchill, we say, white meat or dark meat," his hostess replied, a little prissily.

Churchill apologized and the next day sent her an orchid along with a card reading, "I would be most obliged if you would pin this on your white meat."

When told that by the year 2100 women would rule the world, he replied, "Still?"

"Sarah," Churchill told his daughter in commenting on the state of the world, "we have to a large extent succeeded in erasing the lion and the tiger from the human soul. But we have not succeeded in removing the donkey."

"I am ready to meet my Maker," he said on his 75th birthday. "Whether my Maker is prepared for the ordeal of meeting me is another matter."

Churchill could be nearly impossible to work for. Late in his life one of his loyal valets received one undeserved reprimand too many and stood up to him. A loud argument ensued and when it subsided, Churchill said, "You were very rude to me, you know."

"Yes," the manservant replied, "but you were rude, too."

"Yes," Churchill groused, "but I am a great man."

Later the servant would say: "There was no answer to that. He knew, as I and the rest of the world knew, that he was right."

The manservant continued working for him.

It was Churchill's habit to sleep in the nude and when he awoke he often roamed around his rooms at Chartwell in the same state. He frequently dictated letters to his secretaries half-dressed. Wrote his secretary Kathleen Hill: "He would often be dashing around in shorts and undershirt, while I trotted behind him with a pad and pencil struggling to keep pace with the torrential flow of his words."

On April 9, 1963, Churchill was paid the unique honor of being proclaimed a citizen of the United States. President John F. Kennedy's Churchillian official proclamation read as follows:

> In the dark days and darker nights when Britain stood alone—and most men save Englishmen despaired of England's life—he mobilized the English language and sent it into battle. The incandescent quality of his words illuminated the courage of his countrymen...Given unlimited powers by his fellow citizens, he was ever vigilant to protect their rights. Indifferent himself to danger, he wept over the sorrow of others. A child of the House of Commons, he became in time its father. Accustomed to the hardship of battle, he has no distaste for pleasure. By adding his name to our rolls, we mean to honor him—but his acceptance honors us far more. For no statement of proclamation can enrich his name—the name Sir Winston Churchill is already legend.

Winston S. Churchill, the eight-volume biography of Churchill (begun by his son, with six volumes written by Martin Gilbert after Randolph Churchill's death), is the longest biography in the English language, totaling some 9.2 million words.

∇ ∇ ∇

Colley Cibber (1671–1757)

A rude, conceited man, Cibber was a theatrical manager as well as an actor and dramatist. He had a stock answer whenever a playwright asked him to explain why he had rejected a play submitted to him. "Sir," he would say, pausing to take a pinch of snuff, "there is nothing in it to coerce my passions."

∇ ∇ ∇

Theophilus Cibber (1703–1758)

Cibber led a stormy, controversial life like his playwright father, Colley Cibber, before him. As rude and vain as his father, with much less to be vain about, he was involved in financial dishonesty concerning the Drury Lane Theatre and provoked great scandal by encouraging his actress wife to have an affair with a rich man for mercenary reasons. It is common knowledge that Mark Twain came in and went out with Halley's Comet. Cibber, who led such a stormy life, was born during the Great Storm of 1703 and died in the Great Storm of 1758; he drowned when his ship went down while sailing to Dublin.

John Clare (1793–1864)

The son of a farm laborer and a day laborer himself, the "ploughman poet," never of stable mind, was admitted as insane to an asylum in 1837 and spent the rest of his life there. Some time before this, while watching the *Merchant of Venice* in the company of his patron, the bishop of Peterborough, Clare allied himself with Portia and began berating the actor who played Shylock. Suddenly, he leaped up on his seat crying, "You villain, you murderous villain!" Throughout the performance no one could quiet him or hold him down in his seat and he almost succeeded in climbing up on stage. He grew so wild that the performance finally had to be cancelled.

As Byron's funeral passed by in London Clare watched a young girl mourning the poet. Later he wrote, "I looked up at the young girl's face. It was dark and beautiful, and I could amost feel in love with her for the sigh she had uttered for the poet... The common people felt his merits and his powers, and the common people of a country are the best feelings of a prophecy of futurity. They are the veins and arteries that feed...the heart of living fame."

"If life had a second edition," he remarked in a letter to a friend, "how I would correct the proofs?"

▽ ▽ ▽

Charles Langdon Clarke (fl. early 20th century)

The most imaginative of the Canadian newspaper editor's ingenious hoaxes, which included "the unearthing of the whale that swallowed Jonah," was the story he printed in 1922 after archaeologist Howard Carter discovered the tomb of Egyptian pharoah Tutakhamen. "King Tut's Golden Typewriter," Clarke headlined the story, and he went on to describe the instrument, never bothering to explain how a typewriter could possibly type hieroglyphics! The story seemed so authentic (despite the fact that the typewriter was invented in the 19th century) that rival newspapers picked up on it before Clarke admitted to the hoax.

▽ ▽ ▽

Richard W. Clarke (1845–1930)

It is interesting to note that an Englishman was the prototype for one of America's first western heroes, Deadwood Dick. Deadwood Dick became proverbial through many late 19th-century dime novels, especially those written by Edward L. Wheeler, and long stood for a fearless Indian scout and outlaw fighter. The prototype for Wheeler's westerns was Richard W. Clarke, who had been nick-named Deadwood Dick long before his fictional exploits. Clarke, an Englishman attracted to the Black Hills by the gold diggings, won fame as both an Indian fighter and an express guard for gold shipped from the mines in and around Deadwood, South Dakota. Many of the Deadwood Dick myths have been debunked, but he was certainly a real character. Clarke lies in a mountain grave near Deadwood. He did not write the novels about him, as was once thought.

∇ ∇ ∇

John Cleland (1709–1789)

Cleland's *Memoirs of a Woman of Pleasure* (better known as *Fanny Hill* after its heroine) made his publisher £10,000 in 1748 when first published, and has made millions for others over the years. It brought Cleland, however, only 20 guineas. Cleland's classic of brothel life was written to help the author escape debtor's prison. It has been suggested that the Fanny of this hardly euphemistic novel may have given her name to the euphemism "fanny" for the euphemism "backside."

∇ ∇ ∇

William Cobbett (1763–1835)

It was almost as if the irrepressible Cobbett, a Britisher who lived in America at various times, kept trying to get in trouble. He came to America in the first place to escape prosecution for his unsubstantiated exposés of army frauds. While in exile his books and pamphlets included scurrilous attacks on Tom Paine and Joseph Priestley, charges that Dr. Benajamin Rush killed George Washington with poor medical attention, and a vicious attack on the judge who convicted him of libel for the Rush charges. Even after his death Cobbett was irrepressible. In his will he left £5 to lexicographer Noah Webster to pay for a new portrait of author Webster in his famous speller. The old portrait of Webster was so grim, Cobbett felt, that it was frightening thousands of little children out of their wits.

He read his first book, Swift's *Tale of a Tub*, when he was 11 years old, spending his supper money on it one day while traveling through the English countryside seeking a job. He so relished the book that he carried it with him wherever he went for the next 10 years. When it fell overboard while he was at sea "the loss gave me greater pain," he wrote later, "than I have ever felt at losing thousands of pounds."

∇ ∇ ∇

Claud Cockburn (1904–1981)

While an editor for *The Times* in the 1920s the journalist won a contest for "the most boring headline" with the following entry: "Small Earthquake in Chile: Not Many Dead."

Admiral George Cockburn (1772–1853)

Admiral Cockburn led the incendiaries who demolished the *National Intelligencer* when the British burned Washington during the War of 1812. The gentlemanly incendiary had his men melt down all the *c*'s in the newspaper office "so that later they can't abuse my name."

∇ ∇ ∇

Edward Cocker (1631–1675)

According to Cocker, an English proverb, means very accurate or correct, according to the rules. *According to Cocker* could just as well mean "all wrong," though few authorities bother to mention this. The phrase honors Edward Cocker who also taught penmanship and arithmetic. Cocker wrote a number of popular books on these subjects and reputedly authored *Cocker's Arithmetick*, which went through 112 editions, its authority giving rise to the proverb. Then in the late 19th century, documented proof was offered showing that Cocker did not write the famous book at all, that it was a forgery of his editor and publisher, so poorly done that it set back rather than advanced the cause of elementary arithmetic. *Arithmetick* was first published in 1678, three years after Cocker died, and this seems to further substantiate the theory that it was designed to cash in on Cocker's name. Even the critic who cried forgery—Augustus de Morgan in his *Arithmetical Books* (1847)—noted, "This same Edward Cocker must have had a great reputation, since a bad book under his name pushed out the good ones."

∇ ∇ ∇

Hartley Coleridge (1796–1849)

Carlyle described the poet Samuel Taylor Coleridge's unfortunate son as a ghost "with eyes that gleamed like two rainbows over a ruined world." Coleridge wrote two poems about the gifted Harltey ("Frost at Midnight" and "The Nightingale"), whose addiction to drink and drugs caused him to lose his Oxford fellowship and fail at a teaching career, though his sonnets and his unfinished lyric drama *Prometheus* show genius and great promise. Hartley did hack work for several booksellers. It is said that one publisher commissioned him to write *Biographia Borealis* and only got him to finish it by locking him up every day until his day's work was done. (See RICHARD BRINSLEY SHERIDAN for a similar story.)

∇ ∇ ∇

Samuel Taylor Coleridge (1772–1834)

In one of his letters Coleridge recalled his precocious reading and some of its consequences:

At six years old I remember to have read *Belisarius, Robinson Crusoe,* and *Philip Quarll*—and then I found the *Arabian Nights'* entertainments—one tale of which (the tale of a man who was compelled to seek for a pure virgin) made so deep an impression on me (I had read it in the evening while my mother was mending stockings) that I was haunted by spectres whenever I was in the dark—and I distinctly remember the anxious and fearful eagerness with which I used to watch the window in which the books lay—and whenever the sun lay upon them, I would seize it, carry it by the wall, and bask, and read. My father found out the effect which these books had produced—and burnt them. So I became a dreamer—and acquired an indisposition to all bodily activity—and I was fretful, and inordinately passionate, and as I could not play at anything, and was slothful, I was despised and hated by the boys; and because I could read and spell and had, I may truly say, a memory and understanding forced into almost an unnatural ripeness, I was flattered and wondered at by all the old women—and so I became very vain, and despised most of the boys that were at all near my own age, and before I was eight years old I was a character; sensibility, imagination, vanity, sloth, and feelings of deep and bitter contempt for almost all who traversed the orbit of my understanding were even then prominent and manifest.

Another time Coleridge recalled being flogged as a schoolboy:

When I was about thirteen I went to a shoemaker and begged him to take me as his apprentice. He being an honest man, immediately brought me to Bowyer (the headmaster), who got into a great rage, knocked me down, and...asked me why I had made myself such a fool? To which I answered that I had a great desire to be a shoemaker, and that I hated the thought of being a clergyman. "Why so?" said he.—"Because, to tell you the truth, sir," said I, "I am an infidel." For that, without more ado, Bowyer flogged me.

When a student Coleridge spent his spare time in London bookstores reading whatever he could. One time he was so engrossed in a book that he bumped into a man who mistook him for a pickpocket. After talking to him, however, the man realized his mistake and, charmed by Coleridge's learned conversation, gave him a free subscription to a rental library in Cheapside. For as long as he had the subscription Coleridge took out and read the two volumes a day he was entitled to.

Drinking heavily, rejected in a love affair, pressed by debt, having published only one poem by the time he was 21, and having received only one guinea for it, Coleridge in desperation decided to try the military life. In 1793 he enlisted in the 15th Light Dragoons under the outlandish name Silas Tomkin Cumberbatch, Within hours the poet knew that he was absolutely unfit for an army career, but there was little he could do about it. So often did he fall off his horse in this regiment of skilled horsemen that the cry "Silas is off again!" became a signal for general laughter. Coleridge, or Cumberbatch, could do nothing right. One time an officer during an inspection of the barracks cried out, "Whose rusty gun is this?"

"Is it very rusty, sir?" the poet asked.

"Yes, Cumberbatch, it is," said the officer sternly.

"Then, sir, it must be mine!" Coleridge replied.

Luckily, an old friend learned of the poet's whereabouts and informed his brother, Captain James Coleridge, who could manage to get him out of the army only under an "insanity clause."

Coleridge once explained how he would prepare for writing an epic poem, a task he did not take lightly. " I should not think of devoting less than twenty years..." he said. "Ten years to collect materials and warm my mind with universal science. I would be a tolerable mathematician. I would thoroughly understand Mechanics; Hydrostatics; Optics and Astronomy; Botany; Metallurgy; Fossilism; Chemistry; Geology; Anatomy; Medicine; then the minds of men, in all Travels, Voyages, and Histories. So I would spend ten years; the next five in the correction of it..."

Most famous of all literary works inspired by a dream is Coleridge's "Kubla Khan" (1797). Since the story is usually garbled, here is Coleridge's account of his dream, which was in a note prefixed to the original manuscript:

> In the summer of 1797, the Author, then in ill health, had retired to a lonely farm-house between Porlock and Linton, on the Exmoor confines of Somerset and Devonshire. In consequence of a slight indisposition, an anodyne had been prescribed, from the effects of which he fell asleep in his chair at the moment that he was reading the following sentence, or words of the same substance, in "Purchas's Pilgrimage":
>
> "Here the Khan Kubla commanded a palace to be built, and a stately garden thereunto. And thus ten miles of fertile ground were inclosed with a wall."
>
> The Author continued for about three hours in a profound sleep, at least of the external senses, during which time he has the most vivid confidence that he could not have composed less than from two to three hundred lines; if that indeed can be called composition in which all the images rose up before him as *things*, with a parallel production of the correspondent expressions, without any sensation or consciousness of effort. On awaking he appeared to himself to have a distinct recollection of the whole, and taking his pen, ink, and paper, instantly and eagerly wrote down the lines that are here preserved. At this moment he was unfortunately called out by a person on business from Porlock, and detained by him above an hour, and on his return to his room, found, to his no small surprise and mortification, that though he still retained some vague and dim recollection of the general purport of the vision, yet, with the exception of some eight or ten scattered lines and images, all the rest had passed away like the images on the surface of a stream into which a stone has been cast, but, alas!, without the restoration of the latter.

After reading Coleridge's explanation of metaphysics, Lord Byron remarked that he would like to have "an explanation of the explanation."

When in April 1798 the publisher Joseph Cottle agreed to publish *Lyrical Ballads* he wanted to use the authors' names on the cover. Coleridge said no. "Wordsworth's name is nothing," he said, "and mine stinks." Another time he advised a would-be writer: "Never pursue literature as a trade."

He was shocked by changing times. "I am pestered every ball night to dance, which very modestly I refuse," he declared in 1798. "They dance a most infamous dance called the Waltzen. There are perhaps twenty couples—the Man and his partner embrace each other, arms and waists, and knees almost touching, and then whirl round and round...to lascivious music."

Charles Lamb told the following story of Coleridge the conversationalist:

> He drew me within the door of an unoccupied garden by the roadside...took me by the button of my coat, and, closing his eyes, commenced an eloquent discourse, waving his right hand gently, as the musical words flowed in an unbroken stream from his lips... I saw that it was no use to attempt to break away, so taking advantage of his absorption in his subject, I, with my penknife, quietly severed the button from my coat, and decamped. Five hours afterwards, in passing the same garden, on my way home, I heard Coleridge's voice and, looking in, there he was, with closed eyes—the button in his fingers—and his right hand gracefully waving, just as when I left him.

The Bath bookseller Joseph Cottle recorded an experience he had with the highly impractical poets Coleridge and his friend William Wordsworth in trying to reverse a horse's collar:

> I removed the harness...but...could not get off the collar. In despair I called for assistance. Mr. Wordsworth first brought his ingenuity into exercise: he relinquished the achievement as altogether impracticable. Mr. Coleridge now tried his hand, but, after twisting the poor horse's neck almost to strangulation... he gave up the useless task, pronouncing that the horse's head must have grown (gout or dropsy!) since the collar was put on! for it was a downright impossiblity for such a large *os frontis* to pass through so narrow a collar! At about this juncture, the servant girl appeared, turned the collar upside down, and removed it.

Coleridge was sitting in a coffeehouse when someone at another table read aloud a newspaper account of his suicide. He asked to see the paper, which the man handed him, remarking, "It was very extraordinary that Coleridge the poet should have hanged himself just after the success of his play [*Remorse*] but he was always a strange mad fellow."

"Indeed, sir," Coleridge replied, "it is a most extraordinary thing that he should have hanged himself, be the subject of an inquest and yet he should at this moment be speaking to you."

It developed that a man without any identification except a shirt marked S. T. Coleridge had hanged himself from a tree in Hyde Park and that the absentminded Coleridge had probably lost the shirt in his travels.

The word for the habit of referring to oneself excessively in the third person singular is *illeism*. A nonce word modeled on the Latin *ille* (he) and *egoism*. *Illeism* was apparently invented by Coleridge, or at least he is the first author recorded to have used this coining for "a consummate *egoist*" (in about 1809). Using *he* does sound better than employing the royal *we*, and even a little better than constantly using *I*, for which Victor Hugo was called "a walking personal pronoun." The first English king to use the royal "we" in the place of "I" was Richard the Lionhearted.

Speaking of the English weather, he said to his friend Lamb: "Summer has set in with its usual severity."

"He talked on forever," his friend William Hazlitt observed of him, "and you *wished him* to talk on forever."

Lamb claimed that the poet was "talking bawdy" to a young lady when she objected. "To the pure all things are pure," he told her.

"Either we have an immortal soul, or we have not," he remarked during a religious discussion with friends. "If we have not we are beasts; the first and wisest of beasts, but still true beasts."

His using opium since he was 19 caused terrible dreams later in life, dreams in which a "fiendish crowd of shapes and thoughts...tortured me," as he put it in a poem. In his notebooks he wrote of strange dream visions like the moon creatures "exactly like the people of this world in everything except indeed that they eat with their Backsides, and stool in their mouths...they do not kiss much."

Sailing to Malta in 1804, supplied with an ounce of opium and nine ounces of laudanum, he wrote a heartrending prayer in his journal:

"O dear God! give me strength of soul to make one thorough Trial—if I land at Malta / spite of all horrors to go through one month of unstimulated nature...I am loving and kind-hearted and cannot do wrong with impunity, but O! I am very, very weak—from my infancy have been so—and I exist for the moment!— Have mercy on me, have mercy on me, Father and God!"

On the verge of suicide, unable to conquer his opium addiction, which he had possibly acquired as early as his first year at Cambridge, Coleridge spent the last 18 years of his life in the Highgate household of Dr. James Gillman, trying to cure himself and slowly beginning to write again after a long silence. During this time he rarely left the house, but Thomas Moore told of someone seeing the poet, dressed in "strange shabby" clothing, riding about with a friend at Keswick. When company approached them, "Coleridge offered to fall behind and pass for his companion's servant," but the man refused. "I am proud of you as a friend," he said, surveying Coleridge, "but, I must say, I should be ashamed of you as a servant!"

A year before his death he wrote an epitaph upon himself:

> Beneath this sod
> A poet lies, or that which once seemed he—
> Oh, lift a thought in prayer for S.T.C.!
> That he, who many a year, with toil of breath,
> Found death in life, may here find life in death.

Charles Lamb wrote touchingly of him in a letter to a mutual friend: "Coleridge is dead, having lived just long enough to close the eyes of Wordsworth, who paid the debt to nature but a week or two before. Poor Col. but two days before he died wrote to a bookseller proposing an epic poem on the 'Wanderings of Cain' in twenty-four books. It is said he has left behind him more than four thousand treatises in criticism and metaphysics, but few of them in a state of completion. They are now destined, perhaps, to wrap up spices."

∇ ∇ ∇

John Colet (1467–1519)

The scholar and twice lord mayor of London was among the first to hold that the first four chapters of *Genesis* should be considered poetry rather than fact. Sir Thomas More called the founder of St. Paul's School his "spiritual director" and Erasmus was his good friend. Dr. Colet was buried, according to John Aubrey, in a lead coffin "which was closed like the coffin [crust] of a Pye and was full of a Liquor which conserved the body."

∇ ∇ ∇

William Collingham (fl. late 15th century)

Possibly the author who got in the most trouble for the slightest trifle, this poet wrote:

> The Rat, the Cat and Lovell the Dog,
> Rule all England under the Hog.

In his couplet the "Rat" was royal adviser Ratcliff, the "Cat" minister Catesby, the "Dog" Viscount Lovel, and the "Hog" King Richard III, whose crest was a boar. Collingham was executed for his witticism.

▽ ▽ ▽

William Collins (1721–1759)
Son of the rich mayor of Chichester, the lyric poet squandered his fortune. Suffering from severe melancholia for the last nine years of his life, he wrote little in that time, his madness becoming so violent that he had to be confined in an asylum at Oxford for a period. Nothing was heard of him, Dr. Johnson and all his friends assuming he was dead, and when he did die three years later not a single newspaper or magazine noted his passing.

▽ ▽ ▽

William Combe (1741–1923)
The satirist, author of *The Tours of Dr. Syntax*, was known as Count Combe for his extravagant ways. His immense literary output (including "2000 columns for the papers" and over 200 biographies) couldn't keep up with his expenses. After squandering a fortune bequeathed to him by his father this Beau Brummel of authors contracted great debts and spent most of the last 38 years of his long life in debtor's prison, where his only consolation were the visitors who sought him out for his inexhaustible supply of stories and anecdotes.

▽ ▽ ▽

William Congreve (1670–1729)
The playwright had a number of affairs, including one with the duchess of Marlborough, who bore him a child, and a lifetime liaison with the noted actress Mrs. Bracegirdle. He uniquely interpreted the Ten Commandments. "For my part I keep the Commandments," he once wrote to a married lady. "I love my neighbour as my selfe, and to avoid Coveting my neighbour's wife I desire to be coveted by her; which you know is quite another thing."

Of Congreve's first novel *Incognita* (1691), written under the pseudonym Cleophil, Dr. Johnson remarked, "I would rather praise it than read it."

Visiting Congreve in 1726, Voltaire highly praised his plays. Congreve, who had written little for the stage after Jeremy Collier attacked him in *A Short View of the Immorality and Profaneness of the English Stage* (1698), pointed out that he was from an old, noble family and insisted that his plays were but forgotten trifles. "Perhaps you could just consider me a gentleman," he told the French philosopher.

"If you had been merely a gentleman," said an annoyed Voltaire, "I should not have come to see you."

▽ ▽ ▽

Cyril Connolly (1903–1974)

Suggested the journalist, critic and literary wit: "I should like to see the custom introduced of readers who are pleased with a book sending the author some small cash token: anything between half a crown and 100 pounds. Authors would then receive what their publishers give them as a flat rate and their 'tips' from grateful readers in addition, in the same way that waiters receive a wage and also what the customer leaves on the plate. Not more than 100 pounds—that would be bad for my character. Not less than half a crown—that would do no good to yours."

"Just as repressed sadists are said to become policemen or butchers," he observed, "so those with an irrational fear of life become publishers."

Connolly remarked of one contemporary poet and novelist unfortunate enough to invoke his wrath: "She looks like Lady Chatterley above the waist and the gamekeeper below."

▽ ▽ ▽

Joseph Conrad (Teodor Josef Konrad Korzeniowski; 1857–1924)

For years part of the romantic legend surrounding the great novelist and short-story writer included the tale that he had been badly wounded in a duel when a young man. But after his death it was revealed that Conrad—born of Polish parents in the Russian-controlled Ukraine and for whom English, the language he wrote in, was his *third* language—had tried to commit suicide while serving as an ordinary seaman on a French vessel. Only 21, Conrad had been involved in a smuggling operation that eventually lost money. In an effort to repay his creditors, he tried the tables at Monte Carlo and went deeper into debt. Finally, seeing no way out, he invited a creditor to dinner and as a grand gesture shot himself just before the man arrived. Fortunately, the bullet missed his heart and Conrad recovered. He felt so ashamed when he did that he invented the dueling story.

Conrad made it a policy not to read reviews. Instead, he measured them with a ruler. The longer the review the better he felt.

While rushing to meet a deadline for the second installment of *The End of the Tether*, which was appearing serially in *Blackwood's*, Conrad accidentally knocked over an oil lamp and burned everything on his desk beyond recognition. He had to rewrite the entire installment from memory. (See ISAAC NEWTON.)

It is said that Conrad received his offer of a modest Civil List pension in a long blue official envelope, bearing the legend "On His Majesty's Service." This lay unopened on the author's desk for weeks until the prime minister sent someone to discover what had happened. It seems that Conrad had never opened the envelope because he thought it was his income tax.

Robert Bontine Cunningham-Graham described Conrad's burial, in a piece aptly titled "Harboured": "Handsomely, as he who lay in it might well have said, they lowered the coffin down. The priest had left his Latin and said a prayer or two in English, and I was glad of it, for English surely was the speech of the Master Mariner most loved, and honoured in the loving with new graces of his own."

Conrad's widow is said to have written her malicious memoirs to get back at her husband for all he put her through while he was alive. One time, for example, she served a meal to a table full of unexpected guests. Instead of words of gratitude, Conrad came up behind her and whispered, "A damn bad tea, my dear. A damn bad tea."

▽ ▽ ▽

Thomas Cooper (1517–1594)
After he had worked eight years collecting some 33,000 new words for his learned *Latin Dictionary*, Dr. Cooper's shrew of a wife maliciously burned all his notes, pretending that she feared he would kill himself by working so hard. She boldly flaunted the act, but he said only, "Oh, Dinah, Dinah, thou has given me a world of trouble!" and quietly sat down to begin another eight years of work to replace his burned notes. He published his book in 1548. (See ISAAC NEWTON.)

▽ ▽ ▽

Richard Corbet (1582–1635)
A proud man, the eloquent poet and bishop of Oxford once insisted that he not walk but ride a mare "in procession about the Cathedral church" wearing his surplice and hood and reading from his prayer book. A stallion, however, "happened to break loose, and smelt the mare, and ran and leapt her, and held the Reverend [Corbet] all the time so hard in his Embraces, that he could not get off till the horse had done his bussinesse." John Crowley, who tells the story, adds: "[He] would never ride in a procession afterwards."

The poet, son of a gardener whose mind was "as pure and neatly kept / As were his nourseries," according to Ben Jonson, became bishop of Oxford under James I, whom he served as chaplain. Corbet had a strong baritone voice and loved to sing for anyone who appreciated music. On at least one occasion when he was bishop he stopped at a tavern, shed his clerical robes and donned the tavern singer's traditional leather jacket to sing all day for the patrons.

▽ ▽ ▽

Noel Coward (1899–1973)

The actor and playwright tried to keep his homosexuality a secret, lest receipts from his plays should diminish. In the 1960s a biographer tried to convince him that he could reveal his sexual nature in a much more tolerant era, citing the example of drama critic T.C. Worsley, who had done so with no trouble. "There is one essential difference between me and Cuthbert Worsley," Coward replied. "The British public at large would not care if Cuthbert Worsley had slept with mice."

"I've always thought I'd be particularly good in Romeo," he once remarked. "As the nurse."

One time he was mistaken for actor Rex Harrison. He replied, rather indignantly, "Do I look as if I sold Bentleys in Great Portland Street?"

Coward was among the fastest and most facile of playwrights. "I write at high speed," he once said, "because boredom is bad for my health."

It is said that when his childhood friend actress Gertrude Lawrence married Robert Aldrich, Coward cabled her this poem: "Dear Mrs. A / hooray, hooray / At last you are deflowered / I love you this and every day / Yours truly, Noel Coward."

He was a great practical joker. It's said that he once sent identical anonymous notes to the 20 most prominent Londoners: "All is discovered. Escape while you can." All 20 left town by morning.

Coward corrected singer Elaine Stritch when she pronounced the town of Babel to rhyme with scrabble.

"It's *bayble*, Stritch," he advised.

"I've always said *babble*," she countered. "Everyone says *babble*. It means mixed up language, doesn't it? Gibberish. It's where we get *babble* from."

"That's a fabble," Coward said.

"Mr. Coward, have you anything to say to the *Sun*?" a reporter asked him one cloudy day.

"Shine," he pleasantly replied.

Coward had a six-month-old elephant delivered to songwriter Cole Porter's Beverly Hills house with an attached card reading: "This trunk call says it all. To Coley from Noely." Not one to be bettered, Porter soon sent a live alligator to Coward's house with the attached note: "Here are some teeth to match your tongue. To Noeley from Coley."

The playwright, a friend and the friend's young son were walking by the shore when they passed two copulating dogs. "What are they doing?" the child asked innocently. "It's like this, dear boy," Coward explained. "The one in front is blind and the kind one behind is pushing him."

"Did you see my last play, *Private Lives*?" Coward asked the actress Lady Diana Manners.

"Yes," she replied, "Not at all amusing. Speaking of plays, did you see me play the role of the Virgin in *The Miracle*?"

"Yes," said Coward. "*Very* amusing."

Coward heard that a rather obtuse acquaintance had "blown his brains out." "He must have been a marvelously good shot," the playwright observed.

∇ ∇ ∇

Abraham Cowley (1618–1667)
Cowley, whose father died before he was born, began his career with the poem "Pyramus and Thisbe" written when he was only 10. His first book of poems, *Poetical Blossoms*, appeared before his 15th birthday. A Royalist spy, he performed dangerous missions for the Stuarts and ciphered and deciphered coded letters for Charles I and Henrietta Maria. When he died Charles II wrote as his epitaph: "Mr. Cowley has not left a better man behind him in England."

∇ ∇ ∇

William Cowper (1731–1800)
Cowper's name is sometimes pronounced "Cooper." Originally the family name was Cooper, until his ancestor John Cooper, a London alderman who died in 1609, began spelling it and pronouncing it Cowper. All the family from that day since, including the poet, have so pronounced and spelled it.

Cowper's grandfather Spencer Cowper was tried for murder as a youth and exonerated. He went on to become a judge of the court.

Cowper wrote a poem in praise of halibut, or himself, concluding:

Thy lot thy brethren of the slimey fin
Would envy, could they know that thou wast doomed
To feed a bard and to be prais'd in verse.

Observed critic Ivor Brown over a century later: "The notion of fish pining to become the raw material of indifferent, or even of the best, poetry and to serve as the sustenance of human authorship is one which is beyond comment."

In discussing the genius of John Dryden, the poet commented: "Never, I believe, were such talents and such drudgery united."

Though most of his poems are noted for their cheerfulness, Cowper suffered from severe depression all his life, ever since his mother died when he was six. He tried to commit suicide at least six times, trying to poison, stab and hang himself instead of facing an examination for a clerkship in the House of Lords in 1763. Though he died of natural causes, he spent the last four years of his life in a severe depression from which he never emerged.

During one of his depressions, Cowper told a friend, "I have no more right to the name of a poet than a maker of mousetraps has to that of an engineer."

∇ ∇ ∇

George Crabbe (1754–1832)

Crabbe's most lyrical poems were written while he was under the influence of opium, which he had become addicted to in his later years after first using it in 1790 on a doctor's recommendation. Ironically enough this author who became an opium addict began his career with *Inebriety* (1775), a poem about the evils of drink.

While he was away from home for a few days his granddaughter neatly arranged all the many books in his study. On his return he promptly put them back into the disorder in which she had found them. "My dear," he told her, "grandpa understands his own confusion better than your order and neatness."

On the death of the "English Juvenal," as Sir Walter Scott called Crabbe, British Home Secretary and later Prime Minister Lord Melbourne had this to say about the poet (and all poets): "I am always glad when one of these fellows dies, for then I know I have the whole of him on my shelf."

∇ ∇ ∇

Richard Crashaw (1613?–1649)

The poet wrote this epitaph for his wife and himself:

> To these whom death again did wed
> This grave's the second marriage-bed.
> For though the hand of fate could force
> 'Twixt soul and body a divorce,
> It could not sever man and wife,
> Because they both lived but one life.
> Peace, good reader, do not weep;
> Peace, the lovers are asleep.

∇ ∇ ∇

James Crichton (1560–1585)

Like many characters in fiction—witness Don Juan, Hamlet, Madame Bovary, and even Moby Dick—the butler hero of James M. Barrie's play *The Admirable Crichton* (1902) is based on an actual prototype. But no butler was the model for Barrie's resourceful hero, though the historic figure did personify the same admirable qualities as Lord Loam's man. The real Crichton, a son of Scotland's lord advocate, was born in 1560 and while still in his teens was acknowledged the leading mental and physical prodigy of his day. James Crichton earned his Master of Arts degree when only 15. By the time he turned 20 he had mastered over a dozen languages, as well as all the sciences, in addition to being a poet and theologian of some note. The fabled prodigy was also said to be handsome—"all perfect, finish'd to the fingernail," wrote Tennyson—and without peer in his ability as a swordsman. He served with the French army, then tutored the scions of royalty. Unfortunately, this ideal gentleman proved unwise or human enough to steal the heart of a prince's lady while traveling in Italy. He was, in all probability, assassinated, run through from behind by three masked men in the prince's hire. Another verison has it that Crichton met his end at the hands of a pupil in a street quarrel, but in any event he died when only 25 or so. The epithet "Admirable Crichton" first came into use in 1603, but all record of the man's genius might have died had it not been for Barrie's genius.

John Wilson Croker (1780–1857)

The appellation "Conservative" for the British political party is said to have been coined by this Tory politician and editor, an outspoken man hated by historian Thomas Macaulay "more than cold boiled veal."

▽ ▽ ▽

James Croll (1821–1890)

The Scottish geologist and author of a number of scientific books had never taken a drink all his life, but accepted one on his deathbed, explaining, "I don't think there's much fear o' me becoming a drunkard now."

▽ ▽ ▽

George Croly (1780–1860)

Byron dubbed Croly "Rowley Powley" in *Don Juan*, taking revenge on the clergyman turned poet, who had imitated several of his poems:

The Muses upon Sion's hill must ramble
With poets almost clergymen or wholly
And Pegasus has a psalmodic amble
Beneath the very Reverend Rowley Powley.

One time Croly asked a critic if he had read a certain book. "Yes, I reviewed it," the man replied.

"What!" Croly exclaimed. "Do you read the books you review?"

"Yes," the man assured him, "as a rule I do."

"That's wrong," said Croly. "It creates a prejudice."

▽ ▽ ▽

Oliver Cromwell (1599–1658)

The English lord protector has been depicted as everything from a divine patriot to a satanic hypocrite, but there is no doubt that his policies influenced the course of English literature. He was the subject of hundreds of books and pamphlets in his day, including a sonnet by Milton, his secretary. Cromwell's name was once pronounced "Crumwell," hence the historic Royalist toast, "God send this crumb well down!" Royalists had every reason to wish no good to this brilliant military leader and forceful statesman. A devout Puritan and member of Parliament who vigorously supported the Roundheads, Oliver Cromwell eventually led his modernized army to victory over Charles I's forces in battle, had the king executed in 1649, and abolished the monarchy. In 1653 he became England's lord protector, rejecting the offer of the crown but accepting what was an undisguised dictatorship. He who had established the Commonwealth and began his career as an opponent of absolutism had become an absolutist himself. To this day, his name is a synonym for dictator. Cromwell died a natural death, and he was buried in Westminster Abbey, but when the Royalists regained power in 1660, his body was exhumed, hanged from a gallows, and beheaded. Such was their revenge on the man who said of Charles I, "I tell you we will cut off his head with the crown upon it."

Cromwell's name "fairly stank" to the Royalists, which is why they dubbed their chamber pots Oliver's Skulls. The term was popular slang in England from 1690 to 1820 and puts Cromwell in the select company of the relatively small handful of people who have been discommoded by commodes. (See also RICHARD TWISS.)

Printing paper measuring 13 1/2 x 17 inches is named foolscap because the watermark of a fool's or jester's cap was formerly used on such paper. One old story holds that in 1653 Cromwell invented the design to replace the royal crown used on the paper, but most experts say the fool's cap design dates back at least a century earlier.

∇ ∇ ∇

Aleister Crowley (1875–1947)
The prolific poet and devil worshipper claimed to be the Beast from the Book of Revelation. Yet he took objection to remarks about him in 1934 and brought a suit for defamation of character, which he lost. Said the presiding judge in his summation: "I have been over forty years engaged in the administration of justice in one capacity or another. I thought that I knew every single form of wickedness. I thought that everything which was vicious had been produced at one time or another before me. I have learned in this case that we can always learn something more if we live long enough...I have never heard of such dreadful, horrible, blasphemous and abominable stuff as that which has been produced by the man who describes himself to you as the greatest living poet."

∇ ∇ ∇

John Crowne (1640?–1703)
Crowne hated court life but was a favorite of Charles II, who helped him plot his play *Sir Courtly Nice*. The playwright thought his fortune was made when the play went into rehearsal, since the king had had a hand in it, but then Charles suddenly suffered a stroke and died on the last day of rehearsal. The despondent Crowne wrote little after this, although his play was eventually published in his lifetime.

Alexander Cruden (1701–1790)

Cruden would be considered a mad poet if it weren't that he was a bookseller more than a writer. He believed himself divinely appointed to reform England, suffered periodic attacks of insanity, and was confined in lunatic asylums several times. Cruden compiled a highly regarded *Biblical Concordance*, but he would be more valued today for his highly peculiar form of censorship. He was called "Alexander the Corrector" because he had a penchant for going about London with a sponge and erasing all the "licentious, coarse and profane" graffiti he saw.

∇ ∇ ∇

Richard Cumberland (1732–1811)

Cumberland, a writer of popular sentimental comedies and turgid tragedies, was attending a performance of Richard Brinsley Sheridan's *The School for Scandal*. All through the performance the jealous Cumberland tried to keep his children from laughing at Sheridan's highly successful comedy, often pinching them as he asked, "What are you laughing at, my dear little folks? You should not laugh, my angels; there is nothing to laugh at…Keep still, you little dunces!" The story eventually got back to Sheridan, and the author pretended to be deeply hurt. "That was very ungrateful of Cumberland to have been displeased with his poor children for laughing at my comedy," he said gravely, "for I went the other night to see his tragedy, and laughed at it from beginning to end." Sheridan took further revenge on Cumberland by caricaturing him in *The Critic* as the savage, inept theater critic Sir Fretful Plagiary.

Cumberland was dubbed "The Man Without a Skin" by actor David Garrick because "he was so extremely sensitive that he could not bear to be touched by the finger of criticism." This despite the fact that in the epilogue to his first comedy Cumberland had gone out of his way to compliment Garrick.

∇ ∇ ∇

Robert Bontine Cunninghame Graham (1852–1936)

The writer, social reformer and adventurer, who traveled to and wrote about remote areas of the world, was one of the few British authors elected to Parliament, where he was an outspoken M.P. So outspoken, in fact, that he was suspended an entire year for uttering the word *damn* in a speech.

∇ ∇ ∇

Edmund Curll (1683–1747)

Curll could certainly be called history's most hated publisher. John Arbuthnot remarked that the publisher's inaccurate biographies were "one of the new terrors of death," but Curll was more notorious for the obscene books he published, including *Venus in the Cloister; The Memories of John Kerr of Kersland; The Nun in her Smock*; a book on flagellation; and other inspirational works. Today, "the unspeakable Curll" might be a rich man, but in his time he was fined, put in the pillory and imprisoned for his efforts. His conviction on the grounds of obscenity in 1727 for *Venus in the Cloister* was the first such publishing conviction in the English-speaking world. Among the greats who lampooned him were Jonathan Swift, Daniel Defoe, and Alexander Pope, whose "Dunciad" described him as "a fly in amber." No one has identified the anonymous wit who coined the word *curlicism*, meaning literary indecency, from his name. When Curll was exhibited in the pillory the crowd began to throw rotten eggs, vegetables, mud and rocks at him, as they generally did in such cases, often killing the condemned. But Curll was rich enough not only to pay the attendant to wipe his face free of garbage so he wouldn't suffocate, but to buy off the crowd. "Filthiness drivels in the very tone of his voice," Defoe said of Curll. Pope tried to poison him by slipping ground glass into his drink, but the glass only caused him a few unpleasant hours.

∇ ∇ ∇

George Nathaniel Curzon
(First Baron and First Marquess Curzon of Kendleston; 1859–1925)

The Conservative politican and statesman George Nathaniel Curzon, first marquess of Kedleston, was in his long career a member of Parliament, viceroy of India, chancellor of Oxford, foreign secretary, and author of noted books on foreign affairs. A witty man whose sheer willpower overcame serious physical weakness (a curvature of the spine), Curzon failed in his ambition to become the prime minister in 1923, when Stanley Baldwin was chosen over him. It is said that Curzon died of overwork. The Curzon Line, marking Poland's eastern frontier, was suggested by Curzon in 1919. Although Poland violated the line before World War II, it was confirmed again at Yalta in 1945. Curzon, who was noted for his love of pomp and ceremony and his aloof regal manner, was the butt of many jokes from the time he was at Balliol College in the late 1870s. This anonymous rhyme was circulated about him:

My name is George Nathaniel Curzon,
I am a most superior person.

∇ ∇ ∇ ∇ ∇ ∇ ∇ ∇ ∇

James Daly (fl. late 18th century)

Though the tale may be apocryphal, it's said that toward the end of the 18th century Dublin theater manager and author James Daly bet that he could introduce a new meaningless word into the language almost overnight. He proceeded to pay Dublin urchins to chalk the word "quiz" on every wall in town. By morning almost all Dubliners had seen the word, and because no one knew what it meant, the meaningless "quiz" came to mean "a test of knoweldge."

∇ ∇ ∇

Clemence Dane (Winifred Ashton; 1888–1965)

The novelist and playwright, on whom Noel Coward based Madame Arcati in *Blithe Spirit*, was known for her innocent double entendres. One time a friend asked about the condition of her goldfish, which when last seen were ailing in a shadeless pool. "Oh, they're all right now!" she replied. "They've got a vast erection covered with everlasting pea!"

∇ ∇ ∇

Charles Darwin (1809–1882)

"You care for nothing but shooting, dogs, and rat-catching, and you will be a disgrace to yourself and all your family," Darwin's father once told him in a fit of anger. For Darwin did poorly in school all the way through his medical course at Edinburgh University, which he failed miserably. It wasn't until he embarked with Captain Fitzroy as a naturalist on the *Beagle* in 1831, at the age of 22, that he began to come into his own. In this respect he resembled a good number of other early scientific underachievers, including Newton, Watt, Edison, Ehrlich and Einstein.

Darwin almost wasn't hired by the *Beagle*'s master as naturalist on the famous voyage that led to his epochal *Origin of Species*. The great scientist had a snub nose, and Vice-Admiral Fitzroy, a devotee of physiognomy, believed this to indicate a lack of energy and determination.

Though he later (in his *Descent of Man*) described our common ancestor as "a hairy quadruped, furnished with a tail and pointed ears," Darwin did not do so in his controversial *On the Origin of Species by Means of Natural Selection, or the Preservation of Favoured Races in the Struggle of Life*. The book is one of the few masterworks instantly recognized as such and financially rewarded for its merits. The whole first edition of the book, 1,250 copies, sold out on the first day it was published, November 24, 1859.

Though he is constantly associated with it, Darwin did not originate the expression "survival of the fittest." It was coined by Herbert Spencer, the founder of evolutionary philosophy, in his *Principles of Biology* (1864) and earlier works, but Darwin did accept it as an apt description.

"I love fools' experiments," he remarked to a friend. "I am always making them."

While Darwin was staying at the country house of a friend, his host's sons thought they'd play a practical joke on him. The two boys glued together a grasshopper's legs, a butterfly's wings, and a beetle's head and brought it to Darwin, asking him to please identify it for them.

"Did you notice whether the bug hummed before you caught it?" Darwin asked, suppressing a smile.

"Yes," the boys answered in unison.

"Well then," Darwin said, "it must be a humbug."

Darwin collected over 10,000 barnacles for a study that took him a full eight years. He kept the myriad crustaceans in the house, and his family came to regard the collection as nothing out of the ordinary, as, in fact, something rather indispensable. Said Darwin's young son when he noticed none in a friend's house: "Where does your father keep his barnacles?"

Reflecting on his theories in a letter to friend, he wrote: "Believing as I do that man in the distant future will be a more perfect creature than he now is, it is an intolerable thought that he and all other sentient beings are doomed to complete annihilation after such long-continued slow progress. To those who freely admit the immortality of the human soul, the destruction of our world will not appear so dreadful."

Wanting to detemine exactly what "slow as a tortoise" meant, Darwin measured the speed of a Galapagos turtle by walking beside it. He found that it "walked at the rate of sixty yards in ten minutes, that is 360 yards in an hour, or four miles a day—allowing a little time for it to eat on the road."

An invalid prone to fainting during the last 40 years of his life, Darwin was once thought to suffer from hypochondria or other mental problems. But recent research indicates that he most likely contracted Chagas's disease, unknown at the time, when bitten by a bug during his long scientific studies in South America. This would account for his fainting and other symptoms.

William D'Avenant (1606–1668)

According to one story, Shakespeare was the father of a child born to Mrs. Davenant, the proprietress of an inn at Oxford where the playwright used to stop in his frequent travels from London to Stratford-on-Avon. One day Shakespeare, who had been made the child's godfather, arrived at the inn and the boy was called from school to see him. Running home, he encountered an old gentleman quite familiar with the affairs of the family and asked where he was going in such a rush. "To my godfather, Shakespeare," the boy said. "Fie, child," replied the old man, "why are you so superfluous? Have you not learned yet that you should not use the name of God in vain?" The boy, later Sir William D'Avenant, was made England's poet laureate in 1638. Credited as the founder of English opera with his *Siege of Rhodes*, he also is noted for adapting Shakespeare's *Tempest*.

After the poet laureate contracted syphilis and lost his nose to the disease, those he encountered either sympathized with his impairment or laughed at him. D'Avenant was surprised then when an old woman he met commiserated with him and blessed his *eyesight*. On questioning she explained that he would really be in trouble if his eyes failed because he had nowhere to prop a pair of eyeglasses.

During his final illness he apologized for not having finished his romantic epic *Gondibert*, which already totaled about 1,700 quatrains. "I shall ask leave to desist," he said, "when I am interrupted by so great an experiment as dying."

∇ ∇ ∇

John Davidson (1857–1909)

The poet received £250 from George Bernard Shaw, who wanted to free him from hack work to write the great poem Shaw believed he was capable of. Davidson, however, was so grateful that he decided to write a successful melodrama and immediately repay his benefactor. "The result was disastrous," Shaw recalled years later. "He forgot that if he could not do this for himself, he could not do it for me...He had thrown away his big chance; and instead of asking me for another £250, which I would have given him, he drowned himself." The unfinished poem that the mortified Davidson left behind was entitled "God and Mammon."

∇ ∇ ∇

John Davies (1569–1626)

In 1596 the poet dedicated his *Orchestra or a Poeme of Dancing* to "his very good friend, Master Richard Martin." The very next year Davies, also a barrister, was expelled from the bar for having brutally beaten Martin with a cudgel. Davies' wife, Eleanor, developed an eccentricity verging on madness. She believed and wrote that she had supernatural prophetic powers similar to the Biblical Daniel's because her name made the imperfect anagram "Reveal O Daniel!" She only renounced such claims when a judge anagramized "Dame Eleanor Davies" into "Never so mad a ladie."

∇ ∇ ∇

Sir Humphrey Davy (1778–1829)
The scientist and author was friend to many great literary figures of the day, including Scott and Wordsworth, the proofs of whose *Lyrical Ballads* he helped correct. Davy employed Coleridge and Southey in his chemical laboratory to sample and classify gases by inhaling them and nearly killed himself by inhaling poisonous water gas. He was so admired by Napoleon for his discoveries that the emperor sent him a prize awarded by the Institut National even though France was at war with England.

Davy was a poet of some note, as well as a friend of Cottle, Wordsworth's publisher. A great humanitarian, he refused to take out a patent on his invention of a safety lamp for mines. He was presented with a valuable, silver dinner service by grateful coal mine owners for his invention of the Davy lamp. In his will he decreed that the silver be melted down and sold, and interest from the proceeds be used to establish the Davy Medal of the Royal Society.

So great and widespread was Davy's fame that a letter from Italy reached him with only the address: SIROMFREDEVI/LONDRA.

∇ ∇ ∇

John Day (1574–c. 1640)
Though noted for his dramatic allegory *The Parliament of Bees* (c. 1607) and as the collaborator of Thomas Dekker and other playwrights, Day seems always to have been in debt. His money troubles, in fact, never changed from the time he was a student, when he was expelled from Caius College, Cambridge, in 1592, for stealing a book.

∇ ∇ ∇

Thomas Day (1748–1789)
The eccentric or mad author of the celebrated children's book *Sandford and Merton* wanted to "educate a wife" for himself. He said he desired his new wife to be as "simple as a mountain girl, in her dress, her diet, and her manners, fearless and intrepid as the Spartan wives and Roman heroines." Selecting two pretty 11-

year-old foundlings, he "tested" Sabrina and Lucretia, as he named them, by dropping melted sealing wax on their bare skin to see if they would scream, and by firing blank cartridges at them to see if they would jump. Fortunately for the young women, neither Sabrina nor Lucretia worked out for Day and he returned them to their respective foundling hospitals before they had completed his "training program." Day later married an heiress who agreed with his "ascetic program of life."

Day, a fanatic animal lover who also wrote *The History of Little Jack* (1787), about a boy suckled by wild goats, died in a fall from an unbroken colt. All his life he refused even to kill insects. A lawyer friend once spied a spider near his leg and shouted out, "Day, kill that spider!"

"No," Day replied, "I don't know that I have a right. Suppose that a superior being said to a companion, 'Kill that lawyer.' How should you like it? And a lawyer is more noxious to most people than a spider."

∇ ∇ ∇

Augustus De Morgan (1806–1871)

"He was the kindliest as well as the most learned of men—benignant to everyone who approached him, never forgetting the claims which weakness has on strength," a contemporary wrote of the mathematician, logician and author, who was also an unrivaled teacher whose extemporaneous lectures outshone even his witty writings. In 1871 De Morgan contributed to a book about eccentric English authors a sketch of the Reverend John Dobson, whose two-volume *The Elements of Geometry* (1815) had no stops except for periods at the end of each paragraph. De Morgan's short biography of Dobson was written without punctuation.

∇ ∇ ∇

Dr. John Dee (1527–1608)

Dr. Dee, an astrologer, scholar and writer, was considered so wise by some "that he must have been allied with the devil." As a result a mob broke into his house, assaulted him and destroyed all his library, museum of natural history and scientific instruments.

∇ ∇ ∇

Daniel Defoe (1660–1731)

The author, the son of James Foe, a butcher, changed his name to Defoe at about the time that he became a writer in 1695 or so. In producing his more than 500 books and pamphlets he also used a number of pen names, including Eye Witness, T. Taylor, and Andrew Morton, Merchant. His most unusual pen name—one of the most unusual used by any writer—was "Heliostropolis, secretary to the Emperor of the Moon," used on his *The Consolidator, or Memoirs of Sundry Transactions from the World in the Moon* (1705), a political satire that supplied Swift some hints for *Gulliver's Travels*.

Defoe took part in Monmouth's rebellion, and while hiding as a fugitive in a churchyard after the rebellion was put down and Monmouth beheaded in 1685, he noticed the name Robinson Crusoe carved on a stone. The name stuck in his mind, and 34 years later he gave it to the eponymous hero of his famous novel.

He is said to have been the first English journalist of national importance. His weekly *Review*, begun in February 1704, was a forerunner of the *Tatler* and in it Defoe probably originated that old newspaper standby, the serial story.

The author's *Robinson Crusoe* was based on the true adventures of Alexander Selkirk (1676–1721), a seaman who in 1704 asked to be put ashore on the tiny island of Más a Tierra off South America because he objected to conditions aboard ship. Selkirk spent more than four years alone on the island before being rescued and returning to England, where he became a celebrity. Defoe, a journalist, certainly heard of Selkirk's story and possibly interviewed him. In any case, he wrote the immensely successful *The Life and Strange Adventures of Robinson Crusoe* in 1719, embellishing Selkirk's account and presenting it as a true story. In truth it was the first book to reveal Defoe's genius for vivid fiction and it was written when the author was almost 60. Selkirk never did go back to the Pacific island, as Defoe had Crusoe do in two sequels, which appeared the same year. His experiences had made him quite eccentric, however, and for a time he lived in a cave near his home in England, where it is said he taught alley cats how to do strange dances.

Defoe, who wrote over 560 books, pamphlets and journals, was as prolific at espionage as he was at his literary pursuits. The author worked as a spy for the Tories under Queen Anne and then for the Whigs under George I, hardly missing a beat. For 11 years beginning in 1703 he did his best work traveling the country gathering information and testing the political climate.

For his notorious pamphlet *The Shortest Way with Dissenters* (1702) Defoe was imprisoned and pilloried, but his punishment turned out to be one of the great triumphs of his life. While he stood in the pillory for three days in the heat of July, the crowd chanted his mock-Pindaric ode "Hymn to the Pillory," which he had written in prison. The poem was sold in the streets around him, flower girls of the Cheapside district wreathed the pillory with chaplets they had woven, and the audience drank to his health while reading aloud his verses.

Walter de la Mare (1873–1956)

The poet lay close to death for three weeks in 1928. One day during his long illness his youngest daughter visited him in the hospital. "Is there nothing I could get for you, fruit or flowers?" she asked him as she left. "No, no, my dear," de la Mare replied weakly, "too late for fruit, too soon for flowers."

∇ ∇ ∇

Abraham De Moivre (1667–1754)

The British mathematician, a good friend of Newton and author of *The Doctrine of Chance* (1716), gives his name to two trigonometry theorems. As he grew older De Moivre required more and more sleep, until in his last year he was sleeping some 23 hours a day. At that point he confided that he needed 10 or so minutes more sleep every day than the day before. On the day he reached 24 hours sleep he never awoke.

∇ ∇ ∇

John Denham (1615–1669)

The poet George Wither sided against the Crown at the beginning of the English Civil War and even seized some of loyalist poet John Denham's lands. Nevertheless, Denham pleaded that Wither be spared from hanging when the Cavaliers captured him. So long as Wither lived, Denham explained, he, Denham, "would not be accounted the worst poet in England."

Sir John was addicted to gambling, losing much of his fortune to card sharps, and was noted for his pranks when he was drunk. Early one morning, after a night of drinking with friends, he took a brush and "potte of inke" and blotted out all signs between Temple-barre and Charring-crosse, "which made a strange confusion the next day."

When he was an old man Denham married for a second time. His wife, Margaret Brookes, became the duke of York's mistress and this drove him mad; he once, for example, visited the king and proclaimed himself the Holy Ghost. But he recovered and outlived his wife by two years after she was poisoned with chocolate bonbons by the Countess Rochester.

∇ ∇ ∇

John Dennis (1657–1734)

"Our author, for the advantage of this play, had invented a new species of thunder...the very sort that is presently used in the theatre. The tragedy itself was coldly received, not withstanding such assistance, and was acted but a short time. Some nights after, Mr. Dennis, being in the pit at the representation of

Macbeth, heard his own thunder made use of; upon which he rose in a violent passion and exclaimed, 'See how the rascals use me! They will not let my play run, and yet they steal my thunder.'"

This early account of the origin of the expression "steal my thunder," from the *Biographia Britannica*, is accurate in all respects, according to most authorities. Restoration playwright John Dennis had invented a new and more effective way of simulating thunder on the stage (by shaking a sheet of tin) for his play *Appius and Virginia* (1709). The play soon closed, but a rival company stole his thunder, inspiring his outburst and giving us the expression "steal my thunder."

∇ ∇ ∇

Robert Devereux (Second Earl of Essex; 1566–1601)

This literary patron and poet, who figures so prominently in English history and literature, pardoned the famous hangman Godfrey Derrick (who gives his name to the crane, which resembled the gallows) when Derrick was a young soldier in his army and had been convicted of rape. In return for the pardon, Derrick agreed to become executioner at the infamous Tyburn Prison just ouside London (where he eventually hanged or beheaded 3,000 people). The young and handsome Essex, long a favorite of Queen Elizabeth, was later condemned for treason and sentenced to be executed at Tyburn in 1601. By an odd twist of fate, Derrick became his executioner, though as a headsman, for even then nobles were exempt from hanging.

∇ ∇ ∇

Charles Dickens (1812–1870)

Dickens's strange relationship with his wife Catherine ended when they separated after 22 years, after having produced 10 children. In his courtship letters the novelist called his Kate "dearest Mouse" and "dearest darling Pig," but the year after she married him, in 1836, her younger sister Mary moved into their house and won his affections. When Mary died a year later, Dickens requested that he be buried next to her when he died (a request that was denied him). He wore Mary's ring all his life, yet after her death another of Kate's sisters, Georgiana, moved in with the Dickenses, and the novelist fell in love with *her*. He lived with Georgiana until his death.

When Dickens was 12 years of age his father, John Dickens, was sentenced to debtor's prison and Charles had to help support his mother and seven siblings by working in a blacking factory, where he tied and labelled pots of blacking. He wrote of this darkest period in life, when he bitterly referred to his father as "the Prodigal Father," in the early chapters of his novel *David Copperfield*.

Boz, the pen name Dickens used in the *Pickwick Papers*, was, in Dickens's own words, "the nickname of a pet child, a younger brother, whom I had dubbed Moses, in honour of the Vicar of Wakefield; which being facetiously pronounced...became Boz."

Dickens's *The Old Curiosity Shop* probably commanded greater interest among the reading public than any novel ever had up to that time. In New York City, for example, 6,000 people crowded the wharf where the ship carrying the magazine with the last installment of the novel was to dock. Finally, the ship approached, but the crowd could not wait. Spying the captain on deck, all cried out as one the burning question: "Did little Nell die?"

Probably no fictional death in history affected readers more in its day than the death of Little Nell (Trent) in Dickens's *The Old Curiosity Shop*. For just one more example, the Irish revolutionary and Member of Parliament Daniel O'Connell is said to have been reading Dickens's book in a railway carriage. When he read the passage where the child died, he burst into tears and groaned, "He should not have killed her!" and threw the book out the train window.

The benevolent brothers Cheeryble in Dickens's *Nicholas Nickleby* (1838–39) were based on the real-life merchants William and Daniel Cheeryble, model progressive employers whom the novelist met several times and turned into two of the nicest characters in literature. The novel doesn't record that William Cheeryble, a magistrate, read the riot act to striking weavers in 1826, which led to soldiers opening fire on them and killing at least six people, or that Daniel Cheeryble scandalized the family name by keeping a woman who bore him an illegitimate son.

Dickens, more than any writer of his time, was the favorite of the world's great authors. Tolstoy and Dostoyevsky were among the many eminent writers who counted *Great Expectations* their favorite novel.

His friend Henry Burnett recalled his intense concentration while working:

One night in Doughty Street, Mrs. Charles Dickens, my wife and myself were sitting round the fire cosily enjoying a chat, when Dickens, for some purpose, came suddenly into the room. "What, you here!" he exclaimed; "I'll bring my work." It was his monthly portion of *Oliver Twist* for *Bentley's*. In a few minutes he returned, manuscript in hand, and while he was pleasantly discoursing he employed himself in carrying to a corner of the room a little table, at which he seated himself and recommenced his writing. We, at his bidding, went on talking our "Little nothings,"—he, every now and then (the feather of his pen still moving rapidly from side to side), put in a cheerful interlude. It was interesting to watch, upon the sly, the mind and the muscles working (or, if you please, playing in company, as new thoughts were being dropped upon the paper). And to note the working brow, the set of the mouth, with the tongue tightly pressed against the closed lips, as was his habit.

In 1850 Dickens started his weekly magazine, *Household Words*, which he edited until his death (the name changed to *All the Year Round* in 1859). He published the first work of many famous writers, including Wilkie Collins and George Meredith, but had to read much dross for the gold. One time a poet named Laman Blanchard sent him an interminably long poem entitled "Orient Pearls at Random Strung." Dickens mailed it back with the note: "Dear Blanchard, too much string—Yours. C.D."

Dickens loved his many grandchildren but disliked the name "grandpa" and forbade them to use it. Instead they called him "Wenerables" (venerable), which, according to one earwitness, usually came out "wenbull," "winnible," or "wenapple."

Many of his contemporaries were of the opinion that Dickens could have been as great an actor as he was an author. His dramatic reading tours in Great Britain and the United States played to sell-out crowds unequaled by any author anywhere. Dickens read so passionately that he sometimes worked himself up to a fever pitch and fainted in the midst of a performance, his poor state of health unable to bear such stress.

So great was Dickens's fame as a writer and dramatic reader that the line of people waiting at the box office for tickets to his first American reading in New York City stretched almost a mile long.

The press criticized him for his brilliant reading of Sikes's brutal murder of Nancy in *Oliver Twist*, in which he played both the victim and the snarling, screaming murderer. The performance was so realistic that women fainted in the aisles.

Dickens's lecture manager, Geoerge Dolby, told the following story:

> During the progress of a [Dickens] reading, my attention was drawn to a gentleman who was in a most excited state. Imagining him to be ill and wanting assistance, I said, "What's the matter with you?"
> "Say, who's that man on the platform reading?"
> "Mr. Charles Dickens," I replied.
> "But that ain't the *real* Charles Dickens, the man as wrote all them books I've been reading all these years?"
> "The same."

"Well, all I've got to say about it then is that he knows no more about Sam Weller'n a cow does of pleating a shirt, at all events that ain't my idea of Sam Weller, anyhow." And he clapped his hat on his head and left in a state of high dudgeon.

Dickens, an inveterate letter writer, corresponded with friends and associates almost every day of his life. On one day he mailed over a hundred letters.

Toward the end of his life he burned in a great bonfire all his correspondence, including letters from the famous and obscure, from friends and family. "He had no belief in our commitment to the idea of a public record about private matters," Fred Kaplan observes in his *Dickens* (1988). "His books would speak for him. All other voices would be silenced. His art, not his life, was public property."

Today's royalty system for paying authors only became common in the late 19th century, although authors were sometimes paid a stipulated sum for the first printing of a book and a further sum if another printing was called for. (Milton, for example, got £15 for each of three printings of *Paradise Lost*.) Agreements were often very informal, witness the arrangement Dickens's publisher, Edward Chapman, wrote about in a letter to a friend in 1837: "There was no agreement about *Pickwick* except a verbal one. Each number was to consist of a sheet and a half, for which we were to pay 15 guineas, and we paid him [Dickens] for the first two numbers at once, as he required money to go and get married with. We were also to pay more according to the sale, and I think *Pickwick* cost us altogether £3,000."

After a quarrel with his wife, shortly before he left her, Dickens performed what he would later refer to as his "celebrated feat." He jumped out of bed at 2 a.m. and walked more than 30 miles from his home in London to his home at Gads Hill in Kent.

He loved horseplay. A friend remembered his following a father with a baby held on his shoulder through a London slum. Dickens trailed them down street after street, popping cherries into the baby's gaping mouth while the father walked on unaware.

Dickens could be incredibly kindhearted. When he discovered that a long-time servant had been stealing, he dismissed the man. But realizing that the man would never get another job as a servant, he set up the thief in a small business.

In December 1843 an English magazine published, only weeks after "A Christmas Carol" itself had been published, what was entitled "A Christmas Ghost Story Re-originated from the Original by Charles Dickens Esquire and

Analytically Condensed." Dickens sued, pointing out that "even the language is the same" in the "ghost story," where the language wasn't "degraded." The disreputable publishers, however, using an ancient and still common ploy, quickly declared bankruptcy and Dickens, though he won a moral victory, lost about £700 in legal fees.

It is said that Dickens often mimed his characters as he wrote. He would actually run to his mirror, gesture and make faces, then run back to his desk, where he described his characters as he had portrayed them in the glass.

One would be hard put to find a better brief description of a cold than this sentence from a letter he wrote to a friend: "I am this moment deaf in the ears, hoarse in the throat, red in the nose, green in the gills, damp in the eyes, twitchy in the joints and fractious in temper."

All of the 15 books he wrote in his 34-year career became bestsellers, enabling him to leave an estate of over £93,000 (perhaps $10 million today).

∇ ∇ ∇

Sir Kenelm Digby (1603–1665)

A Renaissance man, the well-rounded author, diplomat, scientist and naval hero at Scanderoon is unfortunately most remembered for his theory that "the powder of sympathy," presumably a form of copper sulfate, could heal wounds without even touching them. Digby, who tried to convert Oliver Cromwell to Catholicism and once killed a Frenchman in a duel for insulting Charles I, wrote of his miraculous powder in a treatise on immortality. His father, Sir Everard Digby, was executed in 1606 for his part in the Gunpowder Plot, so perhaps "powder" had some unknown psychological significance for the son. Sir Everard Digby may have been hanged for his treason, but one old story claims that his heart was plucked out by the executioner, who then cried, "Here is the heart of a traitor!" A heartless Digby is then ("credibly reported") to have indignantly replied, "Thou liest!"

Digby, one of the initial members of the Royal Society, discovered the importance of oxygen to plant life. Aubrey says that "He was such a goodly handsome person, gigantique and great voice, and had so gracefull Elocution and noble address, etc., that had he been drop't out of the Clowdes in any part of the World, he would have made himself respected." It is said that when he was imprisoned by Parliament as a Royalist "his charming conversation made the prison a place of delight." Digby married the celebrated courtesan Venetia Stanley, who always remained faithful to him. (He had said a "handsome wise man, and lusty, could make an honest woman out of a Brothell houre.") When she died, spiteful and false rumors were spread that Digby had caused her death by making her drink viper wine (a supposedly restorative wine medicated by an abstract obtained from vipers) to preserve her beauty.

No author has a better epitaph:

> Under this Stone the Matchless Digby lies
> Digby the Great, the Valiant, and the Wise:
> This Age's Wonder, for his Noble Parts;
> Skill'd In six Tongues, and learn'd in all the Arts.
> Born on the day he died, th'Eleventh of June,
> On which he bravely fought at Scanderoon.
> 'Tis rare that one and self-same day should be
> His day of Birth, of Death, of Victory.

$$\triangledown \ \triangledown \ \triangledown$$

Benjamin Disraeli (1804–1881)

Conversing with Queen Victoria on literary subjects the prime minister and novelist more than once used the words, "We authors, Ma'am." Another time the great flatterer told her: "Your Majesty is the head of the literary profession."

A very busy man, dividing his time between his political and literary pursuits, Disraeli had a standard reply, unmatched for diplomatic ambiguity, for would-be authors who sent him manuscripts to read. "Many thanks," he would write back, "I shall lose no time in reading it."

After he published *Tancred* in 1847 Disraeli was asked what novels he had read recently. "When I want to read a novel," he replied, "I write one."

Disraeli had a low opinion of books for a literary man. "Books are fatal," he once declared, "they are the curse of the human race. Nine-tenths of existing books are nonsense, and the clever books are the refutation of that nonsense. The greatest misfortune that ever befell man was the invention of printing."

At an 1873 banquet in Glasgow he rose to say: "An author who speaks about his own books is almost as bad as a mother who speaks about her children."

At a trade union meeting in Dublin his enemy Daniel O'Connell rose to say: "Disraeli's name shows he is by descent a Jew. His father became a convert. He is the better for that in this world, and I hope he will be the better for it in the next. I have the happiness of being acquainted with some Jewish families in London, and among them more accomplished ladies, or more humane, cordial, high-minded, or better-educated gentlemen I have never met. It will not be supposed, therefore, that when I speak of Disraeli as the descendant of a Jew, that I mean to tarnish him on that account. They were once the chosen people of God. There were miscreants among them, however, also, and it must certainly have been from one of these that Disraeli descended. He possesses just the qualities of the impenitent thief who died upon the Cross, whose name I verily believe, must have been Disraeli."

To this attack Disraeli soon replied: "Yes, I am a Jew, and when the ancestors of the right honorable gentleman were brutal savages in an unknown island, mine were priests in the temple of Solomon."

Disraeli was long Prime Minister William Ewart Gladstone's arch political rival. One time Disraeli offered a friend a definition of the difference between a misfortune and a calamity. "If Gladstone fell into the Thames, it would be a misfortune," he explained. "But if someone dragged him out again, it would be a calamity."

Another time he described Gladstone in an 1878 speech at Riding School, London: "A sophisticated rhetorician, inebriated with the exuberance of his own verbosity, and gifted with an egotistical imagination that can at all times command an interminable and inconsistent series of arguments to malign an opponent and to glorify himself."

Though it has never been confirmed, Gladstone attributed this remark to Disraeli: "Never complain and never explain."

Disraeli and his wife spent a few days at a friend's house, where Mrs. Disraeli found the pictures hung on the walls quite indecent. "There is a most horrible picture in our bedroom," she complained to her hostess. "Disraeli says it is 'Venus and Adonis!' I have been awake half the night trying to prevent his looking at it."

Disraeli particularly loathed the lack of literary ability in his liberal opponent Gladstone. "Gladstone, like Richelieu, can't write," he complained in a letter of October 3, 1877. "Nothing can be more unmusical, more involved or more uncouth than all his scribblement."

Gladstone doubted that Disraeli could make a joke or riposte on any subject, as popular opinion held. Disraeli countered that he could. "Then I challenge you to make a joke about Queen Victoria," Gladstone said. "Sir," Disraeli replied, "Her Majesty is not a subject."

For all his urbane intelligence Disraeli could be preoccupied and absentminded. One time he called on Lady Bradford only to be told by her servant that she had gone to town, as she usually did Mondays.

"I thought you would know that, sir," the servant said.

"I did not," replied Disraeli, "nor did I know that it was Monday."

Disraeli's friends gathered round him on February 27, 1868, to ask if he had been appointed prime minister. "Yes," he told them, "I have climbed to the top of the greasy pole."

Someone told Disraeli that his contemporary, the renowned political agitator and orator John Bright, was a self-made man. "I know he is," Disraeli replied, "and he adores his maker."

When he was advised that his rival Lord John Russell had been elected leader of the House of Commons, Disraeli remarked, "If a traveler were informed that such a man was leader, he may well begin to comprehend how the Egyptians worshipped an insect."

The phrase *on the side of the angels* has long been used for someone who takes a spiritual view of things, or for someone who is on "our" side. Disraeli coined it in 1864, before he became Britain's prime minister, in a speech he made at the Oxford Diocesan Conference opposing the Darwinian theory of organic evolution proposed in *Origin of Species*. "The question is this," he asserted. "Is man an ape or an angel? I, my lord, am *on the side of the angels*." Two years later Disraeli gave us another famous quotation. "Ignorance," he told the House of Commons, "never settles a question."

Matthew Arnold was allegedly speaking to Disraeli sometime in 1880 about his relationship with Queen Victoria when the subject of flattery came up. "Everyone likes flattery," Disraeli said, "and when you come to royalty you should lay it on with a trowel."

As a seemingly frail old man of 68 he addressed a large audience at the Free Trade Hall, speaking vigorously for 3 1/4 hours while consuming two bottles of brandy.

On his deathbed Disraeli was told that Queen Victoria, whose consort had died years before, would like to visit him. "What's the use?" he replied wearily. "She would only want me to take a message to dear Albert."

∇ ∇ ∇

Sydney Dobell (1824–1874)

The poet's long, unfinished *Balder* (1854) is considered perhaps the most extreme example of the "Spasmodic School," a term applied in his day to violent, wordy dramatic poems characterized by obscurity and wild imagery. Two of its lines went: "Ah! Ah! Ah!/Ah! Ah! Ah! Ah! Ah! Ah! Ah! Ah! Ah! Ah!" Dobell inverted his first name to form the pseudonym he used when he wrote his poem *The Roman* (1850)—Sydney Yendys.

∇ ∇ ∇

Charles Lutwidge Dodgson   See LEWIS CARROLL.

∇ ∇ ∇

John Donne (1573?–1631)

Sir George Moore was so angry when the poet John Donne married his daughter Anne that he not only ordered his daughter out of his house but saw to it that Donne lost his political office as secretary to the Great Seal. Donne was so downcast that when the couple moved into a modest house nearby he scratched on the window pane:

John Donne
An Donne
Undone

Walton in his *Lives* tells of how King James I sent for and honored Donne: "When His Majesty was sat down, he said after his pleasant manner, 'Dr. Donne, I have invited you to dinner and though you sit not down with me, yet will I carve to you of a dish that I know you love well. For knowing you love London I do hereby make you Dean of St. Paul's and when I have dined, then do you take your beloved dish home with you to your study, say grace there to your self and much good may it do you.'"

Despite his sonnet "Death, be not proud," Donne, like actress Sarah Bernhardt long after him, made it a practice to prepare himself for death, or rehearsed for it, by habitually lying in a coffin for hours at a time.

Donne wrote his great poem "Hymme to God the Father" on his deathbed. It is said that he also preached his last sermon as "his own funeral sermon" and that on his deathbed he donned his shroud and had his portrait painted in it. The portrait was used as a model for the Donne statue installed in St. Paul's.

As Donne lay dying a famous doctor of the day told him he might restore his health by drinking milk and cordials for 20 days. The poet, who "loathed milk and passionately refused to drink it" did try the regimen for 10 days on his doctor's insistence. But then he told the doctor he didn't fear death and would rather die than continue.

Donne's actual epitaph reads:

> Reader, I am to let thee know,
> Donne's body only lies below;
> For, could the grave his soul comprise,
> Earth would be richer than the sky.

▽ ▽ ▽

William Douglas (1672–1748)

> Her braw is like the snow-drift;
> Her throat is like the swan;
> Her face it is the fairest
> That e'er the sun shone on—
> And dark blue is her ee;
>
> And for bonnie Annie Laurie
> I'd lay me doun and dee ...

The lyrics of the famous old song, "Annie Laurie"—in the 1835 revision by Lady John Scott above—have lasted for nearly 300 years, but few are aware that there was a real Annie Laurie. Poet William Douglas sang about his love for the eldest daughter of Sir Robert Laurie of Maxwelton, Scotland, some 10 years his junior. Annie, however, wasn't impressed enough, for she married a rival suitor, Alexander Fergusson, in 1709. Douglas, for his part, did not expire of a broken heart, living until 1748, when he died at the age of 76. Annie Laurie (1682–1764) lived on even longer to become the grandmother of still another Alexander Fergusson, who was the hero of yet another son—Robert Burns's "The Whistle."

Sir Arthur Conan Doyle (1859–1930)

Early in his career Conan Doyle's first novel, *The Narrative of John Smith*, was lost in the mails. Having no copy, he was shocked and saddened by its loss, but looking back years later and realizing how bad and possibly libelous it was, the author remarked, "My shock at its disappearance would be as nothing to my horror if it were suddenly to appear again—in print."

Conan Doyle probably named his detective after sage American author Oliver Wendell Holmes (1809–1894), who was also a professor of anatomy and physiology at Harvard. Sherlock Holmes, however, was modeled in large part on Dr. Joseph Bell (1837–1911), an eminent Edinburgh surgeon under whom Doyle studied medicine and who, like Holmes, often deduced the life and habits of a stranger just by looking at him. Doyle once admitted: "I used and amplified his methods when I tried to build up a scientific detective who solved cases on his own merits." It is said that Dr. John H. Watson, Holmes's Boswell, was intended as a parody of Doyle. In none of their 60 cases did Holmes ever say "Elementary, my dear Watson," and although he was addicted to cocaine, the great detective never once cried, "Quick, Watson, the needle!"

Conan Doyle received many letters and packages from all over the world with instructions that they be forwarded to Sherlock Holmes. Among them were often gifts, offers of assistance (several ladies wanted to keep house for Sherlock) and, most often, descriptions of cases his correspondents wanted the detective to solve.

A French cab driver decided to play a joke on Sir Arthur when he picked him up at the railroad station.

"Merci, Monsieur Conan Doyle," he said after driving him to the hotel and collecting his fare.

"How do you know my name?" Sherlock Holmes's creator asked.

"Elementary, my dear sir. I had seen in the papers that you were coming from the south of France to Paris; your general appearance told me that you were English; your hair had been clearly last cut by a barber of the south of France. I put these indications together and guessed at once that it was you."

"That is remarkable. You had no other evidence to go upon?"

"Well," said the driver, "there was also the fact that your name was on the baggage."

∇ ∇ ∇

William Drennan (1754–1820)

Not only was he an Irish poet; Doctor William Drennan also claimed that in 1795 he and he alone invented the term *Emerald Isle* for Ireland, obviously because the island is so brilliantly green. He may be right, for the expression is first recorded in his poem "Erin," which contains the lines:

> Arm of Erin! Prove strong, but be gentle and brave,
> And, uplifted to strike, still be ready, to save,
> Nor one feeling of vengeance presume to defile
> The cause of the men of the Emerald Isle.

∇ ∇ ∇

Sir William Drury (1527–1579)

The long-famous street and theater in London called Drury Lane get their name from the Drury House, which once stood just south of the present site. The house was built by statesman and soldier Sir William Drury during the reign of Henry VIII. There have been four Drury Lane theaters, including the present one; the first was originally a cock-pit that was converted into a theater under James I. All the great English actors, from Booth and Garrick on, have performed at one or another Drury Lane.

∇ ∇ ∇

John Dryden (1631–1700)

England's poet laureate and historiographer royal, Dryden was given the name "the Poet Squab" by John Wilmot, the earl of Rochester, because he was so fat. But then Rochester, a former patron of Dryden, had the poet waylaid and beaten by masked thugs at Rose Alley in Covent Garden because he suspected that Dryden had anonymously attacked the king and himself in a book of the day. It is almost certain that Dryden had nothing to do with the satiric attack.

Dryden lived across from the playwright Thomas Otway in Queen Street. One evening, Otway, stumbling home from a tavern, chalked on the poet's door: "Here lives John Dryden; he is a wit." Recognizing the hand-writing the next day, Dryden chalked on Otway's door: "Here lives Tom Otway; he is oppo-site."

Thinking herself neglected by the poet, Dryden's wife, Elizabeth exclaimed, "Lord, Mr. Dryden, how can you always be poring over those musty books? I wish I were a book, and then I should have more of your company."

"Pray, my dear," Dryden replied, "if you do become a book let it be an almanack, for then I shall change you every year."

The following jubilant epitaph, often erroneously attributed to Dryden, actually comes from an Edinburgh, Scotland, graveyard:

Here snug in grave my wife doth lie!
Now she's at peace and so am I.

Dryden greatly admired Milton's *Paradise Lost* but was a champion of rhyme and asked Milton if he could turn his blank verse into a rhymed drama. Surprisingly, Milton agreed. "Well, Mr. Dryden," he said, "it seems you have a mind to tag my points, and you have my leave to tag them. But some of them are so awkward and old-fashioned that I think you had as good leave them as you found them." The result was Dryden's opera *The State of Innocence and the Fall of Man* (1667), which he finished in less than a month.

Legend has it that whenever Dryden sat down to write he first had himself "blooded and purged."

The poet was envious of the success of dramatist John Crowne's elaborately and expensively staged comedies and tragedies, which were very popular in his day. Once in a while Dryden would admit that Crowne did have some genius, but he would always quickly add that his father and Crowne's mother were very well acquainted.

∇ ∇ ∇

Thomas D'Urfey (1653–1723)

A playwright, poet and songwriter who liked to sing his songs in public, Tom D'Urfey, as he was known, was a favorite of England's Charles II, who once leaned on his shoulder and sang a song with him. When princess Anne asked him to write a song about the Electress Sophia, the next heir in succession to the crown, D'Urfey responded with a song favoring the princess that began: "The crown's far too weighty, for shoulders of eighty..." Princess Anne gave him 50 guineas.

∇ ∇ ∇ ∇ ∇ ∇ ∇ ∇ ∇

Sir Arthur Stanley Eddington (1882–1944)

The scientist and author was asked, "Is it true, Professor, that you are one of the three people in the world who understand Einstein's theory of relativity?"

Eddington hesitated.

"I'm sorry," said his interviewer. "I should have realized a man of your modesty would find that question embarrassing."

"Not at all," Eddington replied. "I was just trying to think who the third might be."

▽ ▽ ▽

George Eliot (Mary Ann Evans; 1819–1880)

The author's father, Robert Evans, was noted for his great physical strength, which enabled him to carry loads that three average men could barely handle. One time he took a rude sailor by the scruff of his neck and stuffed him beneath a coach seat, holding him there with one hand for the whole journey. Eliot used some of her father's characteristics and "incidents connected with him" as the model for Adam Bede in her novel of that name.

A clergyman complained to George Eliot that he had recognized himself as an unpleasant character in her *Scenes of Clerical Life*. "I'm sorry," she told him, "I thought you were dead."

In an 1865 letter to Miss Sara Hennell, the novelist wrote: "It seems to me better to read a man's own writing than to read what others say about him, especially when the man is first-rate and the 'others' are third-rate."

"I have the conviction," she wrote to Alexander Main in 1871, "that excessive literary production is a social offense."

▽ ▽ ▽

T.S. (Thomas Stearns) Eliot (1888–1965)

In 1927, the poet, 39 at the time, became a British subject, like Henry James before him, but he had settled in England as early as 1914. At the same time he became a member of the Anglican Church. James had become a British subject in 1915, only a year before he died.

Artist Marie Laurencin met him at a London party. "Eliot? Eliot the writer?" she said. "But they told me you were a woman!"

"No, I assure you," Eliot said, "the facts are the other way."

"But surely I can't be mistaken," Laurencin insisted, "I was given to understand you were a woman."

"No, no," Eliot replied patiently, "I have known myself for quite a long time, and I am convinced that I am not and never have been a woman."

"But aren't you *George* Eliot?" Laurencin demanded

On his 62nd birthday Eliot told a reporter, "The years between fifty and seventy are the hardest. You are always being asked to do things and yet are not decrepit enough to turn them down."

Eliot, like Dostoyevsky before him and his contemporary Bertrand Russell, married his secretary. Though Valerie Fletcher was 30 and he was 68 at the time, this second marriage was as happy as his first marriage had been miserable.

Groucho Marx was a great Eliot fan, to the poet's pleasure. In 1964 Eliot wrote to Groucho: "The picture of you in the newspaper saying that, amongst other reasons, you have come to London to see me has greatly enhanced my credit line in the neighborhood, and particularly with the greengrocer across the street."

"An editor should tell the author his writing is better than it is," Eliot believed. "Not a lot better, a little better."

Henry Sherek, the British impresario who produced T. S. Eliot's *The Confidential Clerk*, was opening congratulatory telegrams with Eliot on the night the play opened in 1954. According to Sherek:

> When I had read half a dozen, I said, "Really, Tom, the ego of some people! Every wire I have read up to now is simply signed with the sender's Christian name. How on earth do they expect me to know who they are? I suppose it's because they think they are so famous. Anybody who does that sort of thing is a conceited nincompoop." At the precise moment that I finished my tirade, Tom Eliot had just finished reading the first wire he had opened. He peered at me over his spectacles, and said slowly, with an absolutely impassive expression: "I say, Henry, I wonder who this telegram is from? It's simply signed 'Henry.'"

This possibly apocryphal palindrome is said to have been uttered by an American publisher on visiting the London firm of Faber and Faber, where Eliot worked: "Was it Eliot's toilet I saw?"

An incurable practical joker, Eliot was never in better form than when he worked as an editor for Faber and Faber. Among his many pranks it was his custom to seat visiting authors in chairs with whoopee cushions and offer them exploding cigars.

"Don't you find this little gathering extraordinarily interesting?" a woman asked him at a cocktail party. "Yes, it is," Eliot replied, "if you concentrate on the essential horror of the thing."

"Do you really think it is necessary...for a poet to write verse at least once a week?" Eliot was asked.

"I had in mind Ezra Pound when I wrote that passage," he replied. "Taking the question in general, I should say, in the case of many poets, that the most important thing for them to do is to write as little as possible."

"Please, sir," a student asked him, "what do you mean by the line, 'Lady, three white leopards sat under a juniper tree'?"

"I mean," he replied: "Lady, three white leopards sat under a juniper tree."

▽ ▽ ▽

Jane (Jean) Elliot (1727–1805)
A heroine who saved her father from the Jacobites, Jane or Jean Elliot is known to have written only one poem, the beautiful ballad "The Flowers of the Forest" (1763), which has often been anthologized. It is said that she wrote the piece after her brother Gilbert, an author, bet her that she could not write a poem.

▽ ▽ ▽

Henry Havelock Ellis (1859–1939)
Though a pioneer in the field of sexology (his *Studies in the Psychology of Sex* [1898] was seized and burned in the United States) and free with sexual advice in his books and conversation, Ellis in fact suffered from impotency until he was about 60. At that time, with the help of a devoted lover, he finally cured the problem.

▽ ▽ ▽

Edward Essex (d. 1658)
This Leveller ironically dedicated his pamphlet *Killing No Murder* (1657) to Oliver Cromwell, the dedication pointing out that the Great Protector was "the true father of your country; for while you live we can call nothing ours, and it is from your death that we hope for our inheritances." The pamphlet advocated Cromwell's assassination.

▽ ▽ ▽

Laurence Eusden (1688–1730)
Honors and prizes often mean nothing, as witness the official poet laureates whose work came to naught and all the unread authors who have received Nobel

and Pulitzer prizes. Politics has frequently played a part in such honors, particularly in the case of Laurence Eusden, England's poet laureate from 1718 until his death. Eusden, a notorious drunkard with little talent, was only given the laureateship on the death of Nicholas Rowe, because he fawningly celebrated the duke of Newcastle's marriage in a poem, knowing that as lord chamberlain the laureateship was Newcastle's to give. None of Eusden's work is read today. About all that is remembered of him is Pope's satire in *The Dunciad*:

> Know, Eusden thirsts no more for sack or praise;
> He sleeps among the dull of ancient days.

∇ ∇ ∇

John Evelyn (1620–1706)

The great diarist was also a gardening writer and kept extensive gardens at his estate, Wotton House, in Surrey. After his death a tenant sublet Wotton House to Russia's Peter the Great, then visiting England. The czar is said to have caused great damage to the beautiful gardens, his favorite amusement being to ride through the flowers in a wheelbarrow.

∇ ∇ ∇ ∇ ∇ ∇ ∇ ∇ ∇

George Farquhar (1677–1707)

Farquhar became a dramatist after vowing never to act again when he nearly fatally wounded another actor in a fencing scene he played in Dryden's *Indian Emperor*. His life was a constant struggle against poverty and it was only a present of 20 guineas from his friend the comedian Robert Wilks that enabled him to write his last play, *The Beaux' Strategem* (1707). Taken mortally ill before he had finished this play, he managed to complete it, but lived only long enough to hear of its success, without reaping any financial reward.

∇ ∇ ∇

Henry Fielding (1707–1754)

The novelist and playwright was "uncommonly versed" in the classics from an early age, but his great knowledge of them was often exaggerated and he qualified his learning in a remark he made to Sir Robert Walpole in 1730:

Tuscan and French are in my head;
Latin I write, and Greek I read.

Why does one branch of your family spell your name with the *e* first and your other branch spell it with the *i* first, the novelist was asked. "I cannot tell," Fielding replied, "except it be that my branch of the family were the first that knew how to spell."

Fielding assumed the pen name Captain Hercules Vinegar in writing most of the columns in the satirical journal *The Champion*. A justice of the peace, he on one occasion wrote a piece demanding that Poet Laureate Colley Cibber be tried for murder of the English language.

Though Fielding was a justice of the peace, making in his words £300 per year "of the dirtiest money upon earth," he lived a hard life. "Handsome Harry Fielding" was early a victim of gout; his first wife (on whom Sophia Western in his immortal *Tom Jones* is patterned) died in his arms, and he lived for a time on the edge of insanity after her demise. Finally, his broken health forced him to resign his magistrate's post and he died in Lisbon at the age of 47 while seeking a cure. At one point in Fielding's life he was in such desperate financial need that he wished he could owe *more* money. Someone told him that a mutual friend was unhappy because the man was deeply in debt. Replied Fielding: "How happy I should be if I could only get 500 pounds deeper in debt than I am already."

∇ ∇ ∇

Sir John Fielding (1722–1780)

Sir John Fielding, the younger stepbrother of English novelist Henry Fielding, was a writer himself, publishing several works on criminal justice that gave him an honored place in the history of modern jurisprudence. But Sir John was much more famous in his own time as a justice of the peace or police magistrate, a position he gained on his brother's death, after serving as Henry Fielding's appointed assistant. Sir John, blinded by an accident at age 19, was one of the few literally blind justices who administered over the ages. Known as "the Blind Beak," he was said to be able to recognize some 3,000 thieves by their voices alone.

∇ ∇ ∇

Ronald Firbank (1886–1926)

Firbank insulted the memory of Rupert Brooke with a flippant remark and offended the poet's friend and literary executor Edward Marsh, who thereafter refused to speak to him or acknowledge his presence. But Firbank wasn't one to be snubbed for long. One evening Marsh spotted him in a theater lobby and turned his back on him, sticking his hands in his pockets. Firbank, however, stole up behind him, took his right hand from his pocket, shook it, and gently pocketed it again before he turned and left.

The innovative novelist paid for the publication of most of his work, and no publisher took him on until the last two years of his life. Firbank hated to talk shop. Siegfried Sassoon once tried to draw him out about literature and art and succeeded only in eliciting the response, "I adore italics, don't you?"

▽ ▽ ▽

John Fitchett (1766–1838)
Perhaps the longest poem in English, Fitchett's 129,807-line epic on the life of King Alfred took over 40 years to write. Its last 2,585 lines were written by Fitchett's editor after the poet's death.

▽ ▽ ▽

Edward Fitzgerald (1809–1883)
Fitzgerald published *The Rubaiyat of Omar Khayyam* at his own expense in 1859. So few copies sold that the bookseller who printed it soon placed it on sale for a penny a copy. When these penny copies fell into the hands of Swinburne and other influential authors the poem was finally appreciated. (See also ROBERT BROWNING.)

▽ ▽ ▽

Thomas Flatman (1637–1688)
When a young man the painter and poet had a cynical view of marriage and wrote a widely recited poem with verses that described matrimony as:

> Like a dog with a bottle tied to his tail,
> Like a Tory in a bog, or a thief in a jail...

When he turned 35, however, he fell in love "with a fair virgin" and "did espouse her." On his marriage night, "while he was in the embraces of his mistress," all his friends gathered outside his window and serenaded him with his cynical song.

Ian Fleming (1908–1964)

James Bond, the scholarly British author of *Birds of the West Indies*, seems an unlikely candidate for the prototype of James Bond, 007, Fleming's fabled hero. But Fleming did name his hero after this ornithologist neighbor of his in Jamaica, where Fleming and Bond, who died in 1988, indulged in birdwatching. The secret agent's attributes, however, were based on many people Fleming knew.

"For Ian, women were like fishcakes," one of his former girlfriends said of 007's creator. "Mind you, he was very fond of fishcakes, but he never pretended there was any great mystique about eating them."

∇ ∇ ∇

Marjorie Fleming (1803–1811)

Before she died of complications from measles, or from meningitis, in Kirkeaddy, Scotland, at the age of eight, "Pet Marjorie" wrote some 10,000 words of diary entries and poems. A favorite of Sir Walter Scott, who called her "my bonnie wee croodlin' doo [cooing dove]" and "the most extraordinary creature I ever met with," Pet Marjorie became the youngest world-famous author in history a half-century after her death, when her diary was finally published and proved a bestseller around the world.

∇ ∇ ∇

John Florio (1553–1625)

Protestant refugee, the lexicographer and translator was the son of an Italian thought to have been ridiculed in Shakespeare's *Love's Labour's Lost* as Holofernes, the pedantic schoolmaster. Holofernes is supposed to be an imperfect anagram of his name.

∇ ∇ ∇

Samuel Foote (1720–1777)

When a habitually drunk nobleman asked the dramatist and actor in what disguise he should go to a costume ball, Foote suggested: "Why don't you go sober, My Lord."

In 1755 Foote composed the following speech when pompous fellow actor Charles Macklin boasted that he could repeat anything after hearing it once: "So she went into the garden to cut a cabbage left to make an apple pie; and at the same time, a great she-bear coming up the street pops its head into the shop— What! no soap? So he died; and she very impudently married the barber; and there were present the picaninnies and the Jobilies, and the Garyulies, and the great Panjandrum himself, with the little round button at top."

"Old Macklin" (he lived to be 100) gave up in disgust, unable to memorize this nonsense, but the mnemonic exercise gave the language both the phrase *no soap*, for the failure of some mission or plea, and *great Panjandrum*, the big boss or someone who imagines himself to be the big boss.

Finding that his more prominent victims had his satiric impersonations of them suppressed under the licensing laws of the theater, Foote would invite the audience to join him for tea the next day, promising some diverting comedy. While the tea was being made he would render his uproarious mimicry of prominent people.

It was hard to know when to believe Foote—he used to say, for example, that he was married to his washerwoman, but no one has ever proved this. Foote often bragged of his exploits, and in 1766 his friend the duke of York took advantage of this, teasing him into boasting of his great horsemanship and then taking him "out to hounds" on a dangerous mount. The playwright was thrown and broke his leg, which had to be amputated. Trying to compensate him, the duke of York gave him a life-patent for the Haymarket Theatre. Foote not only profited from his misfortune with the patent, he also turned his affliction to good use in his plays *The Lame Lover* and *The Devil on Two Sticks*.

"It's a very good match she has made," an actor said of an actress with a bright scarlet past. "And they say she made to her husband a full confession of all her past affairs."

"What honesty she must have had!" another remarked.

"Yes," Foote added, "and what a memory!"

He tearfully asked when his recently deceased friend Sir Francis Delavel would be buried. "Not till the end of next week," he was told, "as I hear the surgeons intend first to dissect his head." "And what will they get there?" he said, still crying. "I am sure I have known Frank these five and twenty years, and I never could find anything in it."

A friend asked Foote's advice after having been thrown out of a second-floor window for cheating at cards. "Do not play up so high," suggested Foote.

"I've given my dear wife a thousand pounds," a friend told the playwright.

Foote, known as "the English Aristophanes" for his literary wit, shook his head sagely. "She is truly your dear wife," he replied.

Foote was asked by Charles Howard if he had read Howard's book *Thoughts, Essays, and Maxims*.

"No, I wait for the second volume," Foote replied.

"And why so?" asked Howard.

"Because I have heard that *Second Thoughts* are best."

"Why do you always sing the same tune?" the playwright asked an acquaintance.

"Because it haunts me," the man replied.

"No wonder," Foote said. "You continually murder it."

Foote's forte was his thinly disguised "take offs" of famous people. Among those his plays satirized were medical quacks, religious zealots, and Squire Long, the 70-year-old lover of young Elizabeth Linley, who later married Sheridan. But when he decided to pillory a certain Dr. Jackson as The Viper in *The Capuchin* (1776), Jackson bribed a discharged servant of Foote's to accuse him of assault. Though Foote disproved this eventually, the year-long struggle to do so broke his health and caused his death at a comparatively young age.

∇ ∇ ∇

Ford Maddox Ford (1873–1939)

One day young Ford had not gone to Sunday School and Rudyard Kipling, older by eight years, was told to repeat to him the lesson. "If you are *good*, Fordie," Kipling explained, "you will go to a place on the clouds and there will be harps. You will sit on a cloud and sing praises unto the Lord, and that is what you will do for ever and ever. You will wear a kind of white dress. And there will be creatures like mama, but with great wings..." Ford's face fell. "But if you are *bad*," Kipling went on, "if you are *bad*...you will go to a *much worse place*."

Ford began signing his books Ford Maddox Ford in place of Ford Hermann Hueffer (his actual name) with the publication of the *Marsden Case* (1923). Ford claimed that his publisher suggested the new name, telling him his books would sell better if his name were pronounceable. "And how does one pronounce your beastly name?" he said. "Hoo-fer? Hweffer? Hoifer? Hyoofer? It's impossible to know." Tired of Ezra Pound calling him "Forty Mad-dogs Hoofer," among other mispronunciations, Ford agreed to the change and made it legal. But he would yet have to cope with Osbert Sitwell calling him "Freud Madox Fraud."

Although he was a great editor, Ford ran the *English Review* very inefficiently, like "an infant in charge of a motor car," as Violet Hunt put it. One day the American poet Ezra Pound was visiting the *Review* offices and looked around, shaking his head. "Ford," he said, "if you were placed naked in a room without furnishings, I could come back in an hour and find total confusion."

"Only two classes of books are of universal appeal," he said: "the very best and the very worst."

Robert Frost once said that writing free verse is "like playing tennis with the net down." That is just about the way Ford and Ezra Pound played tennis. A friend described a typical game between them: "[They looked] readier to spring at each other's throats than the ball...It seemed to matter little how often they served fault after fault. They just went on till the ball was where they wanted, then one or another cried 'Game' or 'Hard luck,' 'My set,' or 'That's love-all' or 'Six sets to one!' It was beyond anyone to umpire or score."

∇ ∇ ∇

E.M. (Edward Morgan) Forster (1879–1970)

In June 1924 Forster published his masterpiece *A Passage to India*. As he feared, it proved to be his fifth and final novel, and he retired from fiction writing, announcing, "I have nothing more to say." (His novel *Maurice*, written and privately circulated in manuscript among friends in 1913, was published after his death, as was a collection of his short stories.)

When D.H. Lawrence died in 1930, Forster wrote a letter to *The Nation and the Athenaeum* reading in part: "Now he is dead, and the low-brows whom he scandalized have united with the high-brows whom he bored to ignore his greatness...All that we can do...is to say straight out that he was the greatest imaginative novelist of our generation." The next week T.S. Eliot wrote a letter to the magazine daring Forster to be more specific. Wrote Forster in reply: "Mr. T.S. Eliot duly entangles me in his web. He asks exactly what I mean by 'greatest,' 'imaginative,' and 'novelist,' and I cannot say. Worse still, I cannot even say what 'exactly' means—only that there are occasions when I would rather feel like a fly than a spider, and that the death of D.H. Lawrence is one of these."

∇ ∇ ∇

Charles James Fox (1749–1806)

The great Whig statesman and orator was a scholar noted for his personal charm (as well as his drinking and gambling), but he had been spoiled by his indulgent father. One story has it that as a boy he urinated all over a pig roasting over the fire, and the cook could do nothing except watch him because it was his father's standing order that the child never be contradicted or reprimanded. The cook did, however want to warn the guests that night of the "sauce" they'd be eating, so he wrote the following lines, which he put in the pig's mouth before sending it to the table:

If strong and savory I do taste,
'Tis with the liquor that did me baste,
While at the fire I foam'd and hiss'd,
A Fox's cub upon me.———

∇ ∇ ∇

Henry Richard Vassall Fox (Third Baron Holland; 1733–1840)

The Whig statesman greatly influenced both literature and politics through the hospitality that his Holland House in London provided for the brilliant and talented people of his day. He counted Sidney Smith, George Selwyn and other great wits among his friends. Selwyn, a very popular wit, was fond of seeing corpses and executions, a peculiarity that was widely known. Said Fox, as his last words on his deathbed: "If Mr. Selwyn calls again, show him up; if I am alive I shall be delighted to see him; and if I am dead he would like to see me."

∇ ∇ ∇

Sir James Frazer (1854–1941)

Frazer, among the most industrious of scholars, consulted so many sources while writing the 12-volume *Golden Bough* that his apartment was often piled to the ceiling with books. The Scottish author used so many books that his future wife later requested him not to bring any more into his rooms, for the weight of the books on the floor had already made the ceiling below look "like an inflated sail."

∇ ∇ ∇

E.A. (Edward Augustus) Freeman (1823–1892)

Freeman was long on shortcomings, including his "almost paranoid hatreds," but even his most vocal critics conceded that the historian was capable of warm friendships. One such was with fellow historian William Stubbs (1825–1901), whose work he often praised. In fact, both men praised each other's work so often that they inspired this anonymous doggerel, written about 1890:

Ladling the butter from adjacent tubs,
Stubbs butters Freeman, Freeman butters Stubbs.

Thomas Gaisford (1779–1855)

At the end of a Christmas Day sermon in the Oxford cathedral, Reverend Gaisford advised the congregation: "Nor can I do better, in conclusion, than impress upon you the study of Greek literature, which not only elevates above the vulgar herd, but leads not infrequently to positions of considerable emolument."

▽ ▽ ▽

John Galsworthy (1867–1933)

A chance meeting with Joseph Conrad turned the British Nobel Prize winner to writing. In a letter written while traveling home on a clipper ship from Australia in 1893, he noted: "The first mate is a Pole called Conrad, and is a capital chap though queer to look at; he is a man of travel and experience in many parts of the world, and has a fund of yarns on which I draw freely."

PEN is the acronym for the International Association of Poets, Playwrights, Editors, Essayists, and Novelists, which was founded in 1921 by Catherine Dawson Scott and Galsworthy, who set up a trust fund for the organization in 1932 with his Nobel Prize money. The organization was named PEN when someone pointed out at the first meeting that the initial letters of *poet, essayist* and *novelist* were the same in most European languages and could serve as the appellation.

▽ ▽ ▽

Heathcoate William Garrod (1878–1960)

The brilliant classical scholar worked for the government during World War I, but a woman stopped him on the street, exclaiming, "I am surprised that you are not fighting to defend civilization!" Replied the erudite Garrod: "Madam, *I* am the civilization they are fighting to defend."

▽ ▽ ▽

Samuel Garth (1672–1719)

Pope described the free-thinking Garth as "the best Christian without knowing it." Once Richard Steele asked the physician and poet why he remained drinking at the Kit Kat Club when he had patients to attend to. Garth pulled a list of his patients from his pocket. "It is no great matter whether I see them tonight or not," he said, "for nine of them have such bad constitutions that all the physicians in the world can't save them, and the other six have such good constitutions that all the physicians in the world can't kill them."

John Gay (1685–1732)

Gay's play *The Beggar's Opera* (1728) is said to have made Gay rich and Rich (the producer) gay (not in today's sexual meaning of the word). Few know that Gay took the prostitute Lucy Locket as the model for Lucy Lockit in his play. Lucy and another prostitute were also celebrated in the well-known nursery rhyme "Lucy Locket lost her pocket,/Kitty Fisher found it;/There was not a penny in it./But a ribbon round it." Lucy Locket and Kitty Fisher were celebrated courtesans in the time of the lascivious Charles II, so celebrated that their names were used by the anonymous inventor of the innocuous rhyme, which was first a bawdy popular song. Kitty Fisher was also depicted as Kitty Willis in Mrs. Cowley's *Belle's Stratagem* and she was painted several times by Sir Joshua Reynolds. During the Revolution, the song "Kitty Fisher's Locket" provided British troops with the music for "Yankee Doodle Dandy."

The Beggar's Opera is one of the few plays at which someone literally died laughing. Fifty years after Gay's death, at an April 1782 performance, a certain Mrs. Fitzherbert broke into laughter at the sight of a male actor, dressed up as a girl, playing the part of Polly. She laughed all the way through the second act and had to be ejected from the Drury Lane Theatre. Mrs. Fitzherbert's laughter never ended, however. Her hysterical laughter lasted all that Wednesday, and all of Thursday until she died of laughter early Friday morning.

A genial, much-loved man, Gay's attitude toward life is apparent in his epitaph, which he wrote himself and which he is buried under in Westminster Abbey:

> Life is a jest, and all things show it;
> I thought so once, and now I know it.

▽ ▽ ▽

King George III (George William Frederick; 1738–1820)

The king of Great Britain and Ireland is possibly the only monarch to have written under a pseudonym. George III suffered bouts of madness all his life from the time he was 27, and died both insane and blind, but rural folk loved "farmer George," who was one of their own despite his "What? What?" at the end of every sentence and his mother's constantly whispered injunction, "George be a king," which he tried too hard to live up to. George the Third was not always absurd, as the clerihew has it, and loved to gossip with the country people about their crops and their families. Though a staunch conservative ("I will have no innovations in my time!"), he was very interested in agricultural improvements and contributed to the *Annals of Agriculture*, first published in 1784, under the pen name Ralph Robinson.

During one of his attacks of insanity George III insisted on ending every sentence in all his speeches with the word *peacock*. His ministers cured him of this by telling him that *peacock* was a beautiful word but a royal one, which a king should whisper when speaking before his subjects so they couldn't hear it. As a result the speeches of George III were less absurd.

∇ ∇ ∇

Balthasar Gerbier (fl. late 17th century)

Sir Balthasar may hold the record for the most people honored by an author in a book dedication. A small work he wrote in 1663 is dedicated to no less than 41 different people, from Great Britain's Queen Mother to the "courteous reader."

∇ ∇ ∇

Edward Gibbon (1737–1794)

Henry Digby Beste, in his *Personal and Literary Memorials* (1829), tells the full story of the famous "scribble scribble" remark made to historian Edward Gibbon.

"The Duke of Gloucester, brother of King George III, permitted Mr. Gibbon to present him with the first volume of *The History of the Decline and Fall of the Roman Empire*. When the second volume of that work appeared, it was quite in order that it should be presented to His Royal Highness in like manner. The prince received the author with much good nature and affability, saying to him, as he laid the quarto on the table, 'Another damn'd thick, square book! Always scribble, scribble, scribble! Eh! Mr. Gibbon?'"

He remembered exactly when and where he had begun *The Decline and Fall of the Roman Empire*: "It was at Rome, on the 15th of October, 1764, as I sat musing amidst the ruins of the Capitol, while the barefoot friars were singing vespers in the Temple of Jupiter, that the idea of writing the decline and fall of the city first started to my mind."

His college days he considered totally wasted. "To the University of Oxford I acknowledge no obligation," he wrote in summing up his life, "and she will as cheerfuly renounce me for a son, as I am willing to disclaim her for a mother. I spent fourteen months at Magdalen College: they proved the fourteen months the most idle and unprofitable of my whole life."

A French physician, jealous of Gibbon's courtship of Lady Elizabeth Foster, told him, "When my lady Elizabeth becomes sick of your nonsense I shall cure her." Replied Gibbon, "When my lady Elizabeth dies from your prescriptions I shall *immortalize* her." Lady Elizabeth, however, surprised both of them, wedding the duke of Devonshire.

He hated exercise. After staying at Lord Sheffield's country house for a few weeks, he decided to leave for home but couldn't find his hat. It was outside in the hall where he had left it on his arrival—he hadn't taken a step outside in all that time.

It was a "hydrocele," a swelling in his left testicle which had afflicted him for many years, that caused his death. He himself described it as "almost as big as a small child," adding that he only managed to "crawl about with some labor and much indecency." Although four quarts of "transparent watery liquid" were drained from him in one operation, the fluid collected again and became septic, resulting in his death.

∇ ∇ ∇

Sir William S. Gilbert (1836–1911)
The lyricist half of Gilbert and Sullivan outraged fellow members of London's Garrick Club by making fun of Shakespeare. "All right then," he said when they strongly protested, "what do you make of this passage then:

"'I would just as lief be thrust through a quickset hedge, as cry, "Plosh," to a callow throstle.'"

"Why that's perfectly clear," one club member said, defending the Bard. "It just means that the bird-lover would rather get himself all scratched up in the thorny bush than disturb the bird's song. What play is the passage from?"

"No play," said Gilbert, "I made it up—and jolly good Shakespeare, too."

Unaware of the recent death of a famous composer, a friend asked Gilbert what the man was doing.

"Nothing," Gilbert replied.

"Surely he is composing," the friend persisted.

"On the contrary," Gilbert said, "he is decomposing."

"See here, sir," a young actor told the dictatorial Gilbert, "I will not be bullied. I know my lines!"

"Possibly," replied Gilbert, "but you don't know mine."

After enduring a terrible performance by an actor in his company, Gilbert hurried from his seat and burst into the man's dressing room, crying, "My dear chap! Good isn't the word!"

"No good play is a success," he once confided; "fine writing and high morals are useless on the stage. I have been scribbling twaddle for thirty-five years to suit the public taste, and I should know."

In addition to his lyrics for comic operas like *The Mikado, The Pirates of Penzance* and *H.M.S. Pinafore,* all peerlessly combining social satire with grand opera, Gilbert was the author of many songs and hymns, including the famous "Onward Christian Soldiers." He died a hero's death, suffering a heart attack while trying to save a girl who had fallen into a lake in Middlesex, an effort all the braver because he was 75 at the time.

▽ ▽ ▽

George Gissing (1857–1903)
Gissing, who experienced extreme poverty and misery as a writer, only escaped his lot by writing an imaginary journal (*The Private Papers of Henry Ryecroft,* 1903) of a recluse who is released from poverty and worry among his books. The author thought that anyone who recommended writing as a permanent livelihood ought to be horsewhipped. "With a lifetime of dread experience behind me," he once asserted, "I say that he who encourages any young man or woman to look for a living to 'literature' commits no less than a crime."

▽ ▽ ▽

Hannah Glasse (fl. 1747)
Writers still attribute the humorous directions "First catch your hare" to a recipe in Mrs. Hannah Glasse's *The Art of Cooking Made Plain and Easy* (1747). What the good lady really wrote was "Take your hare when it is cased and make a pudding..." To "case" a hare is to skin it. The joke, which is all the humorous phrase was, is first recorded in Thackeray's *The Rose and the Ring* (1855), and he used the words as if his readers would be familiar with them.

▽ ▽ ▽

Elinor Glyn (née Sutherland; 1864–1943)
Elinor Glyn sent her first novel to a publisher with an attached note intended to impress him: "Would you please publish the enclosed manuscript or return it without delay, as I have other irons in the fire." The publisher returned the novel quickly; his rejection slip read: "Put this with your other irons."

Three Weeks (1907) was the biggest *succès de scandale* of all Elinor Glyn's sensational romantic novels, many of which were made into hit Hollywood silent movies. In her book Miss Glyn, said to be as exotic in appearance as any of her characters, wrote a seduction scene that took place on a tiger rug. ("Beautiful one! Beautiful one!" the heroine purrs. "And I know all your feelings and your passions, and now I have got your skin—for the joy of my skin!") It wasn't long before the following anonymous verse was being recited almost everywhere English was spoken:

Would you like to sin
with Elinor Glyn
on a tiger skin?
Or would you prefer
to err
with her
on some other fur?

▽ ▽ ▽

William Godwin (1756–1836)

Godwin, the husband of Mary Wollstonecraft and father of Mary Shelley, remarked that before he became an atheist and philosopher he was a follower of John Glas, whom he called: "A celebrated north-county apostle who, after Calvin had damned ninety-nine in a hundred of mankind, has contrived a scheme for damning ninety-nine in a hundred of the followers of Calvin."

▽ ▽ ▽

Thomas Goffe (1591–1629)

"Do not marry her," his friend Thomas Thimble warned the poet while he was courting a widow with three children. Ignoring this advice, Goffe settled down to a brief, miserable life in which, for example, he had to converse with his friends in Latin to prevent her from interrupting and scolding him. The shrewish widow and her brood so persecuted him that Goffe died not long after his marriage, at the age of 38. His last words as he lay dying were: "Oracle, Oracle, Tom Thimble."

▽ ▽ ▽

Oliver Joseph St. John Gogarty (1878–1957)

One of Gogarty's exploits put him in the company of great literary swimmers like Bryon, Poe and Swinburne, not to mention cold water literary swimmers who swam all year round like Eugene O'Neill. On January 20, 1923, the Irish author and surgeon, portrayed as Buck Mulligan in Joyce's *Ulysses*, and then a senator of the Irish Free State, was held at gunpoint by his political enemies in his house at the edge of the Liffey River. Sure he would be killed in this deserted location, Gogarty pleaded "a natural necessity" and got out into the garden, where, as Yeats put it in telling the story, "he plunged under a shower of revolver bullets and as he swam the ice-cold stream promised it, should it land him in safety, two swans." Yeats was with him "when he fulfilled that vow."

Gogarty let his friend Joyce stay in the rented Martello tower the novelist made famous in *Ulysses*. Staying there at the same time was Samuel Chenevix Trench, Joyce's model for Celtophile Haines, who had the recurring nightmare that he was being attacked by a black panther. One night, Trench seized his gun in his sleep and began firing at the panther, narrowly missing Joyce. Gogarty took away the gun and when Trench awoke again screaming for it, Gogarty shouted "Leave him to me!" and he began firing, knocking down some pans near Joyce's bed. Joyce dressed quickly and left the castle that same night.

During an Irish Senate debate on censorship, Gogarty rose to make this observation: "I think it is high time that the people of this country found some other way of loving God than by hating women."

Gogarty entered a pub and encountered a friend wearing a patch over his eye. He hailed him with, "Drink to me with thine only eye."

▽ ▽ ▽

Oliver Goldsmith (1730?–1774)

It is said that Dr. Johnson came upon a drunken Oliver Goldsmith arguing over the rent with his landlady who was threatening to have him arrested for not paying. Johnson convinced the writer to find something, anything, that he could raise money on, and after some searching, Goldsmith gave him the unfinished manuscript of a novel. Johnson took this to the bookseller (publisher) Newberry and managed to get an advance of £60, which save Goldsmith from debtor's prison and resulted in the publication of his classic *The Vicar of Wakefield* (1764), one of the most popular works of fiction in the English language. Unfortunately, it's hard to reconcile this tale, initiated by Dr. Johnson, with the fact that Goldsmith had already sold a third of the *Vicar* to the same bookseller, or his printer, over two years earlier.

Goldsmith studied medicine but earned no degree. "I make it a rule to prescribe only for my friends," he once told an acquaintance who had questioned his ability to practice. "Pray, dear Doctor," the man replied; "alter your rule and prescribe only for your enemies."

Among the five or six professions he tried was the ministry. When he applied for ordination, however, he appeared in bright scarlet clothes and was, in Macaulay's words, "speedily turned out of the episcopal palace."

Few if any authors can match Goldsmith's brilliant versatility. It has been pointed out that he wrote masterpieces in all the literary forms: his play *She Stoops to Conquer*, his poem "The Deserted Village," his novel *The Vicar of Wakefield*, and his essay *Citizen of the World*. He also wrote a lasting nursery tale, *Goody*

Two-Shoes, and produced more than 40 volumes of hackwork in order to make a living.

His natural history book *Animated Nature* was filled with more errors than even his histories were, telling, for example, of monkeys that preached sermons and gigantic Patagonians. "If he can tell a horse from a cow," Dr. Johnson said, "that is the extent of his knowledge of zoology."

"If a dog bites a man," editors used to instruct cub reporters, "that's an ordinary occurrence. But when a man bites a dog, that's *news*." The advice and the saying "man bites dog" can be traced back to Goldsmith's poem "Elegy on the Death of a Mad Dog," about a dog that "went mad and bit a man," which concludes with the lines:

The man recovr'd of the bite,
The dog it was that died.

According to Eric Partridge, this touching poem passed into folklore in a number of versions (possibly including a funny one where a man *did* bite a dog), and finally evolved into the journalistic advice.

When Horace Walpole dubbed Goldsmith "the Inspired Idiot," he wasn't aware that the ancient Greeks had often termed prose writers idiots. The word idiot first meant an uneducated, ignorant person, whom the Greeks considered prose writers (but not poets) to be.

An advertisement he wrote for *The Vicar of Wakefield* (1766) advised: "A book may be amusing with numerous errors, or it may be very dull without a single absurdity."

"There is no arguing with [Dr.] Johnson," he told Boswell, "for when his pistol misses fire, he knocks you down with the butt end of it."

When Boswell told him that Johnson was so superior a man he should go unchallenged, Goldsmith replied, "Sir, you are for making monarchy of what should be a republic."

"No man," Dr. Johnson said of him, "was more foolish when he had not a pen in his hand, or more wise when he had." Johnson laughed when Goldsmith said that the little fishes in a proposed fable should talk like little fishes. "Why, Dr. Johnson," he said, "this is not so easy as you seem to think; for if you were to make little fishes talk, they would talk like whales." Dr. Johnson's epitaph for him read: "To Oliver Goldsmith, Poet, Naturalist, Historian, who left scarcely any style of writing untouched, and touched nothing that he did not adorn."

"His heart was soft even to weakness," Macaulay wrote, "... he forgave injuries so readily he might be said to invite them, and was so liberal to beggars that he had nothing left for his tailor and his butcher... [He had] the simplicity of a child. When he was envious, instead of affecting indifference, instead of damning with faint praise, instead of doing injuries slyly in the dark, he told everybody he was envious. 'Do not, pray, do not, talk of Johnson in such [laudatory] terms,' he said to Boswell; 'you harrow up my very soul.'"

"Is your mind at ease?" a doctor asked him as he lay on his deathbed. His last words were: "No, it is not."

Not long after Goldsmith died, some friends dining with Dr. Johnson were discussing his work. Certain things he wrote showed no talent, they insisted, others showed no originality, some were lacking in both, etc. Finally, Johnson could take this abuse of his friend no longer. Rising, he looked the group squarely in the eye, thundering, "If nobody were allowed to abuse poor Goldsmith but those who could write as well, he would have few censors."

∇ ∇ ∇

Sir Edmund Gosse (1849–1928)

The eminent critic, translator and biographer had been attacked by John Churton Collins for the inaccuracies in his *From Shakespeare to Pope* (1885) and for a time his name was synonymous for an ass; in certain university circles "He made a Gosse of himself" was bestowed on anyone who made a blatant error. But this man of letters was a wit in his own right. Soon after his friend Swinburne died, Gosse was hosting a party at his home. His maid, ignorant of Swinburne's death, misunderstood a telephone call, came to the door and announced: "Mr. Swinburne to speak to you on the telephone, sir!" Gosse loved Swinburne's memory, but he better loved a good riposte. Turning slowly, all eyes upon him, he replied: "Mr. Swinburne to speak to me on the telephone? I shall certainly not speak to Mr. Swinburne. I don't know *where* he may be speaking from."

Gosse and Dante Gabriel Rossetti were standing on a crowded London bus. "I understand you are an anarchist," Gosse suddenly said in a loud voice. Rossetti quickly went along with him. "I am an atheist," he replied, half-shouting. "My daughter is an anarchist." Both men got seats almost immediately as people deserted the bus.

Lady Gough (fl. late 18th century)

Little is known of this Victorian lady outside of her very properly British *Lady Gough's Book of Etiquette*. But that is enough. Among other library bookshelf strictures, her manual forbids the placing of books written by male authors next to books written by female authors—though married authors like the Brownings could be placed together without embarrassment.

▽ ▽ ▽

James Granger (1723–1776)

Reverend Granger clipped over 14,000 engraved portraits from other books to use as possible illustrations for his *Biographical History of England*. Some of the books he pillaged were rare ones, and to make matters worse, he suggested in his preface that private collections like his might prove valuable someday. This resulted in an unfortunate fad called *grangerizing*, or extra-illustration, with thousands of people mutilating fine books and stuffing pictures and other material into Granger's. Editions following the 1769 *Biographical History...adapted to a Methodical Catalogue of Engraved British Heads* provided blank pages for the insertion of these extra illustrations, and the book eventually expanded to six volumes from its original two. Sets of Granger illustrated with up to 3,000 engravings were compiled, and so many early English books were ravaged that "to grangerize" came to mean the mutilation that remains the bane of librarians today.

▽ ▽ ▽

Robert Graves (1895–1985)

Graves was reported killed in action in World War I, but lived to read his own obituary. One time a friend wondered why the poet hadn't worked in a more remunerative field; there was just no money in poetry, he told Graves. "It's true that there's no money in poetry," the poet replied, "but there's no poetry in money, either."

Graves's *The White Goddess* was rejected by the first editor to whom he sent the book, and the "goddess" promptly began working "her" black magic, according to literary tradition. The editor died of a heart attack within a month. A second editor found the book of no consequence and he shortly after hanged himself from a tree, wearing a bra and panties. T.S. Eliot, the first editor to pass on the manuscript, insisted that *The White Goddess* must be published "at all costs" and Eliot of course later won the Nobel Prize.

Thomas Gray (1716–1771)

All of Gray's 12 brothers and sisters died in infancy. He survived only because his mother, seeing him go into convulsions, opened his vein with a scissors.

The author of the famous "Elegy Written in a Country Church-Yard," wrote the inscription on his mother's grave in the same Stoke Pages churchyard: "Mother of many children one of whom alone had the misfortune to survive her."

So great was Gray's fear of fire that he kept in his room at Peterhouse a 65-foot rope ladder that he could fasten by strong hooks to an iron bar across his window and drop in the event of an emergency. One night young pranksters, aware of his fears, shouted "Fire!" outside his window and Gray hastily threw out his ladder. He descended rung by rung in the dark only to drop finally into a carefully placed tub of cold water.

The laureateship was offered to him on the death of Colley Cibber in 1757. Explaining his refusal to a friend that year he observed, "It has been usual to catch a mouse or two (for form's sake) in public once a year."

Said Dr. Johnson to Boswell of him: "Sir, he was dull in company, dull in his closet, dull everywhere. He was dull in a new way, and that made people think him GREAT."

Gray could not stand Dr. Johnson either and was responsible for a derisive nickname that attached itself to the Great Cham. Out walking with a friend one evening in 1769, Gray, who had been berating Johnson, suddenly pointed to the sky and exclaimed bitterly, "Look, look Bonstetten! the great bear! There goes *Ursa Major!*"

Gray is probably the only poet ever to add his own epitaph to a poem he wrote. It is appended to his famous *Elegy Written in a Country Church-Yard* (1751):

Here rests his head upon the lap of Earth
    A youth to Fortune and to Fame unknown.
Fair Science frown'd not on his humble birth.
    And Melancholy mark'd him for her own.

Large was his bounty, and his soul sincere,
    Heav'n did a recompense as largely send:
He gave to Mis'ry all he had, a tear,
    He gained from Heav'n ('twas all he wish'd) a friend.

No farther seek his merits to disclose,
    Or draw his frailties from their dread abode,

(There they alike in trembling hope repose),
  The bosom of his Father and his God.

Seventeen years after the publication of *Elegy Written in a Country Church-Yard* (1751) he wrote to his longtime friend Horace Walpole predicting, "I shall be but a shrimp of an author."

▽ ▽ ▽

Joseph Henry Green (1791–1863)

Coleridge's faithful friend and literary executor was a famous surgeon well known for his objectivity. On his own deathbed the laconic Green diagnosed his condition in one word, "Congestion." Saying no more, he then took his own pulse and died immediately after he said, "Stopped."

▽ ▽ ▽

Robert Greene (1558–1592)

The dramatist and miscellaneous writer may really have died of the plague, but he is traditionally said to have died of "a surfeit of pickled herring and Rennish wine" that he had partaken while dining at a banquet for Thomas Nashe. As he lay dying in the home of a poor shoemaker, he wrote to his wife: "Doll, I charge thee, by the love of our youth and by my soules rest, that thou wilte see this man paide; for if hee and his wife had not succoured me, I had died in the streetes— Robert Greene." Greene had long since forsaken his beautiful wife, however. In fact, this chronicler of London crime lived with a notorious thief called "Cutting Ball," the mother of his illegitimate son, Fortunatus Greene. (For Greene's famous criticisms of Shakespeare, see WILLIAM SHAKESPEARE.)

▽ ▽ ▽

Kate Greenaway (1846–1901)

The children's books she wrote and illustrated were so popular in England and throughout the world that parents tried to dress their sons and daughters like the characters she depicted. It was said that "Kate Greenaway dressed the children of two continents."

▽ ▽ ▽

Frederick Greenwood (1830–1909)

The distinguished journalist was given a copy of the sensational newspaper *The News of the World* to read by its new publisher, Lord Riddell. Several days later Riddell asked him what he thought of the tabloid. "I looked at it and then I put it in the wastepaper basket," he replied, "and then I thought, 'If I leave it there the cook may read it,' so I burned it."

Julian Grenfell (1888–1915)

A courageous soldier and a poet, Grenfell died on the battlefield in World War I. His poem "Into Battle" appeared in the *Times* on the day of his death.

∇ ∇ ∇

Sir Thomas Gresham (1519–1579)

The economist and founder of Gresham College is said to have re-enacted the episode of Cleopatra's pearl with Queen Elizabeth. That episode is based on the great lengths to which Antony and Cleopatra are said to have gone to demonstrate their devotion. Legend has it that she once filled a room ankle high with rose petals so that he would not hear his footsteps when he walked, and that he was so pleased with the dinner a chef prepared for Cleopatra that he made the cook the gift of a city all his own. Cleopatra's pearl concerns a sumptuous banquet Cleopatra gave to Antony. Her lover, the story tells us, expressed astonishment at the costly meal, and she promptly removed a pearl earring, dropped it in a cup of vinegar, and let it dissolve, saying "My draft to Antony [the cost of this banquet] shall far exceed it." Vinegar would not dissolve a pearl, however, and anything strong enough to do so wouldn't have conveniently been on Cleopatra's table. Unless the wileful woman planted it there— in which case it is just as possible that she used a fake pearl. In any case, Gresham is said to have done the same with Queen Elizabeth—grinding a precious £15,000 stone to dust, mixing it in his glass of wine and drinking to the Virgin Queen's health. Gresham, incidentally, was not the author of the famous Gresham's law ("bad money drives out good") so often attributed to him. The principle was stated long before his time by Copernicus and others, and Gresham did not even formulate it.

∇ ∇ ∇ ∇ ∇ ∇ ∇ ∇ ∇

H. Rider Haggard (1856–1925)

The African warrior M'hlopekazi (d. 1897), son of the king of Swaziland, provided Haggard with the model for Umslopogaas in *King Solomon's Mines* (1886). When the warrior heard that the novel was fantastically successful, he suggested that he receive a share of the profits, but he never received more than the hunting knife Haggard had originally given him as a present. The novel and

Haggard's other African novel, *She* (1887), were favorites of the Swiss psychiatrist Carl Gustave Jung, who used them to illustrate several of his concepts. Incidentally, *King Solomon's Mines*, written on a bet that Haggard couldn't turn out as exciting a tale as *Treasure Island*, was completed in only six weeks. Haggard decided only at the last minute to accept a royalty contract for his gold mine of a book; he had been thinking of taking a flat fee.

Reviews in English periodicals up until fairly recently were often anonymous, even in the *Times Literary Supplement*. So much so that Haggard got 20 rave reviews for his *King Solomon's Mines*, all written by his friend Andrew Lang.

▽ ▽ ▽

Joseph Hall (1574–1656)

> I first adventure, follow me who list
> An be the second English satirist—
> *Virgidemiarum Sex Libri*

Hall claimed to be the first English satirist, and if he was not, he was certainly among the best of satirical writers. The English bishop published 10 volumes of satires and a bawdy satirical novel, *Virgidemiarum Sex Libri*, written in Latin. He initiated several literary genres, including the first collections of his letters, the first character-writing (portrayals of "types"), and the first Juvenalian satire. Hall was thrown in the Tower of London for five months in 1641. Milton and the syndicate of Puritan divines called Smectymnuus (*q.v.*) virulently attacked him, but he continued preaching and writing, until, as he put it, "at first forbidden by man" he was "at last disabled by God."

▽ ▽ ▽

Marguerite Radclyffe Hall (1883–1943)

Impressed by the sales of Hall's banned novel *The Well of Loneliness* (1928), Samuel Goldwyn instructed his staff to purchase the movie rights. "You can't film that," he was told. "It deals with lesbians."

"So all right," Goldwyn replied. "Where they got lesbians, we'll us Albanians."

▽ ▽ ▽

Philip Gilbert Hamerton (1834–1894)

"The art of reading," wrote the English art critic and man of letters to a friend, "is to skip judiciously." Skip on.

Thomas Hardy (1840–1928)

It is said that Hardy, who lived so long with fame, had inauspicious beginnings. At birth the author appeared not to be breathing and was thrown aside for dead. He would have died, too, if the nurse attending his mother hadn't suddenly glanced at him, noticing movement and cried: "Dead, no! Stop a minute! He's alive enough, sure!"

The scene in Hardy's novel *Tess of the D'Urbervilles* (1891) where Angel Clare wheels Tess and her dairymaid friends across a flooded lane in a wheelbarrow did not originate with Hardy. Rather, it was the result of censorship. The novelist had had Angel carry the girls across in his arms, but according to Hardy's wife, his publisher thought "it would be more decorous and suitable...if the damsels were wheeled across the lane in a wheelbarrow." In any case, the book created a sensation when it was published, and many critics called it "immoral."

The horrors he created in *Jude the Obscure* (1895), the last of his novels, helped turn Hardy from a full-time novelist to a full-time poet. Some readers felt just as strongly. The book was called "dirt, drivel and damnation," by one critic; another found it "grimy and indecent." Irish novelist George Moore called Hardy "an abortion of George Eliot [the pen name of Mary Ann Evans]." A bishop, whose name goes unrecorded, actually burned *Jude* and sent Hardy the ashes. The author commented that the man had probably burned the book "in his dispair at not being able to burn me."

Although the first parts of *The Dynasts* received poor reviews, Hardy went on to finish the third part. Completing it on Holy Thursday 1907, he wrote in his diary: "Critics can never be made to understand that the failure may be greater than the success...To have the strength to roll a stone weighing a hundredweight to the top of a mount is a success, and to have the strength to roll a stone of ten hundredweight only halfway up that mount is a failure. But the latter is two or three times as strong a deed."

According to Robert Graves, Hardy regarded critics "as parasites no less noxious than autograph hunters," but he did humorously admit that he might have been guilty of coining too many words. "[He] said that once or twice recently he had looked up a word in the dictionary for fear of being again accused of coining, and had found it there right enough—only to read on and find that the sole authority quoted was himself in a half-forgotten novel."

Irish poet William Butler Yeats once asked Hardy how over his long career he handled the problem of books sent to him for his signature: How long did he hold them, what did he write, how did he send them back? Without explaining,

Hardy led him up to the third story of the house, and opened a door that revealed a large room covered from floor to ceiling with books. "Yeats," Hardy said, "these are the books that were sent to me for signature."

Hardy was proud of his many years and when preparing his book *Winter Words* for publication in 1928 wrote in the preface, "So far as I am aware, I happen to be the only English poet who has brought out a new volume of verse on his————birthday..." He had intended to write "eighty-ninth" in the blank space, but didn't quite make another birthday—the book appeared posthumously.

Hardy's first wife, Emma Lavinia Gifford, whatever her faults, put up with much more than she dished out, especially regarding Hardy's ardent pursuit of other women, which began not long after their marriage. She got some revenge, however, by keeping a diary that she titled "What I Think of My Husband."

In Somerset Maugham's *Cakes and Ale*, Edward Driffield, the Grand Old Man of Letters, is almost surely based upon Hardy. Maugham, for instance, mentions Driffield's dislike of water. Hardy apparently had the same aversion to it, for his housekeeper during the last seven years of his life never remembered his taking a bath.

Hardy's heart was to be buried in Stinsford, England, his birthplace, after the rest of his body was cremated in Dorchester. All went according to plan until a cat belonging to the poet's sister snatched the heart off her kitchen table and disappeared into the woods with it.

▽ ▽ ▽

James Harrington (1611–1677)
The author of *The Commonwealth of Oceana* (1656), a model system of a moderately aristocratic commonwealth, was so devoted to Charles I that the monarch's execution "gave him such great a griefe" that he became profoundly depressed for years afterward. This would appear likely in a man who once refused to kiss the pope's toe because he "would not kiss the foot of any prince after kissing the King's hand."

▽ ▽ ▽

Sir John Harrington (or Harington) (1561–1612)
A godson of Elizabeth I, the poet is said to have been reproved by the queen for translating an indelicate selection from *Orlando Furioso* for the ladies of the court, and he was ordered to translate the whole work under the queen's direction as

a punishment. Harrington was banished from Elizabeth's court for his Rabelaisian "Metamorphosis of Ajax [a jakes]," and one story makes him the inventor of the flush toilet. Some four centuries after his birth the *Times Literary Supplement* reviewed *The Cherry Pit*, a work written by a direct descendant of his. The reviewer noted that "Mr. Harrington is less successful than his ancestors at dealing with fundamentals."

▽ ▽ ▽

Frank Harris (1856–1931)

A U.S. citizen, Harris is covered in *American Literary Anecdotes*, but the Irish-born writer spent so much of his life in England that he deserves at least one anecdote here. During Harris's London period, when he edited several influential magazines, he acquired a scandalous reputation, though H.G. Wells thought him "too loud and vain...to be a proper scoundrel." Oscar Wilde, however, quipped that "the greatest Shakespearean of the day," as Harris called himself, "has been received in all the great houses—once."

▽ ▽ ▽

James Harris (1709–1780)

The author was most noted for his *Hermes, or Philosophical Inquiry on Universal Grammar* (1751), but he also wrote a work on human goodness. Just before he gave his maiden speech after being elected to Parliament, a fellow M.P. told another that Harris was the celebrated author of several books about grammar and virtue. "What the devil brings him here then?" the man replied. "I am sure he will find neither the one nor the other in the House of Commons."

▽ ▽ ▽

Charles Hart (d. 1683)

Probably the only one of Shakespeare's relatives to be active in the theater, Charles Hart was the grandson of the Bard's sister Joan. He first played women's parts, but after serving in the Civil War as a lieutenant of horse, had leading parts in Dryden's plays. Pepys mentions him frequently in his famous diary, and he was especially praised for his acting of such Shakespearean parts as Othello, Brutus and Hotspur. Legend has it that Hart was Nell Gwyn's first lover and trained her for the stage.

▽ ▽ ▽

William Harvey (1578–1657)

Harvey, the first to discover how blood circulates in the body, published his pioneering work *De Motu Cordis, Exercitatio de Motu Cordis et Sanguinis* or *An*

Anatomical Treatise on the Movement of the Heart and Blood in Animals in 1628. The little book was one of the most important in the history of medicine and possibly the shoddiest. The German printer who published it used the cheapest paper possible, so that the book quickly began to deteriorate, and the book was filled with typographical errors, because neither the printer nor Harvey had bothered to read proof for it.

∇ ∇ ∇

Stephen Hawes (c. 1475–1511)
Groom of the chamber to Henry VII, Hawes is remembered chiefly for his poem *The Passetyme of Pleasure...*, which influenced Spencer. It is said that Hawes could repeat by heart most of the work of all the English poets.

∇ ∇ ∇

Benjamin Robert Haydon (1786–1846)
While at school the artist and writer thought of becoming a doctor, but was so shocked at an operation he witnessed that he abandoned the idea. From a survival standpoint, he should have remained in medicine, for although he won fame as an artist and pioneering art critic and his outrageous behavior made him well known in literary circles (Dickens used him as the model for Skimpole in *Bleak House*), he earned little from his work and argued with most of his patrons. Deeply in debt, overcome with disappointment and ingratitude, he finally ended his life with a pistol shot, leaving behind a note reading, "Stretch me no longer on the rough world."

∇ ∇ ∇

Sir John Hayward (c. 1564–1627)
Hayward, who emulated the style of the great Roman historians, dedicated his *The First Part of the Life and Raigne of King Henrie IV* (1599) to the Earl of Essex. Queen Elizabeth disliked the dedication and ordered Francis Bacon to search for "places in it that might be drawn within case of treason." Bacon read the book and replied: "For treason surely I find none, but for felony very many, for many of his sentences are stolen from Tacitus." Nevertheless, Elizabeth threw the historian in prison for two years, which amounts ot literary history's only imprisonment for a dedication.

∇ ∇ ∇

Eliza Haywood (1693?–1756)
The former actress wrote 70 or so scandalous and licentious novels, which made her many enemies. Stories were circulated about her, Swift and Walpole con-

demned her, and Pope attacked her in the *Dunciad* with a note calling Miss Haywood one of a tribe of profligate, impudent, libelous "shameless scribblers." The real reason the novelist inspired such vehemence wasn't her licentiousness but the fact that she based her characters on barely disguised real people. In several books she even appended a key in which the characters were explained by the initials of living persons! (The names are supplied to these people in the British Museum copy of *Memoirs of a Certain Island Adjacent to Utopia*, 1825.)

∇ ∇ ∇

William Hazlitt (1778–1830)

When Hazlitt surrendered to his emotions he was at grave risk. The time he fell in love with Sarah Walker, his landlady's daughter, his friends feared for his sanity over the next three years (see his *Liber Amoris*, 1823, which De Quincy described as "an explosion of frenzy"). That Hazlitt was happier in the world of intellect is witnessed by a story told by poet Thomas Moore. It seems that Hazlitt had been rude to John Lamb (Charles's brother) and Charles Lamb knocked him down. A mutual friend who was present begged Hazlitt to shake hands with Lamb and forgive him. "Well, I don't care if I do," Hazlitt agreed. "I am a metaphysician, and do not mind a blow; nothing but an idea hurts me."

Hazlitt was annoyed by people who never returned books they borrowed. "I visit my friends occasionally," he once said, "just to look over my library."

"What we read from your pen, we remember no more," wrote a critic of Hazlitt's work. Hazlitt made the remark a couplet, replying: "What we read from *your* pen, we remember before."

Hazlitt was a fitful, stubborn, moody man, impatient and difficult to restrain. "His manners," wrote Coleridge to a friend, "are 99 in a 100 singularly repulsive."

The author once observed that he had "loitered his life away, reading books, looking at pictures, going to plays, hearing, thinking, writing on what pleased me best." His last words were: "Well, I've had a happy life."

∇ ∇ ∇

Gerald Heard (1899–1971)

The Irish polymath and close friend of Aldous Huxley was more reader than writer. He is said to have read 2,000 books a year over most of his life, probably over 100,000 in all.

Thomas Hearne (1678–1735)

Authors have often inveighed against their publishers, but few have been more explicit than this antiquary and author. Said Hearne of his bookseller, Stephen Fletcher: "He was a very proud, confident, ill-natured, impudent, ignorant fellow, peevish and forward to his wife (whom he used to beat), a great sot, and a whoring prostituted wretch, and of no credit."

∇ ∇ ∇

Richard Heber (1773–1833)

"The fiercest and strongest of all the bibliomaniacs," as a contemporary called him, Heber began while an undergraduate to collect a library that eventually "overran eight houses" in England and on the continent and numbered far more than 150,000 volumes. "His library is superior to all others in the world," said Sir Walter Scott, who dedicated a book to him. Heber, the Atticus of Dibdin's *Bibliomania*, never purchased just one copy of a book. "No gentleman," he claimed, "can be without three copies of a book: one for show, one for use, and one for borrowers."

∇ ∇ ∇

John Henley (1692–1756)

Henley, an eccentric preacher, author and journalist who was caricatured by Hogarth and ridiculed by Pope, attracted a large audience of shoemakers to a sermon by announcing that he would reveal a quick, novel way to make shoes. After he had preached to them he revealed his secret: cut the tops off boots.

∇ ∇ ∇

Mary Herbert (1561–1621)

The countess of Pembroke was Philip Sidney's younger sister and he dedicated his *Arcadia* to her, probably in part because she suggested the poem to him. After his death she revised and added to *Arcadia*, oversaw its publication and went on to complete literary projects her brother hadn't finished. It is said that the countess wrote a letter, since lost, saying that "we have the man Shakespeare with us." In any case, she was patron to many great men of letters, including Spenser, Daniel, Moffat, Nashe, Harvey, Donne, and Jonson. William Browne wrote her well-known epitaph:

Underneath this sable herse
Lies the subject of all verse:
Sidney's sister, Pembroke's mother:
Death, ere thou hast slain another,
Fair, and learn'd, and good as she,
Time shall throw a dart at thee.

John Aubrey in his *Brief Lives* describes her as blonde, witty, beautiful and salacious. "She had a Contrivance," he wrote, "that in the Spring of the Yeare, when the Stallions were to leape the Mares, they were to be brought before such a part of the house where she had a *vidette* (a hole to peepe out at) to looke on them and please herselfe with their Sport; and then she would act the like sport herselfe with *her* stallions. One of her great Gallants was Crookeback't Cecill, Earl of Salesbury."

∇ ∇ ∇

George Herbin (fl. early 17th century)
Herbin's book *Hereditary Rights of the Crown of England* was so hated by the Crown that even Hilkaiah Bedford, the messenger who delivered the manuscript to the printer in 1714, was thrown into jail, where he died.

∇ ∇ ∇

Robert Herrick (1591–1674)
Some 16 months after Herrick's birth on August 24, 1591, his goldsmith father fell to his death from a fourth-floor window in their London house, an apparent suicide. However, judging from Herrick's poems, it appears that this tragedy never affected his temperament. "The greatest song-writer ever born of the English race," as Swinburne called him, was brought up by his uncle, the richest goldsmith in England. If he suffered poverty at times in his life, it was probably due to living too lavishly. Ben Jonson early adopted him as his "poetical son" and Herrick went on to become an Anglican minister. He never married, but before settling down permanently at the village of Dean Prior in South Devonshire, he lived with Tomasin Parsons, a woman 27 years younger than himself by whom he may have had an illegitimate daughter. Finally settling at Dean Prior in 1660 for the last 14 years of his life, he continued writing the little lyrical poems one critic called "like jewels of various value heaped in a casket." Herrick seems to have been a witty happy man loved by the neighboring gentry for such lighthearted pranks as keeping a pet pig that he taught to drink from a tankard. But he apparently had his irascible side, too. Local tradition has it that he once threw his prepared sermon at his congregation, and cursed them for not paying attention.

In those pre-toilet paper days the poet began his book *Hesperides, Works both Humane and Divine* (1648) with the admonitory lines:

Who with thy leaves shall wipe (at need)
The place where swelling Piles do breed;
May every ill that bites or smarts
Perplexe him in his hinder parts.

John Hervey (1696–1743)

One of the most vilified writers of the 19th or any other century, Lord Hervey was known as Lord Fanny because of his effeminate bearing and fragile build. The epileptic Hervey was also called Narcissus and Adonis both behind his back and to his face, but it was the waspish Pope who really did him in after he co-authored a thinly veiled attack on Pope (*Verses Addressed to the Imitator of Horace*) with Lady Mary Wortley Montagu. Pope dubbed him Sporus ("this painted child of dirt, that stinks and stings") after the effeminate favorite of the Emperor Nero.

∇ ∨ ∨

John Heywood (1497?–1580?)

The author's *The Four P's*, "a merry interlude," has four principal characters: "a Palmer, a Pardoner, a Poticary [apothecary], and a Peddlar." (See WILLIAM BALDWIN.)

∇ ∇ ∇

Thomas Heywood (1574?–1641)

Heywood, called "a prose Shakespeare" by Charles Lamb, was "a model of light and rapid talent." One of the most prolific writers in English literary history, he once said that he had "an entire hand or at least a finger in 220 plays," and this was seven years before death ended his writing career. Heywood always insisted that he wrote for the stage, not the press; he was one of those few writers who protested against the printing of his work because he claimed he had no time to polish it.

∇ ∇ ∇

Thomas Hobbes (1588–1679)

Up until the time he was 70—when he became a teetotaler and a vegetarian—Hobbes led a by-no-means retiring life. He estimated that he had been drunk about 100 times, appears to have fathered an illegitimate daughter, and was physically active, being a devoted tennis player. Hobbes shaved his beard to avoid the appearance of a venerable philosopher and was of course intellectually bold, but despite all his efforts he remained at heart a timid man. This he traced to his being born prematurely when his mother was frightened by reports of the Spanish Armada coming. It didn't help, either, that his father, who was a vicar, caused a scandal by deserting his family after brawling with parishioners at the church door. All his life Hobbes, the rational philosopher, had a terrible fear of ghosts.

Hobbes, a voracious reader, was, according to John Aubrey, "wont to say that if he had read as much as other men he should have known no more than other men." Tall and erect in carriage, but genial and humorous, the philosopher sometimes did lose his temper in arguments, especially when the wits at court tried to bait him. King Charles II, in fact, used to call him "the bear." Charles, who relished Hobbes's wit and kept his picture in his room, would see him coming and cry out, "Here comes the bear to be baited!"

Hobbes's philosophic awakening is said to have come when he picked up a copy of Euclid and opened it to the book's 47th proposition. "By God!" he exclaimed, "this is impossible!" But he soon read the proof and, in his own words, "fell in love with geometry."

When he was sick in France, divines "both Roman Catholic, Church of England, and Geneva" found amusement tormenting him at his bedside. He turned on them, growling, "Let me alone, or else I will detect all your Cheates from Aaron to yourselves!"

Every night after going to bed, Hobbes would take a book of written music from his bedside table, and behind locked doors, sure that nobody heard him, the venerable philosopher would begin to sing at the top of his lungs. He didn't think he had a good voice, but believed that singing "cleared his pipes...he did believe it did his lungs good, and conducted much to prolong his life."

When he wasn't singing in bed, "to do the lungs good," Hobbes was often writing there. He would use his sheets for paper and jot words and computations on his thighs when he ran out of sheet space. It is said that all of the author's *Dialogue on Physics or on the Nature of Air* (1661) was written in bed in this manner. When he wasn't in bed working, the industrious author invariably walked about with a pen and an inkhorn in the head of his staff and a notebook in his pocket to record any worthwhile scheme that came into his head.

The philosopher, who lived until the age of 91, was very bald in his old age, but never wore a hat, claiming that he "never took cold in his head." His "greatest trouble," he said, "was to keep off the flies from pitching on the baldness."

Hobbes was 87 when his last book published in his lifetime appeared; his final work, written when he was 90, wasn't published until the year after his death. A few months before his death he wrote these optimistic love verses:

> Tho' I am now past ninety, an too old
> T' expect preferment in the Court of Cupid,

And many Winters made me ev'n so cold
I am become almost all over stupid.

Yet I can love and have a Mistresse too,
As fair as can be and as wise as fair;
And yet not proud, nor anything will doe
To make me of her favour to despair.

To tell you who she is were very bold;
But i' th' Character your Selfe you find
Thinke not the man a Fool tho he be old
Who loves in Body fair, a fairer mind.

His last words were "I am about to take my last voyage, a great leap into the dark."

▽ ▽ ▽

James Hogg (1770–1835)
The Scottish poet known as "the Shepherd" came from a family that had been shepherds for generations. Hogg taught himself to write by copying letters from a printed book as he lay watching his flock. Soon after Sir Walter Scott discovered his genius, he was invited to Scott's house. Dressed like a herdsman, hands dirty, Hogg had no idea of how to conduct himself at first, and when he saw Mrs. Scott, who was quite ill at the time, reclining on a sofa, he stretched himself out similarly on the sofa opposite her. "I thought" he recalled later, "I could never do wrong to copy the lady of the house."

▽ ▽ ▽

James Holman (1786–1857)
Invalided out of the British navy in 1810, Holman became totally blind, but nevertheless began traveling around the world and writing books about his experiences. "The Blind Traveler," as he was called, was arrested in Siberia as a spy but, undiscouraged, resumed his journey from another point after being escorted out of Russia and managed to accomplish his goal. His travels are recounted in a number of books, including the four-volume *A Voyage round the World, Including Travels in Africa, Asia, Australia, America, etc., from 1827 to 1832.* (1834–35).

▽ ▽ ▽

John Home (1722–1808)
Patriotic enthusiasm made the Scottish minister's tragedy *Douglas* (1756) a tremendous success in Edinburgh. Audiences went wild, especially after hearing the long soliloquy beginning "My name is Norval ..." On opening night, in fact,

a loyal Scottish voice cried from the pit when the speech ended: "Whaur's yer Wully Shakespeare noo!"

▽ ▽ ▽

Thomas Hood (1799–1845)

Hood was a remarkable and inveterate punster, the most famous punster of the age, which annoyed some of his stuffier serious readers, so much so that several wrote to the *Comic Annual*, which he edited, condemning him for his punning. But Hood immediately defended himself with the jingling couplet:

> However critics may take offense,
> A double meaning has double sense.

One time while he was sick and solicitous doctors and nurses crowded around him, Hood punned: "The undertaker is too eager to earn a livelihood" (that is, urn a lively Hood).

▽ ▽ ▽

Theodore Edward Hook (1788–1841)

The wit and writer of light verse, a friend of the Prince of Wales, was entertaining friends with comic song improvisations when the butler tapped him on the shoulder, telling him, "Sir, Mr. Winter, the tax collector, is here to collect taxes." Without missing a beat, Hook knocked out the following song:

> Here comes Mr. Winter, collector of taxes.
> I advise you to pay whatever he axes;
> Excuses won't do; he stands no sort of flummery.
> Though Winter his name is, his presence is summary.

A great practical joker, Hook once walked on stage in Elizabethan dress during a performance of *Hamlet* and delivered a letter to the melancholy Dane.

Hook was once insulted by a Mrs. Tottenham. He soon sent out hundreds of letters to Londoners of every social rank, inviting them to attend a party or make repairs at her house on Berners Street. He and a few confederates later sat and watched as visitors ranging from chimney sweeps to the lord mayor of London tied up traffic for hours in the fashionable neighborhood.

Hook, who had been imprisoned once for embezzlement, understood the uses of pretension, but he never tolerated it in others. Once he approached a very pompous man swaggering down the street and bowed low. "I beg your pardon, sir," he asked, "are you anyone in particular?"

∇ ∇ ∇

Anthony Hope (Anthony Hope Hawkins; 1863–1933)
The barrister and author of *The Prison of Zenda* (1894) attended the opening of James Barrie's *Peter Pan* in 1904. On leaving, he was heard to comment, "Oh, for an hour of Herod!" (A century before a similar remark, "Oh, for the days of Herod!," was made by the mistress of King William IV about a play featuring one of the myriad child prodigies on the stage at the time.)

∇ ∇ ∇

John Hoskyns (1566–1638)
For his bold spirit he was granted the crest of a lion's head breathing fire. He liked to joke that it was the only lion in England that smoked tobacco.

Imprisoned in the tower behind boarded windows for speaking too critically of the king in Parliament, Hoskyns wrote this verse to his infant son Bennet during his confinement:

My litle Ben, whilst thou art young,
And know'st not how to rule thy Tongue,
Make it thy Slave whil'st thou art free,
Least it as mine imprison thee.

It is said that while in the Tower he read and revised fellow prisoner Sir Walter Raleigh's *History of the World*. Later Ben Jonson would say that Hoskyns polished his verses so well that he considered him his father. The brilliant scholar was also friendly with John Donne and Sir Henry Wotton, among other London wits, and wrote a huge book of poems, including "verses on the fart in the Parliament house," that his son lent to someone and was lost to history.

Hoskyns was killed by a lumbering country bumpkin who stepped on his toes. Gangrene set in the wound and he died after his toes were amputated. He had his wit until the end, however. Shortly after his toes were cut off he said to the clubfooted minister of his parish: "Sir Hugh, I must get acquainted with your shoemaker."

Geoffrey Household (1901–1988)

The English master of suspense's first novel, *Rogue Male* (1939), was the story of a sportsman who assassinated the dictator of an unnamed European country. The dictator Household actually had in mind was Adolf Hitler, because, as the author later confided, "the man had to be dealt with and I began to think how much I would love to kill him."

∇ ∇ ∇

A.E. (Alfred Edward) Housman (1859–1936)

Housman was a professor, an authority on Manilius, one of the minor Roman poets, as well as a poet, and may never have been able to choose between the two. A perhaps apocryphal story has him put it this way in a speech he made at Trinity College, Cambridge: "This great College, of this ancient University, has seen some strange sights. It has seen Wordsworth drunk and Porson sober. And here am I, a better poet than Porson, and a better scholar than Wordsworth, betwixt and between."

Asked to give his definition of poetry, the poet replied, "I could no more define poetry than a terrier can define a rat."

Instructed Housman when told that a reporter wanted to interview him: "Tell him that the wish to include a glimpse of my personality in a literary article is low, unworthy, and American. Tell him that some men are more interesting than their books but my book is more interesting than its man. Tell them that Frank Harris found me rude and Wilfred Blunt found me dull. Tell him anything else that you think will put him off."

Wrote the poet to his brother Laurence, a fellow poet whose work was widely parodied: "I had far, far rather that people should attribute my verses to you than yours to me."

Literary logrollers long ago formed the first literary mutual admiration societies, favorably reviewing each other's books in order to promote sales and reputations. Commenting on one instance of such a practice, Housman said there had been nothing like it since the passage in Milton where Sin gave birth to Death.

Trying to cheer him up while he lay dying, a friend told Housman a risqué tale. "Yes, that's a good one," Housman said when he finished, "and tomorrow I'll be telling it on the Golden Floor."

As he lay on his deathbed the poet remembered a passage from Arnold Bennett's novel *Clayhanger* describing Cheyne-Stokes breathing—gasping breath that ceases for up to a minute, continues and keeps alternating between gasping and breathlessness until death comes. Housman remembered Bennett's description of the "death breathing" named for William Cheyne and William Stokes, the physicians who first were known to have described it, and this may have been his last memory, for just as he remembered it he began the same death breathing himself.

∇ ∇ ∇

Margaret Hughes (fl. late 17th century)
Women in other countries had acted before she did, but the first woman to appear on an English stage was Prince Rupert's mistress Margaret Hughes, who on December 8, 1660, played Desdemona in Shakespeare's *Othello*. Previous to this female parts were always played by boys. (One Edward Kynaston, who died in 1706, seems to have been the last male to play a woman's part in a serious drama.)

∇ ∇ ∇

Richard Hughes (1900–1976)
The Welsh author of *A High Wind in Jamaica* (1929) wrote the world's first radio drama. His *Danger*, commissioned by the BBC in 1924, concerned three English visitors trapped in a Welsh coal mine. The play also introduced the first radio sound effects, calling for the echoes occurring underground in the tunnel to be simulated by the actors speaking into a large bucket.

∇ ∇ ∇

T.E. (Thomas Ernest) Hulme (1883–1917)
A constable once rebuked a drunken Hulme for urinating in Soho Square. "Do you realize you are addressing a member of the middle class?" Hulme replied indignantly, rendering the man speechless.

The writer, who strongly influenced the modernist movement even though he died young in World War I, was expelled from Cambridge for some unknown reason. He made a spectacular departure from the university as he sat astride a coffin carried by undergraduate friends dressed in deep mourning.

Hulme was a big, blunt man who brooked no nonsense. One time Wyndham Lewis, believing Hulme liked sculptor Jacob Epstein's work better than his, worked himself into a rage and ran into Hulme's home screaming that he was going to kill the philosopher. He leaped at Hulme's throat but Hulme lifted him up, carried him outside and hung him upside down by his trousers from a tall wrought-iron fence.

Like so many British writers, the poet and philosopher was killed in the trenches in World War I. In his case a large shell made a direct hit and he was obliterated, not even enough left of him for a grave.

According to Ezra Pound, in his *Canto XVI*, Hulme went to war in France with "a lot of books" from the London Library: "...and a shell buried 'em in a dugout. / And the Library expressed its annoyance."

∇ ∇ ∇

David Hume (1711–1776)

The brilliant Scottish philosopher did not look the part. "The powers of physiognomy were baffled...to discover the smallest trace of the faculties of his mind in the unmeaning features of his visage," an acquaintance said of him. "His face was broad and fat, his mouth wide, and without any other expression than that of imbecility...The corpulence of his whole person was far better fitted to communicate the idea of a turtle-eating alderman than that of a refined philosopher."

People were always making fun of his corpulence. At a party in Paris someone remarked in Latin when he entered, "Et verbum caro factum est [And the word was made flesh]." However, a witty woman admirer defended him, quickly retorting, "Et verbum carum factum est [And the word was made lovable]."

He had great wit about his weight, even proposing a tax on obesity, though he saw no chance of such a law's passage, because some "divines might pretend that the church was in danger."

The agnostic philosopher was chided about going to church regularly to hear an orthodox Scottish minister preach. "I don't believe all he says," Hume replied, "but *he* does, and once a week I like to hear a man who believes what he says."

Hume had an excellent income from other literary works and took his time writing his *History of Great Britain* (1754–62), despite the urging of his friends, who wondered why he was taking so long. "Gentlemen, you do me too much honor," Hume explained to a particularly urgent group, "but I have four reasons for not writing: I am too old, too fat, too lazy, and too rich."

While Hume was dying, Boswell persisted in asking him if he believed in a future life. "It is a most unreasonable fancy that we should exist forever," he replied. "But surely it is pleasing to think of such a possibility now," Boswell insisted. "Not at all," Hume said. "It is a very gloomy thought."

The philosopher's headstone in the Calton Hill, Edinburgh, graveyard reads:

> Within this circular idea,
> Call'd vulgarly a tomb,
> The ideas and impressions lie,
> That constituted Hume

∇ ∇ ∇

(James Henry) Leigh Hunt (1784–1859)

Hunt, an author and magazine editor, was imprisoned for libel after calling King George IV "a fat Adonis of 50." One time Hunt had been ill for several weeks during an influenza epidemic that had taken many lives, when he suddenly recovered and unexpectedly visited his friend Jane ("Jenny") Welsh Carlyle. Mrs. Carlyle impulsively jumped up and kissed him as he came in the door. This inspired Hunt's famous verse:

> Jenny kissed me when we met,
>   Jumping from the chair she sat in;
> Time, you thief, who love to get
>   Sweets into your list, put that in:
> Say I'm weary, say I'm sad.
>   Say that health and wealth have missed me,
> Say I'm growing old, but add,
>   Jenny kissed me.

Harold Skimpole, a character in Dickens's *Bleak House* "who disguises his utter selfishness under an assumption of childhood innocence," is based on Leigh Hunt. Dickens once said that the character was only "drawn in the light externals" and passionately denied that the later knavery of Skimpole was related in any way to Hunt, but in a letter to a friend he wrote, "I suppose he [Skimpole] is the most exact portrait that was ever painted in words...it is an absolute reproduction of a real man."

∇ ∇ ∇

Aldous Huxley (1874–1963)

When only 16, at Eton, Huxley suffered an attack of keratitis punctata and became nearly totally blind for a period of about 18 months. By using the dilatant atropine and special glasses he became able to read "tolerably well" for the rest of his life. His poor vision, however, made the scientific career he had planned impossible and he turned to literature instead.

Huxley often wrote with his *nose*, though he produced none of his master work this way. "A little nose writing," he notes in *The Art of Seeing*, "will result in a perceptible temporary improvement of defective vision." Huxley's eyesight was so bad from the time he was at Eton that he learned braille to relieve his eyes; he often read at night in bed, hands and book under the covers. A follower of Dr. William Bates, this near-blind author who shed so much light on the world practiced the ophthamologist's exercises for improving eyesight. Any myopic writer or reader who wants to try needn't dip his nose in ink. Simply fix your eyes on the end of your nose and move your head as if you were writing a word, sentence, or anecdote.

The author always took at least one volume of the *Encyclopedia Britannica* with him wherever he traveled, even a short distance, and had the opportunity to read. When he went on a world cruise he had a special traveling case made so that he could take the whole set.

Late in his life Huxley remarked, "It is a bit embarrassing to have been concerned with the human problem all one's life and find at the end that one has no more to offer by way of advice than 'Try to be a little kinder.'"

▽ ▽ ▽

Thomas Huxley (1825–1895)

The defender of Darwin's views, "Darwin's bulldog," as he was called, debated Bishop Samuel Wilberforce at Oxford in 1860. In his speech Wilberforce asked Huxley, "If anyone were to be willing to trace his descent through an ape as his *grandfather*, would he be willing to trace his descent similarly on the side of his *grandmother*?" After the applause subsided, Huxley replied, "A man has no reason to be ashamed of having an ape for his grandfather. If there were an ancestor whom I should feel shame in recalling, it would rather be a man who, not content with an equivocal success in his own sphere of activity, plunges into scientific questions with which he has no real acquaintance."

▽ ▽ ▽ ▽ ▽ ▽ ▽ ▽ ▽

William Ralph Inge (1860–1954)

A pessimistic moralist, the dean of St. Paul's hated anything called progress and anything modern. "The Gloomy Dean" made his opinions known in his public writings and his private conversation. Of a difficult volume of free verse he remarked, "I hate loose meter even more than loose living."

A woman incensed at one of Inge's pessimistic articles wrote this note to him: "I am praying nightly for your death. It may interest you to know that in two other cases I have had great success."

∇ ∇ ∇

William Henry Ireland (1777–1835)

Ireland was a master forger who specialized in Shakespeare documents, which he forged on blank Elizabethan parchments he had discovered. His masterworks were two new "Shakespeare" plays: *Vortigern and Rowena* and *Henry II*. Playwright Richard Brinsley Sheridan actually purchased *Vortigern* for £300 and half of any royalties, and produced it at Drury Lane on April 2, 1796. A complete fiasco, it was even laughed at by its actors and practically hooted off the stage, not to be played again. Ireland, never punished for his crimes, went on to write several forgettable novels.

∇ ∇ ∇

Henry Isaacson (1581–1654)

The theologian and chronologer presented a copy of his *Tabula Historico-Chronologica* (1633) to Charles I. The king quickly turned to his own birth in the chronology and found that the wrong date had been given. "And here's one Lye to begin with," he said, and an ashamed Isaacson "immediately sneak't away."

∇ ∇ ∇ ∇ ∇ ∇ ∇ ∇ ∇

Henry James (1843–1916)

The American-born novelist, who lived in England his last 42 years and became a British subject the year before he died, was something of a hypochondriac, complaining overly of toothaches, common colds, and even the constipation he was cursed with, which he compared to having "terminal cancer." The long-suffering James imagined he had severe stomach troubles in 1910, but Sir William Osler found nothing wrong with him and pronounced him physically "splendid" for his age. His brother William diagnosed a nervous breakdown, as did Edith Wharton in a letter describing a visit with James. "I could hardly believe," she wrote, "[that] it was the same James who cried out to me his fear, his despair, his craving for the 'cessation of consciousness,' & all his unspeakable loneliness & need of comfort & inability to be comforted! 'Not to wake—not to wake'—that was his refrain, '& then one does wake & one looks again into the blackness of life, & everything ministers to it—one reads & sees & hears.'"

H.G. Wells used James as the model for George Boon in his *Boon* (1915) but had his hero claim that novels should be used for propaganda not art. James promptly wrote him: "It is art that makes life, makes interest, makes importance, and I know of no substitute whatever for the force and beauty of its process. If I were Boon I should say that any pretense of such a substitute is helpless and hopeless humbug; but I wouldn't be Boon for the world, and am only yours faithfully, Henry James."

James's literary feud with H.G. Wells began in earnest when he implied that Wells threw information at the reader as if emptying his mind like a perpetual chamber pot from a window: "The more he knows and knows—or at any rate learns—the more, in other words, he establishes his saturation—the greater is our impression of his holding it good enough for us, such as we are, that he shall but turn his mind and its contents upon us by any free familiar gesture and as from a high window forever open…" (For another anecdote about the James-Wells feud see H.G. WELLS.)

James, who constantly experimented with the English language and probably used more synonyms for words than any writer before or since, once gave the following order to a waiter in a restaurant: "Bring me…fetch me…carry me…supply me…in other words (I hope you are following me) serve—when it is cooked…scorched…grilled, I should say—a large…considerable…meaty (as opposed to fatty)…chop. In other words: Burn one chop!"

Though he did sometimes strain for the choice word or phrase, the Master's conversation was usually as impeccably woven as his written prose, which, after injuring his hand, he often dictated to a typist, as was the case with all of *The Ambassadors, The Golden Bowl* and other novels. Said one friend: "He talked as if every sentence had been carefully rehearsed; every semicolon, every comma was in exactly the right place, and his rounded periods dropped to the floor and bounced about like tiny rubber balls."

Wrote James in a letter to his friend, American novelist Edith Wharton: "Summer afternoon—summer afternoon; to me these have always been the two most beautiful words in the English language."

When Edith Wharton sent him a letter bemoaning her unhappy marriage, he replied: "Keep making the movements of life."

"I'm glad you like adverbs," he wrote in a 1912 letter to Miss M. Betham Edwards—"I adore them; they are the only qualifications I really much respect."

Though he occasionally didn't practice what he preached, James instructed his nephew Billy that the three most important things in life were: "To be kind, and then to be kind, and then to be kind."

Remarked Shaw of James's conversion to British citizenship: "James felt buried in America; but he came here to be embalmed."

James counted January 5, 1895, the worst night of his life. That was the opening night of his play *Guy Domville,* which he described as "a little white Christian virgin" thrown "to the tigers and lions." Not only was the play booed, but when he was led on stage, James, too, was booed. He plunged into a deep depression despite good reviews from Wells and Shaw.

James made little money from his novels, and when he got what he considered a royal advance of $8,000 for *The Ivory Tower,* it was because his friend Edith Wharton secretly arranged to have Scribner's take the money from her own abundant royalty account with the publisher. One time Wharton told James that her last novel enabled her to buy a luxurious motor car. "With the proceeds of my last novel," James replied, "I purchased a small go-cart, or hand-barrow, on which my guests' luggage is wheeled from the station to my house. It needs a coat of paint. With the proceeds of my next novel I shall have it painted."

One time James wove an endless sentence, in Ezra Pound's phrase, to an old Englishman from whom he wanted directions: "My friend, to put it to you in two words, this lady and I have just arrived here from Slough: that is to say, to be more strictly accurate, we have recently passed through Slough on our way there, having actually motored to Windsor from Rye, which was our point of departure; and the darkness having overtaken us, we should be much obliged if you would tell us where we now are in relation, say, to the High Street, which, as you of course know, leads to the Castle, after leaving on the left hand turn down to the railway station...In short, in short, my good man, what I want to put to you in a word is this: supposing we have already (as I have reason to think we have) driven past the turn down to the railway station (which in that case, by the way, would probably not have been on our left hand, but on our right) where we are now in relation to—"

"Oh, please," his companion, Edith Wharton, finally interrupted, "do ask him where the King's Road is."

"Ah—? The King's Road? Just so! Quite right! Can you as a matter of fact, my good man, tell us where, in relation to our present position, the King's Road exactly is?"

"Ye're in it," said the old man.

Writing to a friend about Hawthorne's newfound classic status he noted: "The grand sign of being a classic is that you have 'passed,' as they say at examinations, you have passed; you have become one once for all; you have taken your degree and may be left to the light and the ages."

After James came back to Boston from England in 1910 to spend the winter with his recently widowed sister, Somerset Maugham visited him and found him very sad and lonely. "I wander about these great empty streets of Boston," he told his visitor, "and I never see a soul. I could not be more alone in the Sahara."

On the morning of December 2, 1915, James suffered a stroke and expected to die soon. At this time, not as his last words, as is often reported, he exclaimed: "So this is it at last, the distinguished thing!" He died three months later.

∇ ∇ ∇

William Jenkin (c. 1640)

After the Restoration in England, the Noncomformists were forced to worship in secret places. According to an old tradition, first recorded in *Granger's Biographical History of England* (1769), "one congregation assembled in a barn, the rendezvous of beggars and other vagrants, where the preacher and pamphleteer William Jenkin, for want of a ladder or tub (pulpit), was suspended in a sack fixed to the beam. His discourse that day being on the Last Judgment, he particularly attempted to describe the terrors of the wicked at the sounding of the trumpet—on which a trumpeter to puppet show, who was hidden under the straw in the barn with other vagrants, sounded a charge. The congregation fled in an instant from the place, thinking the king's men were coming, leaving their affrighted preacher to shift for himself. The effects of his terror are said to have appeared at the bottom of the sack, and to have occasioned the opprobrious appellation *shitsack* by which the Non Comformants were vulgarly distinguished."

Douglas Jerrold (1803–1857)

On the first night of his first play, *Fifteen Years of a Drunken Life* (1828), a seasoned, successful playwright kidded Jerrold about his nervousness.

"I," he intoned, "never feel nervous on the first night of my pieces."

"Ah, my boy," replied Jerrold, "you are always certain of success. Your pieces have all been tried before."

Publisher Richard Bentley told Jerrold that before he named his noted magazine *Bentley's Miscellany* he had planned to call it *The Wit's Miscellany*. "Well, that would have been going to the other extreme," Jerrold replied.

Jerrold, who used the pseudonym Q for his journalistic writing, did not have a very happy married life. One time someone at a party asked him who was dancing with his wife. "God knows, my dear boy," Jerrold replied. "Some member of the Humane Society, I suppose."

"If an earthquake were to engulf England tomorrow," he remarked to friends, "the English would manage to meet and dine somewhere among the rubbish, just to celebrate the event."

A very thin man had been boring Jerrold all evening with his rambling stories. "Sir," Jerrold finally said, "you are like a pin, but without either its head or its point."

One afternoon a well-known bore approached Jerrold on the street, ready to buttonhole him. "Well, well, Jerrold," he began "What's going on?"

"I am," said Jerrold, and left.

Jerrold's contemporary, Albert Smith, wrote a piece for *Blackwood's Magazine* and signed it A.S. Jerrold didn't much admire Smith. "What a pity," he said, reading the initials, "that Smith will tell only two-thirds of the truth."

Jerrold agreed with Thomas Carlyle's criticisms of life in the 19th century, but found him wanting in the alternatives he offered. "Here is a man," he said, "who beats a big drum under my windows, and when I come running downstairs, has nowhere for me to go."

"He is a kind man," Jerrold said to a friend, speaking of a mutual acquaintance.

"Why, he has been away from his family for years and never sent them a farthing," his friend said. "You call that kindness?"

"Yes, I do," replied Jerrold. "Unremitting kindness."

A notorious sponger asked a mutual friend to borrow money for him from Jerrold. "How much does he want this time?" Jerrold asked. "Oh, just a four and two naughts will put him straight," his friend advised. "Put me down for one of the naughts," Jerrold replied.

Jerrold was a captive audience at his club, caught between a raucous admirer of the prince of Orange and an enraged admirer of William III. "Bah to you, sir!" one man finally shouted. "I spit upon your prince of Orange!"—only to have his opponent jump up and scream, "And I, sir, spit upon your King William!" This went on for a few moments until Jerrold rang the bell and shouted to a waiter, "Here, boy—spittoons for two!"

Jerrold was not the outdoor type. "The only athletic sport I ever mastered," he confessed, "was backgammon."

He was told that a hack writer planned to dedicate his next book to him. Alarmed, Jerrold replied: "Ah, that's an awful weapon he has in his hands!"

▽ ▽ ▽

C.E.M. (Cyril Edwin Mitchinson) Joad (1891–1953)
When an express train to London made an unscheduled stop at Reading, the philosopher boarded it. "You'll have to get off, sir," a conductor told him. "This train doesn't stop here." "In that case, don't worry," Joad said. "I'm not on it." (Trains figured prominently in Joad's life. He was also a prominent radio personality, but that career is said to have been destroyed when, according to one writer, he was "caught…trying to save a few coppers by evading a transport turnstile.")

▽ ▽ ▽

Samuel Johnson (1709–1784)
Dr. Johnson had a huge, strong athletic build, although he suffered from many physical and mental maladies, including a terrible facial twitch. When in his early London years he applied to a publisher for employment, he was found unfit for the job. "You had better get a porter's knot and carry trunks," he was advised.

While working on his great dictionary, Dr. Johnson invented a definition for *lexicographer* almost as well known as the word itself—"Lexicographer: A writer of dictionaries, a harmless drudge."

Lord Chesterfield refused to support Johnson while he was at work on his dictionary, but reviewed the book favorably on its completion. Johnson wrote to him, in part: "Is not a patron, my lord, one who looks with unconcern on a man struggling for life in the water, and when he has reached ground encumbers him with help?" Said Dr. Johnson, later, on the collected letters of Lord Chesterfield: "They teach the morals of a whore, and the manners of a dancing master." Still later he added: "This man I thought had been a Lord among wits; but I find, he is only a wit among Lords."

Another time he said of his "patron": "Chesterfield ought to know me better than to think me capable of contracting myself into a dwarf that he may be thought a giant."

The Great Cham of Literature advised his former teacher that he would complete his *Dictionary* in three years (though it actually took 11 years). "But the French Academy, which consists of forty members, took forty years to compile their dictionary," he was told. "Sire, thus it is," Johnson explained. "This is the proportion. Let me see; forty times forty is sixteen hundred. As is three to sixteen hundred, so is the proportion of an Englishman to a Frenchman."

Johnson defined pastern as the knee of a horse in his *Dictionary*. When a woman asked why, he replied, "Ignorance madam, sheer ignorance."

A *patron*, ran the definition in his *Dictionary*, was "One who countenances, supports or protects. Commonly a wretch who supports with insolence, and is paid with flattery." A *dedication* was listed as "A servile address to a patron," and a *dedicator* as "One who inscribes his work to a patron with compliment and servility."

He defined "Grub Street" in his *Dictionary* as "Originally the name of a street in Moorfields in London, much inhabited by writers of small histories, dictionaries and temporary poems; whence any mean production is called grubstreet." Though he never resided in Grub Street, he selected that home of needy writers of dictionaries like himself by attaching to the entry a Greek quotation meaning: "Hail, Ithaca! After toil and bitter woe, I am glad to reach your soil."

"Dictionaries are like watches," he told his good friend Mrs. Thrale, "the worst is better than none, and the best cannot be expected to go quite true."

When a woman took him to task for recording "improper" words in his dictionary, Dr. Johnson stopped in mock horror. "Madam," he said, "you have been looking for them!"

Despite his proclamation in the preface that his *Dictionary* was written "with little assistance of the learned," he did convince his friend Thomas Wharton to have Oxford make him an honorary Master of Arts to help sell the great work.

"Your manuscript is both good and original," he told a prospective author; "but the part that is good is not original, and the part that is original is not good."

Boswell told Johnson that he might dislike puns so much because he couldn't make them. "If I were punished for every pun I shed," Johnson replied, "there would not be left a shed for my puny head."

Of his many remarks about Scotchmen perhaps the most famous was his reply when Boswell told him, "I do indeed come from Scotland, but I cannot help it..." Johnson replied: "That, sir, I find, is what a very good many of your countrymen cannot help."

Another time Boswell wondered aloud how he could describe a terrible inn where he and Johnson had stayed in Bristol. "Describe it, sir?" Johnson said. "Why, it was so bad that Boswell wished to be in Scotland."

While touring Scotland with Boswell he visited the MacDonald clan; one of the young MacDonald ladies sat on his knee and kissed him on the cheek. "Do it again," Dr. Johnson told her, "and let us see who will tire first."

He liked the Irish almost as little as the Scots. "The Irish are a fair people," he said—they never speak well of one another.

He bet that he could repeat verbatim a complete chapter of Horrebow's *National History of Ireland*. It proved to be Chapter LXXII, "Concerning Snakes," which read in its entirety: "There are no snakes to be met with throughout the whole island."

Boswell censured a certain widower for marrying a second time, claiming this showed disrespect for the man's dead wife. "Not at all sir," Dr. Johnson disagreed. "On the contrary, were he not to marry again, it might be concluded that his first wife had given him a disgust for marriage, but by taking a second wife he pays the highest compliment to the first by showing that she made him so happy as a married man, that he wishes to be so a second time."

Many famous writers, including Pope, Voltaire, Schiller and Balzac, were gargantuan coffee drinkers. But Dr. Johnson seems to have been the champion tea drinker among Western authors. "No man could eat more heartily than

Johnson," says Boswell in his biography. Macaulay writes of "the sight of food affecting [Johnson] as it affects wild beasts and birds of prey…Whenever he was so fortunate as to have near him a hare that had been kept too long, or a meat pie made with rancid butter, he gorged himself with such violence that his veins swelled and the moisture broke out on his forehead." To wash down such meals, this man who "dressed like a scarecrow and ate like a cormorant" drank pots, lakes, oceans of tea. It is said that he often drank over 25 cups of tea at one sitting.

While enjoying a particularly good meal with Dr. Johnson, Boswell asked him if he didn't think that a good cook was more essential to a community than a good poet.

"I don't suppose," Johnson replied, "that there's a *dog* in the town that doesn't think so."

The actor David Garrick asked Johnson to name life's greatest pleasure. "[He] answered fucking and the second was drinking," Garrick recalled. "And therefore he wondered why there were not more drunkards, for all could drink tho all could not fuck."

"Drinking drives away care. Would you not allow a man to drink for that reason?" Boswell once asked the Great Cham.

"Yes, sir, I would," Dr. Johnson replied. "If he sat next to you."

Johnson so loved his cat Hodge that he would buy oysters for it and shuck them himself. Ironically, his biographer Boswell, forever linked with him in literary history, hated cats, though he was discreet enough to keep this a secret from Johnson.

"If your company does not drive a man out of his house," he told Boswell one day, "nothing will."

"I would rather be attacked than unnoticed," he told Boswell. "For the worst you can do to an author is to be silent to his works." Another time he remarked: "Never mind whether they praise or abuse your writings; anything is tolerable, except oblivion."

Of music Dr. Johnson remarked that it was the only sensual pleasure without vice.

"Do you like music?" a lady friend once asked Johnson.

"No, madam," replied the Great Cham, "but of all noises, I think music is the least disagreeable."

Once he was told that a piece being played by a famous musician was very difficult. "Difficult do you call it, sir?" he replied. "I wish it were impossible."

One of Dr. Johnson's circle was complaining about the playwright Samuel Foote being kicked in Ireland. "He is rising in the world," Johnson said. "When he was in England no one thought it worthwhile to kick him."

Another time he observed of Foote: "If he be an infidel, he is an infidel as a dog is an infidel; that is to say, he has never thought upon the subject."

After a performance of *Irene* his friend Garrick took him backstage to the dressing rooms of the actors. When asked to go backstage another time, he replied: "No, David, I will never come back. For the white bubbies and the silk stockings of your actresses excite my genitals."

He could be childlike. While visiting friends, he advised them that he would like to "take a roll down" a steep hill behind their house. Emptying his pockets, he lay atop the hill and propelled himself sideways, rolling over and over like a joyous boy until he reached bottom.

Johnson correctly believed that the celebrated poems allegedly written by the Scottish bard Ossian were actually forgeries written by their translator James Macpherson. And he thought little of them. "Do you think, sir," Dr. Robert Blair asked him, "that any man of a modern age could have written such poems?" "Yes, sir," he replied, "many men, many women, and many children."

When Johnson finally declared James Macpherson's Ossianic poems to be a fraud (he was later proved right) the poet wrote a threatening letter to him. Replied Johnson: "I hope I shall never be deterred from detecting what I think a cheat by the meanness of a ruffian... I thought your book an imposture, I think it an imposture still... Your rage I defy."

Said Dr. Johnson: "Rousseau, sir, is a very bad man. I would sooner sign a sentence for his transportation than that of any felon who has gone from the Old Bailey these many years. Yes, I should like to have him work in the Plantations."

"Sir," asked Boswell, "do you think him as bad a man as Voltaire?"

"Why, sir," Johnson replied, "it is difficult to settle the proportion of inequity between them."

A certain Miss Brooks had written a tragedy entitled *The Siege of Sinape* and wanted the Great Cham to read and correct it because she was too busy and had too many irons in the fire. Johnson replied: "In that case, madam, I would say: Put your tragedy where your irons are." (This riposte, in various forms, is attributed to several authors.)

Though the magistrate Sir John Hawkins devoted much of his life to the arts, Johnson found him stingy and unsociable. One night Hawkins refused to pay his share of the dinner check at their club. "Sir John, sir," Johnson later told a friend, putting down Hawkins for the ages, "is a very unclubable man."

Johnson could be as kindhearted as he was irascible. According to a woman friend, "As he returned to his lodgings about one or two o'clock in the morning he often saw poor children asleep on thresholds and stalls and he used to put pennies into their hands to buy them a breakfast."

Mrs. Elizabeth Montagu (*q.v.*) was the head of a London literary salon contemptuously dubbed the bluestockings because one of its impecunious male members (Mr. Benjamin Stillingfleet) wore common blue worsted hose instead of gentleman's black silk hose. She had a falling out with Dr. Johnson and broadcast the word that he was persona non grata in her little circle. "Mrs. Montagu has dropt me," Johnson remarked when he heard the news. "Now, sir, there are people whom one should like very well to drop, but would not wish to be dropt by."

At one of Mrs. Montagu's literary gatherings, a group of young women surrounding Dr. Johnson wondered how to treat this great, gruff bear whose hostility they had heard so much about. Finally Johnson assured them: "Ladies, I am tame, you may stroke me."

"To endeavour to make *her* ridiculous," he said of the radical historian Mrs. Catherine Macaulay, "is like blackening the chimney."

In a move to expose literary pretension, Dr. Johnson read a long, difficult poem to a noted critic, who expressed unreserved admiration for the work. The Great Cham then told him that he had omitted every other line.

"No man but a blockhead ever wrote except for money," he told Boswell. (See also BYRON.)

He was told that a man who had been most unhappy in marriage married immediately after his shrewish wife died. "It was a triumph of hope over experience," he said.

Johnson was asked by his friend Maurice Morgann to compare the talents of the poets Christopher Smart and Samuel Derrick, both of whom he thought little of, though history has not upheld his opinion of the insane Kit Smart. In any case, Dr. Johnson's answer did not help either of the poets. "Sir," he replied, "there is no setting the point of precedency between a louse and a flea."

The insane poet Christopher Smart (see the anecdote above) was a brilliant classical scholar and innovative poet but little recognized in his own time. Smart's derangement usually took the form of praying in public, "falling upon his knees and saying his prayers in the street, or in any other unusual place," as Johnson put it. Though Johnson did not appreciate his "poor friend's" genius, he didn't think Smart should be confined to the madhouse. "I did not think he ought to be shut up," he told his friend Dr. Burney after Smart's death. "His infirmities were not noxious to society. He insisted on people praying with him; and I'd as lief pray with Kit Smart as anyone else..."

"Sir, what is poetry?" he was asked.
"Why, sir, it is much easier to say what it is not. We all *know* what light is; but it is not easy to *tell* what it is."

A pretentious shopkeeper asked Johnson to write an epitaph for the man's daughter, advising him that she had always been modest and polite to her inferiors. "An admirable trait," Dr. Johnson said, "but it might not be so easy to discover who the lady's inferiors were."

Henry Hervey, an army officer of noble birth, was very kind to Dr. Johnson when the author was a struggling young writer in London, often inviting him to dinner at a time when Johnson had little if anything to eat. Dr. Johnson never forgot his generosity, despite his shortcomings. "Harry Hervey," he said years later, "was a vicious man, but he was very kind to me. If you call a dog Hervey, I shall love him."

Critics are continually placed in the position of having to say something clever and this is a heavy tax on them, a friend told Dr. Johnson.
"It is indeed," Johnson replied, "a very heavy tax on them, a tax which no man can pay who does not steal."

Johnson hated baby talk and once gave a ride in his coach to a poor woman walking in the rain with her baby on the condition that she wouldn't indulge in it in his presence. When the woman forgot her promise and cooed to her waking child, "The little dearie, is he going to open his eyesy-pysies then," Johnson had the coach stopped and ordered her out into the rain again.

He told Boswell: "An old tutor of a college said to one of his pupils: Read over your composition, and whenever you meet with a passage which you think is particulary fine, strike it out." (See also SYDNEY SMITH.)

"Sir," he said to Boswell, "you have but two topics, yourself and me. I am sick of both."

"I hate a fellow," he said, "whom pride, or cowardice, or laziness drives into a corner, and who does nothing when he is there but sit and *growl*; let him come out as I do, and *bark*."

Discussing Bishop Berkeley's theory of the nonexistence of matter, Boswell remarked that though he considered it untrue, he wasn't able to refute it. Kicking a large stone, Johnson said, "I refute it thus."

He was not much impressed by literary innovation. "A new manner [of writing]!" he exclaimed when the subject arose one evening. "Buckinger had no hands, and he wrote his name with his toes at Charing-cross for half a crown apiece; that was a new manner of writing!"

He considered himself something of a gourmet. "Some people have a foolish way of not minding, or pretending not to mind, what they eat," he said at table one evening. "For my part, I mind my belly very studiously, and very carefully; for I look upon it, that he who does not mind his belly will hardly mind anything else."

"A man should begin to write soon," he remarked, "for if he waits until his judgement is matured, his inability, through want of practice to express his conceptions, will make the disproportion so great between what he sees, and what he can attain, that he will probably be discouraged from writing at all."

He was of the opinion that "Whoever thinks of going to bed before twelve o'clock is a scoundrel."

"Fly fishing may be a very pleasant amusement," he is said to have remarked, "but angling or float fishing I can only compare to a stick and a string, with a worm at one end and a fool at the other."

When Frances Sheridan, the mother of Richard Brinsley Sheridan, published her *Memoirs of Miss Sydney Biddulph* (1763), a novel with an unhappy ending, Johnson was one of the few critics not to receive it warmly. "I know not, madam," he told her, "that you have a right, upon moral principles, to make your readers suffer so much."

He was so good at writing dedications that other authors hired him to devise them for their books. He once boasted that he had "[dedicated] to the Royal Family, 'all round.'"

He was told that he infinitely exceeded all his contemporaries in writing biography. "Sir," he replied, "I believe that is true. The dogs don't know how to write trifles with dignity."

No one could understand why Pope had written the lines:

> Let modest Foster, if he will, excel
> Ten metropolitans in preaching well.

"What do you think?" Dr. Johnson was asked. "Sir, he hoped it would vex somebody," Johnson replied.

When the Great Cham was seriously ill, Bennet Langton brought him texts to read on Christian charity. "What is your drift, sir?" Johnson inquired.

Author Hannah More wondered why Milton, who had written *Paradise Lost*, wrote such awful sonnets. "Milton, madam," replied Dr. Johnson, "was a genius that could cut a Colossus from a rock, but could not carve heads upon cherrystones."

After reading Goldsmith's apology in the London *Chronicle* for beating Evans the bookseller, Dr. Johnson observed, "It is a foolish thing well done."

Of literary criticism he remarked, "You may scold a carpenter who has made a bad table, though you cannot make a table. It is not your trade to make tables."

"Shakespeare never had six lines together without a fault," he claimed. "Perhaps you may find seven, but this does not refute my general assertion."

"If I had no duties, and no reference to futurity," he remarked, "I would spend my life in driving briskly in a postchaise with a pretty woman."

Late in life he observed, "As I know more about mankind I expect less of them, and am ready now to call a man *a good man* upon easier terms than I was formerly."

Dr. Johnson had scathingly attacked the M.P. and poet Soames Jenyns for his optimistic *A Free Enquiry into the Nature and Origin of Evil* (1757). Soames later suggested the following epitaph for him:

> Here lies Sam Johnson:—Reader, have a care,
> Tread lightly, lest you wake a sleeping bear:
> Religious, moral, generous, and humane
> He was; but self-sufficient, proud, and vain,
> Fond of, and overbearing in, dispute,
> A Christian and a scholar—but a brute.

∇ ∇ ∇

David Jones (1881–1967)

Jones, head of the Phonetics Department at University College, London, always claimed that he was the prototype for George Bernard Shaw's Henry Higgins in *Pygmalion*, though Shaw probably didn't base the character on him. Jones claimed that Shaw in gratitude had a free box reserved for him for any production of the play as long as the author lived. He said Shaw chose the name Higgins after glimpsing a sign reading Jones and Higgins over a London shop; Shaw calling the character Higgins because he obviously couldn't use Jones.

∇ ∇ ∇

Henry Arthur Jones (1851–1929)

George Bernard Shaw reviewed the popular playwright's *My Dear Wells* (1921) and, despite the fact that Jones was vehemently critical of him, recommended that everyone read a long sentence in it: "It contains more than 800 words, and stops only because the printer, in desperation, bunged in a full-point. I read that sentence to my wife, and at the end we found ourselves cheering with excitement."

∇ ∇ ∇

Ben Jonson (1573–1637)

Jonson was in the country and his son Benjamin, seven years old, stayed in London when a plague was ravaging the city. At the time the poet had a dream in which he saw his son fully grown with a bloody cross, as if cut by a sword, on his forehead. He soon learned that his son had died of the plague and always believed that the boy, whom he mourned in the touching poem "Ben Jonson, his best piece of poetry," had appeared to him in the shape of a man because that was the form he would take at the resurrection.

While serving as an English soldier in Flanders he fought and killed an enemy soldier in single combat. Later, in a duel he fought at London's Hogsden Fields in 1598, Jonson killed an actor named Gabriel Spenser, probably in self-defense, and was in danger of the gallows. However, a Roman Catholic priest visited him in prison and he converted to Catholicism. Pleading guilty to manslaughter, he served a short term in jail and was finally released by benefit of clergy, forfeiting all his possessions and being branded with an M on his left thumb.

The poet once called on Lord Craven, who had expressed a desire to meet him.

"I understand your lordship wanted to see me," he said when Craven came to the door.

"You, friend?" Craven replied to the shabbily dressed man standing before him. "Just who are you?"

"Ben Jonson."

"Oh now—you can't be the Ben Jonson who wrote *The Silent Woman*. You look as if you would not say *Boo!* to a silly goose."

"Boo, then!" Jonson cried, and Craven laughed, exclaiming, "You are Ben Jonson after all!"

Jonson once remarked in jest that he wanted to be buried standing up. When he died, James I took him at his word and today he still stands below one square foot of Westminster Abbey.

He was a heavy drinker. One story, probably apocryphal, claims that he and poet Michael Drayton visited Shakespeare in Stratford and drank so hard with him as to bring on the fatal fever that killed the Swan of Avon.

Though he loved Shakespeare "on this side of idolatry," Jonson had this reservation: "The players often mention it as an honor to Shakespeare that in his writing, whatsoever he penned, he never blotted out a line. My answer hath been, 'Would he had blotted out a thousand.'"

Jonson took as his model for Volpone, the rich Venetian in his *Volpone or The Fox* (1605), the merchant Thomas Sutton, who was the richest English commoner of his day and who like Volpone had no children and was courted by aristocrats who wanted to be his heirs. Sutton had so many great chests of money in his chamber that at least one visitor feared the room would collapse.

Riding through Surrey he came upon several women "weeping and wailing, lamenting the death of a lawyer who lived there." Why so much grief for a *lawyer*, he asked, and he was told that the advocate was a good charitable man. He quickly improvised this mock epitaph:

God works wonders now and then,
Behold a Miracle, deny't who can,
Here lies a *Lawyer* and an *honest* man.

Saying grace before King James he extemporized:

Our King and Queen the Lord-God blesse,
The Paltzgrave and the lady Besse,
And God blesse every living thing
That Lives, and breath's, and loves the King.
God bless the Councell of Estate,
And Buckingham the fortunate.
God Blesse them all, and keep them safe:
And God Blesse me, and God blesse Raph.

A puzzled James asked him just who this Raph was. When Jonson told him
Raph was the "Drawer at the Swanne Taverne...who drew him good Canarie
[wine]" the king gave him £100 for his jest.

Poet Robert Herrick wrote Jonson's epitaph, one fit for any great writer:

Here lies Jonson with the rest
Of the poets, but the best.
Reader, woulds't thou more have known?
Ask his story, not the stone;
That will speak what this can't tell
Of his glory; so farewell.

▽ ▽ ▽

Thomas Jordan (fl. early 19th century)
Nineteenth-century author Thomas Jordan is remembered for little in literary
history save the dedication pages of his books, which helped him gain patrons
and sell copies. According to a critic of the day, Jordan "prefixed high-flown
dedications to his books with blanks for the name, the blanks being separately
and surreptitiously filled in by a hand-press, so that there was a special dedicatee
for every copy."

▽ ▽ ▽

James Joyce (1882–1941)
When Joyce was a student at Clongowes Wood College in Ireland another
student smashed his eyeglasses. When prefect of studies Father James Daly beat
him, claiming that Joyce himself broke the glasses to avoid his studies, Joyce

complained to Daly's superior. Nor did he let it drop there. A man with a long memory, the novelist depicted Daly as Father Dolan in both *A Portrait of the Artist as a Young Man* (1916) and *Ulysses* (1922).

The difficulties Joyce had in publishing his realistic collection of short stories, *Dubliners*, would make the most scorned of beginning writers take heart. As he said in looking back on his efforts: "Ten years of my life have been consumed in correspondence and litigation about my book *Dubliners*. It was rejected by 40 publishers; three times set up, and once burnt. It cost me about 3,000 francs in postage, fees, train and boat fare, for I was in correspondence with 110 newspapers, 7 solicitors, 3 societies, 40 publishers and several men of letters about it. All refused to aid me, except Mr. Ezra Pound. In the er. 1 it was published, in 1914, word for word as I wrote it in 1905." Joyce forgot to add here that when the book was at last published some fanatic bought out the entire edition and had it burned in Dublin, "a new and private auto-da-fé," as its author later put it.

After his *Portrait of the Artist as a Young Man* (1914–15) was published Joyce wrote this little-known limerick on the book's protagonist:

There once was a lounger named Stephen
Whose youth was most odd and uneven
    He throve on the smell
    Of a horrible hell
That a Hottentot wouldn't believe in.

Joyce studied languages from an early age and was remarkably proficient in them. As early as 1901 he wrote in Dano-Norwegian a letter of profound admiration to Henrik Ibsen.

Struggling to make ends meet all his life—one of his children was born in a pauper's ward—Joyce had no cavalier attitude toward money. One time he expressed some reservations about his hero Ibsen to his brother Stanislaus Joyce. "Absolute realism is impossible, of course," he said. "That we all know… But it's quite enough that Ibsen has omitted *all* question of finance from his thirteen dramas."

"Maybe there are some people who are not so preoccupied about money as you are," his brother suggested.

"Maybe so, by God," said Joyce, "but I'd like to take twenty-five lessons from one of those chaps."

Joyce's American patron John Quinn gave him as much moral, financial and practical support as anyone over the many years it took the author to complete

Ulysses. But the only acknowledgment Joyce ever made was a three-word telegram he sent to Quinn on finishing his magnum opus: "Ulysses published. Thanks."

Perturbed that wealthy American book collector Abraham Rosenbach had paid one-fourth the price ($1,975) for the longhand manuscript of *Ulysses* in 1924 than the manuscript of Joseph Conrad's *Victory* had brought at auction, Joyce sat down and wrote the following petulant verse in a letter to a friend:

Rosy Brook he bought a book
Though he didn't know how to spell it.
Such is the lure of literature
To the lad who can buy and sell it.

The pertinent part of Judge John M. Woolsey's U.S. District Court decision of December 6, 1933, allowing Joyce's *Ulysses* to be brought into the country, reads as follows: "In respect of the recurrent emergence of the theme of sex in the minds of his [Joyce's] characters, it must always be remembered that his locale was Celtic and his season Spring...whilst in many places the effect of 'Ulysses' on the reader undoubtedly is somewhat emetic, nowhere does it tend to be an aphrodisiac. 'Ulysses' may, therefore, be admitted into the United States."

Her printer told Caresse Crosby, who operated the Black Sun Press with her husband, Harry, that "Tales Told of Shean and Shann," a section from Joyce's then work-in-progress *Finnegans Wake*, had only two lines of copy for the last page. It looks awkward, he said; ask the author if he has anything more to go here. Caresse insisted that she could never make such a request of an artist, but the printer himself went to Joyce. Returning with eight additional lines, he informed her, "[Joyce] had been wanting to add more, but was too frightened of you, madam, to do so."

Joyce told a story illustrating his belief that reality is in the eye of the beholder. It seems that an old Blasket islander, who had never left his birthplace, finally ventured to the mainland where in a bazaar he found a small mirror, something he had never seen, and had to purchase it to bring home. All the row back to the Blaskets he would look in the mirror, stare at the image in it and cry, "Oh, Papa! Papa!" Arriving home, he jealously guarded his prized possession, keeping it secret from his wife in his jacket, but she suspected he was hiding something and took the mirror from his pocket one hot day when he stripped to his shirtsleeves while working in the fields. Yet when she looked into the strange object her husband held so precious, she cried out, "Ach, it's nothing but an old woman!" and angrily smashed it against a rock.

The author's father, John Joyce, was known almost as much for his dry wit as for his thirst. When a Dublin friend showed him an abstract portrait the avant-garde artist Brancusi had done of his son in Paris, he observed, "The boy seems to have changed a good deal."

In the opinion of several biographers, though they were happily married, Joyce's loyal wife, Nora Barnacle, did not adequately understand or appreciate his work, and was far more concerned with his difficulty in making a living. In any case, one of her pet nicknames for the foremost literary innovator of the century was "Simpleminded Jim."

One time Nora Barnacle was told that her husband's Molly Bloom soliloquy in *Ulysses* was a masterpiece of female psychology. "Ah, he doesn't understand women at all," Nora replied irritably.

In 1909 a former friend of Joyce lied that he had been sexually intimate with the author's wife, Nora, even while Joyce was courting her. Joyce decided to use this story, which he briefly believed, for the main theme of *Ulysses*. He no longer believed it, however, when he began writing the novel five years later and wanted to again feel the jealousy that had inspired him. His wife complained to a mutual friend at the time: "Jim wants me to go with other men so that he will have something to write about." She refused to do so but did help him by using the salutation "Dear Cuckold" in at least one letter she wrote to him.

Joyce and his wife, Nora, were talking to Hemingway about a possible African trip to increase Joyce's stock of experiences. "Jim can do a spot of lion hunting," Nora suggested.

"The thing we must face," said Joyce, who was going blind, "is that I couldn't see the lion."

But Nora insisted: "Hemingway'd describe him to you and afterwards you could go up to him and touch him and smell him. That's all you'd need."

While she may have been right, the trip was never made.

"The only demand I make of my reader," Joyce once told an interviewer, "is that he should devote his whole life to reading my works."

The American writer Max Eastman asked Joyce why he was writing *Finnegans Wake* (1939) in the way he was, in a then unique and very difficult style with a very wide range of allusion. Replied Joyce with the hint of a smile: "To keep the critics busy for three hundred years."

Joyce's handwriting, due to his blindness, was atrocious. So illegible was the Circe (brothel) episode of Joyce's *Ulysses* that the husband of the third typist trying to decipher it mistook the manuscript for scrap paper and threw it in the fire. Luckily, New York collector John Quinn had a "fair copy" of the section and agreed to supply a photographic copy of this to Sylvia Beach, who first published *Ulysses*. It is said that before the brothel scene was thrown in the fire at least nine other typists found it so objectionable that they refused to work on it. One of them threw what she had done in Joyce's face and refused to accept payment, while another threatened to leap out the window if he came near her.

Joyce felt that the most euphonious word in the English language was *cuspidor*.

Samuel Beckett served as Joyce's secretary, and a conscientious amanuensis he was, faithfully taking down Joyce's every utterance. One time Joyce was dictating a bit of *Finnegans Wake* to him when someone knocked at the door. "Come in," Joyce said and Beckett wrote his words down. Later Beckett read back his transcription and Joyce asked, "What's that 'Come in.'" "Yes, you said that," Beckett replied and Joyce, "quite willing to accept coincidence as a collaboration," as his biographer Richard Ellman commented, let the words stand in his book.

Finding herself fresh out of new playwrights for the Abbey Theatre, Lady Augusta Gregory, a leading figure in the Irish Revival, advertised in the papers for same. The response was overwhelming, as Joyce noted in a limerick he wrote on the phenomenon:

There was a kind lady called Gregory,
Said, "Come to me poets in beggary."
   But found her imprudence
   When thousands of students
Cried, "All we are in that caTEGory!"

Joyce prided himself on his singing voice. When he won only the bronze medal in a Dublin singing contest he angrily threw it into the Liffey River.

"Who in your opinion is the greatest living writer?" Joyce was asked by an American woman. "Aside from myself, I don't know," he replied.

"Shaw's work," he once remarked, "makes me admire the magnificent tolerance and broadmindedness of the English."

His wife Nora scolded him about his attitude toward their children. "You pay no attention to them," she complained. "Why, you've never done a single thing for them!"

"You forget, my dear," said Joyce sweetly, "that I was responsible for their conception."

In 1940, a year before his death, Nora Joyce advised her husband, "Well, Jim, I haven't read any of your books but I'll have to someday because they must be good considering how well they sell."

▽ ▽ ▽ ▽ ▽ ▽ ▽ ▽ ▽

John Keats (1795–1821)

As a boy the poet was known, little as he was, as a great fighter in defending what was right or chivalrous. Remembered his schoolmate Holmes, "He would fight anyone—morning, noon and night, his brother among the rest. It was meat and drink for him."

Writing to Benjamin Bailey, he was skeptical about women who fawned over him. "I do think better of womankind," he remarked, "than to suppose they care whether Mister John Keats, five feet high, likes them or not."

Wrote Keats in a love letter to Fanny Brawne on July 8, 1819: "I love you more in that I believe you have liked me for my own sake and nothing else. I have met with women whom I really think would like to be married to a Poem and given away by a Novel."

There is a famous lapse in Keats's great poem "On First Looking into Chapman's Homer." The poem tells of "stout Cortez...with eagle eyes" discovering and staring "at the Pacific," when it was Balboa who discovered the Pacific Ocean.

No one would argue that Keats's "Ode on a Grecian Urn" isn't among the most beautiful and best-known poems of all time, but the vase that he wrote about might be called kitsch today. The story begins with the great English potter Josiah Wedgwood (1730–1795), who copied from the famous "Grecian" Portland vase that Sir William Hamilton, husband of Lord Nelson's great love, purchased when he served as ambassador to Naples. Hamilton had sold it to the duchess of Portland, who donated the vase to the British Museum in 1784. The Portland vase, however, wasn't a Greek vase as everybody thought, but a heavy-handed Roman imitation from the time of Augustus. The vase that John Keats saw and that inspired him to write his immortal poem was a Wedgwood copy of a Roman copy of a Greek vase—a doubly fake Grecian urn:

> Beauty is truth, truth beauty—that is all
> Ye know on earth and all ye need to know.

"I am convinced more and more day by day," Keats wrote to his close friend John Hamilton Reynolds, "that fine writing is next to fine doing, the top thing in the world." To another friend he confided, "I would sooner fail than not be among the greatest," and to George and Georgiana Keats he predicted, "I think I shall be among the English Poets after my death."

Oscar Wilde was so upset at the sale of the poet's love letters that he wrote this poem:

On The Sale by Auction of Keats' Love-Letters

> These are the letters which Endymion wrote
>   To one he loved in secret, and apart,
> And now the brawlers of the auction mart
> Bargain and bid for each poor blotted note,
> Ay, for each separate pulse of passion quote
>   The latest price—I think they love not Art
>   Who break the crystal of a poet's heart
> That small and sickly eyes may glare or gloat.
>
> It is not said, that many years ago
>   In a far Eastern town some soldiers ran
>   With torches through the midnight, and began
> To wrangle for mean raiment, and to throw
>   Dice for the garments of a wretched man,
> Not knowing the God's wonder or his woe?

Keats did not invent his own epitaph, as is often said. While he lay dying in Rome, listening to the falling water in a fountain outside his room, he remembered words from the play *Philaster, or Love Lies A-bleeding*, written by Beaumont and Fletcher in 1611. "All your better deeds/Shall be in water writ," one of the characters says. Keats mused upon this sentiment and a week or so before he died told his friend the painter Joseph Severn that he wanted no epitaph or even name upon his grave, just the line, "Here lies one whose name was writ in water."

During his final illness Keats asked his doctor, "When will this posthumous life of mine come to an end. I feel the flowers growing over me." His last words, to his friend artist Joseph Severn, were "I shall die easy. Don't be frightened. Thank God it has come."

∇ ∇ ∇

William Paton Ker (1855–1923)
A man of letters and professor of poetry at Oxford, Ker died while on holiday in the Italian Alps, where he was hiking up the slopes of Pizzo Bianco at *Macugnaga*, and was buried there. He had stopped to admire the scenery and died of a heart attack immediately after he remarked to his companions: "I thought this was the most beautiful spot in the world and now I know it."

∇ ∇ ∇

John Maynard Keynes (1883–1946)
The distinguished economist, a member of the Bloomsbury group and a patron of the arts, was asked by a reporter during the Great Depression if there was ever anything like it. "Yes," Keynes replied, "it was called the Dark Ages and it lasted four hundred years."

According to Leon Edel's *Bloomsbury: A House of Lions*, Keynes said that when he was in Berlin he saw "a naughty boy…covered with ink…a sweet imp, pure and giggling" and "had a little flirt with him." Albert Einstein was the "sweet imp" and so far as is known he did not flirt back.

∇ ∇ ∇

Thomas Killigrew (1612–1683)
Killigrew was more esteemed as a wit than as the dramatist and playhouse owner he was. He held the title of king's fool, or jester, and was permitted to revile or jeer even the greatest nobles without fear of punishment. Wrote Sir John Denham of him:

> Had Cowley ne'er spoke, Killigrew ne'er writ,
> Combined in one, they'd made a matchless wit.

∇ ∇ ∇

Rudyard Kipling (1865–1936)
For a brief period early in his career Kipling worked as a reporter for the *San Francisco Examiner*, until he was fired. "This isn't a kindergarten for amateur writers," said the editor who dismissed him. "I'm sorry, Mr. Kipling, but you just don't know how to use the English language."

Kipling based his famous Gunga Din on a real-life regimental water-bearer, an Indian of low caste named Juma who was a hero at the siege of Delhi in 1857 and later served as a much decorated officer in the British Corps of Guides in India.

"I hear that you are selling your work at one dollar a word," an American wrote the author. "Enclosed is one dollar. Please send me a sample."

"Thanks," Kipling wrote, keeping the dollar.

But his correspondent had the last word. "Sold the 'Thanks' anecdote for two dollars," he wrote back a few weeks later. "Enclosed please find forty-five cents in stamps, that being half the profits on the transaction, less the postage."

Even Kipling thought his famous poem "If" had been "anthologized to weariness." Considered the most commercially successful poem of all time, it has been translated into at least 27 languages.

A devoted golfer, he was, while living in America, the inventor of winter golf, painting his golf balls red so that he could play in the snow.

An old story, unproved one way or the other, had it that those good friends Kipling and Mark Twain had a contest to see who could write the bawdiest, most offensive story. An effort of Kipling's beginning "'Shit!' said the Queen ..." was brought to Queen Victoria's attention, which is why Kipling was never knighted and never became poet laureate. "We" were not amused.

Kipling, like Hemingway, Robert Graves and several other writers, lived to see his obituary mistakenly published in a newspaper. That same day he wrote to the editor: "I've just read that I am dead. Don't forget to delete me from your list of subscribers."

It happened that the last poem in the definitive edition of *Rudyard Kipling's Verse* (1940) begins:

> If I have given you delight
>> By aught that I have done,
> Let me lie quiet in the night
>> Which shall be yours anon.

∇ ∇ ∇

Richard Knolles (1550?–1610)

Dr. Johnson took the plot of *Irene* from Knolles's *The Generall Historie of the Turkes* (1603) and Byron later said that the book inspired the "oriental colouring" of his poetry. Knolles, however, had a limited reputation. Johnson explained this by saying that although the book showed "all the excellencies that narration can admit," Knolles wrote of a subject "of which none desires to be informed."

∇ ∇ ∇ ∇ ∇ ∇ ∇ ∇ ∇

Henry Labouchère (1831–1912)
The politician and journalist lay on his deathbed when his nephew accidentally knocked over an oil lamp. Opening his eyes, Labouchère, who was to die the next day, laughed. "Flames? Not yet, I think."

∇ ∇ ∇

James Lackington (1746–1815)
One Christmas Eve the bookseller and his wife were down to their last half-crown, which Lackington was sent out with to buy their Chirstmas dinner. Instead he wandered into a book shop and purchased a copy of Edward Young's poem *Night Thoughts on Life, Death and Immortality*. Explaining himself to his wife, he said, "I think that I have acted wisely; for had I bought a dinner we should have eaten it tomorrow, and the pleasure would have been soon over, but should we live fifty years longer, we shall [still] have the *Night Thoughts* to feast upon."

∇ ∇ ∇

Lady Caroline Lamb (1785–1828)
Shortly after marrying Prime Minister Lord Melbourne, Lady Caroline began a notorious affair with Lord Byron and when the poet broke with her she wrote *Glenarvon* (1816), a Gothic novel featuring thinly disguised versions of herself and Byron that enjoyed a great *succès de scandale*. It is said that her mind began to disintegrate when she met Byron and broke down completely when she accidentally encountered his funeral procession on the road in 1824. She had, however, behaved eccentrically long before the poet came upon the scene. Once, for example, she had herself served to her husband as a dessert dish at his birthday party, emerging naked from a large tureen.

Charles Lamb (1775–1834)

A loud hiss came forth from somewhere in the audience while the poet was delivering a lecture. After a brief silence, Lamb, showing no emotion, simply said: "There are only three things that hiss—a goose, a snake, and a fool. Come forth and be identified."

"I could write like Shakespeare if I had a mind to," Wordsworth told Lamb.

"So, you see, it's the mind that's wanting," Lamb replied.

In an 1823 letter to a friend, Lamb succinctly described the relationship between 19th-century authors and their publishers or booksellers: "Those fellows hate us."

The poet, who had a hearty appetite, was invited to dine with poet Thomas Hood. "We have a hare," Hood told him. "And how many friends?" Lamb anxiously asked.

A talkative woman at a dinner party was irritated at Lamb's inattention. She finally tugged at his arm and declared, "You seem to be none the better for all I am telling you."

"No, madam," Lamb replied, 'but this gentleman on the other side of me must be—for it all went in one ear and out the other.

"I can read anything which I call a *book*," Lamb once wrote. "There are things in that shape which I cannot allow for such. In this catalogue of books which are not books— *biblia a-biblia*—I reckon Court Calendars, Directories, Pocket Books, Draught Boards, bound and lettered on the back, Scientific Treatises, Alamanacs, Statutes at Large, the works of Hume, Gibbon, Robertson, Beattie, Soame Jenyns, and generally, all those volumes which 'no gentleman's library should be without.'"

Songwriter and journalist Barry Cornwall made a witty remark to Lamb.

"V-very well, my dear boy, v-v-very well," Lamb stammered. "B-Ben, Ben Jonson has said worse than that—and b-b-better."

Lamb was watching a game of cards over the shoulder of a friend whose pesonal hygiene offended everyone in the room. "George," he finally said, unable to bear him any longer, "if dirt were trumps, what a hand you'd have."

"Really, Mr. Lamb, you come very late!" said an official at the East India House in reprimanding Lamb for his poor work habits.

"Y-yes," Lamb replied, "b-but consi-sider how ear-early I go!"

Wordsworth sometimes diverged from the everyday language he espoused and used archaic "poetical" terms. One time Lamb read aloud the first line of a new Wordsworth poem, "The Force of Prayer": "What is good for a bootless bene?" Immediately his sister Mary cried out "A shoeless pea!"

Lamb once described his friend Samuel Taylor Coleridge as "an archangel slightly damaged." Coleridge, unquestionably a great poet, was addicted to opium and was a man of many enthusiasms, which he rarely failed to broadcast in a strong voice cultivated by his preaching throughout England's West Country. One day, bragging of his oratorical abilities, he asked Lamb, "Did you ever hear me preach?"

"I never heard you do anything else," Lamb replied.

Lamb had observed a man doing something he strongly disliked when an unknowing friend offered to introduce him to the fellow. "Don't introduce me to that man!" he exclaimed. "I want to go on hating him, and I can't hate a man whom I know."

He was more specific than the myriad writers who've said they don't give two cents for critics. "For critics," he told a friend, "I care the five thousandth part of the tythe of a half-farthing."

His letters are even more charming than his essays. "In him I have a loss the world cannot make up," he wrote of an old friend who had just died. "He was my friend and my father's friend all the life I can remember. I seem to have made foolish friendships ever since. Those are friendships which outlive a second generation. Old as I am waxing, in his eyes I was still the child he first knew me. To the last he called me Charley. I have none to call me Charley now ..."

He was much annoyed by a woman who interminably praised "a charming man," concluding her exegesis by crying, "And well I know him, bless him!" Replied Lamb: "Well, I don't, but damn him, at a hazard."

Dr. Parr asked him how he puffed so much smoke out of his pipe and he replied, "I toil after it as other men after virtue." A dedicated pipe smoker, he once said he would like "to draw his last breath through a pipe and exhale it as a pun."

"This very night I am going to leave off tobacco!" he wrote to Thomas Manning in 1815. "Surely there must be some other world in which this unconquerable purpose shall be realized."

"The greatest pleasure I know," he remarked to a friend, "is to do a good deed by stealth, and to have it found out by accident."

Commenting on William Hazlitt's marriage to the widow Isabella Bridgewater, which was astonishing to his friends because he had just divorced his wife and gotten over a disastrous love affair with Sarah Walker, Lamb wrote to Robert Southey: "I was at Hazlitt's marriage, and had like to have been turned out several times during the ceremony. Anything awful makes me laugh. I misbehaved once at a funeral." The marriage ended a few years later.

He, Coleridge and Thomas Holcroft were fiercely arguing about which was best: "Man as he was, or man as he is to be." Remarked Lamb: "Give me man as he is *not* to be."

"Nothing puzzles me more than time and space," he told a friend, "and yet nothing troubles me less, as I never think about them."

Learning that a sonnet of his had been rejected, he exclaimed, "Damn the age; I will write for Antiquity!"

He jotted down this verse in a copy of *Coelebs in Search of a Wife* (1809), a book of sharp moral observations by Hannah More about the protagonist's (Coelebs) search for the proper wife.

If I ever marry a wife,
    I'll marry a landlord's daughter
For then I may sit in the bar,
    And drink cold brandy and water.

Coleridge had written in "This Lime-tree Bower, My Prison" (1797):

For thee my gentle-hearted Charles, to
    whom
No sound is dissonant which tells of life.

Reading the poem, Lamb wrote to him: "For God's sake (I never was more serious) don't make me ridiculous any more by terming me gentle-hearted in print...substitute drunken dog, ragged head, seld-shaven, odd-eyed, stuttering, or any other epithet which truly and properly belongs to the gentleman in question."

On leaving his "33 years' desk" at the East India House, where he had worked since he was 17, he sat down to write his friend Bernard Barton: "I came home forever!"

∇ ∇ ∇

Hugh Latimer (1492?–1555)

As the preacher and writer was being burned alive for heresy at Oxford, on October 16, 1555, he turned to Nicholas Ridley beside him and said: "Play the man, Master Ridley; we shall this day light such a candle, by God's grace, in England, as I trust shall never be put out."

∇ ∇ ∇

William Laud (1573–1645)

It is said that Laud, the archbishop of Canterbury and eminent scholar, a very short man, insisted upon the dismissal of King Charles's jester Archie when Archie said the following joking grace at a dinner the king gave for him: "Great praise be given to God, but little Laud to the Devil."

∇ ∇ ∇

William Lauder (d. 1771)

Author and classical scholar William Lauder for some unknown reason hated John Milton and tried to prove that a great part of the poet's work was stolen from modern Latin poems. He went to the trouble of translating passages from Milton into Latin, and inserting them into Latin poems, publishing his work as "proof" of Milton's thievery. Even Dr. Johnson was fooled, and wrote a preface and postscript to Lauder's *An Essay on Milton's Use and Imitation of the Moderns* in 1750. It wasn't until the next year that a scholarly book exposed this most ill-intentioned of literary hoaxes.

∇ ∇ ∇

D.H. (David Herbert) Lawrence (1885–1930)

When a high-school student in Nottingham, the great writer placed 13th out of a graduating class of 21 in English. He won the school's mathematics prize.

Lawrence's first love was Louie Burrows, a teacher associate in Nottingham. Lawrence wearied of the relationship and subtly freed himself from it, but Louie Burrows, though she married, loved him all her life; she even carried his love letters in a secret compartment in her corset. Lawrence later partly based his character Ursula Brangwen in *The Rainbow* (1915) on her.

The author recalled his uneducated coal-miner father struggling through half a page or so of his first novel, *The White Peacock* (1911).

"And what dun they gie thee for that, lad?" he asked.

"Fifty pounds, father," Lawrence said.

"Fifty pounds!" His father was dumbfounded and looked at him shrewdly, as if he were a swindler. "An' tha's niver done a day's hard work in thy life."

When *Sons and Lovers* (1913), his first major novel, was rejected by Heinemann, a furious Lawrence got it all off his chest with the following invective he wrote to his friend Edward Garnett. "Curse the blasted, jelly-boned swines, the slimy, the belly-wriggling invertebrates, the miserable sodding rutters, the flaming sods, the sniveling, dribbling, dithering, palsied, pulse-less lot that make up England today. They've got the white of egg in their veins and their spunk is that watery it's a marvel they can breed."

Another time when a critic annoyed him, he jotted down this little rhyme:

I heard a little chicken chirp:
My name is Thomas, Thomas Earp,
And I can neither paint nor write,
I can only put other people right.

When Lawrence's *The Rainbow* was prosecuted under the 1857 Obscene Publications Act in 1915, the novelist later recalled, his publisher, Sir George Methuen, "almost wept before the magistrate...He said he did not know the dirty thing he had been handling, he had not read the work, his reader had misadvised him..." The remaining 1,011 copies of the novel were burned by the examining magistrate's order.

He wrote in a letter to British scholar and champion of modern poetry Edward Marsh: "I think more of a bird with broad wings flying and lapsing through the air than anything when I think of metre."

In a review of *Lady Chatterley's Lover*, the *Field and Stream* magazine's reviewer felt, tongue in cheek, that Lawrence's account of an English gamekeeper's daily life "is full of considerable interest to outdoor-minded readers, as it contains many passages on pheasant raising, the apprehending of poachers, ways to control vermin and other chores and duties of the professional gamekeeper. Unfortunately one is obliged to wade through many pages of extraneous material in order to discover and savor these sidelights on the management of a midland shooting estate."

The novelist used the talented English composer and songwriter Philip Hesel-tine (1894–1930) as the basis for Julius Halliday in *Women in Love* (1920). Hesel-tine, an alcoholic who sometimes used the pseudonym Rab Noolas (saloon bar spelled backward), never forgave him and vowed vengeance. Revenge came when a manuscript of philosophical essays by Lawrence fell into Heseltine's hands after the author's death. No other copy of the essays existed and Heseltine used each sheet of the manuscript as toilet tissue. The composer, who had changed his name to Peter Warlock, committed suicide not long after by gassing himself after putting the cat out.

When a mutual friend told Lawrence that the philosopher Bertrand Russell had complained that he "had no mind," Lawrence replied, "Have you ever seen him in a bathing suit? Poor Bertie Russell! He is all Disembodied Mind!"

Wrote the author to a friend in 1912: "I always say, my motto is, 'Art for my sake.'"

Lawrence never trusted the opinions of John Middleton Murry, the British critic and novelist who was the husband of Katherine Mansfield. As he lay dying in Venice he was told that Murry had come to the conclusion that there was no God. "Now I know there is," Lawrence replied.

∇ ∇ ∇

T.E. (Thomas Edward) Lawrence (1888–1935)

Lawrence of Arabia lost most of his famous *The Seven Pillars of Wisdom* while changing trains at Reading in 1919 and had to rewrite it from memory. This was at about the same time that Hemingway's wife Hadley on a train somewhere in France, lost a suitcase containing all of Hemingway's early work except three short stories.

Wrote George Bernard Shaw to Lawrence while editing the adventurer's *Seven Pillars of Widom* (1926): "Confound you and your book, you are no more fit to be trusted with a pen than a child with a torpedo...you have no rules and you sometimes throw colons around with an unhinged mind ..."

The almost mythical Lawrence of Arabia wasn't without a sense of humor. One hot afternoon a celebrity hunter approached him on the steps of a Cairo hotel. "Imagine, Colonel Lawrence," she said, trying to make conversation. "Ninety-two already!"

"Indeed!" Lawrence replied with a bow. "Many happy returns of the day!"

Stephen Leacock (1869–1944)

The Canadian author and economist, whose best work has been described as "balanced between cutting satire and sheer absurdity," was told by his friend, a professor of Greek, that the classics had truly made the professor what he was. Replied Leacock: "This is a very grave statement, if well founded."

▽ ▽ ▽

Edward Lear (1812–1888)

Lear always claimed that he got the idea for the nonsense verse he wrote from a book called *The Anecdotes and Adventures of Fifteen Gentlemen* (1822).

The poet and painter's verses were labeled *learics* by M. Russell, a Jesuit wit of the day. The new word was not only a play on the poet's name, it is also implied that his lyrics weren't dignified and that some of his verses inspired *leering* grins. Fifty-two years after Lear's book was published the one-stanza poems, by now immensely popular, were dubbed *limericks*. This name may have come from the chorus of a popular song that went, "We'll all come up, come up to Limerick." The refrain was sung during a party game after each guest would invent and recite a *learic*. It is also possible that the *learic* became the *limerick* because people believed that the verses were invented in Ireland, the land of poetry. In any case, despite his fame, the poet, an epileptic, suffered from depression and great loneliness all his life.

▽ ▽ ▽

Nathaniel Lee (1653?–1692)

The dramatist Nathaniel Lee began his career as an actor but couldn't earn a living due to acute stagefright. Lee wrote a number of tragedies with passages of great beauty despite their extravagances. He eventually lost his mind and was committed to Bedlam twice in his short life, escaping from his keepers the last time and later dying in a drunken fit. During one of his confinements the English journalist Sir Roger L'Estrange visited Lee in the madhouse. L'Estrange couldn't conceal the sorrow he felt for the gifted writer, but Lee sensed and spurned his pity, improvising:

> Faces may alter, names can't change,
> I am strange Lee altered, you are still Le-Strange.

During another of his stays in Bedlam, Lee asked a visitor to jump off the roof of the building with him. "Let us immortalize ourselves; let us leap down this moment!" he urged his friend. "Any man could leap *down*," his friend replied, thinking quickly, "so we could not immortalize ourselves that way. But let us go down and see if we can leap *up*." Lee immediately forgot about jumping off the building and ran downstairs and began trying to leap up to the roof.

While writing a play when confined in Bedlam the mad actor turned dramatist looked up to see a cloud cover the moon. "Jove, snuff the moon!" he cried out in ecstasy.

"'Tis very difficult to write like a madman," Lee once said while in Bedlam, "but 'tis a very easy matter to write like a fool."

▽ ▽ ▽

Alexander Leighton (1568–1649)

It is hard to think of an author more horribly punished for his work than Alexander Leighton. Convicted by the Star Chamber, Leighton, the author of the religious tract *An Appeal to the Parliament: or Sion's Plea Against the Prelacie* (1630), was manacled and thrown into a hole filled with mice and rats. Later he was whipped, had his ears cut off, his nose split, and was branded with the letters S.S. (Sower of Sedition). Sentenced to life imprisonment he was released after 11 years.

▽ ▽ ▽

Charles Lever (1806–1872)

The popular Irish novelist lived an exciting early life, including a time when he was adopted into a tribe of Indians in the Canadian backwoods and eventually risked his life to escape. He continued his travels, singing his songs in the streets of Dublin for coins, practicing as a ship's surgeon without license, and finally earning a medical degree. Then he found that writing came most easily to him, remarking after his first success with *The Confessions of Harry Lorreguer* (1839), "If this sort of thing amuses them, I can go on forever." He did go on writing bestsellers until his death, his work praised by Trollope and other master novelists. Lever was so witty a man in company that Lord Derby offered him the lucrative consulship of Trieste. "Here," Derby wrote, "is six hundred a year for doing nothing, and you are just the man to do it."

▽ ▽ ▽

C.S. (Clive Staples) Lewis (1898–1963)

The scholar, critic and novelist never paid much attention to his dress or grooming. Returning from a hike in the country, he boarded a train and entered a first-class compartment. Studying the unwashed, uncombed figure, a prissy old lady asked him, "Have you a first-class ticket?"

"Yes, madam," said Lewis, "but I'm afraid I'll be needing it for myself."

Monk (Matthew Gregory) Lewis (1775–1818)

This highly sensitive novelist was known as Monk Lewis because of his enormously popular gothic novel *The Monk* (1796), which he wrote in under 10 weeks. One morning Lewis, sad and red-eyed, was asked what was the matter. "I am so affected by kindness," he replied, "and just now the duchess of York said something so kind to me that…" Here he started crying again and a very British Colonel Armstrong standing nearby tried comforting him. "Never mind, Lewis, never mind," said the colonel. "Don't cry. She couldn't have meant it."

∇ ∇ ∇

Wilmarth Sheldon Lewis (1894–1979)

British-born scholar and biographer Wilmarth Sheldon Lewis filled a library at Strawberry Hill in Farmington, Connecticut, with what one newspaper called a virtual "day-by-day account of everything known of every day of British author Horace Walpole's life." Starting when he was 26, Lewis amassed a collection at the Lewis-Walpole Library that includes 7,000 Horace Walpole letters, five miles of microfilm, and a million file cards. "By his energy, his persistence, his lavish care," wrote historian J.H. Plumb, "W.S. Lewis collected more information about a single human life [than has ever been done before]."

∇ ∇ ∇

Wyndham Lewis (1882–1957)

The author and artist would go to great lengths, if not any length, to get his work published. One tale has it that he wanted to publish his short story "The Pole" in the influential *English Review* edited by Ford Maddox Ford. Entering Ford's house—Ford always left doors unlocked—Lewis found him in the bathtub and read the entire story aloud while Ford bathed. In any case, Ford did publish the story in the *English Review*.

Among Lewis's lovers was an English novelist and critic who lived with him for several years and bore him two children. Her most painful experience during their stormy relationship came on the day she arrived home from the hospital with their newborn daughter and Lewis made her wait outside until he finished making love to another woman.

Over one mouse-hole in his rodent-infested studio Lewis hung a gong which he sounded to scare off the mice. This seems to be the only protection he had against the rodents, however. It is said that Edith Sitwell walked out on Lewis while he was painting her portrait because of the filthy, mouse-infested studio, or because he kept making advances toward her. His portrait of Sitwell is unfinished, without hands.

As Ezra Pound tells it in his *Canto XVI*, most of Lewis's company was killed in 1914 when a bomb hit their barracks, "While he [Lewis] was out in the privy, / and he was all that was left of that outfit."

Shortly after T.S. Eliot had been knighted, Ezra Pound suggested that Lewis might be interested in a knighthood. Lewis replied indignantly: "As to your implying that my remarks were motivated by envy of the dangling crosses and those letters you stick after your name, oh sir, has my life been that of one prizing the values of the career-man or directing his gaze ahead to covet the dignity of knighthood? I have lived as witness to the contrary."

∇ ∇ ∇

Thomas Linacre (1460?–1524)
The classical scholar, who was one of Henry VIII's physicians, is said to have read the Gospel for the first time toward the end of his life. "Either this is not the Gospel, or we are not Christians," he remarked on finishing.

∇ ∇ ∇

Sir David Lindsay (1490–1555)
Flyting is a word for "word fighting." Flytings (from the Old English *flyte*, "to contend or jeer") were contests held principally by 16th-century Scottish poets in which two persons "assailed each other alternately with tirades of abusive verse." Following is one of fully 32 stanzas directed at Scotland's James V by his former tutor, Sir David Lindsay. Bear in mind that this vitriolic diatribe *lost* the flyting.

> Purse-peeler, hen-stealer, cat-killer, no I qyell thee;
> Rubiator, fornicator by nature, foul befal thee.
> Tyke-sticker, poisoner Vicar, Pot-licker, I mon paz thee.
> Jock blunt, dead Runt, I shall punt when I slay thee.

∇ ∇ ∇

Bernard Lintot (1675–1736)
Alexander Pope, who satirized his uncouth appearance in *The Dunciad*, once asked Lintot, his publisher, how he dealt with critics. The poor ones he bought off with food and drink. As for prosperous critics, he said, "I can silence...the rich ones for a sheet apiece of the blotted manuscript, which costs me nothing. They'll go about with it to their acquaintances, and pretend they had it from the author, who submitted to their correction: this has given some of them such an air that in time they come to be consulted with, and dedicated to, as the top critics of the town."

John Locke (1632–1704)

The great philosopher, called by John Stuart Mill the unquestioned founder of the analytic philosophy of mind, lay dying at the home of Sir Francis Masham in Essex. Lady Masham was at his bedside reading the Psalms to him when he uttered his last words. "Oh! The depth of the riches of the goodness and knowledge of God," he said. Then he said to her, "Cease now," and died.

▽ ▽ ▽

John Gibson Lockhart (1794–1854)

The ferocious Scottish critic, nicknamed "the Scorpion," savaged practically all his contemporaries except his father-in-law, Sir Walter Scott. At one time or another, his victims included Keats, Hazlitt and Leigh Hunt, whom he castigated as constituting the low-born "Cockney School of Poetry." He is best remembered, however, for his attack on the high-born Lord Peter Robertson, about whom he wrote this mock epitaph:

Here lies the Christian, judge and poet Peter,
Who broke the laws of God, and man, and
metre.

▽ ▽ ▽

Frederick Lonsdale (Lionel Frederick Leonard; 1881–1954)

Famed for his lighthearted comedies, Freddy Lonsdale, as he was known, was a member of the celebrated Garrick Club in London. One New Year's Eve a friend asked him to make up with a club member he had quarrelled with, to go over and wish the man a happy New Year. Lonsdale approached his enemy and stuck out his hand. "I wish you a happy New Year," he said, "but only one."

▽ ▽ ▽

Richard Lovelace (1618–1658)

Stone walls do not a prison make,
    Nor iron bars a cage;
Minds innocent and quiet take
    That for an hermitage;
If I have freedom in my love
    And in my soul am free,
Angels alone, that soar above,
    Enjoy such liberty.

These famous words by the Cavalier poet Richard Lovelace are from his "To Althea, from Prison," which he wrote in 1642 while serving seven weeks in the Gatehouse Prison at Westminster for presenting a petition to the House of

Commons on behalf of King Charles I. The poem also contains words praising Charles (The sweetness, mercy, majesty/And glories of my King), yet Lovelace was freed not by any action of the monarch but on a large bail of from £4,000 to £40,000 that he posted. In 1648 Lovelace was again imprisoned, by the Commonwealth, and while in prison he prepared for press another famous poem, "To Lucasta, Going to the Wars," which contains the famous lyric "I could not love thee, Dear, so much/Loved I not Honour more." Lovelace named "Lucasta" for his beloved Lucy Sacheverell, who married another man when it was reported that the Cavalier poet had been killed fighting for the French king in France. By the time Lovelace finished his second jail term, his great fortune had been exhausted in support of the monarchy. It is said that he died in a cellar, without money to buy food, just before his 40th birthday.

The historian Anthony à Wood, who knew him at Oxford, called Lovelace "the most amiable and beautiful person that ever eye beheld."

▽ ▽ ▽

Malcolm Lowry (1909–1957)
Of the great critical reception accorded *Under the Volcano* in 1947, the novelist, a chronic alcoholic, observed: "Fame, like a drunkard, consumes the house of the soul." Lowry, like several of his major characters, died as a result of his alcoholism.

▽ ▽ ▽

Martin Lucas   See ROBERT BARKER.

▽ ▽ ▽

Thomas Lyttelton (1744–1779)
The "wicked Lord Lyttelton," as he was called, was noted for both his literary ability and the dissipated life he led. That life ended when he was only 35, and it is said that he was warned of his death in a dream three days before he died.

▽ ▽ ▽ ▽ ▽ ▽ ▽ ▽ ▽

Thomas Babington Macaulay (1800–1859)

The historian was a walking library who had filled his head with learning ever since he began reading at age three. He was a "book in breeches," the Reverend Sydney Smith claimed, but Smith had some reservations about his loquacity. "Yes, I agree, he is certainly more agreeable since his return from India," Smith once said of the historian. "His enemies might perhaps have said before (though I never did so) that he talked rather too much; and now he has occasional flashes of silence that make his conversation perfectly delightful." But then everyone had a bad word for Macaulay. "His conversation was a procession of one," said Florence Nightingale of him. "Macaulay is well for a while, but one wouldn't want to live under Niagara," said Carlyle. "I wish I was as cocksure of anything as Tom Macaulay is of everything," said Viscount Melbourne.

Macaulay seems almost always to have had an astounding vocabulary. When he was only four years old he and his family were visiting the Walpoles and a servant spilled scalding hot coffee on his legs. "How are you feeling?" Mrs. Walpole asked soon after he was treated for burns.

"Thank you, madam, the agony has abated," he replied.

Though his *History of England* brought him some fame, Macaulay wasn't as well known as he thought. But he did believe that he was famous, as this excerpt from a letter to a friend clearly shows. Macaulay is describing his visit to see the first hippopotamus displayed at the London Zoo: "Two damsels were just about to pass [the hippo's area]...when I was pointed out to them. 'Mr. Macaulay!' cried the lovely pair. 'Is that Mr. Macaulay? Never mind the hippopotamus.' And having paid a shilling to see Behemoth, they left him in the very moment at which he was about to display himself—but spare my modesty. I can wish for nothing more on earth."

"I met Sir Bulwer Lytton, or Lytton Bulwer," he confided to a friend. "He is anxious about some scheme for some association of literary men. I detest all such associations. I hate the notion of gregarious authors. The less we have to do with each other, the better."

Lord Macaulay was of course a Whig politician as well as a historian and his hatred of the opposition ran deep. He allegedly remarked to the publishers of his *History of England* (1848): "Let no damn Tory index my History."

While Macaulay was standing for Parliament, a heckler in the audience threw a dead cat that hit the candidate in the face. "I'm sorry," the man quickly apologized, "I intended it for your opponent." "Well," Macaulay said, "I wish you had meant it for me and hit him."

Arthur Machen (1863–1947)

The journalist was fired from the *London Daily News* in 1906 when he wrote an obituary on Oscar Wilde's lover, Lord Alfred Douglas, calling him a "degenerate." It turned out that Douglas wasn't dead after all. Douglas won £1,000 in a libel action against the paper and Machen lost his job.

∇ ∇ ∇

Julian Maclaren-Ross (d. 1964)

The author had a wardrobe consisting of just the pearl-colored suits and silk ties he preferred to write in. When his novels and stories failed to sell and he was forced to take a job as a gardener, Maclaren-Ross had only these elegant outfits to wear, and large crowds often gathered around him while he worked.

∇ ∇ ∇

Fiona Macleod (William Sharp; 1856–1905)

Here is one of the few cases in literature of a male posing as a female author. Fiona Macleod was the pen name of William Sharp, the Scottish poet and man of letters who was such a brilliant talker that he was known as "Conversation" Sharp. Under his own name Sharp wrote a number of noted biographies and several novels. But it was as Fiona Macleod that he triumphed in his double life; the mystic stories and sketches he wrote under her name made him the most prominent Scottish writer of the modern "Celtic twilight" movement. Sharp kept his authorship of the Fiona Macleod books secret while he lived—even going to the extent of writing letters to magazines over the name of Fiona Macleod and supplying an entry to *Who's Who* for her. His secret was not revealed until after his death. Sharp once confided to a friend that whenever he wrote as Fiona Macleod he dressed as a woman. When the sententious scholar William Paton Ker was told this, he replied, "Did he?—the bitch!"

∇ ∇ ∇

Sir John Pentland Mahaffy (1839–1919)

Another shooter in his hunting party slipped and fell, causing his gun to discharge a bullet through the Irish classical scholar's hat. Mahaffy studied the hat. "Two inches lower," he said, "and you would have shot away ninety percent of the Greek in Ireland."

Mahaffy had published a newspaper article about a poor old woman whom superstitious villagers had buried alive because they thought her a witch. His fellow professor at Trinity College, Dublin, Dr. Robert Yelverton Tyrell, took exception to the piece because he came from the village in question. "After all," he said, putting down his paper, "it is only a question of premature burial, which is not such an obnoxious thing as delayed burial, which Mahaffy so obtrusively represents."

∇ ∇ ∇

"Ern Malley" (putatively 1919–1944)

> Swamps, marshes, barrowpits and other
> Areas of stagnant water serve
> As breeding grounds.
> —"Culture and Exhibit," Ern Malley

According to the editor of *Angry Penguins*, an Australian literary journal, Ern Malley, who had "recently died at the age of 25," was "one of the two giants of contemporary Australian poetry." *Angry Penguins* published a large selection of Malley's poems in 1944, including the lines above. The work was supposedly submitted by his sister. Unfortunately, the journal had been hoaxed. Ern Malley turned out to be two Australian servicemen, Lieutenant James MacAuley and Corporal Harold Stewart, who had whiled away some time by constructing "Malley's" poems from lines pieced together from whatever books they had on hand; the lines quoted above were taken verbatim from a United States bulletin on mosquito control.

∇ ∇ ∇

Sir Thomas Malory (d. 1471)

Not quite fit for the Round Table, the author of the famous romance *The Noble Histories of King Arthur and Certain of His Knights* hardly resembled the chivalrous knights he depicted. Malory, who probably died in prison, where he wrote much of his work, is said to have extorted 100 shillings from two people, stolen nine cows and 335 sheep, and twice looted a Cistercian abbey. Punished for breaking into the house of one Hugh Smyth and raping his wife, he learned nothing. He broke in a second time and raped her again.

∇ ∇ ∇

Thomas Malthus (1766–1834)

The curate published *An Essay on the Principle of Population As It Affects the Future Improvement of Society* in 1798, and his name almost immediately aroused a storm of controversy throughout the world. His essay contained what came to be called the Malthusian theory: that population increases faster, geometrically, than the means of susbsistence, which increases arithmetically. According to this theory, population would always outstrip food supply unless checked by natural controls such as war, disease or famine. Malthus later revised and refined his pessimistic outlook by including control that he called "moral restraint," a combination of late marriage and sexual abstinence. Most of the economist's predictions haven't been borne out, but his analysis remains correct in many respects and the Malthusian principle still operates in parts of the world where the birthrate has not dropped through birth-control practices. It is interesting to note that Charles Darwin was struck by the phrase "struggle for existence" when he read Malthus's *Essay*. The words stimulated him to find the key to biological change in the process of natural selection.

∇ ∇ ∇

Katherine Mansfield (Kathleen Mansfield Beauchamp; 1888–1923)
"Looking back," the New Zealand-born writer confessed, "I imagine I was always writing. Twaddle it was, too. But better far write twaddle or anything, anything, than nothing at all."

As part of the treatment to cure her tuberculosis in 1922 at the Institute for the Harmonious Development of Man at Fontainebleu, Mansfield had to spend a few hours every day on a platform suspended over a cow manger, deeply breathing the noxious odors emanating from below. The treatment did no good and she died of her illness the following year.

She wrote of a literary party she attended: "A silly, unreal evening. Pretty rooms and pretty people, pretty coffee, and cigarettes out of a silver tankard…I was wretched. I have nothing to say to 'charming' women. I felt like a cat among tigers…"

Her last words were: "I love the rain. I want the feeling of it on my face."

∇ ∇ ∇

Margaret of Scotland (1425–1444)
Wed to Louis XI when she was only 11 and he 13, Margaret lived for her poetry while her young husband devoted himself to collecting mistresses. She died when she was only 19. Her last words were, "Fie upon life! Speak to me no more of it!"

∇ ∇ ∇

Christopher Marlowe (1564–1593)
The eldest son of a shoemaker, the great poet, whose work prepared the way for Shakespeare, was educated at Corpus Christi College, Cambridge. He seemed to be in trouble from the time he left school. Though he had four great theatrical successes in London he was reviled by many for his atheism, and his violent nature caused him to run afoul of the law several times. In 1592 an injunction

was brought against him for his part in a street brawl three years earlier, in which a man was killed, and that same year he was deported from the Netherlands for counterfeiting gold coins. He may also have been involved in espionage for England on the continent.

On May 30, 1593, Marlowe was dining at a tavern not far from London with Ingram Frizer, Nicholas Skeres and Robert Poley, three government spies. "[Frizer and Marlowe] uttered one to the other divers malicious words for the reason that they could not...agree about the payment [bill for the meal]," according to coroner William Danby's report. Marlowe grabbed Frizer's dagger from his belt and wounded him superficially, but Frizer seized Marlowe's hand and turned the weapon on him, "gave the said Christopher then and there a mortal wound over his right eye, of the depth of two inches [reaching the brain]...of which the aforesaid Christopher Marlowe then and there instantly died." Marlowe was buried two days later in a grave still unknown; his killer pleaded self-defense and was set free.

▽ ▽ ▽

Frederick Marryat (1792–1848)
The former Royal Navy captain and prolific author of sea stories was a meticulous, thrifty man whose economies extended to his penmanship. Marryat's handwriting was so small that his copyreaders had to leave pins in his manuscripts when they stopped reading in order to find their place later.

▽ ▽ ▽

John Marston (1575?–1635)
Several of the dramatist's satirical works were ordered burned by the archbishop of Canterbury, and he published his *The Scourge of Villanie* (1599) under the pseudonym Kinsayder. The work nevertheless contains one of the most immodest, and sincere, dedications in publishing history, Marston dedicating it "To his most esteemed and beloved Selfe..."

▽ ▽ ▽

Andrew Marvell (1621–1678)
Marvell might be considered an English poet laureate, since he became unofficial laureate to Cromwell after writing "An Horatian Ode upon Cromwell's Return from Ireland," among the greatest political poems in the language. But in his time he was better known as a wit, patriot and spy than as a lyric poet. In fact, the exquisite poems for which he is famous today were published after his death by his housekeeper, Mary Palmer, who found them among papers in his house. In order to get £500 that belonged to Marvell, she signed the preface to the poems

"Mary Marvell" and had them printed in 1681. Even then the poems were neglected for over a century before their worth was recognized.

He died of an overdose of an opiate taken during an attack of ague. When Aubrey writes that "some suspect that he was poysoned by the Jesuits" he is referring to the belief at the time that Marvell was in danger of assassination because of his outspoken *An Account of the Growth of Popery and Arbitrary Government in England* (1676). This work, published anonymously, charged the court with plans to establish an absolute monarchy and the Roman Catholic religion at the same time, and prompted the *London Gazette* to offer a reward for any information leading to the author's identity.

Charles II, admiring Marvell's great wit, sent Lord Danby to offer him a place at court and a gift of 1,000 guineas. Marvell graciously declined, telling the lord treasurer at length that he had no need of anything since he was able to live and eat well. As soon as Lord Danby left, Aubrey says, he "Sent to his bookseller for the loan of one guinea."

∇ ∇ ∇

W. Somerset Maugham (1874–1965)

Enormously successful as a playwright, novelist and short-story writer, Maugham lived a full 91 years and always had the means to enjoy the best of everything. He traveled by sea as much as any modern author and was asked why he always sailed abroad French ships. "Because there's none of that non-sense about women and children first," he replied.

Scandal over his homosexual affairs eventually persuaded Maugham to leave England for the south of France. One of many stories about his sexual preferences has him attending a party given by society hostess Emerald Cunard. Pleading that keeping sensible hours kept him young, Maugham, as was his habit, left the party early. When his hostess protested, he told her, "I can't stay, Emerald, I have to keep my youth."

"Then why don't you bring him with you?" asked Lady Cunard. "I should be delighted to meet him."

Disguised as a reporter, Maugham worked for British Intelligence in Russia during the Russian Revolution in 1917, but his stuttering made it difficult for him to transmit secret messages. This combined with his poor health made him rate his performance as a failure. His experiences did, however, supply him with material for his spy tales.

Maugham's most famous story, which became the play *Rain* and was made into several movies, was inspired by a missionary and prostitute among his fellow passengers on a trip to Pago Pago.

Maugham thought he had stumped Dorothy Parker in a party game in which players challenged each other to complete rhymes. He presented her with: "Higgledy, piggledy, my white hen/She lays eggs for gentlemen."

Added Miss Parker: "You cannot persuade her with gun or lariat/To come across for the proletariat."

British actor Ernest Thesiger's favorite pastime was embroidery; in fact, he shared the interests of most of his women friends, from sewing to cooking and housekeeping. One time Thesiger complained to Maugham that the playwright never wrote any parts for him. "But I am always writing parts for you, Ernest," Maugham replied. "The trouble is that somebody called Gladys Cooper *will* insist on playing them!"

Harpo Marx never succeeded in shocking the distinguished Maugham. One night he even climbed chimplike over rows of theater seats to the author's side and gestured and chattered at him. "Sorry, I haven't got a banana for you," Maugham said affectionately.

Angered by Maugham's ridicule of him as the obvious prototype for Alroy Kear in *Cakes and Ale* (1930), novelist Hugh Walpole portrayed Maugham as the arrogant pessimist in his own *John Cornelius* (1937). Maugham seems to have been the basis for more fictional characters than any contemporary author. These number at least eight, including the cynical John Blair-Kennedy in Noel Coward's *South Sea Bubble* (1956); the ungrateful Leverson Hurle in *Gin and Bitters* by A Riposte (a pen name of Evelyn May Wiehe)—the book was withdrawn when Maugham sued for libel; the old homosexual novelist Sir Hugo Latymer in Noel Coward's *A Song at Twilight* (1966); the celebrated writer Mortimer Quinn in Coward's *Point Valaine* (1935); Kenneth Marchal Toomey in Anthony Burgess's *Earthly Powers* (1980); Willie Tower in S.N. Behrman's *Jane* (1946); and Gilbert Hereford Vaughn in Ada Leverson's *The Limit* (1911). Maugham's wife, Syrie, whom he divorced, is also the prototype of three or four fictional characters.

"I haven't anything to write about," protested a young man whom Maugham had encouraged to write a book.

"My boy," he replied, "that is the most inconclusive reason for not writing that I have ever heard."

He wanted to keep his beliefs to the end. As he lay dying it is said that he arranged for Sir Alfred Ayer, professor of logic at Oxford University and an atheist noted for his persuasiveness, to visit him and reassure him that there was no life after death.

∇ ∇ ∇

Thomas May (1595–1650)

This obese poet and historian, who also suffered from a bad speech impediment, didn't like the way his double chins wobbled. To remedy the problem, he tied his drooping chins tight with strips of cloth, which unfortunately caused his death one day when he swallowed a huge mouthful of food and choked.

∇ ∇ ∇

William McGonagall (1830–1902)

> Swans sing before they die; 'twere no bad thing
> Did certain persons die before they sing.
>   —Samuel Taylor Coleridge

Nineteenth-century Scottish poet William McGonagall is probably the only writer to have his work collected solely because it is so bad. In his introduction to McGonagall's selected poems, published by the Stephen Greene Press, James L. Smith writes that the poet is "unquestionably the great master of Illiterature in the language." McGonagall, who never lost faith in his greatness, and actually outsells Browning and Tennyson in Great Britain today, attracted audiences to his poetry reading because people who had read his poems wanted to pelt him with rotten tomatoes and eggplants. There have been others who have produced "art" with more mechanical regularity than McGonagall; present-day Indian poet Sri Chinmoy composed 843 poems a day in 1975 and another time turned out 16,031 paintings in a day. But no one's poetry has been as consistently bad as the Scottish bard's. It has been called the worst poetry ever written, in any language, at any time. A sample of his work from "The Battle of Abu Klea":

> Oh, it was an exciting and terrible sight,
> To see Colonel Burnaby engaged in the fight;
> With sword in hand, fighting with might and main
> Until killed by a spear thrust in the jugular vain.

W.H. Auden remarked that "with inverted commas round his verses...Mc-Gonagall becomes one of the greatest comic poets in English."

George Meredith (1828–1909)

In 1856 the young poet and novelist sat for Henry Wallis's painting "The Death of Chatterton." Soon after the painting was finished Wallis ran off with Meredith's wife, Mary Ellen, in what became the literary scandal of the day.

Reading a George Meredith contribution to the *English Review*, Henry James remarked, "Poor old Meredith, he writes these mysterious nonsenses and heaven alone knows what they all mean." Later, Meredith read an article by James in the same issue. Without knowing what James had said of his piece, Meredith made this comment: "Poor old James, he sets down on paper these mysterious rumblings in his bowels—but who could be expected to understand them." Both pieces were entirely comprehensible.

∇ ∇ ∇

John Stuart Mill (1806–1873)

Possibly the most brilliant child prodigy among literary figures, Mill's I.Q. is estimated to have been over 200. As his autobiography (1873) shows, he was rigorously educated by his stern father, philosopher James Mill, from an early age; he was studying Greek at the age of three and history by the time he was four. The intellectual pressures on his were so great that he went into an acute depression until he was inspired by Wordsworth's poetry to find a new will to live.

His disciplinarian father believed, as Plato did, that poets should be banned as the enemies of truth. It took Mill years of struggle to abandon this doctrine, as it did to throw off his father's stern rule of "few acquaintances, fewer friends, no familiarities."

∇ ∇ ∇

Andrew Millar (1707–1768)

Just before the publisher brought out Henry Fielding's *Amelia* in 1751, a critic warned him that the novel wasn't nearly as good as Fielding's last book, the vastly successful *Tom Jones*. Millar saved his large investment in the book by holding an auction of all his stock and advising the trade: "Gentlemen, I have several works to put up for which I shall be very glad if you will bid. But as to *Amelia*, every copy is bespoke." As a result England's booksellers quickly put in orders for the entire second edition of *Amelia*, which actually was the first edition.

Joseph Miller (1684–1738)

Joe Miller didn't write the famous joke book that bears his name. The comic actor and barfly Joseph or Josias Miller, a favorite at Drury Lane Theatre in parts such as *Hamlet*'s first gravedigger, was an illiterate. He married his wife, in fact, only so that she could read his parts for him. When Miller died leaving his family in poverty, his friend playwright John Mottley gathered a collection of jokes attributed to him—and there were many, either because he was famed for his wit, or because it was something of a joke to credit this "grave and taciturn" actor with any joke making the rounds of the pubs. The proceeds of the 72-page book went to Miller's family, and since it was the only joke book extant for many years, it went into numerous editions over the next two centuries. Eventually the original 272 jokes increased to well over 1,500. Because the jokes were widely quoted and imitated on the stage so long, any stale joke began to be called a "Joe Miller." The full title of the joke book was: *Joe Miller's Jests: or, The Wit's Vade-Mecum, being a collection of the most brilliant jests, the polite repartees, the most elegant bon mots, the most pleasant short stories in the English language. First carefully collected in the company, and many of them transcribed from the mouth of the facetious gentleman whose name they bear*. Some writers have gone so far as to say that the book is the basis for all stage and screen humor, and professional comedians such as Fred Allen have acknowledged their indebtedness to the collection. But poor Joe Miller probably had very little to do with it at all.

∇ ∇ ∇

A.A. (Alan Alexander) Milne (1882–1956)

"Almost anyone can be an author," remarked Winnie-The-Pooh's creator; "the business is to collect money and fame from this state of being." Though one of the most prolific authors of his day none of his work but his classic children's stories survives today.

∇ ∇ ∇

John Milton (1608–1674)

Milton was a very handsome youth with, in his own words, "a certain niceness of nature, an honest haughtiness." At least for his first two or three years at Christ's College, Cambridge, he was generally unpopular among his fellow students, who were alienated by his peculiarly grave, good looks and haughty manner. Thinking him prudish and far too fastidious, they sneeringly dubbed him "the Lady," a nickname that stuck and was converted to "the Lady of Christ's" by students of the other colleges. Only when his great intellectual preeminence because apparent was the nickname forgotten.

While a student at Christ's College, Cambridge, Milton quarreled with his tutor and started a fist fight with him, for which he was expelled for a term. Before he left, in the words of Samuel Johnson, "Milton was one of the last students in either university that suffered the public indignity of corporal corrections," that is, a paddling in public.

The first published work of Milton, who is generally regarded as second only to Shakespeare in English literature, was an anonymous eulogy on the bard prefacing the 1632 second folio of Shakespeare's plays.

When Milton was 33 he married 17-year-old Mary Powell, a frivolous, flighty girl who grew bored with the life of a poet soon after the honeymoon was over. She soon begged him to let her go home for a visit and Milton agreed, if she promised to make the visit a brief one. When she didn't return as promised, perhaps persuaded not to by her Royalist parents, Milton was inspired to write his famous essays on divorce, in one of which he maintained that those who lived loosely in youth were more likely to have lasting marriages than those who kept chaste and modest. It was three years before Mary returned to the poet, through the interventions of friends, and she bore him three daughters before she died in childbirth in 1652. (Milton's second wife, Katherine Woodcock, also died in childbirth, and his third wife, Elizabeth Minshull, survived him.)

Milton was hardly kind to his first wife, Mary Powell. But after he went blind he married a shrew who was more punishment than he deserved. One time, however, the duke of Buckingham called the woman a rose. "I am no judge of colors anymore," replied Milton, "but it may be so, for I feel the thorns daily."

Though Milton used the phrase "the last infirmity of noble mind" in his elegy *Lycidas* (1637) on the death of his old friend Edward King, the poem *Sir John van Olden Barnevalt* called glory "that last infirmity of noble minds" 16 years before. An amazed Swinburne was sure that this was "the most inexplicable coincidence in the whole range of literature," but the idea was simply in the air at the time and can be traced back even earlier. Incidentally, both *Bartlett* and the *Oxford Dictionary of Quotations* still credit the words to Milton.

Few haven't heard the British term *Bobby* or *Peeler* for a policeman, in honor of Sir Robert Peel, home secretary from 1828 to 1830 when the Metropolitan Police Act remodeled London's police force. *Miltonian*, however, comes as a surprise. In fact, John Milton resided in Scotland Yard while working for Oliver Cromwell from 1649 to 1651, and two centuries later his name, in the form of *miltonian*, became a slang term for a policeman. At the same time *miltons* were slang for oysters. Thackeray called oysters "mute inglorious miltons," and this pun on

Gray's words in his "elegy" (not necessarily original with Thackeray) may be the source of the expression.

Aubrey tells us that Milton was an early riser who went to bed at nine and got up at four in the morning. His chief exercise was walking—three or four hours a day—and he was a man of temperate habits, who was known to be extremely pleasant in conversation but was considered "Satyricall."

In 1638 Milton located and visited the great Galileo in Florence, where he was still officially a prisoner of the Inquisition for his scientific heresy. Milton recorded his conversation with the blind, aged Galileo in his famed *Areopagitica*, which attacked censorship. Thirteen years later, when only 44, he would be totally blind himself. When his daughters grew old enough, they would walk him about and read to him, but as time passed they "made nothing of neglecting him." Rebelling against the drudgery of attending him and reading books they understood not a word of, his daughters, in Aubrey's words, "did combine together and counsel his maid-servant to cheat him in her marketings," and actually stole "some of his books and would have sold the rest." Only when Milton married his third wife, Elizabeth Minshull, in 1662, were his daughters restrained, and for the rest of his life a series of amanuenses read and wrote for him as he composed his greatest poems, including *Paradise Lost*, one of the monumental works of world literature.

The copyright of *Paradise Lost: A Poem Written in Ten Books: By John Milton* (1667) was sold to London printer Samuel Symons for what one biographer called a "waste-paper price," though it was about average for books of the day: "The author received 4 pounds down, was to receive a second 5 pounds when the first edition should be sold, a third 5 pounds when the second was sold, and a fourth 5 pounds when the third edition should be gone." Milton lived to receive the second five pounds, and no more: 10 pounds in all for *Paradise Lost*. Symons printed a 1,300-copy first edition, which did relatively well, selling out in 18 months. When the poet died, his wife Elizabeth Minshull surrendered all future claims on the poem for another eight pounds.

A Cambridge mathematician was urged to read Milton's *Paradise Lost* and did so. "I have read your famous poem," he complained when he finished. "I have read it attentively but what does it prove? There is more instruction in a half page of Euclid! A man might read Milton's poem a hundred, aye, a thousand times, and he would never learn that the angles at the base of an isosceles triangle are equal!"

Since Roman times *R* has been thought of as the "dog's letter," or the snarling letter, because its sound resembles the snarling of a dog—r-r-r-r. Ben Jonson, in his *English Grammar Made for the Benefit of all Strangers* (1636), put it this way: "R is the dog's letter, and hurreth in the sound; the tongue striking the inner palate, with a trembling about the teeth." Shakespeare has Juliet's nurse in *Romeo and Juliet* call *R* the dog-name, when she tells Romeo that his name and rosemary, an herb associated with weddings, both begin with an *R*. In parts of the United States, especially the Midwest, *R* is still pronounced as the dog letter, while in other regions, particularly parts of New England and the South, it is pronounced as *ah*. Milton is probably the most famous example of a literary light who used the dog letter. "He pronounced the letter *r* very hard," Aubrey tells us, adding Dryden's comment on the subject: "*literia canina*, the dog letter, a certain sign of satirical wit." In fact, Milton's tendency to be satirical and sarcastic in conversation was connected by some of his friends with "his peculiarity of voice and pronunciation."

Grub Street cannot be found in London today. Since 1830 it has been called Milton Street, which, ironically, suggests the poet. But, contrary to popular opinion, it was not renamed for the blind, impoverished Milton, who lived in the neighborhood for many years and is buried in St. Giles in the ward. The name commemorates a builder and landlord named Milton who owned most of the houses on Grub Street at the time.

Many writers believe that Milton's grave in the parish church of St. Giles, Cripplegate, was desecrated by church officials and workers in 1790, when the church was undergoing repairs. Cowper even wrote an indignant poem called "On the Late Indecent Liberties Taken with the Remains of Milton." According to antiquary Philip Neve, there was little left of Milton when the ghouls got through. One man "pulled hard at the teeth, which resisted, until someone hit them with a stone, when they easily came out." All the teeth, and "a large quantity of the hair" were taken as souvenirs by grave-robbers, who later charged the curious anywhere from twopence to sixpence to view the remains.

∇ ∇ ∇

John Mitford (1782–1859)

An early biographer said of Mitford that he "took to journalism and strong drink." The author was paid a shilling a day by his Grub Street publisher, "of which he expended tenpence on gin and twopence on bread, cheese and an onion." Rent he had not, as he "lived in a gravel pit, with pen, ink and paper, for the last 43 days of his life."

Mary Russell Mitford (1787–1855)

The novelist and playwright was forced into writing by her eccentric father's gambling and other extravagances. Dr. George Mitford spent not only his wife's entire fortune on himself, he also went through a £20,000 lottery prize Mary had won at the age of 10. His daughter's books sold well, but her income never matched his expenditures, and there was barely enough to live on. She worked incessantly, encouraged by Coleridge and her close friend Elizabeth Barrett Browning, who knew something of tyrannical fathers, managing to produce a substantial body of work and maintain a pleasant disposition despite her virtual enslavement to her eccentric father, which entailed working for him, reading to him, keeping house and nursing him, and refusing all social engagements beause he constantly wanted her at his side.

∇ ∇ ∇

Nancy Mitford (1904–1973)

The author, famous for her provocative remarks on "U" and "Non-U" vocabulary terms and behavior, as well as for her entertaining novels, apparently thought prostitution was U behavior. When the authorities were trying to eliminate prostitution in London, she protested, "But where will the young men learn?"

∇ ∇ ∇

Elizabeth Montagu (1720–1800)

"A bluestocking," said Rousseau, "is a woman who will remain a spinster as long as there are sensible men on earth." Undoubtedly a male chauvinist point of view, especially when we look at the word bluestocking's origins. The original bluestockings were a group headed by Mrs. Elizabeth Montagu (her first name is variously given, and "Montagu" is often spelled with an "e") that first met in her London home and the homes of friends about 1750. Their purpose was to replace idle evenings of chatter with a literary salon based on Parisian models, and they hoped to attract the era's leading intellectuals. The club members dressed simply as a reaction against the sumptuous evening clothes of the time. The group of intellectuals were soon held in contempt by "proper" society and a noted wit dubbed them The Bluestocking Club, or *bluestockings*, for the blue-colored hose that one *male* member wore in place of gentlemen's black silk hose. For no good reason, a bluestocking came to mean an intellectual or affectedly literary, dowdy woman, although the group probably did have a few such members. The appellation seems all the more unfair when one considers that only a Mr. Benjamin Stillingfleet wore the homely blue-gray tradesman's stockings responsible for the club's name. Ironically, the word bluestocking originally applied to a man.

One room in the Queen of the Blue's house in Portman Square—a room big enough to hold a literary party for over 700 guests—had it walls and ceiling covered with feathers from every bird species she could obtain.

∇ ∇ ∇

Lady Mary Wortley Montagu (1689–1762)

The great English letter writer (Smollett said her letters "were never equalled") was always sure of the enduring fame of her correspondence. "The last pleasure that fell my way was Madame de Sévigné's letters," she once told her friends, "very pretty they are, but I assert, without the least vanity, that mine will be full as entertaining forty years hence. I advise you, therefore, to put none of them to the use of waste paper."

Lady Mary had been Pope's good friend until he offended her sensibilities by including in a letter he wrote to her an epitaph he had written about two lovers struck by lightning:

Here lye two poor lovers, who had the mishap
Tho very chaste people, to die of a *Clap*.

The savage satirists Swift and Pope were of humble origins but liked to brag of aristocratic origins. Lady Mary saw through them. "It is pleasant to consider," the "Lady of Quality" wrote to the countess of Bute, "that, had it not been for the good nature of these very mortals they contemn, these two superior beings were entitled by their birth and hereditary fortune, to be only a couple of link boys [caddies]."

In a 1755 letter to her daughter she wrote: "Clarissa [the eponymous heroine of Richardson's famous novel] follows the maxim of declaring all she thinks to all the people she sees, without reflecting that in this mortal state of imperfection, fig leaves are as necessary for our minds as for our bodies, and 'tis as indecent to show all we think as all we have."

Despite her feud with Alexander Pope and a disfiguring skin disease that brought her close to madness in later years, the English letter writer and literary light led a full life and traveled widely. Her last words were: "It has all been most interesting."

C.E. (Charles Edward) Montague (1867–1928)

Montague was 47 when World War I began, but he dyed his gray hair black, lied about his age and joined the army as a private. The novelist was said to be the only man on record whose hair turned black in a single night from fearlessness. Once he saw what war was really like he became bitterly disillusioned, as is reflected in his novel *Disenchantment* (1922).

▽ ▽ ▽

James Montgomery (1771–1854)

The popular poet and hymn writer was a favorite of Byron. When Montgomery's house was robbed in 1812 (a precious inkstand among the items taken) the whole town of Sheffield was shocked and sorry. Even one of the burglars, who returned the inkstand with the following note: "Honored sir: When we robbed your house we did not know you wrote such beautiful verses as you do. I remember my mother told some of them to me when I was a boy. I found what house we robbed by the writing [engraving] on the inkstand. Honored sir, I send it back. It was my share of the booty, and I hope you and God will forgive me."

▽ ▽ ▽

Francis Moore (1657–1714)

Among the most famous of English almanacs was *Old Moore's Almanac* (1699), published by Francis Moore to promote the sale of his pills to cure almost everything. Moore would make weather predictions by just writing down whatever came into his head. He established a reputation for uncanny accuracy when his secretary woke him one afternoon to ask what prediction should be printed for June 3, Derby Day. "Cold and snow, damn it!" Moore replied irritably and went back to sleep. His prediction was recorded, however, and it *did* happen to snow that Derby Day. People never forgot and Moore was forgiven every mistake he made afterward because of that one lucky prediction. Incidentally, his alamanac still sells close to 2 million copies a year.

▽ ▽ ▽

George Moore (1852–1933)

Ever since his first novel, *A Modern Lover* (1883), the Anglo-Irish author was gossiped about in London literary circles as a great lover, and in fact he had many affairs that he was not at all secretive about. At least one woman, however, did not take kindly to his bragging about their romance. "Some men kiss and do not tell, and some men kiss and do tell," she let it be know, "but George Moore told and did not kiss."

Moore, an Anglo-Irish aristocrat, knew little of the working class. For his acclaimed novel *Esther Waters* (1894), the story of the life of a servant, he paid his cook an hourly wage to interview her about life backstairs.

At his 80th birthday reporters asked Moore how it was that he continued to enjoy such excellent health. Replied Moore, "It's because I never smoked, or drank, or touched a girl—until I was eleven years old."

∇ ∇ ∇

George Edward Moore (1873–1958)
Moore's *Principia Ethica* (1903), dealing with the concept of goodness, began a new era in British philosophy, and his views were very influential on members of the Bloomsbury group, among others. He was a very modest, unassuming, scrupulously honest man. "I have never but once succeeded in making him tell a lie and that was by a subterfuge," philosopher Bertrand Russell said. "'Moore,' I said, 'do you *always* speak the truth?' 'No,' he replied. I believe this to be the only lie he ever told."

∇ ∇ ∇

Thomas Moore (1779–1852)
The Irish poet came of poor but proud stock and never pretended otherwise. When Moore was invited to join a fashionable London club, a single lord objected to his membership.

"I understand, Mr. Moore, that your father was a shopkeeper," he intoned.

"Indeed he was," Moore replied, "and a very honest one, too."

"How very interesting," said the lord, "and may I enquire why you didn't follow in his footstep?"

"Because," Moore said, "my talents were limited." Then he paused and added, "I have heard that *your* father was a gentleman. May I ask why you have not followed in *his* footsteps."

In a book on the dead Byron, Leigh Hunt blamed Tom Moore (still Ireland's national poet, but whose statue for some reason stands above Dublin's largest public urinal) for publishing Byron's *Letters and Journals*, which Hunt found objectionable. In fact, Moore found it hard to dislike anyone and people had trouble disliking him. Moore and the critic Francis Jeffrey became friends while waiting for the pistols to be loaded during a duel between the two men, but even this mild-mannered poet had his limits. He replied to Hunt with "The Living Dog and the Dead Lion":

> Nay, fed as he was (and this makes *dark* case)
> With sops every day from the Lion's own pan,
> He lifts up a leg at the noble beast's carcase,
> And does all a dog so diminutive can.
>
> However, the book's a good book, being rich in
> Examples and warnings to lions high-bred,
> How they suffer small mongrelly curs in the kitchen,
> Who'll feed on them living, and foul them when dead.

∇ ∇ ∇

Sir Thomas More (1477?–1535)

An author asked More, then chancellor of Henry VIII, his opinion of a book he had written. Sir Thomas told him to turn the prose into rhyme. When he did so and submitted it to More, the chancellor said, "Ay! ay! that will do, that will do. 'Tis rhyme now, but before it was neither rhyme nor reason."

"What did Nature ever create milder, sweeter, and happier than the genius of Thomas More?" Erasmus asked. He told how More kept in his house a monkey and many other pets and observed that "all the birds in Chelsea came to him to be fed."

More entitled his famous book *Nusquama*, or *Nowhere*, but someone—nobody knows who it was—changed his title to the Greek equivalent, *Utopia*, during the printing at Louvain and gave a new word to the language. More's account seemed so authentic that one missionary planned to travel to Utopia and convert the Utopians to Christianity.

In his *Utopia* one of More's laws states that young people must see each other stark naked before they are married. He apparently practiced this law in his private life. According to John Aubrey, Sir William Roper came to More's house early one morning with a proposal to marry one of his daughters. More's daughters were both asleep in the same bed and he led Roper into their room and suddenly whipped off the sheet covering them: "They lay on their backs, and their smocks up as high as their arme-pitts. This awakened them, and immediately they turned on their bellies. Quoth Roper, 'I have seen both sides,' and so giving a patt on the buttock, he made choice, saying, 'Thou art mine.'"

More liked to sit atop the gatehouse at his country place in Chelsea and contemplate the Thames and the fields far beyond. One day a wandering Tom o'Bedlam, among the mentally ill homeless of his time, climbed up to the flat roof while More stood there and threatened to throw him off, crying "Leap, Tom, leap!" The elderly More couldn't repulse the strong young man and had to think fast. He pointed to his little dog beside him. "Let us throw the dog down," he said, "and see what sport that will be." When the dog was thrown over, More went on, "This is very fine sport, let us fetch him up and try once more!" The madman agreed and while he was climbing down to retrieve the dog, More let himself in the gatehouse, locked the door, and cried for help.

More's son-in-law reported that Sir Thomas tried to comfort his wife, who was distraught at seeing him imprisoned in the Tower of London by Henry VIII for refusing to take any oath that would impugn the pope's authority or justify the king's divorce from Queen Catherine:

"'Is not this house,' quoted he, 'as nigh heaven as mine own?' To whom she, after her accustomed homely fashion, not liking such talk, answered, 'Tilly vally, Tilly vally.'"

On July 7, 1535, More, weak and trembling, began to ascend the scaffold where he would be beheaded. He then turned to the governor of the Tower of London, saying, "I pray you, I pray you, Mr. Lieutenant, see me safe up, and for coming down let me shift for myself."

More carefully placed his long gray beard so that it would be out of the axeman's way when he laid his head upon the block. It would be a "pity that should be cut," he said, "that hath not committed treason."

After he was beheaded his head was displayed on London Bridge. According to an old story in the family, "one day one of his daughters was riding under the bridge," looked up at her father's head, and said, "That head has lain many a time in my lap. Would to God it would fall into my lap as I pass under." Suddenly her wish came true, the head fell into her lap and the family soon had it "preserved in a vault in the Cathedral Church at Canterbury."

∇ ∇ ∇

Evan Morgan (1893–1949)

A Bloomsbury character who later became Viscount Tredegar, Morgan threw many parties for the English literati. Among his many tricks was one that involved his pet parakeet. Morgan trained it to climb up inside his pants' leg and then pop out chirping through his fly.

William Morris (1834–1896)

Like Balzac, who once fled screaming from what he called its colossal vulgarity, the poet and architect couldn't stand the sight of the Eiffel Tower. But during one long visit to Paris, he stayed in the restaurants of the tower as long as he could, even doing his writing there.

"You must really be impressed by the tower, hardly ever leaving it," a French friend remarked.

"Impressed!" said Morris, "I stay here because it's the only place in Paris where I can't see the damn thing!"

The painter and poet Dante Gabriel Rossetti and his sister Christina were well regarded in the England of their day, but their brother, art critic William Rossetti, didn't enjoy their reputation. Certainly not in the eyes of William Morris. One time Morris sent Dante Rossetti a copy of his epic poem *Sigurd the Volsung* and grew angry when Rossetti failed to acknowledge the gift. Finally encountering Rossetti, he said, "Evidently you do not like my book, or you would have written to tell me about it."

"To tell you the truth, Topy," Rossetti said, "I must own I find it difficult to take much interest in a man whose father was a dragon."

Stomping out of the room, Morris shouted, "I don't see it's any odder than having a brother who's an idiot!"

∇ ∇ ∇

Thomas Morton (1764?–1838)

> They eat, and drink, and scheme, and plod,
>   And go to sleep on Sunday—
> And many are afraid of God—
>   And more of Mrs. Grundy.

These lines from Frederick Locker-Lampson's poem "The Jester" (1857) were inspired by a character in playwright Thomas Morton's comedy *Speed the Plough*, first staged at London's Covent Garden in 1800. Actually Mrs. Grundy is something less than a character, for she never appears on stage and is never described physically. She is the epitome of propriety, the narrow-minded, straitlaced neighbor of Farmer Ashfield and Dame Ashfield, his wife, who is obsessed with Mrs. Grundy's opinion of things. "What will Mrs. Grundy say? What will Mrs. Grundy think?" is on Dame Ashfield's lips so often that the words became proverbial for "What will that straitlaced neighbor say? What will the neighbors think?" and Mrs. Grundy herself became a symbol of prudish propriety or social convention. Dickens's Mrs. Harris, the mythical friend of Sara Gamp in *Martin Chuzzlewit* (1843), is a similar character.

∇ ∇ ∇

R.K. (Richard Kendall) Munkittrick (d. 1911)
The editor tired of a young poet who kept submitting his painful verse to *Judge*. Wrote Munkittrick on the final rejection slip: "Please curb your doggerel."

∇ ∇ ∇

Arthur Murphy (1727–1805)
Murphy, a prolific author and barrister, was told that publishers commonly published books they couldn't be expected to understand. "True," he replied, "some of 'em *do* deal in morality."

∇ ∇ ∇

Sir James Murray (1837–1915)
All the countless authors who are indebted to the great *Oxford English Dictionary*, a monument to scholarship in our time, should know that up until his death in 1915 the English philologist and lexicographer James Murray was *by himself* responsible for fully one-half of the vast work.

∇ ∇ ∇

Robert Murray (1635–1660)
Though this writer on business and economics left no literary work of much value today, he is still remembered as the originator of the penny post and the inventor of the ruled copybook.

∇ ∇ ∇ ∇ ∇ ∇ ∇ ∇

Thomas Nashe (1567–1601)

In 1592 the playwright and satirist rebuked Gabriel Harvey for inventing the words *conscious, extensively, jovial, notoriety*, and *rascality*. They would never last, he laughed, and characterized Harvey as: "Cowbaby, Gorboduck, Huddle-duddle, Gogmagog, Jewish Talmud of absurdities, coarse himpenhempen Slampant, stale Applesquire Cocledemoy—creator of rascally hedge raked-up terms, familiar to roguish morts and doxies, ridiculous senseless sentences, finical flaunting phrases, and termagant inkhorn terms...hermaphrodite phrases, half Latin, half English."

▽ ▽ ▽

Sir Isaac Newton (1642–1727)

Perhaps the greatest figure in the history of science, the scientist and much published author was essentially as modest and unassuming as Galileo before him and Einstein after him. "If I have seen a little farther than others," he once said, "it is because I have stood on the shoulders of giants." As for his modest opinion of himself, from Brewster's *Memoirs of Newton*: "I do not know what I may appear to the world, but to myself I seem to have been only a boy playing on the sea-shore, and diverting myself in now and then finding a smoother pebble or a prettier shell than ordinary, whilst the great ocean of truth lay all undiscovered before me."

Newton's mother told him that he was so weak at birth that there was little hope that he would live more than a few days. He was such a small baby, she said, that he would have fit into a quart mug.

The first mention of the legendary apple falling on Newton's head and inspiring him to ponder the question of gravitation came in Voltaire's *Philosophie de Newton* (1738): "One day, in the year 1666, Newton, then retired to the country, seeing some fruit fall from a tree, as I was told by his niece, Mme. Conduit, fell into profound meditation upon the cause which draws all bodies in a line which, if prolonged, would pass very nearly through the center of the earth."

According to another, more likely, story, a stranger asked Newton, "How did you discover the laws of gravitation?"
"By thinking of them without ceasing," the great man replied.

Everyone knows the story of the apple falling on Newton's head, but less familiar, and perhaps even less reliable, is the story of his little dog Diamond. It seems that Diamond upset a candle on his master's papers one winter morning, setting on fire and destroying the results of many years' experiments. But

Newton didn't turn the dog out in the cold. "Oh, Diamond, Diamond, thou little knowest the mischief done!" he is said to have exclaimed, sitting down at his desk and beginning all over.

A probably apocryphal but persistent story about the animal-loving philosopher has it that Newton cut a hole in the bottom of his outside door for his cat and cut a smaller one next to it when the cat had kittens.

Newton had no ear for music, especially opera. "He said he never was at more than one opera," the Reverend William Stukeley wrote in a 1720 diary entry. "The first act he heard with pleasure, the 2nd stretch'd his patience, at the 3rd he ran away."

To a woman who asked him his opinion of the immortality of the soul, Newton replied, "Madam, I am an experimental philosopher."

In his posthumously published *Autobiography and Journals* the artist Benjamin Robert Haydon (*q.v.*) tells of the "immortal dinner" he gave for Lamb, Wordsworth and Keats. At the party, "in a strain of humour beyond description" Lamb abused Haydon for putting Sir Isaac Newton's head in his picture "Christ's Entry into Jerusalem," declaring Newton "a fellow who believed nothing unless it was as clear as the three sides of a triangle." Lamb and Keats then agreed that Newton "had destroyed all the poetry of the rainbow by reducing it to the prismatic colors." Then all three great poets drank "Newton's health and confusion to mathematics."

After his monumental early discoveries, even while serving as president of the Royal Society, Newton worked primarily on alchemy, seeking magical potions and the like. Working mostly in secret the great scientist accumulated over 100 books on alchemy and wrote some 650,000 words on the decidedly unscientific subject.

His absentmindedness was legendary when he taught at Trinity. He forgot to comb his hair, forgot appointments, forgot to eat. Always absorbed in scientific problems, he would even forget where he was. Often he would rise in the morning and sit on the edge of his bed for hours, pondering some problem and forgetting to get dressed.

He sagely observed that he could predict the movements of the heavenly bodies but not the madness of men and sold his shares in the South Sea Company at a good profit before the South Sea Bubble burst in the great English crash of 1720. Unfortunately, he reinvested his money and lost everything.

Lord Norbury (John Toler, 1745–1831)

England's chief justice and literary wit was talking about the notorious Caroline of Brunswick, wife of King George IV, and her affair with the dey, or governor, of Algiers. "She was as happy as the dey was long," he remarked.

∇ ∇ ∇

Viscount Northcliffe (Alfred Charles William Harmsworth; 1865–1922)

The British press baron once asked a young reporter if he was happy at his job and the man said that he was. "Then you're dismissed," Northcliffe barked. "I don't want any one here who's content on five pounds a week."

∇ ∇ ∇ ∇ ∇ ∇ ∇ ∇

Torlogh O'Carolan (1670–1738)

On his deathbed the poet asked for a cup of Irish whiskey. His last words, as he sipped it, were: "It would be hard if two such friends should part at least without kissing."

∇ ∇ ∇

Sean O'Casey (1880–1964)

The Irish playwright was a laborer in his youth. "When I stepped from hard manual work to writing," he observed in later years, "I just stepped from one kind of hard work to another."

He called himself the "flying wasp" of playwright critics and couldn't silence a restless tongue. At his son's funeral he is reported to have said: "It gives me a kind of trespassin' joy."

∇ ∇ ∇

Simon Ockley (1678–1720)

Ockley's financial difficulties take up a chapter in Isaac D'Israeli's *Calamities of Authors*. Jailed for debt after working 10 years on his three-volume *History of the Saracens*, he managed to complete the work in prison. He died in poverty when he was only 37, never realizing that his masterpiece was fatally flawed because he had unknowingly chosen an Arabic romance rather than a reliable history as the major basis for his work.

∇ ∇ ∇

John Boyle O'Reilly (1844–1890)

The Irish poet and revolutionary joined a British cavalry regiment with the intention of persuading the large number of Irishmen in it to join the revolutionary cause. He succeeded but was caught, court-martialed and transported to Australia, where he escaped after serving two years of his 20-year sentence. Making his way to America, he became the editor of a Catholic newspaper, *The Pilot*, and in 1876 led an expedition to Western Australia that freed Irish military prisoners there.

∇ ∇ ∇

George Orwell (Eric Arthur Blair; 1903–1950)

Writing to his publisher about his celebrated novel *Nineteen Eighty-Four* (1949) Orwell advised: "It isn't a book I would gamble on for a big sale." From shortly after he died of the tuberculosis until the year 1984, when it became a bestseller again, his book, which added "Big Brother" and many other words to the language, sold well over ten million copies.

∇ ∇ ∇

Thomas Otway (1652–1685)

Otway, the author of 10 or so plays, fell in love with the famous actress Mrs. Barry, who had her first successful role in his *Alcibiades*, but she scorned him for her patron the earl of Rochester and out of despair Otway obtained a commission in the army. When he returned from Holland, he was paid with depreciated money like all the troops. He was poor, ragged and dirty, but managed to resume his writing career. Over the next two years he wrote his tragic masterpieces *The Orphan* and *Venice Preserv'd*, but then his successes turned into a long line of failures. Otway seemed to lose the will to struggle against his misfortunes and nearly starved to death. It is said that one morning he left his room to beg for bread and a passerby gave him a guinea. He hurried to a nearby baker's shop where he bought a loaf of bread and began stuffing it in his mouth to satisfy his ravenous hunger, but he choked to death with the first mouthful.

∇ ∇ ∇

Ouida (Marie Louise de la Ramée; 1839–1908)

This odd pen name (like Boz for Charles Dickens), was the result of a young child's mispronunciation of the popular novelist's name (Louise). Ouida's novels of fashionable society were filled with inaccuracies and peopled by impossible heroes, but were largely redeemed by their narrative force. She once confided what she thought was the secret of her success to Ocar Wilde: "I am the only woman who knows how two dukes talk when they are alone."

∇ ∇ ∇

John Overall (1560–1618)

Overall, one of the revisers of the King James Bible and the dean of St. Paul's, never preached in church because he had written and spoken Latin "so long it was troublesome for him to speak English in a continued oration." He was married to one of the most beautiful and "wondrous wanton" women of his time, a woman much younger than he, who apparently cheated on him, judging by an anonymous verse of the time:

> The Dean of Paule's did search for his wife,
>   and where d'ee thinke he found her?
> Even upon Sir John Selbye's bed,
>   as flatte as any Flounder.

∇ ∇ ∇

Thomas Overbury (1581–1613)

When the poet's friend Robert Carr made plans to marry the divorced countess of Essex, Overbury protested that she was not the wife for him, or anyone, and even wrote a poem called *The Wife*, which he widely circulated in manuscript, giving his idea of what a man should expect from a wife—nothing that Lady Essex could possibly provide. Carr and Lady Essex had the poet thrown into the Tower on a trumped-up charge of disrespect to the king. Then, with the aid of four confederates, including a jailer and an apothecary, they slowly poisoned him with copper vitriol. Overbury died within four months. After more than a year the murder plot was exposed and the murderers tried and found guilty. A disgraced Carr and Lady Essex, now married, went free and the four accomplices were hanged.

∇ ∇ ∇

John Owen (1563?–1622)

This 16th-century author of rhymed Latin epigrams that were translated into several languages compared his book to the world, and men to verses. In each case, Owen said, you could find a few good examples.

William Oxberry (1784–1824)

The author was known as "The Five P's" because he was for his all-too-brief 40 years a Printer, Poet, Publisher, Publican and Player (actor).

∇ ∇ ∇

Earl of Oxford (Edward de Vere, 17th Earl of Oxford; 1550–1604)

A disputatious man who may have planned to kill one rival he argued with, Oxford wrote 15 or so poems, so far as is known, and at least one critic identified him as the author of Shakespeare's poems. According to John Aubrey. "[The] Earle of Oxford, making his low obeisance to Queen Elizabeth, happened to let a Fart, at which he was so abashed and ashamed that he went to Travell, 7 years. On his return the Queen welcomed him home, and say'd, My Lord, I had forgott the Fart."

He lost his great fortune through extravagance, spending, for example, £40,000 a year in the seven years he traveled on the continent. Aubrey tells the story of the poet and philosopher Nicholas Hill, who traveled with him as his steward, being asked for a penny by a beggar. "'A penny!' said Mr. Hill. 'What doest thou say to ten pound?' 'Ah! ten pounds!' said the beggar, 'that would make a man happy!' Hill gave him immediately 10 pounds and putt it downe upon account— 'Item to a Beggar ten pounds, to make him happy,' which his Lordship allowed and was well pleased at it."

∇ ∇ ∇ ∇ ∇ ∇ ∇ ∇ ∇

Dr. Samuel Parr (1747–1825)

Dr. Parr's style seems verbose and mannered today, but in the early 19th century he was highly regarded as a stylist and especially as a writer of Latin epigraphs. Once "the Whig Johnson," as Parr was called, said to a friend, "My Lord, should you die first, I mean to write your epitaph." "Dr. Parr," his friend replied, "it is a temptation to commit suicide."

Not long after the death of Dr. Johnson, Parr was dining with Sir Joshua Reynolds when the topic turned to recent criticism of the Great Cham. Remarked

Parr, who composed the Latin epitaph for Johnson's monument: "Now that the old lion is dead, every ass thinks he may kick at him."

Parr's sermons were as much valued as his epitaphs. The lord mayor of London said he heard only four things he did not like in the clergyman's famous 1800 Easter Tuesday sermon. These were the four times the church clock struck at each quarter of the hour.

Parr hated playing whist with an inferior partner. One evening he was paired with someone totally inept. His hostess came to his table to inquire how the game was going and he replied, "As well as might be expected, madam, considering that I have three opponents."

∇ ∇ ∇

Eric Partridge (d. 1985)
The great etymologist was noted for his pithy definitions. In his *Dictionary of Slang* he notes a term honoring the Great Cham, the combative Dr. Samuel Johnson: "Dr. Johnson, the *membrum virile*: literary: ca. 1790–1880. Perhaps because there was no one that Dr. Johnson was not prepared to stand up to."

∇ ∇ ∇

Walter Pater (1839–1894)
While Pater was an Oxford don, Benjamin Jowett, the master of Balliol, learned of letters signed "Yours lovingly," that Pater had written to a young Balliol student who had written and circulated several homosexual sonnets. Jowett threatened to make the letters public if Pater ever became a candidate for any university office. Pater had already written his acclaimed *Studies in the History of the Renaissance* (1873), which Wilde called "the holy writ of beauty," but which Jowett and others found morbid and unscholarly. In any case, Pater never again wrote in the same manner and some critics say that he went into hiding from his detractors. He devoted the rest of his life to the cultivation of prose that is, according to one biographer, "the consequence of much sublimation."

∇ ∇ ∇

Thomas Love Peacock (1785–1866)
A witty man whose novels were noted for their diverting, satirical style rather than story or plot, Peacock wrote *Melincourt or Sir Oran Haut-ton* (1817), which featured a trained orangutan that held a seat in Parliament (someone commented that this was an improvement over a number of members). Peacock learned after Jeremy Bentham's death that an oily substance was oozing from the philosopher's body, which he had left to science for dissection. Another

philosopher, James Mill, had told him this. "The less you say about that, the better for you," Peacock advised Mill, "because if the fact becomes known, just as we see in the newspapers that a fine bear is to be killed for his grave, we have be having advertisements that a fine philosopher is to be killed for his oil."

▽ ▽ ▽

Samuel Pepys (1633–1703)

Pepys was admonished while a student at Cambridge for being "scandalously" drunk. In 1660 he began his famous diary, using a secret code to put down, in the words of a biographer, "whatever he saw, heard, felt or imagined, every motion of his mind, every action of his body, and he noted all this, not as he desired it to appear to others, but as it was to his seeing." Nine years later he abandoned the diary, fearing for his eyesight, and it was not deciphered (from a key he left among his papers) until 1825, more than a century after his death.

While he was secretary to the Admiralty Pepys was known as among the most dedicated of government officials. It is said that while the plague raged in London in 1666 he remained at his post while many of his colleagues ran away.

His dramatic criticism left something to be desired. In 1662 he noted in his diary that *Romeo and Juliet* was the worst-written play he'd ever seen. Six months later he changed his mind, noting that "*A Midsummer Night Dream* [is] the most insipid ridiculous play that ever I saw in my life."

In 1669 Pepys viewed the body of Katherine of Valois, interred two centuries earlier in Westminster Abbey. He bent down to kiss her on the mouth, and later remarked: "This was my birthday, thirty-six years old, that I did first kiss a Queen."

▽ ▽ ▽

Sir William Petty (1623–1676)

Among the founding fathers of statistics with his important book *Political Arithmetic* (1690), Petty was so precocious a boy that when he went to sea his jealous shipmates deserted him on a lonely coast of France with a broken leg. In 1650 he and several medical students were appointed to do the autopsy of a serving maid named Nan Green, who was hanged in Oxon Castle for murdering her illegitimate child. After Nan was cut down, the others wanted to proceed with the autopsy, but Petty found life in her and revived her, which was "looked upon as a great wonder" of the day.

John Aubrey tells this tale of him in *Brief Lives*: "I remember about 1660 there was a great difference [argument] between him and Sir Hierome Sanchy, one of Oliver's knights. They pitted one against the other...The Knight had been a Soldier, and challenged Sir William to fight with him. Sir William is extremely short sighted, and being the challenger it belonged to him to nominate place and weapon. He nominates, for the place a darke Cellar, and the weapon to be a great Carpenter's Axe. This turned the knight's challenge into Ridicule, and so it came to naught."

∇ ∇ ∇

William Petty (Second Earl of Shelburne; 1737–1805)
After being shot in the groin in a duel, the wit and scholar shrugged off his wound, assuring his friends, "I don't think Lady Shelburne will be the worst for it."

∇ ∇ ∇

Ambrose Philips (c. 1675–1749)

> Timely blossom, infant fair,
> Fondling of a happy pair,
> Every morn, and every night
> Their solicitous delight,
> Sleeping, waking, still at ease
> Pleasing without skill to please.
> Little gossip, blithe and hale,
> Tattling many a broken tale.

Philips had the bad luck to accidentally tread on Alexander Pope, easily the most venomous and malicious of the great English poets. Politics and envy had more to do with his misfortune than insipid versifying. (See a sample of his seven-syllabled lines on children quoted above.) Philips was a Whig and Pope a Tory, and in 1713 the Whig *Guardian* praised the Whig pastoral poet as the only successor of Spenser. This inane criticism enraged Pope—"the Wasp of Twickenham"—and initiated a quarrel between the two poets that Samuel Johnson described as a "perpetual reciprocation of malevolence." Pope was particularly incensed because *his* pastorals had appeared along with Philips's in *Tonson's Miscellany* (1709)—he thought it obvious that *he*, if anyone, was Spenser's successor. The articles praising Philips in *The Guardian* implied a comparison with Pope's pastorals, which was subtle, veiled revenge on Pope because he had dedicated his poem "Windsor Forest" to Tory Secretary for War George Granville. So Pope ingeniously submitted an anonymous article to the periodical that ostensibly attacked his own poems. In it, as Dr. Johnson observed in *The Lives of the Poets*, he drew a "comparison of Philips's performance with his own, in which, with an unexampled and unequalled artifice of irony, though he himself always has the advantage, he gives the preference to Philips." Pope ridiculed *The Guardian*'s principles and disposed of Ambrose's pretensions in one bold stroke, but Philips was not to be deterred. Pope's rival continued to turn out his pastorals and even indited a few pieces to political powers like Sir Robert Walpole. But it was Philip's juvenile poems that did him most harm. He wrote several sentimental little poems for the infant children of his friends Lord John Carteret and Daniel Pulteney, including his "To Mistress Charlotte Pulteney," quoted above. These adulatory verses were addressed "to all ages and characters, from Walpole steerer of the realm, to Miss Pulteney in the nursery," and if any further inspiration was necessary, may have inspired Pope to criticize Ambrose, among others, in his essay, "Martinus Scriblerus...or the Art of Sinking in Poetry" (1727). Pope scoffed that the verses were "little flams on Miss Carteret" and soon Pope's friend, poet and composer Henry Carey, joined in the fray. Carey, rumored author of the words and music of the British anthem "God Save the King," satirized Ambrose in the same book that included his popular song, "Sally in Our Alley," parodying Philips's juvenile poems and writing: "So the nurses get by heart Namby-Pamby's little verses." The author of *Chrononhotonthologos*, a burlesque which he characterized as "the Most Tragical Tragedy that was ever Tragedized by any Company of Tragedians," even entitled his parody of Philips *Namby Pamby*, taking the *amby* in each word from the diminutive of *Am*brose and the alliterative *p* in the last word from *P*hilips. Pope, ready for the kill, seized upon the contemptuous nickname and included it in the edition of his enormously popular poem "The Dunciad" that appeared in 1733. The phrase immediately caught the public fancy and, much to his distress, Ambrose Philips saw his name, in the form of namby-pamby, come to mean not only feeble, insipidly sentimental writing, but a wishy-washy, weakly indecisive person as well.

∇ ∇ ∇

Katherine Philips (1631–1664)

The Matchless Orinda, as she was called (she used the pen name Orinda), is said to have "read the Bible thorough" before she was four years old, and to have memorized all the sermons that she heard in church. Her early death from smallpox inspired elegies by both Cowley and Temple.

The poet founded one of England's first literary groups, "A society of friendship" that met at her home. Members called each other by fantastic names, Mrs. Philips being called "Orinda," her husband "Antenor" and Sir Charles Cotterel "Poliarchus." Her one book of poetry was entitled *Poems by the Incomparable Mrs. K.*

Peter Pindar (John Wolcot; 1738–1819)

The satirist, who wrote under the name Peter Pindar, was asked if he was a good subject of George III. "I do not know anything about that, madam," he said, "but I *do* know that the king has been a devilish good subject for me."

"You Gifford!" he cried, and with few preliminaries the physician and satirical poet began pummeling another author in a London bookstore. Only after he had been bruised and bloodied, knocked down and thrown out into a mud puddle, did "Peter Pindar" discover that he had challenged the wrong author—a John Gifford had insulted him and he attacked William Gifford.

His last words were: "Give me back my youth!"

∇ ∇ ∇

Sir Isaac Pitman (1813–1897)

The inventor of the first, simple phonetic shorthand, Pitman popularized his method in any way he could. The schoolteacher went as far as having his wife's tombstone engraved in Pitman shorthand:

> In memori ov
> MERI PITMAN,
>   Weif of Mr. Eizak Pitman,
>   Fonetik Printer, ov this Sit.
> Deid 19 Agust 1857 edjed 64
>   'Preper tu mit thei God'
>   —EMOS 4,12.

∇ ∇ ∇

Francis Place (1771–1854)

Place's *Illustrations and Proofs of Principle of Population* (1822) was the first major work to urge contraception as the best means to limit population. The author, who actively campaigned for birth control until the day he died, himself was the father of 15 children, five of them dying in childbirth.

∇ ∇ ∇

Alexander Pope (1688–1744)

The poet was only 4 feet 6 inches tall (or small). Author Colley Cibber, who was feuding with him, published a letter describing how a young nobleman had some fun with the little poet, a charge Pope never denied: "...his lordship's frolic proposed was, to slip his little Homer, as he called him, at a girl of the game...in which he so far succeeded that the smirking damsel, who served us with tea, happened to have charms sufficient to tempt the little-tiny manhood of Mr. Pope into the next room with her; at which, you may imagine, his lordship was in as much joy, at what might happen within, as our small friend could probably be in possession of it: but I...observing he had staid as long as without hazard of his health he might...threw open the door upon him, where I found this little hasty hero, like a terrible Tom Tit, pertly perching upon the mount of love! But such was my surprise that I fairly laid hold of his heels and actually drew him down safe from his danger." (Despite this letter, Pope later made Cibber a hero in the *Dunciad*.)

Pope, crippled and twisted from an early age, could be vicious in his verbal attacks on people and sometimes encountered people as vicious as he. Once he berated a young man for his abysmal ignorance and, with a sneer, finally asked him if he knew what an interrogation was. "Yes, sir," the young man replied. "A little crooked thing that asks questions."

Pope was by far the most popular poet of his day and his work, especially his translations of Homer, sold so well that he became the first English poet who made a living by his poetry alone.

Pope's famous "The Rape of the Lock" was based on a true incident involving a piece of hair. He wrote the mock-heroic poem when one Lord Petre snipped off a lock belonging to a Miss Arabella, which resulted in a quarrel between the two families. Ultimately the poet only made the feud worse.

Lord Halifax interrupted Pope several times while he was reading aloud his translation of the *Iliad*. "I beg your pardon, Mr. Pope," he said each time, "but there is something in that passage that does not quite please me. Be so good as to mark the place and consider it at your leisure. I'm sure you can give it a better turn." Pope returned sometime later and, acting on the advice of intimates of Halifax, said, "I hope you will find your objection to these passages removed, my Lord," and proceeded to read him the passages exactly as he had before. When he finished, Halifax exclaimed, "Aye, now they are perfectly right! Nothing can be better."

His *Dunciad* attacked so many writers that a group of them cornered its publisher and threatened to beat him if he printed any more copies. Other authors executed him in effigy, and relations of authors threatened his life. The little man felt so acutely in danger that he would not go for a walk without his great Dane and two pistols at his side.

His curvature of the spine grew so severe that he had to be laced up in a stiff canvas bodice each morning to enable him to stand erect. He offered several descriptions of himself. He was, he once said, "a lively little creature, with long legs and arms; a spider is no ill emblem of him; he has been taken at a distance for a small windmill."

> Lo, the poor Indian! whose untutored mind
> Sees God in clouds, or hears him in the wind;
> His soul proud sciences never taught to stray.
> For as the solar walk, or milky way;
> Yet simple nature to his hope has giv'n,
> Behind the cloud-topped hill, an humbler heav'n.

Pope's well-known words *Lo, the poor Indian* in the above lines from his *Essay on Criticism* (1711) inspired the now obsolete term *Lo,* for an American Indian. The word isn't recorded in this sense until 1871, but must be considerably older. "Is it longer a matter of astonishment," someone wrote in 1873, "that the *Lo's* are passing so rapidly from the face of the earth?"

"I am rich enough," Pope told Swift, "and can afford to give away a hundred pounds a year. I would not crawl upon the earth without doing good. I will enjoy the pleasure of what I give by giving it alive and seeing another enjoy it. When I die I should be ashamed to leave enough for a monument if a wanting friend was above ground."

As Pope lay on his deathbed, his doctor kept assuring him that his pulse was getting sturdier, his breathing easier, there was good color in his face, and so on, trying to cheer him. "Here I am," Pope said, "dying of a hundred good symptoms."

In an ironic end to an incredibly painful life, during which, as a friend put it, he suffered terrible headaches four days a week and was sick the remaining three, Pope died, in Johnson's words, "so placidly that the attendants did not discern the exact time of his expiration." (See also AMBROSE PHILIPS.)

∇ ∇ ∇

Richard Porson (1759–1808)

The distinguished classical scholar had a wit as sharp as his renowned memory. When a young colleague suggested that they collaborate on a book, Porson replied, "If we put in all I know and all you don't know, it will make a great work."

Porson was talking to Poet Laureate Robert Southey. "My work will be read when Shakespeare is forgotten," Southey said. "Yes, but not till them," Porson replied.

The classical scholar claimed that he could rhyme anything. When someone challenged him to make a rhyme of the three Latin gerund endings—*di, do, dum*—in the old Eton Latin grammar, he quickly came up with this couplet:

When Dido found Aeneas would not come
She mourned in silence, and was Di-do dum(b).

Gibbon's *Decline and Fall* was to Porson the greatest literary work of the century, but he felt it more than lacking in style. The critic once told a friend, "There could not be a better exercise for a schoolboy than to turn a page of it into English."

Porson was a great drinker—"Porson would drink ink rather than not drink at all," as the saying went—but he was rather indifferent about food. When poet Samuel Rogers invited him to dinner one time, he replied, "Thank you, no, I dined yesterday."

▽ ▽ ▽

(Helen) Beatrix Potter (1866–1943)
A lonely child, Helen Beatrix Potter kept a journal of more than half a million words written in an elaborate secret code that wasn't deciphered until 22 years after her death. A number of her 30 or so books, including her first *The Tale of Peter Rabbit*, began as letters to a young friend and were published at her own expense. So lonely and shy was the storyteller as a child that her only real friends were the rabbits, frogs, snails, mice, bats and tame hedgehog that she kept hidden in her nursery and that later became the basis for many of her animal characters.

Thousands of fictional characters have been based on real people, and thousands of animal fictional characters, such as Moby Dick, have been based on real-life animals. But Potter based an animal on a real human being. Johnny Town-Mouse, in her illustrated tale of the same name, is based on her friend Dr. George Parson; her description of Johnny Town-Mouse adopts Parson's facial features and even the long golf bag he used.

▽ ▽ ▽

J.B. (John Boynton) Priestley (1894–1984)
The prolific novelist, short story writer, playwright and Man of Letters was asked about Americn slang during a U.S. radio interview. "I know only two words of

American slang," he said "'swell' and 'lousy.' I think 'swell' is lousy, but 'lousy' is swell."

▽ ▽ ▽

Joseph Priestley (1733–1804)

After the great scientist and author hailed the French Revolution in 1791 a rabid mob burned down his house in their rampage through Birmingham. Priestley addressed an open letter to "My Late Townsmen and Neighbors," which read in part: "…You have destroyed the most truly valuable and useful apparatus of philosophical instruments…You have destroyed a library…which no money can repurchase except in a long course of time. But what I feel far more, you have destroyed manuscripts which have been the result of the laborious study of many years, and which I shall never be able to recompose; and this has been done to one who never did, or imagined you any harm…You are mistaken if you imagine that this conduct of yours has any tendency to serve your cause, or to prejudice ours…Should you destroy myself as well as my house, library, and apparatus, ten more persons, of equal or superior spirit and ability, would instantly spring up. If those ten were destroyed, a hundred would appear…In this business we are the sheep and you the wolves. We will persevere in our character, and hope you will change yours. At all events, we return you blessings for curses, and pray that you may soon return to that industry, and those sober manners, for which the inhabitants of Birmingham were formerly distinguished."

Three years later Priestley immigrated to America.

▽ ▽ ▽

Matthew Prior (1664–1721)

An extempore epitaph the poet wrote for himself went:

> Nobles and heralds, by your leave,
>   Here lies what once was Matthew
>   Prior;
>
> The son of Adam and of Eve;
>   Can Bourbon or Nassau claim
>   higher?

▽ ▽ ▽

William Prynne (1600–1669)

The Puritan pamphleteer criticized Charles I in his *Histriomastix* (1632), a work condemning stage plays, which the king and queen enjoyed. Prynne was sentenced by the inquisitorial court called the Star Chamber two years later to be imprisoned for life and have his ears cut off in the pillory. Archibishop William Laud prosecuted him and had his book burned publicly. Prynne continued to write while he was imprisoned in the Tower of London, where he was branded on the cheeks with the letters *S.L.* (Seditious Libeler). Despite everything, the author never lost his sense of humor—he claimed the branded letters stood for *Stigmata Laudis* (i.e., Laud). In 1640 his sentence was declared illegal and Prynne was released by Parliament. Four years later he was Laud's prosecutor when the archbishop was convicted of high treason and beheaded.

Aubrey tells us he was a learned man of "immense reading," which he accomplished by wearing "a long quilt cap, which came 2 or 3 inches at least, over his eyes, which served him as an Umbrella to defend his eyes from the light." All through the day as he read, his servant would bring him bread and ale "to refocillate his wasted spirits."

When he was allowed to take his seat in Parliament in 1660, he donned his very long, rusty sword and marched into the House. Says John Aubrey: "Sir William Waller marching behind him…Prynne's long sword ran between Sir William's short legs and threw him down, which caused laughter."

∇ ∇ ∇

Henry James Pye (1745–1813)
The constantly ridiculed Pye is still considered the worst of England's poet laureates; he wheedled his way into the office by writing insipid poems praising mad George III. One poem that Pye wrote in the monarch's honor was so filled with allusions to birds, or "feathered songsters," that it inspired Geroge Stevens to write the famous punning lines:

> When the Pye was opened
> the birds began to sing
> Wasn't that a dandy dish
> to set before the king.

∇ ∇ ∇ ∇ ∇ ∇ ∇ ∇ ∇

Sir Walter Alexander Raleigh (1861–1922)

A professor of English at Oxford and a prominent critic, Raleigh stood to the side at a garden party one afternoon in 1914 and watched the other guests. His observations were committed to posterity in his poem "Wishes of an Elderly Man":

> I wish I loved the Human Race;
> I wish I loved its silly face;
> I wish I liked the way it walks;
> I wish I liked the way it talks;
> And when I'm introduced to one
> I wish I thought *What Jolly Fun!*

∇ ∇ ∇

Sir Walter Raleigh (1552?–1618)

John Aubrey in *Brief Lives* tells of

> Sir Walter Raleigh, being invited to dinner with some great person...His son sat next to his father, and was very demure at least half of the dinner time. Then said he: "I, this morning, not having the fear of God before my eyes...went to a whore. I was very eager of her...and went to enjoy her, but she thrust me from her and vowed I should not, 'For your father lay with me but an hour ago.'" Sir Walt, being so strangely suprised...at so great a table, gives his son a damned blow over the face; his son, as rude as he was, would not strike his father, but strikes over the face of the gentleman that sat next to him, and said, "Box about, 'twill come to father anon."

The old story about Sir Walter throwing his plush coat over a puddle for Queen Elizabeth is probably not true. The poet and adventurer did marry Elizabeth Throckmorton, one of the queen's maids of honor. According to John Aubrey's *Brief Lives*, he first made love to this maid against a tree in the forest: "...fearful of her honor, and modest, she cried, 'Sweet Sir Walter, what do you me ask? Will you undo me? Nay, sweet Sir Walter! Sweet Sir Walter! Sir Walter! Sir Walter!' At last, as the danger and the pleasure at the same time grew higher, she cried in the ecstasy, 'Swisser Swatter! Swisser Swatter!"

It came to King James's attention that Raleigh had urged nobles close to Queen Elizabeth to keep the government in their hands after her death by setting up a commonwealth. The next time Raleigh's name was called for the presentment to the king, James remarked, "O my soule, mon, I have heard rawly of thee."

"Fain would I climb, yet fear I to fall," he is said to have written on a windowpane. Queen Elizabeth wrote underneath it: "If thy heart fails thee, climb not at all."

His *History of the World*, written with the help of several assistants during his long imprisonment for high treason, was selling very slowly, his bookseller told him, and he would lose money on it. According to the traditional story, he grew so angry at this that he cried: "The world does not understand it and they shall not have the second part," which he scooped up and threw into the fire.

His drinking companion Charles Chester, a bold, impertinent type who never shut up, was known to make "a noise like a drum in a room." One particularly noisy night in a tavern Sir Walter subdued him and sealed up his mouth with hard wax. It is said that this incident inspired Ben Jonson to pattern his jester in *Every Man out of his Humour* on Chester.

He introduced England to tobacco, which, when he first brought it back from the New World, sold for its weight in silver. Addicted to the weed himself, he took a pipe of tobacco just before he went to the scaffold, thus scandalizing some proper people.

Feeling the edge of the axe before his execution, he observed, "'Tis a sharp remedy, but a sure one for all ills." When asked which way he preferred to lay his head on the axe-man's block, he said: "So the heart be right, it is no matter which way the head lies."

This poem, written the night before his execution, was found in his Bible:

> Even such is time, which takes in trust
> Our youth, our joys, and all we have,
> And pays us but with age and dust,
> Who in the dark and silent grave,
> When we have wandered all our ways,
> Shuts up the story of our days.
> And from which earth, and grave, and dust,
> The Lord shall raise me up, I trust.

∇ ∇ ∇

Terence Rattigan (1911–1977)

Rattigan's play *In Praise of Love* (1973) is about a woman dying of leukemia whose husband tries to keep her illness a secret from her. Rattigan himself had been told he had leukemia 10 years before he wrote the play. He decided to live to the fullest the two or three years he thought he had left and went on a world cruise. When he got back to England, a year later, he was told that there had been a mistake and he didn't have leukemia at all.

Robert Recorde (1510?–1558)

Recorde's *Whetstone of Wit* (1557) introduced the mathematical equal (=) sign to the world. The plus (+) and minus (-) signs had been first used in Michael Stifel's *Arithmetica integra* (1544).

∇ ∇ ∇

Barnaby Rich (1542–1617)

"One of the great diseases of this age," Rich wrote in 1600, "is the multitude of books that doth so overcharge the world that it is not able to digest the abundance of idle matter that is every day hatched and brought into the world." This, however, did not stop the former army captain turned author from churning out more of his romances. His *Apolonius and Silla* was the basis for Shakespeare's *Twelfth Night*.

∇ ∇ ∇

Grant Richards (1872–1948)

The monocled, worldly Richards was a publisher who devoted his life to literature rather than making money from literature. He supported a great many authors, including Housman, Dreiser and Firbank, Dreiser rewarding him by basing his character Barfleur in *A Traveller at Forty* (1913) on the publisher. Twice-bankrupted, Richards was far from financially prudent and was so honest he is said to be the first publisher to quote unfavorable reviews in advertising his books. Richards' *Memories of a Misspent Youth* (1932) and *Author Hunting* (1934) recount his career. Wrote George Bernard Shaw to him about the last book: "You should have called your book *The Tragedy of a Publisher Who Allowed Himself to Fall in Love with Literature*."

∇ ∇ ∇

Samuel Richardson (1689–1761)

The first modern English novel of character, *Pamela, or Virtue Rewarded* (1740–41), by Samuel Richardson, was a great success with the public and sent into two editions even before it was reviewed. Part One had been published in November 1740, and as with Dickens's novels in a later age, extracts appeared in newspapers. Readers throughout England eagerly awaiting the novel's outcome were ecstatic to learn that the heroine triumphed at the end and that virtue had been rewarded. It is said that at Slough "the enraptured villagers rang the churchbells for joy." The same thing happened at Preston in Lancashire, where a maid explained to a woman who asked why the bells were ringing: "Why madam, poor Pamela's married at last; the news came down to us in the morning's paper." Richardson, whose *Pamela* became the model for epistolary novels, had, when he was a boy of 13, regularly written love letters for three young women who didn't know what to write to their lovers.

Richardson's *Pamela* was the first novel printed in America. A reprint of the English edition was published in 1774 by Benjamin Franklin, who, among his myriad "firsts," was the first printer-bookseller in Philadelphia. He also established Philadelphia's first circulating library.

"Length is my principal Disgust," Richardson used to say of his expansive novels, but in conversation he could be curt to suit his purposes. One time a stranger took him aside before a dinner party, saying, "I'm so happy to pay my respects to the author of *Sir Charles Grandison*, for at Paris and the Hague and, in fact, at every place I have visited it is much admired." Richardson said nothing, hoping to bring the subject up again at the dinner table, where more people would hear the compliment. "Sir," he said to the man as soon as all were seated, "I think you were saying something about *Sir Charles Grandison*?"

"No, sir," the man replied. "I do not remember ever to have Heard it mentioned."

In the 1720s the early 1730s Richardson suffered the deaths of his wife and not one but all of his six children to various causes. Though he married again and fathered four daughters, he always believed that the shock of these early tragedies was responsible for the nervous disorders and general malaise of his later years.

▽ ▽ ▽

Joseph Ritson (1752–1803)
The eccentric scholar and lawyer was an irritable but thorough-going man who in his books successfully challenged the authenticity of many accepted works of his day. Ritson, who died insane, was also a fanatical vegetarian, so much so that he would hire only a vegetarian printer to print his book *An Essay on Abstinence from Animal Food as a Moral Duty* (1802).

▽ ▽ ▽

Sir Boyle Roche (1743–1807)
Coleridge defined the "Irish bull" as a "mental juxtaposition of incongruous ideas, with the sensation, but not the sense, of connection." Irish bulls are said to be named for one Obadiah Bull, an Irish solicitor in London, but their foremost practitioner was Sir Boyle Roche, a Dublin politician of whom it was first said, "Every time he opens his mouth he puts his foot in it." Among the many bulls attributed to him are: "Half the lies our opponents tell about us aren't true." "This

piece is chock full of omissions." "A man cannot be two places at the same time, unless he is a bird."

∇ ∇ ∇

Earl of Rochester (John Wilmot, Second Earl of Rochester; 1647–1680)

Rochester "blazed out his youth and health in lavish voluptuousness," as Dr. Johnson said, but the poet certainly led a romantic, adventurous life. When he was only 18 he abducted the beautiful heiress Elizabeth Malet in a coach and six and convinced her to marry him; his many mistresses included famed actress Elizabeth Barry; and he was as renowned for his wit and scurrilous lampoons as he was for his brilliant poems. When John Dryden dedicated a play to Rochester's enemy Lord Mulgrave in 1657, Rochester hired a band of thugs to beat Dryden in Covent Garden; rather than feeling any shame for the brutal attack, he later quipped in a poem, "Who'd be a wit in Dryden's cudgelled skin?" His own acid wit was displayed again when playwright Samuel Pordage left a copy of his rhymed tragedy *Herod and Mariamme* at his house, hoping that Rochester, whom he did not know, would back it. A week later Pordage went to collect the play and found that Rochester had written on the cover:

> Poet, who'er thou art, God damn thee,
> Go hang thyself, and burn they Mariamme

Rochester, a brilliant man who had received his master's degree at Oxford when only 14 years old, was a natural mimic who disguised himself as a beggar and fooled his friends. Once he posed as a German physician and treated hundreds of patients, even curing some, without any of the ladies and gentlemen of the court recognizing him.

He was a poet of genius but a notorious libertine known as one of the most licentious men in Charles II's dissolute court. The English poet Edmund Waller reported this converation between Rochester and his king:

> King Charles: I believe the English are the most untractable people upon earth.
> Rochester: I most humbly beg your majesty's pardon, if I presume in that respect.
> King Charles: You will find them so were you in my place, and obliged to govern.
> Rochester: Were I in your majesty's place, I would not govern at all.
> King Charles: How then?
> Rochester: I would send for my good lord Rochester, and command him to govern.
> King Charles: But the singular modesty of that nobleman—
> Rochester: He would certainly conform himself to your majesty's bright example. How gloriously would the two grand social virtues flourish under his auspices!
> King Charles: What can these be?
> Rochester: The love of wine and women!
> King Charles: God bless your majesty!

Many critics ridiculed the versified Psalms of the joint authors Thomas Sternhold and John Hopkins, but none so effectively as Lord Rochester, who circulated the epigram "Spoken Extempore to a County Clerk after Having Heard Him Sing Psalms":

> Sternhold and Hopkins had great qualms
> When they translated David's psalms
>   To make the heart full glad;
> But had it been poor David's fate
> To hear thee sing, and then translate,
>   By God! 'twould have made him mad.

Madam Cresswell, a notorious brothel owner in London, left £10 in her will for a funeral sermon in which nothing derogatory could be said of her. Wilmot is said to have written the brief sermon, which went: "All I can say of her is this—she was born *well*, she married *well*, and died *well*; for she was born at Shad-well, married to Cress-well, lived at Clerken-well, and died in Bride-well."

Rochester wrote the famous mock epitaph on Charles II:

> Here lies our sovereign lord, the king
>   Whose promise none relies on;
> He never said a foolish thing,
>   And never did a wise one.

But Charles once again got the best of his advisor.

"This is very true," he said upon reflection, "for my words are my own and my actions are my minister's."

He believed that city life cursed him. Aubrey tells us that "He was wont to say that when he come to Brentford the Devill entered into him and never left him till he came into the Country again."

It is hard to say whether liquor or lechery or a combination of both sent an impoverished Rochester to an early grave at the age of 33. Probably drink did the most damage. He once boasted that he had been continuously drunk for *five years*.

∇ ∇ ∇

Samuel Rogers (1763–1855)

The poet, son of a rich banker and a banker himself for a short time, was known as a literary dictator in England for many years and noted for the breakfasts and dinners he held at his magnificently decorated St. James Place house. But a benevolent dictator he was, with "a genius for charity." Rogers gave financial help to Moore, Sheridan, Wordsworth and many others over his long life, asking no recognition and even refusing the poet laureateship when he was offered it upon the death of Wordsworth. He was, however, a great conversationalist noted for his sarcastic and bitter wit; actress Fanny Kemble said, "He had the kindest heart and unkindest tongue of anyone I ever knew." Rogers excused this fault in himself this say: "They tell me I say ill-natured things. I have a weak voice; if I did not say ill-natured things, no one would hear what I say."

At one of his literary dinners Rogers had candles placed above and below the paintings on the walls to best display his excellent art collection. Rogers asked the wit Sydney Smith how he liked this arrangement. "Not at all," Smith said. "Above there is a blaze of light, and below, nothing but darkness and gnashing of teeth."

Thomas Carlyle's wife, Jane, the original of Leigh Hunt's "Jenny Kissed Me," was as good a conversationalist as her husband and usually promptly picked up where he left off. This happened after Carlyle had gone on interminably at one of Rogers's literary breakfast parties, and the host said half under his breath, but intentionally loud enought to be heard, "As soon as that man's tongue stops, that woman's begins!"

Rogers tells in his *Table Talk* of a surgeon named Humphrey Howarth who appeared at a duel stark naked, explaining that he didn't want an infection from his clothing to set in if he was hit by a bullet. The sight of him so upset his opponent that he refused to fight.

Not long after Rogers's famous poem "Pleasures of Memory" (1792) was published, a friend approached him at a party and told him, "Lady X is dying to be introduced to the author of the 'Pleasures of Memory.'"

"Pray let her live," Rogers said, making his way toward the lady.

"Mr. Rogers, madam, author of the 'Pleasures of Memory,'" his friend said, introducing him.

"Pleasures of what?" the woman asked.

∇ ∇ ∇

Robert Ross (1869–1918)

Remembered today as one of Oscar Wilde's two or three loyal friends, who never deserted him, Robby Ross was never rewarded for his loyalty. His was a short, stormy life filled with trouble. Toward the end of his days, he was asked what he would have as the words on his gravestone and Ross, quickly adapting Keats's famous epitaph, replied, "Here lies one whose name is writ in hot water."

▽ ▽ ▽

Dante Gabriel Rossetti (1828–1882)

The painter and poet was no slouch as a salesman. Once, after finishing a painting, he asked a friend to accompany him to the zoo.

"Why the zoo?" asked his friend.

"I want to hire an elephant to wash my windows," Rossetti explained.

"That's ridiculous!" his friend said.

"Of course," Rossetti agreed, "but it *sells*. You see, when people observe such a spectacle in front of my house, they gather in great numbers and many come into my house and buy pictures."

The snark never was until Lewis Carroll created it in his mock-heroic nonsense poem "the Hunting of the Snark" (1876). Its name a portmanteau word formed from *snake* and *shark*, the snark was an elusive creature, and just when its hunters thought they had tracked it down they found that their quarry was the very dangerous *Boojum* (another word Carroll coined). *Snarkhunter* has since been applied to dreamers and visionaries. Rossetti always believed that Carroll was caricaturing him in "The Hunting of the Snark," but this wasn't the case. Rossetti's morals had been viciously attacked by the poet Robert Buchanan in an article in the *Contemporary Review* called "The Fleshly School of Poetry." Published in October 1871 under the pseudonym Thomas Maitland, the article accused Rossetti, Swinburne, William Morris and several others of being decadent, morally irresponsible and obsessed with the sensual and carnal. The piece created great controversy. Swinburne replied at length to the charges in his *Under the Microscope* (1872), and Rossetti, who got the brunt of the criticism, never really recovered from it. His tendency toward gloomy brooding increased, he avoided people, overused narcotics and became paranoid enough for friends to fear for his sanity. Rossetti had many more delusions like the one about the snark until his death in 1882 at age 54.

James Whistler liked a picture Rossetti seemed unable to finish. "You've done nothing at all to it since I saw it last, have you?" he finally complained one day.

"No," said Rossetti, "but I've written a stunning sonnet on the subject."

"Then take out the picture and frame the sonnet," an exasperated Whistler replied.

It is said that Rossetti practiced his poetic craft by playing the versifying game *bouts-rimes* ("rhymes without lines"), in which lines are composed for certain given rhymes. He could write a sonnet from such rhymes in five to eight minutes.

While his wife, Elizabeth, was dying of tuberculosis, Rossetti had been unfaithful to her and he felt great remorse for this the rest of his life. When the beautiful Elizabeth died of an overdose of laudanum in 1862, only two years after their marriage, the painter buried with her the little book in which he had handwritten all his poems, placing the volume close to her lips and wrapping it with her long golden hair. There the poems were meant to stay, for as Rossetti had said to his dead wife at graveside, speaking as though she could hear him, the poems had either been written to her or for her. Yet after seven years Rossetti regretted having renounced poetry and wanted back the only perfect copy of the poems he thought were the most beautiful he could ever write. Finally obtaining official permission, the poet had his wife's grave in Highgate Cemetery opened one night and in the light of a great fire built by the side of the grave (to prevent infection) the buried poems were taken from the coffin, drenched with disinfectants, and dried leaf by leaf. Rossetti noticed that his wife's golden hair had continued to grow after death, filling the coffin, and the scene so unnerved him that despite the fact that he wrote about it in his sonnet "Life in Love," he left instructions in his will that he be cremated and not buried beside Elizabeth. A year after their disinterment, in 1870, Rossetti's *Poems* were published to excellent reviews and became a living monument to his wife.

On the verge of insanity in his last years, Rossetti preferred the company of wild aniamls to that of people. The poet's house pets included an opossum that slept on the dining-room table, a raccoon that made its home in his dresser drawer, an armadillo that once gnawed its way into a neighbor's house, a peacock that died under a sofa, woodchucks, owls, a raven, a zebra and a donkey.

▽ ▽ ▽

Nicholas Rowe (1674–1718)

The playwright, poet laureate and author of what he called "she-tragedies," early in his career was introduced to the earl of Oxford, who asked him if he spoke Spanish. No, but he could learn it in a short time, Rowe replied, thinking Oxford had him in mind for foreign employment. Rowe spent six or seven months learning the language and then went back to Oxford to tell him that he spoke it fairly well now. "Well, then," his lordship told him, "now you'll have the pleasure of reading *Don Quixote* in the original, and 'tis the finest book in the world."

He sat in the theater laughing throughout the premiere of his first comedy, *The Biter* (1704), but no one else in the audience uttered a single laugh all evening. He never again wrote a comedy.

▽ ▽ ▽

John Ruskin (1819–1900)

When John Ruskin condemned several of James McNeill Whistler's paintings in 1877, Whistler brought a libel suit against the critic, and the case became a *cause célèbre* of the 19th century. Ruskin had particularly disliked Whistler's *The Falling Rocket, a Nocturne in Black and Gold*, on which the artist put a 200-guinea price tag. "I have seen, and heard, much of cockney impudence before now," he wrote, "but never expected to hear a coxcomb ask two hundred guineas for flinging a pot of paint in the public's face."

During the trial Whistler was cross-examined by the attorney general.

"Now, Mr. Whistler. Can you tell me how long it took you to knock off that nocturne?"

"I beg your pardon?" (Laughter)

"Oh! I am afraid that I am using a term that applies rather perhaps to my own work. I should have said: How long did it take you to paint that picture?"

"Oh, no! I am too greatly flattered to think that you apply, to work of mine, any term that you are in the habit of using with reference to your own. Let us say then how long did I take to—'knock off,' I think that is it—to knock off that nocturne; well, as well as I remember, about a day."

"Only a day?"

"Well, I won't be quite positive; I may have still put a few more touches to it the next day if the painting were not dry. I had better say then, that I was two days at work on it."

"Oh, two days! The labour of two days, then, is that for which you ask two hundred guineas?"

"No, I ask it for the knowledge of a lifetime." (Applause)

Though Whistler won his case, he was awarded only the derisory damages of one farthing. Ruskin, who had said he would never write another line if he lost, continued writing.

Ruskin's marriage to Euphemia (Effie) Chalmers Gray was an arranged one that brought no happiness to either partner. According to one biographer, "Ruskin was so appalled at the sight of her pubic hair that he was unable to bring himself to have relations with her." The unconsummated marriage lasted six years, until 1854, when Effie obtained a nullification of the marriage under Scots law and Ruskin returned to his parents, with whom he resided until their death.

Bertrand Russell (1872–1970)

In the philosopher's worst nightmare a worker combed the shelves of a great central library, examining each book and either placing it back on the shelves for posterity or dumping it in a huge trash basket he carried. Finally, the worker came upon the world's last surviving copy of Russell's masterwork *Principia Mathematica* (written with Alfred North Whitehead), took it down, turned a few pages, seemed puzzled, closed the volume, and for an interminably long time held it in his hands between the shelf and the trash basket...Here the dream ended.

He told of a woman asked about the state of her recently deceased daughter's soul. "Oh, well," the woman replied, "I suppose she is enjoying eternal bliss, but I wish you wouldn't talk about such unpleasant subjects."

Would you be prepared to die for your beliefs, Russell was asked one time. "Of course not," he said. "After all, I may be wrong."

Though he lived just two years short of a century, Russell read his own obituaries in 1936, when he fell seriously ill in China and journalists there reported him dead. Read one missionary journal's obituary brought to his attention: "Missionaries may be pardoned for heaving a sign of relief at the news of Mr. Bertrand Russell's death." Russell of course went on to live 35 more fruitful years and won the Nobel Prize for literature in 1950. (See also ROBERT GRAVES.)

∇ ∇ ∇ ∇ ∇ ∇ ∇ ∇ ∇

Rafael Sabatini (1875–1950)

The famous words "born with the gift of laughter and a sense that the world was mad" became famous not because they are from Shakespeare, Milton or any of the great classical writers of antiquity, but because they were inscribed as a hoax over a door in the Hall of Graduate Studies at Yale University. The line is from the first sentence of contemporary Italian-born English novelist Rafael Sabatini's rousing adventure story *Scaramouche*, and the full quote, referring to the hero, is "He was born with the gift of laughter and the sense that the world was made, and that was his only patrimony." The words apparently were written on Yale's hallowed walls as the result of a hoax. At least the building's architect, John Donald Tuttle, confessed in a letter to the *New Yorker* (December 8, 1934) that collegiate Gothic repelled him. It is, he wrote, "a type of architecture that has been designed expressly...to enable yeomen to pour molten lead through slots on their enemies below. As a propitiatory gift to my gods...and to make them forget by appealing to their sense of humor, I carved the inscription over the door." Yale authorities apparently didn't enjoy the joke. After employing medievalists, classical scholars and Egyptologists to find the source of the quotation, only to learn it was from a mere adventure novelist, they planted the ivy that hides the words today.

∇ ∇ ∇

Henry Sacheverell (c. 1674–1724)
Not many preachers or writers have been put down as properly as Dr. Sacheverell. "Famous for blowing the coals of dissention," as one biographer put it, the English clergyman had both "the blower of a stove" and a chamber pot named after him. The naming was undoubtedly done by Whigs, whom Sacheverell had violently attacked in 1709 in two sermons, especially lashing out against the government's toleration of dissenters. Charged with seditious libel, the fervent Tory was suspended from preaching for three years. But his trial brought about the downfall of the Whigs and he was rewarded with the important rectory of St. Andrew's immediately after his suspension expired.

∇ ∇ ∇

Thomas Sackville (First Earl of Dorset; 1536–1608)
The poet and statesman's father was so rich that he was called Sir Richard Fillsack. Lord high treasurer of England, the earl died while presenting evidence at the trial of another prominent nobleman. Pulling the incriminating documents out from under his coat with a flourish, he explained, "Here is that will strike you dead!" With these words he himself "fell downe starke dead."

∇ ∇ ∇

Saki (Hector Hugh Munro; 1870–1916)
It is often noted that the author's short stories depict an inordinate number of wild animals as fierce "agents of revenge upon mankind." There may well be a reason for this. In 1793 the son of Saki's ancestor Sir Hector Munro was killed by a tiger in India, where Saki was born and later served in the British military police. The writer must have known the story well, down to the finest details, as it appeared in the July *Gentleman's Magazine* of that year. Wrote the hunter who accompanied young Munro:

The beast was about four and a half feet high, and nine long. His head appeared as large as an ox's, his eyes darting fire...Mr. Downey and myself immediately jumped up to take our guns; mine was the nearest, and I had just laid hold of it when I heard a roar, like thunder, and saw the immense tiger spring on the unfortunate Munro, who was sitting down. In a moment his head was in the beast's mouth, and he rushed into the jungle with him, with as much ease as I could lift a kitten, tearing through the thickest bushes and trees, everything yielding to his monstrous strength. The agonies of horror, regret, and, I must say, fear (for there were other tigers, male and female) rushed on me at once. The only effort I could make was to fire at him, though the poor youth was still in his mouth. I relied partly on Providence, partly on my aim, and fired a musket. I saw the tiger stagger and agitated, and cried out so immediately. Mr. Downey then fired two shots and I one more. We retired from the jungle, and, a few minutes after, Mr. Munro came up to us, all over blood, and fell. We took him on our backs to the boat, and got every medical assistance for him from the *Valentine* East India Main, which lay at anchor near the Island, but in vain. He lived twenty four hours in the extreme torture; his head and skull were torn and broke to pieces, and he was wounded by the claws all over the neck and shoulders; but it was better to take him away, though irrecoverable, then leave him to be devoured limb by limb...

Saki disliked George Bernard Shaw's egotism. "Bernard Shaw discovered himself," he once remarked, "and gave ungrudgingly of his discovery to the world."

The author's last words were to a soldier who had lit up in the trenches in World War I. "Put that bloody cigarette out!" Munro ordered, rising to full height, and at that instant a German sniper's bullet snuffed his life out.

∇ ∇ ∇

Richard Savage (c. 1697–1743)
In his *Life of Mr. Richard Savage*, Dr. Johnson described the last days of the author, who claimed to be a descendant of nobility. Savage, once pardoned of a murder conviction, lived in poverty all his life.

The symptoms grew every day more formidable, but his condition did not enable him to procure any assistance. The last time that the keeper saw him was on July the 31st, 1743, when Savage, seeing him at his bedside, said, with an uncommon earnestness, "I have something to say to you, Sir"; but, after a pause, moved his head in a melancholy manner, and, finding himself unable to recollect what he was going to communicate, said, "Tis gone!" The keeper soon after left him; and the next morning he died. He was buried in the churchyard of St. Peter, at the expense of the keeper.

Such were the life and death of Richard Savage, a man equally distinguished by his virtues and vices; and at once remarkable for his weaknesses and abilities...

Those are no proper judges of his conduct who have slumbered away their time on the down of plenty, nor will any wise man presume to say, "Had I been in Savage's condition, I should have lived or written better than Savage."

Sir Walter Scott (1771–1832)

Scott, a good and honorable man if ever there was one, wrote himself to death after assuming a staggering £130,000 bankruptcy debt (millions today) as his personal responsibility. In his diary he wrote: "I am become a sort of writing automaton, and truly the joints of my knees, especially the left, are so stiff and painful in rising and sitting down, that I can hardly help screaming—I that was so robust and active...My head, too, is bothered with rheumatic headaches..." In another entry he observed that "my fingers begin to stammer—that is, to write one word instead of another very often."

Said Sir Walter when he was trying to work off his enormous debts and was close to death from his literary labors: "If there is a mental drudgery which lowers the spirits and lacerates the nerves, like the toil of a slave, it is that which is exacted by literary composition, when the heart is not in unison with the work upon which the head is employed. Add to the unhappy author's task sickness, sorrow or the pressure of unfavorable circumstances and the labor of the bondsman becomes light in comparison."

When only a year and a half old he was stricken with polio, which left his left leg permanently lame. He was, however, luckier than six of his 11 brothers and sisters, who died in infancy.

"I have the greatest contempt for Aristotle," said Wordsworth to Scott.
"But not, I take it," observed the novelist, "that contempt which familiarity breeds."

"Them are fine novels of yours; they are invaluable to me," Scott's faithful servant told him. The novelist smiled, very pleased—until Tom finished: "Yes, when I come home very tired, and take up one of them I'm asleep directly."

He wrote so much and so often that he required a massive desk with two desktops. With these two surfaces to write upon he could keep two projects going at a time.

Sir Walter and his wife walked through a field filled with frolicking lambs. "Ah, delightful, it's no wonder that poets from the earliest times have made lambs symbols of peace and innocence," said Scott. "Delightful creatures indeed," agreed Lacy Scott, "especially with mint sauce."

He turned out his enormous body of work with the help of at least five pen names, including: Jebediah Cleisbotham, Crystal Croftangry, Malachi Malagrowther, Lawrence Templeton, and Captain Clutterbuck.

Scott told the following story:

> One morning last spring I opened a huge lump of a dispatch...the contents proved to be a MS play by a young lady of New York who kindly requested me to read and correct it, equip it with prologue and epilogue, procure for it a favorable reception from the manager of Drury Lane and make Murray or Constable bleed handsomely for the copyright; and inspecting the cover I found that I had been charged five pounds for the postage! This was bad enough—but there was no help, so I groaned and submitted. A fortnight or so after, another packet, of not less formidable bulk arrived, and I was absent enough to break its seal too without examination.
>
> Conceive my horror when out jumped the same identical tragedy of "The Cherokee Lovers," with a second epistle from the authoress, stating that, as the winds had been boisterous, she feared the vessel entrusted with her former communication might have foundered, and therefore had judged it prudent to forward a duplicate.

Verses from his *Lady of the Lake*, including "Hail to the Chief who in triumph advances!" were put to music by James Sanderson (1769–1841) and became the march traditionally played to honor the president of the United States.

He wrote in his journal for December 11, 1826: "The block-heads talk of my being like Shakespeare—not fit to tie his brogues."

His *The Talisman*, a novel about the Crusaders, painted such a flattering picture of Saladin that it turned some Englishmen away from orthodoxy. What first shook your Christian faith, George Eliot was once asked. "Walter Scott," she replied.

∇ ∇ ∇

John Duns Scotus (1266?–1308?)

Ironically, one of the most brilliant scholars and philosophers of the Middle Ages is the source for the word dunce. Little is known about John Duns Scotus outside of his new theology. He was probably born in 1266 in Scotland, most likely died while still a young man, aged 42 or so, and his middle name is presumably a place name, either from the village of Duns, Scotland; Dunse in Berwickshire; or Dunston in Northumberland. The Subtle Doctor, as he was called, apparently taught at Oxford and the University of Paris, but again there is no hard evidence available. Duns Scotus did found a school of philosophy that attracted numerous followers. A Franciscan, he successfully opposed the teachings of St. Thomas Aquinas and the Dominicans. He challenged the harmony of faith and reason and insisted on the doctrine of the Immaculate Conception, for which he was known as the Marian Doctor. After his death—tradition has it that he died in Cologne, where he was buried alive—Duns Scotus remained a great influence on scholastic thought. His works were studied in all the great universities throughout Europe and his followers, called Scotists, reigned supreme. However, these same Dunsmen sabotaged his reputation some 200 years later. During the Renaissance, blindly resistant to change, "the old barking curs," the Dunsmen, raged from the pulpit against the new learning and were scorned and ridiculed as hair splitters and stupid obstructionists. *Dunsmen* became *dunses* and finally *dunces*, "blockheads incapable of learning or scholarship." Exactly the opposite of the precise, learned mind of the man who started it all.

∇ ∇ ∇

Sir Charles Sedley (c. 1639–1701)

The profligate wit, dramatist and great patron of literature, a friend of Dryden and Rochester, learned that James II had seduced his daughter Catherine and then made her countess of Dorchester. Sedley remarked that he hated ingratitude: Since the king had made his daughter a countess, he would endeavor to make the king's daughter a queen.

∇ ∇ ∇

John Robert Seeley (1834–1895)

Seeley succeeded Charles Kingsley as Cambridge professor of modern history in 1869 and served there with great distinction until his death. The historian's inaugural lecture, however, was, to say the least, disappointing. After hearing it, the master of Trinity College remarked, "I did not think we could so soon have had occasion to regret poor Kingsley."

∇ ∇ ∇

John Selden (1584–1654)

"*Quod Seldenus nescit nemo scit*" ("What Selden doesn't know, nobody knows") was said of the historian and antiquary. The witty Selden was asked why he attended the Westminster Assembly as a lay delegate. "To see wild asses fight," he replied.

∇ ∇ ∇

George Selwyn (1719–1791)

The wit was listening to African traveler James Bruce tell of his visit to Abyssinia, which Bruce had detailed in his *Travels to Discover the Source of the Nile* (1790). Bruce's travels, though they have since been authenticated, were widely disbelieved at the time. After his talk one of the dinner guests asked him if any musical instruments were used in Abyssinia. "I think I saw one *lyre* there," Bruce replied. "Yes," Selwyn whispered to the man at his side, "and there is one less since he left the country."

Selwyn, "the first of the fashionable wits" and a member of England's notorious Hellfire Club, was told that a father, son and grandson all had had the same mistress, passing her on from one generation to another. "There's nothing new under the sun," the man remarked. "Nor under the grandson," Selwyn added.

Selwyn was asked by politician Charles Fox if he had attended the hanging of a highwayman also named Charles Fox. "Oh, no, I never go to rehearsals," he drawled.

▽ ▽ ▽

Elkanah Settle (1648-1724)
A dramatic rival of Dryden in his early days, Settle switched so often from one political side to another that he was known as "Recanting Settle." He was appointed poet of the city of London in 1691, but for all his maneuvering, he "is chiefly remembered today for the elaborate bindings on the presentation copies of his poems." In his old age, when stage plays were forbidden, he helped make his living by keeping a booth at Bartholomew Fair where he presented what he called a "droll humor," playing the part of the dragon in his farce while wearing a green leather suit he designed.

▽ ▽ ▽

Thomas Shadwell (1642?-1692)
The poet laureate and dramatist is said to have died of an overdose of opium when about 50. Satirist Thomas Brown (q.v.), who had also lampooned Shadwell's enemy John Dryden, "eulogized" him with the following wit:

Tom writ, his readers still slept o'er his book;
For Tom took opium, and they opiates took.

▽ ▽ ▽

William Shakespeare (1564-1616)
Little is really known about the personal life of the greatest English poet and dramatist. Shakespeare was born in 1564 at Stratford-on-Avon of substantial, middle-class parents—his father was an alderman—and received a solid grammar school education, well above the standards for the time. There is evidence that the Sweet Swan of Avon, as Ben Jonson called him, left Stratford for London to avoid a charge of poaching. He probably acted in the earl of Leicester's company and by 1592 had achieved fame as a dramatist and actor. By this time Shakespeare had acquired property and lived like a gentleman with his wife, Anne Hathaway, whom he had married 10 years previously, and with their

children, Susanna and the twins Hammet and Judith. Shakespeare was one of the few writers in his day to win fame and wealth. The Bard of Avon died on his own birthday in 1616, aged 52, in Stratford, where he had retired five years before. Countless stories and speculations surround the dramatist's life, ranging from the spelling of his name to the alleged infidelity of his wife, the identity of the dark lady of the sonnets, and the fantastic theory that Bacon actually wrote his plays. Most of these are familiar but none has been proved. It is not even certain that Shakespeare wrote the famous epitaph on his gravestone at Holy Trinity Church in Stratford: GOOD FRIENDS FOR IESUS SAKE FOR-BEARE/TO DIGG TI IE DUST ENCLOSED HERE!/BLESTE BE YE MAN THAT SPARES THES STONES,/AND CURST BE HE THAT MOUES MY BONES.

Shakespeare's plays and poems have appropriately evoked even more comment than his personal life. Thirty-seven plays in all have been attributed in whole or part to him, beginning possibly with *Love's Labour's Lost* in 1588 to *Henry VIII* in 1613. It would be impossible to even try to show in how many ways the 814,780 words in his plays or the 1,277 speaking characters he created have enriched English—the irrepressible Falstaff and all Shakespeare's characters come so alive in the dramas that they have stepped off the stage and into the language forever. Despite his "borrowings," his assimilative temperament and his "lack of education," the "myriad minded" Shakespeare remains "great above rule," "not for an age but for all time," "not England's poet but the world's."

No one really knows how Shakespeare spelled his name. The seven unquestionable genuine signatures are very difficult to decipher. The name is spelled Shakspeare on the Bard's own monument, but Shakespeare on the tombs of his wife and daughter. Other early variations are Shakspere and Shagspere (on his marriage license). In 1869 a Philadelphian named J.R. Wise published a book called *Autograph of William Shakespeare...together with 4000 ways of spelling the name*.

When Shakespeare was a child in Stratford in 1564 the black plague killed one out of seven of the town's 1,500 inhabitants.

"His father was a butcher," Aubrey tells us in *Brief Lives*, "and I have been told...by some of the neighbours, that when he was a boy he exercised his father's Trade, but when he kill'd a Calfe he would do it in a high style, and make a speech."

When Shakespeare was 15 a woman from a nearby village drowned in the Avon. Though her death was ruled accidental, it may have been a suicide. It seems likely that Shakespeare was familiar with the case and it probably influenced the title of his play *Hamlet* and the questions in it about whether Ophelia died accidentally or by her own hand.

According to legend, Shakespeare as a young man of 19 was prosecuted by Justice of the Peace Sir Thomas Lucy for deer poaching from Charlecotte Park. Lucy's family owned the village of Charlecotte and though the village did not have a deer park, it did have a warren that was a preserve for deer and other animals. Additionally, Lucy was well known as a preserver of game and had introduced into Parliament a bill for game preservation. According to the legend, told by Nicholas Rowe in 1710, but mentioned by Archdeacon Davies of Sapperton, Gloucestershire, who died in 1708, and others before him, Shakespeare aggravated his troubles with Lucy by writing a derogatory ballad about him. The trouble arising from the incident is important because it is said to have driven Shakespeare from Stratford to London, and the Bard is said to have caricatured Lucy later as Justice Shallow in the *Merry Wives of Windsor*, though many critics deny this. Nicholas Rowe, writing in 1709, gave the Lucy ballad, perhaps Shakespeare's first published poetry, as follows:

> A parliemente member, a justice of peace,
> At home a poor scare-crowe, at London an asse,
> If Lowsie is Lucy, as some Folke miscalle it,
> Then Lucy is lowsie whatever befall it:
> > He thinks himselfe greate,
> > Yet an asse in his state,
> We allowe by his ears but with asses to mate.
> > If Lucy is lowsie, as some Folke miscalle it,
> > Sing lowsie Lucy, whatever befall it.

The unsubstantiated tradition that Shakespeare was a poacher in his youth, which some scholars say is supported by evidence in his plays, is first recorded by one Richard Davies in about 1681, some 60 years after the Bard's death: "[Shakespeare was] much given to all unluckiness in stealing venison and rabbits, particularly from Sir [Thomas] Lucy, who had him oft whipped and sometimes imprisoned."

The Bard was known in his day as a very rapid writer. "His mind and hand went together," his publishers Heminges and Condell reported, "and what he thought, he uttered with that easiness that we have scarce received from him a blot in his papers." (Even if he should have blotted out a thousand lines, as his friend Ben Jonson quipped.)

Shakespeare was not the inspired uneducated writer he has often been made out to be. He possessed a large vocabulary for his day, having used 29,066 different words in his plays as compared to the 6,000 different words used in the entire Bible. Today the average English-speaking person uses something like 2,000 words in everyday speech.

It has been pointed out that one out of every 10 words Shakespeare uses in his plays and poems is used for the first time anywhere. A sample of his word inventions include aerial, auspicious, assassination, barefaced, bump, clangor, critic, countless, laughable, hurry, eventful and road.

According to some numerologists, Shakespeare wrote the Bible—or at least he helped write it. Their "evidence":

1. The King James Version of the Bible was published in 1610, when Shakespeare was 46.
2. *Shake* is the 46th word of the 46th *Psalm*.
3. *Spear* is the 46th word from the end in the 46th *Psalm*.

Not many anecdotes survive about Shakespeare and examples of his real-life wit are rare. Only one pun—and a rather poor one it is—has been attributed to him. Shakespeare seems to have been talking with Ben Jonson about what he would give Jonson's newborn son, Shakespeare's godson, for a present. "I' faith, Ben," he finally said, "I'll e'en give him a dozen of good latten spoons, and thou shalt translate them."

It is often forgotten that perhaps the greatest writer of all time could not make a living from writing. Shakespeare was paid no more than £8 apiece for his plays (which was the highest price any playwright got at the time), and since he wrote fewer than 40 plays, his income from writing during his 20 years in the theater was less than £20 a year. He was not unusual in this regard—Ben Jonson estimated that he made less than £200 from writing plays—but the Swan of Avon had to support himself as a working actor all his life. His income from all sources may have been the equivalent of about $50,000 a year after 1599, according to one biographer.

Despite all the praise of his genius, many famous writers have criticized the Bard in no uncertain terms:

- Playwright Robert Green, a contemporary of Shakespeare: "There is an upstart Crow, beautiful with our feathers, that with his *Tygers hart wrapt in a Players hyde*, supposes he is well able to bombast out a blanke verse as the best of you: and being an absolute *Johannes factotum* is in his owne conceit the onely Shake-scene in a countrey." (Greene parodied here a line from *Henry VI, Part 3*, "Oh Tiger's heart wrapt in a woman's hide.")

- Poet John Dryden: "[Shakespeare] writes in many places below the dullest writers of ours or any precedent age. Never did any author precipitate himself from such heights of thought to so low expressions...He is the very Janus of poets; he wears almost everywhere two faces; and you have scarce begun to admire the one ere you despise the other."
- Samuel Pepys hated many of Shakespeare's plays and called *A Midsummer Night's Dream* "the most insipid, ridiculous play that I ever saw in my life."
- John Dennis thought Shakespeare "utterly devoid of celestial fire."
- Pope sneered at the Bard when he wrote: "Shakespeare (whom you and every play-house bill/Style the divine, the matchless, what you will)."
- Addison failed to include Shakespeare in his *Account of the Greatest English Poets*.
- Hume considered Shakespeare "a disproportionate and misshapen giant."
- Byron sneered at: "One Shakespeare and his play so dating./Which many people pass for wits by quoting."
- Sardou called Hamlet an "empty wind-bag hero" and declared that there is "nothing good in the play...except the scene with the actors."
- Voltaire wrote: "Shakespeare is a drunken savage with some imagination whose plays can please only in London and Canada," and "Shakespeare is the Corneille of London, but everywhere else he is a great fool," elsewhere comparing him to "a mean or vicious ape."

"I hear a great deal, too, of Shakespeare, but I cannot read him," George II said of the Bard, "he is such a *bombast* fellow."

His contemporary Thomas Fuller (1608–61) compared the Bard and his friend Jonson: "Many were the wit-combats betwixt him and Ben Jonson, which two I behold like Spanish great gallion, and an English man of war: Master Jonson (like the former) was built far higher in learning; solid, but slow, in his performances. Shakespeare, with the English man of war, lesser in bulk, but lighter in sailing, could turn with all the tides, tack about, and take advantage of all winds, by the quickness of his wit and invention."

It has been pointed out recently that Shakespeare did *not* blunder, as is so often asserted, when he wrote of a seacoast in (landblocked) Bohemia. According to one biographer, "Under King Premysl Ottocar II (1258–78), the Kingdom of Bohemia stretched to the Adriatic Sea, and in 1526, upon the accession of the first

Hapsburg to the throne of Bohemia, the realm of the King of Bohemia comprised the Archduchy of Austria, which bordered the Adriatic between the territories of the Venetian Republic."

Not much is known about Shakespeare's Romeo and Juliet, but they were real lovers who lived in Verona, Italy, and died for each other in the year 1303. The Capulets and Montagues were among the inhabitants of the town at that time, and as in Shakespeare's play, Romeo and Juliet were victims of their parents' senseless rivalry. Their story was told in many versions before the Bard of Avon wrote of his "star-crossed lovers." The tale can be traced to Masuccio's *Novellino* (1476) and even before that to *Ephesiaca* by the pseudonymous third-or fourth-century writer Xenophon of Ephesus. Shakespeare found the tale in Arthur Brooke's poem "The Tragical Historye of Romeus and Juliet," containing "a rare example of love's constancie…" (1562).

When Mercutio is dying in *Romeo and Juliet*, Shakespeare has him say, "Look for me tomorrow and you will find me a *graveman.*" Shakespeare was a devoted punster. *Macbeth* contains at least 114 puns and *Shakespeare's Pronunciation* by Helge Kokeretz takes 89 pages to merely list the Bard's puns.

It was in Shakespeare's *Othello* on December 8, 1660, that the first woman appeared on the English stage. Prince Rupert's mistress Margaret Hughes played Desdemona that night at a new theater in Clare Market, London. Before that boys had always played women's parts and they kept doing so up until 1706.

In *Henry IV, Part 1* Shakespeare mentions a starling "taught to speak nothing but 'Mortimer.'" His sentence inspired a group of literary enthusiasts who wished to introduce all the birds in Shakespeare's plays to America. These bardologists brought a score of starlings across the Atlantic in 1890 and released them in Central Park in New York City. The starling has since become the most numerous of all American birds and a pest that preys on gardens—including the many public Shakespeare gardens in which are planted all the flowers and vegetables mentioned in Shakespeare's work.

With the passing of time there have been many variations, one more risqué than the other, on the old joke about Shakespeare, actor Richard Burbage, and their lady friend. The incident may or may not have occurred, but here is the original story from the diary of 17th-century English author John Manningham:

> Upon a time when Burbage played Richard the Third there was a citizen grew so far in liking him, that before she went from the play she appointed him to come that night unto her by the name of Richard the Third. Shakespeare, overhearing their

conversation, went before, was entertained and at his game ere Burbage came. Then, message being brought that Richard the Third was at the door, Shakespeare caused return to be made that William the Conquerer was before Richard the Third.

A nice but probably apocryphal story says that Queen Elizabeth tried to distract Shakespeare while he was playing the role of a king by dropping her handkerchief on the stage at his feet. Without missing a beat, Shakespeare turned to one of the play's courtiers and ordered him to "Take up our sister's handkerchief."

Shakespeare never made the Roman Catholic Church's *Index Librorum Prohibitorum* but several of his plays were censored or banned in other places. Queen Elizabeth disliked th scene where the king is deposed in *Richard II* and had it deleted from all copies of the play. From 1788 to 1820 *King Lear* was forbidden on the English stage, due to George III's apparent insanity. Thomas Bowdler (*q.v.*) bowdlerized Shakespeare, as Coleridge had suggested before him, and in recent times *The Merchant of Venice* has been banned on the grounds that Shylock is a vicious characterization of a Jew. Moreover, Shakespeare has often been revised to the point of bowdlerization over the centuries. Conspicuous among examples are Nahum Tate's rewrite giving *King Lear* a happy ending; the Honorable James Howard, Dryden's brother-in-law, rewriting *Romeo and Juliet* so that the young lovers are happily married; and Poet Laureate Sir William Davenant's jolly production of *Macbeth*, complete with dancing and singing.

Shakespeare left London in 1613 to settle in Stratford-on-Avon, where he died three years later. If we are to believe the diary of a Mr. Ward, the vicar of Stratford: "Shakespeare, [Michael] Drayton and Ben Jonson had a merry meeting, and, it seems, drank too hard, for Shakespeare died of a fever then contracted."

In a mock trial held in Washington, D.C., in 1987, three United States Supreme Court justices unanimously ruled that the works of William Shakespeare were written by William Shakespeare and no one else. The following year, at a mock trial in England, three Law Lords, the British equivalents of U.S. Supreme Court justices, came to the same conclusion.

∇ ∇ ∇

George Bernard Shaw (1856–1950)

Londoners first became aware of Shaw's name in a series of scurrilous interviews published in an evening newspaper. The interviewer claimed that he had forced his way into Shaw's apartment and browbeat and insulted him into talking. People couldn't understand why this Shaw put up with a boorish newspaper man, why didn't he bodily eject him or at least call the police, do *something*? No one could figure it out—until it was revealed that the "interviews" were written by none other than the formerly unknown Shaw himself.

A young Irish actress asked Shaw why he'd come to England instead of seeking his inspiration in Ireland, the land of his birth. "I could not stay there, dreaming my life away on the Irish hills," he explained. "England had conquered Ireland, so there was nothing for it to do but come over and conquer England. Which, you will notice, I have done rather thoroughly."

When Shaw and Fabian union organizer Annie Besant decided to marry, Mrs. Besant, an atheist, drew up a marriage contract to replace the traditional religious vows. But when she presented the long, tedious document to Shaw he began laughing hysterically and refused to sign it. "Good God!" he finally managed to say. "This is worse than all the vows exacted by all the churches on earth." The two never married.

Shaw was master of the outrageous remark designed to attract attention to himself. Perhaps his most outrageous was his famous comparison of himself and two or three literary immortals. "With the single exception of Homer," GBS said, "there is no eminent writer, not even Sir Walter Scott, whom I can despise so entirely as I despise Shakespeare, when I measure my mind against his."

Shaw belonged to the Writing-for-Posterity, or Anything-for-Art School. He once remarked: "The true artist will let his wife starve, his children go barefoot, his mother drudge for his living at seventy, sooner than work at anything but his art."

To H.G. Wells Shaw once wrote: "The longer I live the more I see that I am never wrong about anything, and that all the pains I have so humbly [!] taken to verify my notions have only wasted my time."

Shaw printed the following as his review of a play when he was drama critic for the *London Saturday Review*:

> I am in a somewhat foolish position concerning a play at the Opera Comique, whither I was bidden this day week. For some reason I was not supplied with a program; so that I never learned the name of the play. At the end of the second act the play had advanced about as far as an ordinary dramatist would have brought it five minutes after the first rising of the curtain; or say, as far as Ibsen would have brought it ten years before that event. Taking advantage of the second interval [intermission] to stroll out into the strand for a little exercise, I unfortunately forgot all about my business, and actually reached home before it occurred to me that I had not seen the end of the play. Under these circumstances, it would ill become me

to dogmatize on the merits of the work or its performance. I can only offer the management my apologies.

After switching occupations from critic to playwright, Shaw addressed a dinner of London critics. "I used to be a critic," he told them. "I still regard it as one of the professions I keep in reserve. I gave it up because the profession of playwright which I adopted is very much easier, very much more illustrious and much more attractively remunerative. You will notice I don't say it was better paid."

Though married, GBS carried on a passionate correspondence over the years with the actress Mrs. Patrick Campbell, a widow. Later in their lives Mrs. Campbell begged Shaw to let her publish 128 of his love letters to her. An indignant Shaw cabled her: "I will not, dear Stella, at my time of life, play the horse to your Lady Godiva."

For all his Shavian wit, the bearded Irishman could be bettered. The actress Cornelia Otis Skinner got the best of Shaw in the following exchange of telegrams after a revival of his *Candida*.

Shaw: Excellent. Greatest.

Skinner: Undeserving such praise.

Shaw: I meant the play.

Skinner: So did I.

One perhaps apocryphal story has it that Eleanora Duse wrote Shaw telling him that every eugenical principal cried that they should have a baby. "Think what a child it would be," she added, "with my body and your brain!"

Wrote Shaw in reply: "Think how unfortunate it would be if the child were to have my body and your brain."

Mrs. Shaw occasionally outdid the master.

"Isn't it true, dear, that male judgement is superior to female judgement?" Shaw once asked his wife.

"Of course, dear," she replied. "After all, you married me and I you."

When in 1935 a country parson wrote Shaw asking for his recipe for brewing coffee, at which Shaw excelled, the author obliged but replied saying that he hoped the man hadn't really written just to get his autograph. The parson wrote back thanking him for the recipe and enclosing the great man's signature, which he had neatly cut from Shaw's letter.

"People must not be forced to adopt me as their favourite author," he remarked to Alma Murray, "even for their own good."

Lady Randolph invited GBS to lunch and he wired back: "Certainly not; what have I done to provoke such an attack on my well known habits?"

The lady countered with another telegram: "Know nothing of your habits; hope they are not as bad as your manners."

The portly novelist G.K. Chesterton thought he had scored when he told the stringbean of a vegetarian, "Looking at you, Shaw, one would think there was a famine in England."

"Looking at you," Shaw replied, "one would think you caused it."

In a complete turnabout of the above anecdote, Shaw tells Chesterton, "If I were as fat as you I'd hang myself." Replies the corpulent Chesterton in his shrill little voice, "And if I had it in mind to hang myself, I'd use you as the rope."

Shaw received an invitation from a celebrity hunter that read, "Lady Blank will be home Thursday between four and six." He returned the card with the message, "Mr. Bernard Shaw likewise."

"Oh, Mr. Shaw, what made you ask me to dance?" said a dowager to GBS at a benefit affair.

"This is a charity ball, isn't it?" Shaw replied.

A visitor asked why Shaw kept no vases of flowers. "I thought you were so fond of flowers," he said.

"So I am," Shaw retorted. "I'm very fond of children, too. But I don't cut off their heads and stick them in pots all over the house."

Mrs. Pat Campbell got the starring role in Shaw's *Pygmalion* because all the reigning London actresses refused to say the taboo word "bloody" that the playwright put in the mouth of Eliza.

At various times Shaw used the pen names Redbarn Wash, G.B. Larking, Corno di Bassetto and Horatio Ribbonson. He even employed the riposte on his name originated by Oscar Wilde (*q.v.*), signing himself P-Shaw.

"Did you know that 'sumac' and 'sugar' are the only two words in English that begin with *su* and are pronouncd *shu*?" historian B.H. Liddell Hart said to Shaw.

"Sure," replied Shaw.

Shaw came across a book of his in a second-hand bookstore. The volume had been inscribed to a friend, beneath whose name GBS had written "With the compliments of George Bernard Shaw." Shaw bought the book and sent it back to his friend, writing under the original inscription: "With renewed compliments, G.B.S."

One opening night Shaw stepped forward on stage to accept the plaudits of the audience. Amid all the applause, however, a lone dissenter shouted out: "Shaw, your play stinks!" GBS hardly missed a beat after the brief silence that followed. "My friend," he said almost immediately, "I agree with you completely, but what are we two"—he gestured toward the audience—"against the great majority?"

Captain Shotower in Shaw's *Heartbreak House* (1917) was modeled on either Commander Charles Ashwell Boteler Pocock or Gordon Craig, both of whom led full and fascinating lives. Both of these possible prototypes refused on his deathbed, in Shaw's words, "to take the bread of Extreme Unction unless he could have some cheese with it."

When playwright St. John Ervine lost a leg in World War I, the outrageous Shaw wrote him, offering this strange consolation: "For a man of your profession two legs are an extravagance...The more the case is gone into the more it appears that you are an exceptionally happy and fortunate man, relieved of a limb to which you owed none of your fame, and which indeed was the cause of your conscription; for without it you would not have been accepted for service."

"Obscenity," he said in defending authors from censorship, "can be found in every book except the telephone directory."

Shaw did not like receiving manuscripts to read from aspiring authors and made it a policy to insult people who imposed upon him in this way. To a young man who sent him a long boring novel, he wrote: "The covers of your book are too far apart."

William Douglas Home asked Shaw if there was any sense for him aspiring to be a dramatist. "Go on writing plays, my boy," he advised. "One of these days a London producer will go into his office and say to his secretary, 'Is there a play from Shaw this morning?' and when she says, 'No,' he will say, 'Well, then we'll have to start on the rubbish.' And that's your chance, my boy."

A prodigious letter writer, Shaw probably holds the literary record for the most letters written in a lifetime— over 250,000.

When he left on a trip to Russia Shaw's wife asked Lady Astor to look after him. According to one biographer: "These instructions Nancy carried out faithfully, to the point of washing Shaw's beard personally, in the Metropole Hotel, Moscow, watched by the fascinated hotel staff."

Shaw could be outrageously, even weirdly, wrong, especially in matters political, as this excerpt from a 1936 letter he wrote to *The New Republic* shows: "I hold with Adolf Hitler, that our political democracy is a lie. Its 'waning' means presumably its being found out. The faster it 'wanes' in this sense the better I shall be pleased.

"There is no antithesis between authoritarian government and democracy. All government is authoritarian; and the more democratic a government is the more authoritarian it is; for with the people behind it it can push its authority farther than any Tsar or foreign despot dare do."

When Sylvia Beach's Shakespeare and Company brought out James Joyce's *Ulysses*, subscriptions were solicited from prominent literary figures. Shaw replied that the magazine serial fragments he had read of the novel were "a revolting record of a disgusting phase of civilization," adding that, anyway, no Irishman would pay 150 francs for a book. Yeats, for one, proved him wrong in this last regard; he subscribed immediately.

"You must not suppose," Shaw told a correspondent, "because I am a man of letters, that I never tried to earn an honest living."

Mrs. Patrick Campbell liked to taunt the vegetarian Shaw about his prowess as a lover. "Some day you'll eat a pork chop, Joey," she once told him, "and then God help all women."

Though a staunch vegetarian, Shaw refused an invitation to a testimonial where the bill of fare was strictly vegetarian. Said GBS: "The thought of two thousand people crunching celery at the same time horrifies me."

Friends told him that his vegetarianism would kill him and he replied that at least his funeral could be attended by a procession of all the animals he had never eaten. "And they will look better than most pallbearers I have seen," he added.

He was asked during the Great War to let his name be used as an example of vegetarianism in newspaper ads to help ease the meat shortage. Refusing, he explained: "There are millions of vegetarians in this world but only one Bernard Shaw. You do not obtain eminence quite so cheaply as by eating macaroni instead of mutton chops."

In an early edition of *Who's Who* GBS gave his hobbies as "cycling and showing off."

A shrewd literary negotiator, he was once overheard saying to a motion picture producer, "There's no use in our talking about it [anymore] because, obviously, you're a great artist and I'm just a businessman."

Sam Goldwyn telephoned Shaw, trying to drive down his price for the film rights to several of his plays. Argued Goldwyn: "Think of the millions of people who would get a chance to see your plays who would otherwise never see them. Think of the contribution it would be to art."

"The trouble is, Mr. Goldwyn," said Shaw, "that you think of nothing but Art and I think of nothing but money."

Producer Gabriel Pascal acquired the film rights to Shaw's plays after far richer men had failed. Pascal had made a successful film in London and then immigrated to Hollywood where he could get no work. Arriving back in London, he impulsively called on Shaw, whom he had never met, without an invitation, and told him he wanted to film his plays. "How much capital do you have?" Shaw asked him. "Fifteen shillings and sixpence—but I owe a pound," Pascal replied.

Delighted with Pascal's admiration, effrontery and wit, Shaw gave him a pound to pay his debts and signed a contract.

Shaw was standing alone in a corner at a cocktail party. "Are you enjoying yourself, Mr. Shaw?" his hostess anxiously asked him. "Certainly," he replied. "There is nothing else here to enjoy."

Wrote Shaw to Oswald Garrison Villard in 1921: "You are right in your impression that a number of people are urging me to come to the United States. But why on earth do you call them my friends?"

George Bernard Shaw despised the Eros fountain the sculptor Sir Alfred Gilbert had erected in London's Piccadilly Circus. Later Gilbert was charged with taking payment for another sculpture that he never even began. When the sculptor's friends came to the playwright seeking his support, an outraged Shaw refused to do anything except help Gilbert drown himself in the fountain he'd built.

When Shaw visited William Randolph Hearst's opulent, baroque estate at San Simeon, he turned to a companion and said: "This is probably the way God would have done it if He'd had the money."

Most newspaper editors howled in protest when Shaw criticized virtually all things American in a widely reported interview. But a Miami editor held his fire until the writer visited there. The editor's paper published a long article on *Mrs. Shaw's* activities during the visit, reporting that she ate lunch here, went to dinner there, atttended this party, said this, did that. At the tail end of the piece came the afterthought: "Accompanying Mrs. Shaw was her husband George Bernard, a writer."

The leader of a rather mediocre orchestra playing at a London restaurant recognized Shaw, then a music critic, and sent a note to his table asking him what he'd like the group to play next. "Dominoes," Shaw replied.

Few are the humans who have the wit or will to impose their own names on the language, but Shaw, no ordinary mortal, did just that. Shaw did not like the way "Shawian" sounded and so Latinized his name to Shavius and coined the word Shavian from it. Shavian, meaning characteristic of the work or style of George Bernard Shaw, soon bred the phrases Shavian wit or Shavian humor, referring to the dramatist's brilliant written or impromptu lines. Shaw, who began as a music reviewer and novelist, should be an inspiration to every fledgling author, for he earned exactly £6 in his first nine years of writing.

"I often quote myself," he assured a critic. "It adds spice to my conversations."

As he lay dying, Shaw turned and spoke to the attending nurse. "Sister," he said, "you're trying to keep me alive as an old curiosity, but I'm done, I'm finished, I'm going to die." These were his last words.

Shaw was cremated after he died. It was his wish that his ashes be mixed with those of his wife, Charlotte, and scattered over the garden they both loved so much at their home in Ayot St. Lawrence, England. As his wife died seven years before him, her ashes had to be saved in an urn seven years to make this possible.

GBS, who lived until the age of 94, once suggested the following epitaph for himself: I knew if I stayed around long enough, something like this would happen.

▽ ▽ ▽

Mary Wollstonecraft Shelley (1797–1851)

Before she wrote *Frankenstein* (1818), Mary Shelley was in the habit of staying up all night telling ghost stories with her husband Percy Bysshe Shelley and Lord Byron, the three inspired by the popular German ghost stories of the time. The stories could be spine-tingling. On one occasion her husband suddenly became hysterical and ran shrieking from the room.

After she died, the ashes of Shelley's heart were found in her copy of his "Adonais," an elegy on the death of Keats that ends with the prophetic words "my spirit's bark is driven/Far from the shore..."

∇ ∇ ∇

Percy Bysshe Shelley (1792–1822)

English author Edward Trelawny once left Shelley standing by the mantel in his study reading at 10 o'clock in the morning. When he returned that evening at six, he found the poet, who generally read 16 hours a day, in the same position, still reading without having moved an inch.

While at Oxford Shelley dabbled in chemistry experiments and his room was cluttered with scientific books and materials. One afternoon the future husband of the creator of Dr. Frankenstein nearly blew himself up.

His best friend, Thomas Jefferson Hogg, wrote that in consequence of Shelley's "almost incessant" insatiable reading far into the night, "he would often fall asleep in the daytime—dropping off in a moment—like an infant. He often quietly transferred himself from his chair to the floor, and slept soundly on the carpet, and in the winter upon the rug, basking in the warmth like a cat; and like a cat his little round head was roasted before a blazing fire..."

Shelley was expelled from Oxford in 1811 along with his friend Thomas Jefferson Hogg. Both had refused to answer any questions about a pamphlet called *The Necessity of Atheism*, which they had sent to the heads of the colleges and a number of bishops, among other prominent people. Shelley, who had at Eton been called "Mad Shelley" and "Shelley the Atheist," almost certainly wrote the pamphlet. He was expelled for "contumaciously refusing to answer questions" and for "repeatedly declining to disavow" authorship of the "little syllabus."

While living at Tanyrallt in Carnarvonshire, Wales, in 1813, Shelley was attacked on the night of February 26th by an assassin who fired three shots at him. The poet once claimed it hadn't been a human assassin but "the devil." Actually it was later learned that three shepherds incensed by some well-meaning acts of Shelley in ending the lives of diseased, dying sheep had tried to throw a scare into him; a shepherd named Robin Pant Evan played the "assassin" and fired the shots.

A confirmed cat hater, Shelley once conducted an electrical experiment with a neighborhood cat. Capturing it, he tied the doomed creature to a kite string that he was flying during a violent thunderstorm. Luckily no harm came to the cat.

Shelley was a vegetarian with little taste for food, hardly knowing whether he had partaken of a meal or not and satisfied with a plain loaf of bread to eat. The poet tried to impose his beliefs on his entire family, but not upon guests, whom ne would permit his wife to serve what he called "a murdered chicken."

Shelley's father, Timothy, an M.P., thought more of his reputation than he did of his son. When Shelley visited the family at Field Place with his wife, Harriet, and two children, years after he had eloped with Harriet and broken with his father, Timothy made no real attempt at a reconciliation. So afraid was he of being associated with this atheist liberal that he made his son wear an army uniform while visiting Field Place and go by the name of Captain Jones.

In the letter he wrote to his wife Harriet telling her that he had run off to the continent with Mary Godwin and asking Harriet to join them, he included the instructions: "Please bring my flute."

When he visited a monstery in Switzerland he was irritated by the pious entries in the guest book. He wrote, in Greek: "I am a lover of mankind, a democrat, and an atheist." Soon after Byron visited the same monastery and crossed out the word "atheist" in the vain hope that what he had written hadn't already gotten back to England.

He told of his extreme sensitivity in an 1821 letter to Claire Clairmont, Byron's mistress: "You ask me where I find my pleasure. The wind, the light, the air, the smell of a flower, affect me with violent emotions."

The poet was fascinated by water and many times forecast his death by drowning. As much as he was near and on the water he never learned to swim or navigate. It was as if he fatalistically accepted his prediction of his death. One time his friend Trelawny, a strong swimmer, had to save Shelley when the poet jumped into the Arno and Shelley protested, saying that the truth always lay "at the bottom of the well" and that "in another minute I should have found it." Another time, in Geneva, he and Byron got caught in a storm and thought their open boat would sink. They sat there arguing—Byron, an excellent swimmer, insisting that he'd save Shelley, and Shelley arguing that he would not be saved. Even after this close call Shelley did not make any attempt to learn how to swim.

Shelley drowned when his small schooner the *Ariel* sank in the Gulf of Spezia. The ship has been described as "the reverse of safe," but its condition when recovered suggested that it was run down by a felucca or fishing-smack rather than having capsized in a squall. There is a rumor, "not strictly verified and certainly not refuted," according to one authority, that an old Italian seaman confessed on his deathbed that he had been a crewmember on a felucca that collided intentionally with Shelley's ship in order to steal money hidden on board. There was, in fact, money on the *Ariel* and Shelley's friend Edward Trelawny, the best authority on the subject, always accepted the collision theory as true.

When Shelley's body was found on the beach near Viareggio after he drowned nothing was left of a face said to be not handsome but almost beautiful, its complexion brilliant beneath abundant, wavy, dark-brown hair, the deep blue "stag-eyes" large, fixed and beaming. His fish-eaten corpse might not have been identified were it not, according to his friend Trelawny, for "the volume of Sophocles in one pocket and Keats' poems in the other, doubled back, as if the reader, in the act of reading, had hastily thrust it away ..." It was his spirit not his body that Trelawny referred to when he added three lines from Shelley's favorite play, *The Tempest*, to his tomb:

Nothing of him that doth fade,
But doth suffer a sea change
Into something rich and strange.

When he recovered Shelley's body after the poet drowned, Trelawny wrote: "Byron asked me to preserve the skull for him; but remembering that he had formerly used one as a drinking cup, I was determined Shelley's should not be so profaned." Shelley's skull was thus cremated with the rest of his body, except his heart, which was given to his wife, who carried it with her in a silken shroud everywhere she went for the rest of her life.

Fanny Kemble, asked by Mrs. Shelley to help her choose a school for the dead poet's son, advised her to send him someplace where they would teach him to think for himself.

"Teach him to think for himself?" the poet's wife replied, almost horrified, remembering her husband's life. "Oh, my God, teach him rather to think like other people!"

Viscount Sherbrooke (Robert Lowe; 1811–1892)

The British statesman, journalist and author, widely known as Bobby Lowe in his day, was as well known for his wit as his tall striking figure and albino complexion and hair. Inevitably, other wits were out to get him. One anonymous rhymster wrote his mock epitaph in the seventies:

Here lies poor old Robert Lowe;
Where he's gone to I don't know;
If to realms of peace and love,
Farewell to happiness above;
If, haply, to some lower level,
We can't congratulate the devil.

∇ ∇ ∇

Richard Brinsley Sheridan (1751–1816)

Sheridan fought two duels with a so-called Captain Mathews over his wife Elizabeth Linley, whom the overbearing Mathews continued to pursue even after Sheridan had married her, unknown to her ardent suitor. The duels were to an extent farcical, suggesting in part Sheridan's first play, *The Rivals*, but in the latter duel Sheridan was badly wounded, as one of the seconds recorded in his diary:

> Mr. Mathews advanced fast on Mr. Sheridan; upon which he retreated, till he was very suddenly ran in upon Mr. Mathews, laying himself exceedingly open and endeavoring to get hold of Mr. Mathews' sword. Mr. Mathews received him on his point, and I believe disengaged his sword from Mr. Sheridan's body, and gave him another wound.
>
> Mr. Mathews, I think, on finding his sword broke, laid hold of Mr. Sheridan's sword-arm and tripped up his heels; they both fell; Mr. Mathews was uppermost, with the hilt of his sword in his hand, having about six or seven inches of the blade to it, with which I saw him give Mr. Sheridan, as I imagined, a skin-wound or two in the neck—for it could be no more, the remaining part of the sword being broad and blunt; he also beat him in the face either with his fist or the hilt of his sword. Mr. Sheridan's sword was bent, and he slipped his hand up the small part of it, and gave Mr. Mathews a slight wound in the left part of the belly; I that instant turned again to Captain Paumier [Sheridan's second], and proposed again our taking them up [stopping the fight]. He in the same moment called out, "Oh! he is killed—he is killed!"
>
> I as quick as possible turned again, and found Mr. Mathews had recovered the point of his sword, that was before on the ground, with which he had wounded Mr. Sheridan in the belly; I saw his drawing the point out of the wound. By this time Mr. Sheridan's sword was broke, which he told us. Captain Paumier called out to him, "My dear Sheridan, beg your life, and I will be yours for ever." I also desired him to ask his life: he replied, "No, by God, I won't!"

It was charged that Mathews, who had lost the first duel, had cheated in the second by wearing protective armor beneath his clothes. He fled to France.

Sheridan recovered from his very serious wounds, but soon saw a comical side to the whole affair and mined it for his play.

Said Sheridan's friend Lord Holland on one occasion: "Sheridan assured me at the same time that his treatment at school had created in his mind such an aversion for the stage that he had never seen a play when he wrote *The Duenna* [his second play]; that he engaged in that work from absolute indigence; and that throughout his life he had never seen a representation from beginning to end, except for his own pieces at rehearsal!" Later Sheridan confirmed this to the marquis of Abercorn, saying "he did not remember ever previously sitting out a play in his whole life."

The dilatory Sheridan was so relieved when he finished writing *The School for Scandal* at the last possible moment on opening night that he wrote on the final page of the manuscript, "Finished at last, Thank God!" To this the harassed prompter added the coda: "Amen. W. Hopkins."

Sheridan's old fencing master, Angelo, told how a friend of his was passing a block away from the Theatre Royal in Durry Lane on May 8, 1777, when he heard a sudden noise like an explosion. Wondering what it might be, he made his way toward the theater. He soon realized that the loud sudden noise which had startled him and still continued was the prolonged applause when the curtain fell after the fourth act of *The School for Scandal.*

Sheridan's farce *The Critic* (1779), in which he created Sneer the critic and Puff the unscrupulous literary advertiser, among other lifelike literary characters, had no last scene up until two days before its first night's performance at the Drury Lane. The actors rehearsed what they could but were afraid the play would never go on. Finally, Sheridan's father-in-law, Thomas Linley, stepped in. Sheridan was invited to a rehearsal at the theater and when he got there was asked to step into the green room for a moment to discuss a matter of some concern. As soon as Sheridan stepped in the room, it was locked behind him. Inside he found a roaring fire, a comfortable chair, a large table, a platter of anchovies, two bottles of claret and pen, ink and paper. Through the door his father-in-law told him that he would be locked in the room until he wrote the last scene. Sheridan sat down, ate the anchovies, drank the claret and finished his play. (See HARTLEY COLERIDGE.)

In *The Critic* Sheridan mischievously cast the role of Lord Burleigh with a Mr. Moody, a very stupid actor who "looked profound." The actor couldn't possibly blunder, Sheridan bet a friend, for his directions clearly said: "Mr. Moody as Lord Burleigh will advance from the prompter's side—proceed to the front of the stage—fall back to where Mr. Waldron stands as Sir Christopher Hatton—shake his head, and exit." Sheridan lost. On opening night, instead of shaking his own head, Moody walked over to Waldron-Hatton, took *his* head in two hands and slowly shook it from side to side before making his exit.

In 1776 Sheridan had acquired a share in the famous Drury Lane Theatre and produced his plays there. He rebuilt the theater 18 years later. In 1809 the new Drury Lane Theatre was destroyed by fire and Sheridan sat at the Piazza coffeehouse watching it burn to the ground. "How can you bear your misfortune so calmly?" a friend inquired. Replied Sheridan: "A man may surely be allowed to take a glass of wine by his own fireside."

One of the biggest hits Sheridan produced at the new Drury Lane Theatre was Frederick Reynolds's play *The Caravan,* in which the trained dog Carlo jumped nightly into a pool to save a drowning child. After opening night, an elated Sheridan, sure he had a hit that would save him from financial ruin, rushed backstage shouting, "Where is my Preserver?" Reynolds, the play's author, modestly stepped forward to receive the great man's plaudits. "Pooh, not you—*the dog,*" Sheridan said. Another evening during *The Caravan*'s long run a principal actor ran up to Sherican indicating that something terrible had happened.
"What is it?" Sheridan asked.
"I've lost my voice, can't you tell!" the actor finally said.
"Oh, is that all?" Sheridan replied. "I thought something had happened to the dog."

The Irish composer and actor Michael Kelly heard that Sheridan had advised the king, who loved the immensely popular *The School for Scandal,* that he was writing another comedy. Kelly asked him if this was true and Sheridan told him it was.
"Not you," Kelly said, "you will never write again, you are afraid to write."
"Of whom am I afraid?" an amused Sheridan inquired.
"You are afraid of the author of *The School for Scandal.*"

Sheridan's classic comedy *The Rivals* was badly received on its first night at the Covent Garden on January 17, 1775, due to a poor performance by John Lee, who played Sir Lucius O'Trigger. Lee was so incensed when an apple hit him in the head that he strode to the edge of the stage and cried out: "By the powers, is it *personal?—*is it me or the matter [the character he was playing]?"

Despite his theatrical successes, Sheridan valued politics over playwriting and considered his finest accomplishment not *The School for Scandal* or *The Rivals,* but his famous speech as an M.P. during the impeachment trial of Warren Hastings, for which he was offered £1,000 for the copyright two hours after he made it.

Ironically, his great-grandson Thomas Sheridan, the Victorian marquess of Dufferin and Ava, chose a career in government and wound up as viceroy of India, equivalent to the same position (governor general) that Hastings had held.

Sheridan's son Thomas couldn't understand his father's love of politics, though he later became a politician himself. "If I were in Parliament," Thomas told him one evening, "I would write on my forehead, 'To Let.'" Sheridan made a point of studying the boy's head for a moment and replied: "Add 'Unfurnished.'"

Edward Gibbon was at first full of praise for Sheridan's parliamentary speech during the trial of Warren Hastings, noting that Sheridan had complimented him. "Mr. Sheridan's eloquence commanded my applause," the historian noted, "nor could I hear without emotion the personal compliment which he paid me in the presence of the British Nation. Sheridan said, 'I do say, that if you search the history of the world, you will not find an act of tyranny or fraud to surpass this; if you read all past histories, peruse the annals of Tacitus, read the luminous pages of Gibbon…'"

Gibbon, however, was not so happy when he heard Sheridan's reply to his remarks.

"I did not say luminous," he told a fellow Whig, "I said *vo*luminous."

"There is French fraternity for you!" Edmund Burke exclaimed, suddenly plunging a dagger into the floor of the House of Commons. "Such is the poniard which French Jacobins would plunge into the heart of your sovereign!" Sheridan, then sitting as an M.P., responded to the dagger with a cutting remark: "The gentleman has brought his knife with him; but *where's the fork*?"

Sheridan rose to make a point of order when a fellow M.P. stopped to pour a glass of water in the middle of a long, boring speech.

"What is your point, sir?" the Speaker asked.

"Why, I think, sir," Sheridan replied, "that it is *out of order* for a windmill to go by water."

During a parliamentary debate Sheridan was asked to apologize for insulting a fellow M.P. "Mr. Speaker," Sheridan replied, "I said the honorable member was a liar it is true and I am sorry for it. The honorable member may place the punctuation where he pleases."

Social status meant everything to Sheridan. He badly wanted to become a member of the exclusive Whig club Brook's, but two members, the earl of Bessborough and George Selwyn, wanted to exclude him because he was associated with the theater. Members had to be elected unanimously and night after night the two men blackballed him, but finally Sheridan was for some reason elected. According to one old story, Sheridan accomplished this by sending Selwyn a note saying that his daugher had suddenly fallen ill, and sending the earl a note saying that his house was on fire. Before the men got back and realized that they were hoaxed, Sheridan was elected.

Two noblemen greeted Sheridan playfully, one of them quipping, "I say, Sherry, we were just discussing whether you were a rogue or a fool."

Taking each man by the arm, Sheridan replied, "Why I believe I am midway between both."

While he was visiting friends in the country, a persistent woman tried to get Sheridan to take her for a walk. The playwright pleaded bad weather, but she looked up at the sky and advised him that it was clearing. Sheridan, too, looked out the window. "Yes," he replied after a brief scrutiny, "enough for one, but not enough for two."

"Won't you come into the garden?" he asked a beautiful young woman. "I would like my roses to see you."

The playwright had told a joke to the earl of Lauderdale, who began laughing hysterically and said he'd be sure to repeat it over and over. "Pray don't, my dear Lauderdale," Sheridan replied. "A joke in your mouth is no laughing matter."

Byron remarked that Sheridan often "got drunk very thoroughly and very soon" and that it often "fell to my lot to convey him home..." Once he described "conducting Sheridan down a damned corkscrew staircase, which had certainly been constructed before the discovery of fermented liquors..." In fact, Sheridan was arrested for drunkenness on the streets the very night of his success with *The School for Scandal*; he often took a bottle of wine to bed with him and he took at least a pony of brandy in the morning with breakfast. But Byron concluded that Sheridan was well worth his efforts. "Poor fellow," he said, "his very dregs are better than the first sprightly runnings of others."

Forever in debt, Sheridan and his wife, Elizabeth, moved from one place to another; they rented 12 homes in London alone. Often these places were nearly bare. One time the playwright had to get the family silver out of pawn for a dinner party at his Bruton Street house. He also had to call in the bookseller Beckett to fill his empty floor-to-ceiling bookshelves for the affair—it wouldn't do for a gentleman's house to be without books. Beckett agreed, but on one condition.

Two of his assistants had to disguise themselves as servants for the evening—so that they could keep an eye on the books while waiting on table.

In a letter to his wife Sheridan wrote: "There is no Person who has been near to me...that has not been confirmed or improved in principle and integrity in his views and transactions...it may be egotism but is is Fact."

Sheridan was known throughout England for the great sums he owed and as often as not failed to pay back. One time when he stood for Parliament, mobs sang this popular ditty in the streets.

> Oh, Sherry! red Sherry!
> You'd make us all merry.
> With your drolls, your stage tricks and curvets;
> But don't, on old Davy
> Draw drafts for the Navy:
> Nor pay 'em as you pay your debts.

"I'll cut you off without a shilling!" Sheridan said to his son Thomas in the heat of an argument.

"Ah, father," Thomas quickly replied, "but where will you borrow the shilling?"

A tailor dunned Sheridan for at least the interest he owed on a bill. Replied Sheridan, "It is not my interest to pay the principal, nor my principle to pay the interest."

Without money, as usual, Sheridan wondered how he would pay for the coach he had hired over two hours ago. Then the playwright spied his friend Joseph Richardson, celebrated for his persistent argumentativeness, strolling down the street. He gave Richardson a lift and managed to start an argument with him. Eventually, pretending to be very angry, Sheridan shouted that he could not remain in the same coach with a person who used such foul language. Asking the coachman to let him out, he stuck the still arguing Richardson with the fare.

A friend recorded in his diary how a certain Mr. Vaughan found Sheridan and his wife in the playwright's terrible last few days:

> He said that he found him and Mrs. Sheridan both in their beds, both apparently dying, and both starving! It is stated in Mr. Moore's book that Mrs. Sheridan attended her husband in his last illness; it is not true. She was too ill to leave her own bed, and was in fact already suffering from the disease [cancer] of which she died a couple of years after. They had hardly a servant left. Mr. Sheridan's maid she

was about to be sent away, but they could not collect a guinea or two to pay the woman's wages. When Mr. Vaughan entered the house, he found all the reception rooms bare, and the whole house in a state of filth and stench that was quite intolerable. Sheridan himself he found in a truckle bed in a garret with a coarse blue and red coverlet, such as one sees as horse-cloths, over him; out of this bed he had not moved for a week, not even for the occasions of nature, and in this state the unhappy man had been allowed to wallow, nor could Vaughan discover that anyone had taken any notice of him, except one lady, whose name I hardly know whether I am authorized to repeat, Lady Bessborough, who sent 20 pounds.

Sheridan was always joking, even to the point of masquerading as a policeman one time in Bath and arresting people. His last joke was made on the day of his death, July 7, 1816, at about noon. He looked up at a woman friend several hours before he died and spoke words he had put in the mouth of his creation Mrs. Justice Credulous: "I won't die Bridget, I don't like death."

After his death Sheridan was laid out at a relative's house in London. In a few days a well-dressed man called and, claiming he had come a long way and was an old friend of Sheridan, asked to view his remains. On his insistence Sheridan's coffin was opened and the corpse unshrouded. The man promptly drew his bailiff's wand, touched Sheridan on the forehead and declared that he was arresting him in the name of the king for a debt of £500. Since the corpse was arrested, the funeral and burial could not go on until George Canning and another of Sheridan's friends pulled out their purses and paid the man. (See also GEORGE GORDON BYRON.)

∇ ∇ ∇

Thomas Sheridan (1687–1738)

Father of the actor Thomas Sheridan and grandfather of the playwright and politician Richard Brinsley Sheridan, Thomas Sheridan was a close friend of Jonathan Swift and an author and scholar in his own right. A confidant of Swift in the affair of the Drapiers Letters, which made Swift an Irish hero, he helped prepare *Gulliver's Travels* for publication at the Sheridan family house in Dublin. Early in their friendship, however, Swift made him promise to tell the Dean if ever he saw signs of avarice in him. Sheridan's word was his bond and when he did see what he thought were signs of greed in the great man, he told him so. Swift never spoke another word to him, not even interceding when he fell upon bad times. Sheridan died in poverty.

Wrote Swift of Richard Brinsley Sheridan's grandfather: "He was a generous, honest, good natured man, but his perpetual want of discretion and good judgement made him act as if he were neither generous, honest or good natured." Swift never approved of Sheridan's wife, Elizabeth; he called her Xantippe, after

Socrates' supposedly shrewish wife, and once declared her "the greatest beast in Europe." Sheridan, for his part, tried to laugh away his troubles—a family trait. Besides the nine children "Ponsy" had presented him with, he at one time or another had a tribe of poor relations living with him and eating him out of house and home. One time he complained to Swift good-naturedly that he was "entirely be-Sheridaned."

▽ ▽ ▽

Thomas Sheridan (1719–1788)
Thomas Sheridan, father of the playwright Richard Brinsley Sheridan, was an outstanding actor second only to Garrick in his time, but Dr. Johnson, his friend and fellow member of the Literary Club, found him rather obtuse: "Sherry is dull," he once told Boswell, "naturally dull; but it must have taken him a great deal of pains to become what we now see him as. Such an excess of stupidity, sir, is not in nature." (Ironically, Sheridan's son would become perhaps the only English wit who might be said to be wittier than Johnson.)

▽ ▽ ▽

Thomas Sheridan (1775–1817)
Playwright Richard Brinsley Sheridan remarked to his son Tom that their family was descended from the kings of Ireland and that their rightful name was O'Sheridan. Said his poet son to the brilliant but ever impoverished playwright: "Yes, that is true, for we owe everybody."

▽ ▽ ▽

Sir Philip Sidney (1554–1585)
Sir Philip's *Arcadia*, written for his younger sister, the countess of Pembroke, a charming if "salacious" lady, is another work—like Virgil's *Aeneid* and Kafka's novels—that was never meant to be published. On his deathbed he ordered the uncorrected romance burned, but it was saved, edited and published five years later.

"The President of Noblesse and of Chivalry," as Spenser called him, was both a poet and one of the greatest literary patrons of his time, but he was attacked by the Puritan playwright Stephen Gosson in an unusual way. Gosson dedicated his *School of Abuse* (1579) to him, but the title page described the book as "a pleasant invective against poets, pipers, players, jesters, and such like caterpillars of the commonwealth." Gosson probably was reacting to Sidney's scorn of him, but in any case he stimulated the poet to write his *The Defence of Poesy*, the first Elizabethan classic.

Known today more as the perfect English Renaissance man than as a poet, Sidney died a hero's death at the battle of Zutphen as a result of a thigh wound he received because he gallantly refused to wear leg armor, since the marshal of his camp wore none. It is said that after he was wounded, he refused a bottle of water offered to him. He gave it to a dying soldier, saying, "Thy need's greater than mine." In any case, he died of gangrene three weeks later. Aubrey, however, further embellishes the tale by asking us to believe that Sidney died because he refused to obey the injunctions of his physicians. To "forbeare his carnall knowledge" of his comely wife until his wound healed. "Some roguish verses" were thus made upon his death, Aubrey reports. Another biographer claims that Sidney welcomed death, declaring on his last day, "I would not change my joy for the empire of the world." His funeral in London was the greatest of his day.

∇ ∇ ∇

Dame Edith Sitwell (1887–1964)

The eccentric, controversial author only wrote prose to pay for her poetry. Accustomed to invective rather than praise about her poetry during the early years, Dame Sitwell was surprised when a woman came up to her after a reading and lavishly praised her poems. She was going to say thank you, but on reflection replied, "Now please don't say anything more. You mustn't spoil me. It isn't good for me to be spoiled." Though one critic claimed she belonged to the history of publicity, rather than that of poetry, her work has endured.

She had a low opinion of Virginia Woolf's work. "I enjoyed talking to her," she wrote to a friend in 1955, "but thought *nothing* of her writing. I considered her 'a beautiful little knitter.'"

∇ ∇ ∇

John Skelton (1460?–1529)

Cardinal Wolsey imprisoned the poet more than once for his fierce satires of him. A traditional, possibly fictional, story has Skelton kneeling before Wolsey begging for pardon. The cardinal keeps ranting and raving at him. Finally Skelton says, "I pray you let me lie down and wallow, for I can kneel no longer."

Henry VIII playfully gave the title Vicar of Hell to Skelton, who was his "poet laureate." The term was a pun on Skelton's being the rector of Diss in Norfolk. *Dis* is a Roman name for Pluto, the mythological ruler of the infernal regions.

Christopher Smart (1722–1771)

A highly regarded classical scholar as well as a brilliant poet, Smart wrote under his own name and a number of pseudonyms, including "Mrs. Midnight." He drank himself into a madness that included periods when he knelt down and prayed in the middle of the street, prompting Dr. Johnson to say, "I'd as lief pray with Kit Smart as anyone else." Committed to hospitals for the insane from 1757 to 1763, Smart wrote such lines therein as "Let Ross, House of Ross, rejoice with the Great Flabber Dabber Flat Clapping Fish with hands." Suffering great poverty after his release, Smart died "within the rules of the king's bench" (that is, while living in an area specified by a court that had imprisoned him for debt).

▽ ▽ ▽

Smectymnuus (fl. 1641)

Using the pseudonym Smectymnuus, five Presbyterian divines (Stephen Marshall, Edmund Calamy, Thomas Young, Matthew Newcomen and William Spurstow) published a pamphlet in 1641 attacking Bishop Joseph Hall (q.v.) and episcopacy. There followed a long controversy to which Milton contributed five pamphlets attacking Hall and his early satires, one of which (possibly by Hall's son) had accused Milton of youthful "harlotting" and charged that he had been "vomited out" of Cambridge. Hall was eventually thrown in the Tower.

▽ ▽ ▽

Adam Smith (1723–1790)

The philosopher led a simple life, contributing most of his income to secret charities. If his life contained any adventures, they are unknown and likely to remain so, for he ordered that most of his papers be burned on his death. Smith's adventures seem all to have been intellectual, but he began life like a character in a romance novel. When he was three years old a band of tinkers or gypsies kidnapped him from his home at Kirkaldy; they abandoned him on a lonely road when they were pursued.

So absent minded was Smith that one morning he wandered out of his garden and walked 12 miles to Dumfermline before the Sunday service church bells woke him from his reverie and he realized that he was dressed only in his nightgown.

All England was indebted to Smith's *The Wealth of Nations*. At a dinner that he attended, Prime Minister Pitt rose with the whole room when Smith entered. Said Pitt, "We will stand till you are seated, for we are all your scholars."

Smith met with Dr. Johnson only once. When his friends asked him what the cantankerous Johnson said, he answered, "Why, he said, *you lie!*" What did you reply, he was asked. "I said, *you* are a son of a bitch," he advised.

▽ ▽ ▽

Charlotte Smith (1749–1806)
When her husband was imprisoned for debt, Mrs. Smith moved herself and her family to a run-down chateau in France and began writing novels and poems to provide for them. She finally separated from her husband, and returned to England, where her work was admired by Scott, Hunt and other literary notables, earning her enough to support herself and her 12 children.

▽ ▽ ▽

Horace Smith (1779–1849)
This historical novelist, who also wrote the classic parody *Rejected Addresses* (1812) with his brother James, made a great fortune as a stockbroker before he turned to writing. Said his friend Shelley of him: "Is it not odd that the only truly generous person I ever knew who had money enough to be generous with should be a stockbroker? He writes poetry and pastoral dramas and yet knows how to make money, and does make it, and is still generous."

▽ ▽ ▽

Logan Pearsall Smith (1865–1946)
The last words of this author and consummate bookworm were said to be: "Thank heavens the sun has gone in and I don't have to go out and enjoy it." Earlier he had remarked: "People say life is the thing, but I prefer reading."

▽ ▽ ▽

Sydney Smith (1771–1845)
The clergyman and author almost set off a full-scale war when he asked the famous rhetorical question "Who reads an American book?" in a book review he wrote for the *Edinburgh Review* in 1820. Smith, however, had been reviewing the *Statistical Annals of the United States* by Adam Seybert and was on his way toward making an ironic point that has little to do with literature, as the last paragraph of his essay shows:

> In the four corners of the globe, who reads an American book? or goes to an American play? or looks at an American picture or statue? What does the world yet owe to American physicians or surgeons? What new substances have their chemists discovered? or what old ones have they analyzed? What new constellations have been discovered by the telescopes of Americans? What have they done in mathematics? Who drinks out of American glasses? or eats from American plates? or

wears American coats or gowns? or sleeps in American blankets? Finally, under which of the tyrannical governments of Europe is every sixth man a slave, whom his fellow-creatures may buy, and sell, and torture?

"I never read a book before reviewing it," Smith once commented. "It prejudices a man so."

There were few wittier conversationalists in England than Smith, but even he didn't appreciate the historian Macaulay's brilliant but prolix conversation. Remarked Smith of Macaulay: "He not only overflowed with learning, but stood in the slop."

The clergyman author won an argument with a man who angrily declared, "If I had a son who was an idiot, I would make him a parson."

"Your father was of a different opinion," Smith said.

Smith saw two women angrily shouting at each other, heads stuck out their windows on opposite sides of St. Paul's Close. "They will never agree," he observed, "as they are arguing from different premises."

"You never expected justice from a *company*, did you?" he asked a friend. "They have neither a soul to love nor a body to kick."

Smith studied the outfit worn by eccentric British author Harriet Grote, which was topped off by a Turkish turban. "Now I know the meaning of the word 'grotesque,'" he finally said.

Editors and printers despaired of reading Smith's handwriting, which was close to being indecipherable. Smith himself wouldn't read it. "I must decline reading my own handwriting twenty-four hours after I have written it," he once told an editor. "My writing is as if a swarm of ants, escaping from an ink bottle, had walked over a sheet of paper without wiping their legs."

Referrring to his friend and co-founder of the *Edinburgh Review*, the invariably severe critic Lord Francis Jeffrey, who was once challenged to a duel by Thomas Moore for his strictures, Smith made this observation: "No one minds what Jeffrey says;...it is not more than a week ago that I heard him speak disrespect-fully of the equator." (Harriet Martineau said Mrs. Smith told *her* that when Captain [later Sir John] Ross had approached Jeffrey, interrupting his daily ride, about supporting an expedition to the North Pole, he had snapped "Damn the North Pole!" When an upset Ross reported this to Smith, he replied soothingly. "Never mind him damning the North Pole. *I* have heard him speak disrespect-fully of the equator.")

It was his practice, he told friends, to "Take short views, hope for the best, and trust in God."

George Canning, a witty parodist himself, became prime minister in 1827, much to Smith's dismay. Smith couldn't understand how the Tory had been elected. "Canning in office is like a fly in amber," he remarked. "Nobody cares about the fly: the only question is, 'How the devil did he get there?'"

In his diary Tom Moore wrote that Smith was so funny he could actually make people in a room cry with laughter.

"Correspondences," he wrote to Mrs. Crowe, "are like small-clothes [knee-britches] before the invention of suspenders. It is impossible to keep them up."

"I am just going to pray for you at St. Paul's," he told a caller, "but with no very likely hope of success."

He once boasted that his sermons were "long and vigorous, like the penis of a jackass."

"I look upon Switzerland," he wrote to Lord Holland, "as an inferior sort of Scotland."

He didn't appreciate rural life. "I have no relish for the country," he wrote to a young lady, "it is a kind of healthy grave." Another time he complained that his parish in Yorkshire "was so far out of the way, that it was actually twelve miles from a lemon."

He advised a would-be author: "In composing, as a general rule, run your pen through every other word you have written; you have no idea what vigor it will give your style." (See SAMUEL JOHNSON.)

"I have, alas, only one illusion left," he was heard to say, "and that is the Archbishop of Canterbury."

"Marriage," he said, "resembles a pair of shears, so joined that they can not be separated; often moving in opposite directions, yet always punishing anyone who comes between them."

He put his recipe for salad into rhyme for his friends:

Let onion atoms lurk within the bowl,
And, scarce-suspected, animate the whole.

"Poverty is no disgrace to a man," he observed, "but it is confoundedly inconvenient."

The imperious hostess Lady Holland once instructed him, "Sydney, ring the bell for the butler." To which he replied, "And shall I sweep the room, too?"

"Lord Dudley was one of the most absent [minded] men I have ever met with in society," he confided. "One day he met me in the street and invited me to meet myself: 'Dine with me today; dine with me, and I will get Sydney Smith to meet you.' I admitted the temptation he held out to me, but said I was engaged to meet him elsewhere."

Of the wide-ranging philosopher William Whewell he said: "Science is his forte, and omniscience his foible."

"Don't tell me of the facts," he declared, "I never believe facts; you know [Prime Minister] Canning said nothing was so fallacious as facts, except figures."

"What you don't know would make a good book," he told an arrogant acquaintance.

Of a moralistic acquaintance, Smith quipped, "[He] deserves to be preached to death by wild curates."

When it was proposed that St. Paul's be surrounded with a wooden pavement, he suggested: "Let the Dean and Canons lay their heads together and the thing will be done."

"What a pity it is," he remarked, "that we have no amusements in England but vice and religion."

In his last, pain-filled days, he had light heart enough to write to a friend: "If you hear of sixteen or eighteen pounds of human flesh, they belong to me. I look as if a curate has been taken out of me."

He died "at peace with himself and all the world," his wife, all of whose friends had advised against marrying him, wrote in her memoirs. Concluding her reminiscences she wrote; "And now dear Children I have done. After passing nearly half a century with *such* a man I am alone...the Light of my Life is extinguished."

William Smith (1769–1839)
The author's *Geological Map of England and Wales* (1815), published in 15 huge sheets, illustrated his finding that "strata regularly slant eastward in a slight ascending grade until they end at the earth's surface." For his discovery he was pensioned off by the British government and earned the sobriquet "Strata Smith."

▽ ▽ ▽

Leonard Smithers (1861–1907)
Publisher Leonard Smithers devoted himself to deflowering virgins and made no secret of his sexual peculiarity. "Smithers loves first editions," Oscar Wilde said of him.

▽ ▽ ▽

Tobias Smollett (1721–1771)
Poverty was no problem for Smollett, one of the richest authors of his day and among the first prose writers to lead a comfortable life. When he wrote his *Universal History* and the eight-volume *Present State of All Nations*, he employed an army of authors that he called his "literary factory."

A discontented person, a grumbler and faultfinder is still sometimes called a *smellfungus*. The first *smellfungus* was clearly Smollett, who was once imprisoned for libel. Smollett's book *Travels in France and Italy* (1766) was entertaining but ill-tempered and novelist Laurence Sterne parodied the author as "Smelfungus" in his *Sentimental Journey through France and Italy* (1768). Within a short time *smellfungus* was being applied to any ill-tempered grumbler.

Smollett was sued for libel, fined £100 and sentenced to three months' imprisonment when in 1757 he called Sir Charles Knowles "an admiral without conduct, an engineer without knowledge, an officer without resolution, and a man without veracity."

▽ ▽ ▽

Ethel Smyth (1858–1944)
The composer and admirer of Virginia Woolf (who said of Ethel's table manners "I had rather dine with a dog") both literally and figuratively kicked the bucket when she died at the age of 86. Dame Ethel died from the fall she took when she tripped over a pail serving her as a chamber pot.

Robert South (1634–1716)

The witty, sarcastic preacher and author once noticed Charles II sleeping through one of his services. When one of the king's courtiers also fell asleep and began snoring, he cried out, "Lord Lauderdale, let me entreat you to rouse yourself; you snore so loud that you will wake the king!"

∇ ∇ ∇

Robert Southey (1774–1843)

The poet laureate congratulated himself for admonishing a young girl who had written him asking whether she had a chance of becoming a writer. "Literature cannot be the business of a woman's life," he had replied, "and it ought not be. The more she is engaged in her proper duties, the less leisure will she have for it, even as an accomplishment and recreation. To those duties you have not yet been called, and when you are you will be less eager for celebrity." The aspiring author was Charlotte Brontë.

The poet was bragging to a woman companion about his vast learning. "I rise at five throughout the year," he went on. "From six till eight I read Spanish; then French, for one hour; Portuguese next, for half an hour—my watch lying on the table; I give two hours to poetry; I write prose for two hours; I translate ..." When he finally finished, his companion asked, "And, pray, when doest thou think, friend?"

∇ ∇ ∇

Robert Southwell (1561–1595)

The poet was seized on the way to celebrate mass and imprisoned under a law forbidding anyone to become a Jesuit priest. Southwell was tortured in the vain hope that he would inform on other priests. So horribly was he tortured that his own father petitioned Queen Elizabeth to bring him to trial and put him to death rather than keep him in "that filthy hole" in the gatehouse at Westminster. Southwell was eventually hanged at Tyburn. He was beatified in 1929.

∇ ∇ ∇

Sir Henry Spelman (1562–1641)

Another of history's slow learners who accomplished much, the author matured late, not understanding Latin well, for example, until he was over 40. "The Spelmans' Witts open late," a family saying went and as a child Henry was considered backward. It is said that whenever his schoolmaster chastised a dull boy he would say, "You are as very a dunce as H. Spelman."

Herbert Spencer (1820–1903)

The founder of evolutionary philosophy attended a reception with many of England's literary lights. G.H. Lewes pointed out that everyone present had written a tragedy, even Herbert Spencer. "Ah," Thomas Huxley interjected, "I know what the catastrophe would be—an induction killed by a fact."

An army officer trounced the philosopher at billiards, running 50 balls before Spencer had a chance to shoot. Said Spencer, rather dryly: "A certain dexterity in games of skill argues a well-balanced mind, but such dexterity as you have shown is evidence, I fear, of a misspent youth."

▽ ▽ ▽

Edmund Spenser (c. 1552–1599)

The Prince of Poets in his Tyme, as his Westminster Abbey monument describes him, always had financial troubles; the earl of Essex, in fact, paid his funeral expenses. There is a story that the earl of Southampton, a great patron of poets, was reading the manuscript of Spenser's *Faerie Queen*, which the poet had hand-carried to him, when he cried out to his servant, "Give the author twenty pounds." A little later, deeper into the manuscript, he cried with delight, "Give the man another twenty pounds!" Still later he shouted, "Give him twenty more pounds!" Spenser, waiting in another room, had received £60 in all, but finally Southhampton, still thrilled with the poem yet finally come to his senses, threw down the manuscript, turned to his manservant and said, "Go, turn that fellow out of the house, for if I read on I shall be ruined!"

After Spenser presented a poem to her, Queen Elizabeth ordered Lord Treasurer Burleigh to send him a royal gratuity of £100, to which Burleigh replied, "What, all this for a song?" Spenser waited a long time without receiving the money and finally wrote these lines to the queen:

I was promised on a time
To have reason for my rhyme.
From that time, unto this season,
I received nor rhyme, nor reason.

Reading this, Elizabeth upbraided Burleigh, who quickly sent Spenser the £100 promised him. (William Cecil, Lord Burleigh, served Queen Elizabeth faithfully for 40 years, but aside from this anecdote he is mainly remembered in history for Cecil's Fast, the synonym for a dinner of fish, because he introduced a bill prescribing the eating of fish on certain days in order to restore England's fishing industry.) Burleigh was later satirized in Richard Sheridan's *The Critic*, in which the character based on Burleigh comes on stage but never talks, just nodding because he is much too busy with affairs of state to do more. This inspired the expression "Burleigh's nod" and "as significant as a shake of Burleigh's head."

It is said that when the great poet died, young and impoverished, the scholars and poets attending his hearse symbolically cast the pens they wrote with into his tomb.

∇ ∇ ∇

Speranza (Jane Francesca Elgee Wilde; d. 1878)

Oscar Wilde's mother, who wrote under the pen name Speranza, was well known as a graceful writer and literary hostess noted for her unconventional behavior and outlandish dress. On one occasion a friend asked her to receive a "reputable" young lady. "You must never employ that description in this house," Speranza replied. "Only tradespeople are respectable."

Speranza was once asked to correct proofs of poems she had written years before but were being published in a new edition of her work. She refused, explaining, "I cannot tread the ashes of that once glowing past."

∇ ∇ ∇

Reverend William Archibald Spooner (1844–1930)

Spooner, dean and later warden of New College, Oxford, was a learned man, but not spell woken, or well spoken, that is. "We all know what it is to have a half-warmed fish inside us," he once told an audience, meaning to say, "half-formed wish." On another occasion he advised his congregation that the next hymn would be "Kingering Congs Their Titles Take," instead of "Conquering Kings Their Titles Take," and he is said to have explained to listeners one time that "the Lord is a shoving leopard." Spooner's slips occurred both in church, where he once remarked to a woman, "Mardon me padom, this pie is occupied, allow me to sew you to another sheet," and where he told a nervous bridegroom that "it is kisstomery to cuss the bride," and in his classes, where he chided one student with, "You hissed my mystery lecture," and dismissed another with, "You have deliberately tasted two worms...and can leave Oxford by the town drain!" Other mistakes attributed to him are "The cat popped on its drawers," for "the cat dropped on its paws"; "one swell foop," for "one fell swoop"; "sporn rim hectacles"; "a well-boiled icicle"; "selling smalts"; "tons of soil" (referring to farmers); "blushing crow"; "Is the bean dizzy?" for "Is the dean busy?" and the "the Assissination of Sassero," for a Roman history lecture. Spooner lived 86 years, and committed many spoonerisms in public, too. "When the boys come back from France, we'll have the hags flung out!" the dean told a gathering of patriots during World War I, and Queen Victoria once became "our queer old dean." Nobody knows how many of these spoonerisms were really made by Spooner but they are among the hundreds attributed to him. Spooner was an albino; his metathetical troubles were probably due to nervousness and poor eyesight resulting form his condition. The scientific name for his speech affliction is metathesis, the accidental transposition of letters or syllables in the words of a sentence. The process was known long before Spooner made it so popular that his slips of the tongue and eye were widely imitated. Some of the best spoonerisms therefore aren't really spoonerisms at all, being carefully devised and far from accidental.

Reverend Spooner was asked whether he thought there was much Christian Socialism at Oxford. "No, I shouldn't say there was much," he replied, "in fact, I think there are only two Christian Socialists in Oxford, Dr. Rashdall and myself. Only Dr. Rashdall and myself; and I'm not very much of a Socialist, and Dr. Rashdall isn't very much of a Christian."

On greeting an old acquaintance, Dean Spooner said, "I remember your name perfectly, but I just can't think of your face."

∇ ∇ ∇

J.C. (John Collings) Squire (1884–1958)
The poet and literary journalist wrote an article about Shakespeare's *A Midsummer Night's Dream*. Finding that the name "Hermia" was misspelled "Hernia" in the proofs, he let the mistake stand, inserting an asterisk and the note: "I cannot bring myself to interfere with my printer's first fine careless rupture."

∇ ∇ ∇

Philip Dormer Stanhope   (Fourth Earl of Chesterfield; 1694–1773)
Wrote Chesterfield in one of his famous letters to his son:

> I know a gentleman who was such a good manager of his time that he would not even lose the small portion of it which the calls of nature obliged him to pass in the necessary-house; but gradually went through all the Latin poets in those moments. He bought, for example, a common edition of Horace, off which he tore gradually a couple of pages, carried them with him to that necessary place, read them first, and then sent them down as a sacrifice to Cloacina: this was so much time fairly gained, and I recommend you to follow his example...

Despite Chesterfield's wise *Letters to His Son*, young Philip Stanhope never measured up to his father. Fanny Burney attested that "[he had] as little good breeding as any man I ever met with."

In his last days, long after his famous quarrel with Dr. Johnson (*q.v.*), he described his old friend Lord Tyrawley and himself: "Tyrawley and I have been dead these two years, but we do not wish it to be known."

∇ ∇ ∇

Henry Morton Stanley (1841–1904)

"Dr. Livingston, I presume!" journalist Henry Morton Stanley said when after a long, arduous journey—only 700 miles in 236 days— he found the ailing Scottish missionary-explorer David Livingstone on the island of Ujiji in the heart of Africa. The star reporter had completed one of the greatest manhunts of all time. Deserted by his bearers, plagued by disease and warring tribes, he was probably too tired and overwhelmed to think of anything else to say. Stanley had been sent to Africa by the *New York Herald* to locate the famous explorer, Livingstone, feared dead or swallowed up by the Dark Continent. Born John Rowlands in Denbigh, Wales, Stanley assumed the name of his adoptive father when he immigrated to America as a youth. He later become a noted explorer in his own right. Dr. Livingstone died, aged 60, a year after the reporter left him in 1873. His body was shipped back to England and buried in Westminster Abbey.

∇ ∇ ∇

William Thomas Stead (1849–1912)

The most tasteless author who ever pursued verisimilitude was possibly journalist William Thomas Stead, who went down with the *Titanic*. To research an article on the evils of prostitution, Stead paid a 13-year-old girl £10 to work as a prostitute in a London brothel and report the conditions to him. Stead, who was later sent to jail for his efforts, did initiate many political and social reforms in England as a journalist and magazine editor.

∇ ∇ ∇

Richard Steele (1662–1729)

Dr. Johnson relates that the Irish man of letters and collaborator with Addison on *The Tatler* and *The Spectator* always lived beyond his means and was constantly in debt. One day some friends came to dinner at his house and were astonished to see the great number of servants who attended them. How can you afford so many servants when you are so deep in debt? Steele was finally asked. Oh, those were *bailiffs*, Steele replied. They had come on official business to collect debts, and as he couldn't pay them and couldn't get rid of them, he dressed them up in servants costumes and stationed them about the house.

The author once invited Richard Savage to dinner in a small tavern, where he dictated a pamphlet to Savage while they ate. At the end of the leisurely meal the pamphlet was finished, but Steele had no money to pay for the meal and Savage had to go out and sell the pamphlet to a bookseller for two guineas before the bill could be paid. There was just enough left over for Steele to pay the creditors who were hounding him.

In a 1707 love letter to his future wife, Mary Scurlock, he wrote:

> Madam, It is the hardest thing in the world to be in love and yet attend to business. All who speak to me find me out, and I must lock myself up or other people will do it for me. A gentleman asked me this morning, "What news from Lisbon?" and I answered, "She is exquisitely handsome." Another desired to know when I had been last to Hampton Court. "It will be on Tuesday. Prythee, allow me at least to kiss your hand before that day."

So quick was his friend English composer Henry Purcell with wordplay that one day Steele dubbed him the Pun-Master General.

∇ ∇ ∇

Laurence Sterne (1713–1768)

The humorist's life was hardly a humorous one. The son of a wandering soldier father and an often malevolent mother, he made an unhappy marriage in which all of his children save one were stillborn. Even before Sterne became a pastor in 1738 he had contracted tuberculosis. His only solace seems to be the women he flirted with or chased. In 1759, soon after *Tristram Shandy* was rejected by a printer, his wife had a mental breakdown. A year later he awoke to find himself famous with the publication of his book, but his happiness was short-lived, for in 1762 his health began to deteriorate, worsening every year until his death. It is said that his last words were "Now it is done," after which "he put up his hand as if to stop a blow, and died in a minute." But trouble followed even after his death. His body was stolen by grave robbers a few days after burial and sold to anatomists at Cambridge, where a friend recognized it on the dissecting table at an anatomy lecture and had it returned to the grave.

For the first 10 years of Sterne's life his mother Agnes dragged him from place to place throughout England and Ireland following his father's regiment. A shrewish, demanding woman, she refused to really let go of her son even when he married the wealthy Elizabeth Lumley. Agnes Sterne consistently demanded money from her daughter-in-law, despite Sterne's objections. His feelings toward Agnes were decidedly negative. When, for example, she was arrested for vagrancy, he refused to pay her bail.

"Men of wit," the duke of Newcastle told Sterne, "are not fit to be employed, being incapable of business."

"They are not incapable of business, my Lord," Sterne replied to the prime minister." "A sprightly generous horse is able to carry a pack-saddle as well as an ass, but he is too good to be put to the drudgery."

By the 18th century, book dedications had become slavish as authors vied for patrons. Writers got up to 50 guineas for a dedication at the time, and some included more than one dedication in a book—Edward Young's *The Complaint, or Night Thoughts* (1742–45), for example, had a dedication for each of the seven nights of the week. It was with such examples in mind that Sterne parodied literary dedications in *Tristram Shandy* (1760–67), inscribing the dedication page with the words: "To be let or sold for fifty guineas."

The novelist asked a woman if she'd read his *Tristram Shandy*. "I have not," she replied, "and to be plain with you, I am informed it is not proper for female perusal." Sterne pointed at her three-year-old son rolling on the floor in his white tunic. "My dear good lady," he said, "do not be gulled by such stories. The book is like your young heir there. He shows at times a good deal that is usually concealed, but it is all in perfect innocence!"

It is said that Sterne's *A Sentimental Journey* (1768) is the first English novel to survive in its author's handwriting. The dash that ends *Sentimental Journey* has the distinction of being the only dash to end a novel and the only dash that is listed as a euphemism for the vagina in a slang dictionary (Farmer and Henley's *Slang and its Analogues*, 1890). The novel ends: "...so that, when I stretched out my hand, I caught hold of the fille-de-chambre's————."

Reverend Sterne shocked his congregation on the Sunday following his Saturday marriage to Elizabeth Lumley in 1741. He preached a sermon that took its text from *Luke* 5:5, "We have toiled all night and have taken nothing."

∇ ∇ ∇

George Alexander Stevens (1736–1800)
The author liked to tell the true story of an art critic deceived by a painting of fruits and flowers:

> The connoisseur would not give his opinion of the picture till he had first examined the catalogue; and finding it was done by an Englishman, he pulled out his eye-glass. "Oh, sir," says he, "those English fellows have no more idea of genius than a Dutch skipper has of dancing a cotillion. The dog has spoiled a fine piece of canvas; he is

worse than a Harp Alley sign-post dauber. There's no keeping, no perspective, no foreground. Why, there now, the fellow has actually attempted to paint a fly upon that rosebud. Why, it is no more like a fly than I am like—" but, as he approached his finger to the picture, the fly flew away.

Stevens, called "the Puck of [Shakespeare] commentators" by the caustic critic William Gifford, wasn't above totally ignoring things he didn't like in the Bard's plays, or making forgeries, or inventing facts and sources. According to one old story, he had been offended by the clergymen John Collins and Richard Amner. He retaliated by ascribing to them all the research he had compiled on the "indecent passages" in Shakespeare.

∇ ∇ ∇

Robert Louis Stevenson (1850–1894)

"In the small hours one morning," the novelist's wife testified, "I was awakened by cries of horror from Louis. Thinking he had a nightmare I awakened him. He said angrily: 'Why did you awaken me? I was dreaming a fine bogey tale.'" The "bogey tale" turned out to be *Dr. Jekyll and Mr. Hyde*, inspired by a dream (as were Mary Shelley's *Frankenstein*, Horace Walpole's *The Castle of Otranto*, A.C. Benson's *The Phoenix* and, of course, Samuel Taylor Coleridge's "Kubla Khan").

In Stevenson's *The Strange Case of Dr. Jekyll and Mr. Hyde*, Dr. Jekyll, a physician, discovers a drug that releases in him a personality that absorbs all his evil instincts. This personality, which he calls Mr. Hyde, is repulsive in appearance and gradually gains control of him until he finally commits a horrible murder. Jekyll can rid himself of Hyde only by committing suicide. Stevenson locked himself in his study and wrote the novel in three days after he had his famous dream about the story (see preceding anecdote). Unconsciously, he had based the main character on an Edinburgh cabinetmaker and deacon named William Brodie (1741–88), who was a "double being," by day a respected businessman and by night the leader of a gang of burglars. Brodie was finally hanged for his crimes, but Stevenson, who was raised in Edinburgh, knew his story well and in fact wrote a play entitled *Deacon Brodie, or The Double Life* when he was only 15. This was the germ of the dream and the later work.

Stevenson's novel *Treasure Island* (1883) was first published in *Young Folks* magazine, July 1881–June 1882. The famous book was the outgrowth of a *map* the novelist, a great game player and inventor, and his stepson Lloyd Osbourne devised while vacationing in Scotland. In the magazine serialization the tale bore the rather less appealing title, *The Sea Cook, or Treasure Island*.

Remarked Stevenson on the literary life: "All who have meant good work with their whole heart, have done good work, although they may die before they have time to sign it."

When Stevenson heard of the death of his friend, poet Matthew Arnold—a stern, demanding moralist—he observed, "Poor Matt, he's gone to heaven, no doubt—but he won't like God."

When ill in the South Seas and unable to hold his pen or even speak, Tusitala, or "The Tale Teller," as the Samoans called Stevenson, dictated his stories by sign language.

The Samoans were devoted to "Tusitala" and when he died buried him on the mountain top, where they tabooed the use of guns and other weapons "so that the birds might sing undisturbed."

In his will Stevenson bequeathed his birthday, November 13th, to his young friend Annie Ide, who always complained that her own fell on Christmas Day. "If, however, she fails to use this bequest properly," his will read, "all rights shall pass to the President of the United States."

▽ ▽ ▽

Dugald Stewart (1753–1828)
The Scottish philosopher and writer often forgot to return books he had borrowed. Stewart was so well known for this that when he confessed that he was deficient in arithmetic, an anonymous punster replied, "That might be true; but he certainly excels in bookkeeping."

▽ ▽ ▽

Marie Stopes (1880–1958)
The paleobotanist, poet and early birth control advocate, published her first book, *Married Love* (1918), after her first marriage was annulled, at a time, she later claimed, when she was still a virgin. Dr. Stopes, according to one biographer, "could not and would not sleep unless her bed was aligned north to south. If unable to move it she would lie across it slantwise, correctly oriented."

▽ ▽ ▽

John Stow (1525–1605)
Abandoning his trade as a tailor, Stow turned to writing the first English historical works based on the systematic study of public records. His chronicles brought him little money, however, especially as he spent as much as £200 a year

for reference books, and in his last year had to be granted a license to beg by James I. He died 11 months later.

∇ ∇ ∇

Lytton Strachey (1880–1932)

When the eminent Victorian author and member of the Bloomsbury group, a conscientious objector, was examined for the draft during World War I, he was asked, "What would you do if you saw a German soldier attempting to rape your sister?" Replied Strachey, "I should try and come between them."

Author Cecil Beaton described him in his diary: "Lytton Strachey peered at everyone through thick glasses, looking like an owl in daylight. He is immensely tall, and could be even twice his height if he were not as bent as sloppy asparagus."

In a 1921 letter to a friend Strachey described the appearance of an eminent poet visiting at Arnold Bennett's house: "Then Edith Sitwell appeared, her nose longer than an anteater's, and read some of her absurd stuff."

As he lay dying of cancer of the stomach, Strachey remarked, "If this is dying, I don't think much of it."

∇ ∇ ∇

John Stubbs (fl. 1579)

Stubbs attacked Queen Elizabeth in his pamphlet *The Discoverie of a Gaping Gulf Where into England Is Likely to Be Swallowed by Another French Marriage.* His pamphlet was burned in a public bonfire, and the author's right hand was hacked off with a meat cleaver at the same time. Stubbs is said to have raised his hat with his left hand immediately afterward and cried, "God, save the Queen!"

∇ ∇ ∇

Sir John Suckling (1609–1641)

Suckling, who invented the game of cribbage and made £20,000 (a huge sum at the time) from his invention, was said to be the greatest gallant and gamester of his day. He gave magnificent parties in London, serving the ladies at one affair silk stockings and garters, then a great luxury, for the dessert course. The poet and dramatist loved to bowl, but his sisters often came down to the bowling green, a contemporary biographer says, "crying for fear that he should lose" their portions of the family estate. Unable to bear the poverty of his exile in Paris after fleeing England, Suckling "tooke poyson, which killed him miserably with vomiting."

Jonathan Swift (1667–1745)

Nearly all of Swift's works were published anonymously and he received payment only for *Gulliver's Travels* (£200). In the case of what has been called the "Bickerstaff Hoax," Swift made no profit and used the pen name Isaac Bickerstaff. The Dean grew prudently indignant in 1708 when an ignorant cobbler named John Partridge, claiming to be an astrologer, published an almanac of astrological predictions, so he parodied the book under the title "Prediction for the Ensuing Year by Isaac Bickerstaff." In his parody, Swift foretold the death of John Partridge on March 29, 1708, and when that day arrived he published a letter affirming his prediction and giving an account of Partridge's death. Partridge indignantly protested that he was very much alive, but Swift wrote what he called a "Vindication," proving that Partridge was dead. Poor Partridge was doomed to a literary death as a result, especially when other writers perpetuated the joke. Benjamin Franklin later emulated Swift's hoax in America.

Trying to please him, a hostess kept asking Swift what he'd have for dinner. On and on she went: "Will you have an apple pie, sir?" "Will you have a gooseberry pie, sir?" "Will you have a currant pie, sir?" "Will you have a plum pie, sir?" "Will you have a pigeon pie, sir..."

"Madam!" Swift finally replied. "Any pie! I'll have any pie but a magpie!"

Esther Vanhomrigh (pronounced "Vanummery") met Dean Swift in 1708, fell deeply in love with him and followed him to Ireland, where she later proposed marriage to him. Swift gently rejected her in his 1713 poem "Cadenus and Vanessa" (Vanessa was his pet name for Esther—"Essa" for Esther and the Van of her last name—and Cadenus is an anagram of *Decanus*, Latin for dean). When in 1723 Swift broke off their relationship, due to her jealousy, she is said to have died of shock or a broken heart. She had preserved his poem among her papers and it was first published three years later.

Swift enjoyed playing tricks so much that he once paid for an ad in a newspaper inviting readers to a certain shop the next day for a nonexistent auction.

The author was shown the motto under the arms of William, prince of Orange, on his accession to the English crown. *Non rapui sed recepi* (I did not steal but I received) it read. "The receiver," Swift said, "is as bad as the thief."

Swift used at least six pseudonyms. these included Isaac Bickerstaff, A Dissenter, A Person of Quality, A Person of Honour, M.B. Drapier and T.R.D.J.S.D.O.P.I.I. The initials conceal The Reverend Doctor Jonathan Swift, Dean of Patrick's in Ireland.

When he became a prominent writer he acted the part, never letting the rich or famous belittle him. Writing to his love Stella (his pet name for Esther Johnson), he asserted, "I am so proud that I make all the lords come up to me...I was to have supped at Lady Ashburnham's, but the drab did not call for us in her coach as she promised, but sent for us, and so I sent my excuses."

Once he convinced the authorities not to pardon a man charged with rape. It was pointed out that the woman "had [willingly] lain with [the man] a hundred times before." "What?" he replied. "Must a woman be ravished because she is a whore?"

Swift was always partial to his strikingly original *The Tale of a Tub* (1704). On reading the work again in later years, he exclaimed, "Good God! What a genius I had when I wrote that book!"

The Houyhnhnms, pronounced "whinims," are the intelligent breed of horses that Swift created in *Gulliver's Travels* (1726). Swift said he coined their name from the characteristic whinny of a horse as it sounded to him. The talking horses, endowed with reason, ruled over the brutish Yahoos, another word coined by Swift in the book. *Gulliver's Travels* also gives us *brobdingnagian*, for any immense thing, after the giants Gulliver encounters in the country of Brobdingnag, and *lilliputian*, after Lilliput, an island of tiny people.

He claimed that an Irish bishop told him *Gulliver's Travels* "was full of improbable lies, and for his part he hardly believed a word of it."

Swift made it a ceremony year after year to read aloud from the book of Job on his birthday.

He could be among the most misanthropic of men in everyday life as well as in his writing. It is said that he once went an entire year without speaking to another person. But this was in his dying years, when he suffered worse from his lifelong affliction with Ménière's disease and many thought him insane. On the other hand, this genius who made just £200 from all his writings (he was paid only for *Gulliver's Travels*), spent a third of his earnings as a churchman on charities and saved another third each year to found St. Patrick's Hospital for Imbeciles in 1757.

In a letter written when he was 62 years old, Swift mused:

"I remember when I was a little boy, I felt a great fish at the end of my line which I drew up almost on the ground, but it dropped in, and the disappointment vexeth me to this day, and I believe it was the type of all my future disappointments."

Swift at the end was like "the ruin of a great empire," as Thackeray put it. He is now thought to have suffered from Ménière's disease all his life. He tried many nostrums to improve his condition, including long walks of up to 38 miles, but his mental state had so deteriorated by 1742 that it was necessary to appoint a guardian for his person and estate and he eventually sank into the dementia that preceded his death. Swift himself had sadly predicted his mental decay when he was about 50 to the poet Edward Young. Gazing at the withered crown of a tree, he had remarked, "I shall be like that tree, I shall die from the top."

Ill and suffering, his eye inflamed to the size of an egg, Swift had little use for life in his last years. As his customary farewell to friends he would say, "Goodnight, I hope I never see you again."

In his "Verses on the Death of Dr. Swift," a mock obituary in verse, Swift took pride in his originality, writing: "To steal a hint was never known,/But what he writ was all his own." Yet he loved trickery as much as his originality. These lines themselves were taken without credit from English poet John Denham. For his epitaph he chose Latin lines meaning: "Where bitter indignation can no longer tear his heart."

∇ ∇ ∇

Algernon Charles Swinburne (1837–1909)

Swinburne's five years at Eton were hard ones because the poet was subjected to the worst kind of hazing. A former schoolmate recalled that "... when I first went to Eton, the head-boy called us together, and pointing to a little fellow with a mass of curly red hair, said, 'If you ever see that boy, kick him—and if you are too far off to kick him, throw a stone.'"

In his youth his lyrical ecstasy made him a poet's poet in England, where his work especially excited the young, freeing them from the restraints of the day. Remarked another young poet: "We all went about chanting to one another these new astounding melodies."

He spoke of his "tendency to the dulcet and luscious form of verbosity which has to be guarded against." In his *Nephelidia*, an amphigouri, or verse composition that sounds well but makes no sense, he became one of the few poets to parody his own style. Its opening lines:

From the depth of the dreary decline of the dawn
    through a notable nimbus of nebulous moonshine,
Pallid and pink as the palm of the flag-flown that
    Flickers with fear of the flies as they float,
Are the looks of our lovers that lustrously lean from
    a marvel of mystic miraculous moonshine,
These that we feel in the blood of our blushes that
    Thicken and threaten with throbs through his throat?

Usually he read his poetry better than any poet of his time, but sometimes, a friend remembered after his death, "he lost control of his emotions, the sound became a scream, and he would dance about the room, the paper fluttering from his finger-tips like a pennon in a gale of wind."

Like Hemingway after him, Swinburne lost one of his manuscripts while traveling. In 1868 Swinburne absentmindedly left the manuscript of his tragedy *Bothwell* in a hansom cab. Unlike Hemingway, he luckily recovered the long drama after offering a reward for it.

Swinburne came close to being dropped from the Arts Club for his constant drunkenness. One time on leaving the club he tried on numerous hats in trying to find his own. Hat after hat failed to fit his huge head. Angry with each hat that failed to fit, he threw each on the floor and stamped it flat.

The poet was asked if he had replied intemperately to Emerson after the American author criticized his *Poems and Ballads*. "Oh, no, I kept my temper, I preserved my equanimity," he said. "But what did you say?" "I called him a wrinkled and toothless baboon, who, first hoisted into notoriety on the shoulders of Carlyle, now spits and sputters on a filthier platform of his own finding and fouling."

∇ ∇ ∇

John Addington Symonds (1840–1893)
It was widely gossiped in literary London that Symonds's wife hated his work. This suggested to Henry James the character Mark Ambient in "The Author of Beltraffo." Symonds, a poet and critic who acknowledged his homosexuality after his marriage, suffered many years from the tuberculosis that killed him before his time.

∇ ∇ ∇ ∇ ∇ ∇ ∇ ∇

John Taylor (1580–1653)

A Thames waterman, the author was called the "Water Poet" and known for his lively, entertaining verse and prose. He was also celebrated for his eccentric journeys, about which he wrote extravagantly titled tracts. One of these, taken on a bet, was his journey to Prague, where he was entertained by the queen of Bohemia. Another resulted in his *A Very Merry, Wherry Ferry Voyage, or Yorke for My Money* (1623). But Taylor's most noted trip, made with a companion said to be "as feather-brained as himself," was from London to Queensborough. This excursion was made in a brown-paper boat, using two cured fish tied to canes for oars. The boat eventually sank and Taylor and his friend nearly drowned.

∇ ∇ ∇

William Temple (1881–1944)

A rugby master discussed one of his schoolboy essays with the future archbishop and author. "Are you not a little out of your depth here?" he inquired. "Perhaps, sir," replied the always confident Temple, "but I can swim."

∇ ∇ ∇

Alfred, Lord Tennyson (First Baron Tennyson; 1809–1892)

An autograph hunter, hoping to trap the poet laureate, who rarely gave his autograph, wrote asking him which was the best dictionary, *Wesbster's* or *Ogilvie's*. Tennyson cut the world *Ogilvie's* out of the man's letter, put it in an envelope and sent it back to him.

Tennyson's father, George Clayton Tennyson, was notoriously absentminded. One morning he went to pay a call on a parishioner and couldn't remember his own name when the servant answering the door asked who was calling. Walking away through the village, he pondered who he was until a local tradesman smiled and said, "Good day to you, Dr. Tennyson."

"By God, my man, you're right!" Dr. Tennyson exulted.

Early in his career Tennyson fell in love with Lady Duff Cooper, who married one of his friends. Visiting her once he got down on the floor and rolled across the carpet to her chair. "Will you please to put your foot on me for a stool?" he implored her.

"Do you know anything about Lowell?" the absentminded Tennyson snapped at a visiting American poet he had invited to lunch.

"Why, my dear," Mrs. Tennyson quickly replied, "this *is* Mr. Lowell!"

Someone said it was a shame that Thomas Carlyle and his wife, Jane, seemingly so incompatible, hadn't each married someone else. "No," Lord Tennyson said. "By any other arrangement *four* people would have been unhappy instead of two."

When Tennyson wrote the line "Every moment dies a man / Every moment one is born," he received a complaining letter from the literal-minded mathematician Charles Babbage. Babbage wrote that "if this were true, the population of the world would be at a standstill" and urged him to change the line to: "Every moment dies a man / Every moment 1 1/6 is born." Tennyson claimed poetic license.

Lady Augusta Gregory told Yeats that "Tennyson had the British Empire for God, and Queen Victoria for Virgin Mary."

The poet's friend Max Mueller told this story about him:

Tennyson's pipe was almost indispensable to him, and I remember one time when I and several friends were staying at his house, the question of tobacco turned up. Some of his friends taunted Tennyson that he could never give up tobacco. "Anybody can do that," he said, "if he chooses to do it." When his friends still continued to doubt and tease him, "Well," he said, "I shall give up smoking from tonight." The very same evening I was told that he threw his tobacco and pipe out the window of his bedroom. The next day he became very moody and captious, the third day no one knew what to do with him. But after a disturbed night I was told that he got out of bed in the morning, went quietly into the garden, picked up one of his pipes, stuffed it with the remains of the tobacco scattered about, and then having had a few puffs came to breakfast all right again.

A pun still remembered is Sir William Harcourt's reply to Tennyson when the poet said his first pipe of tobacco was always the best of the day. Recalling the famous lines from Tennyson's poem "The Princess," the British statesman replied to an unamused poet. "Ah, the earliest pipe of half-awakened *bards*." The lines from Tennyson's poem read:

Ah, sad and strange as in dark summer dawns
The earliest pipe of half-awakened birds.

Tennyson's "Maud" (1855) was found obscure or morbid by critics ranging from George Eliot to Gladstone. "Maud" had one vowel too many in its title, one critic remarked, and it made no difference which vowel that was.

Good poetry is not always the result of long reworking. Lord Tennyson, for example, wrote the celebrated "Crossing the Bar" in a moment or so while crossing over to Yarmouth from Lymington; he jotted down the 16 lines (almost unchanged in the final version) on an old envelope.

In Tennyson's poem "Enoch Arden," Enoch Arden, Philip Ray and Annie Lee grow up together in a little seaport town. Though both boys love Annie, Enoch wins her hand and they live together happily until Enoch sails aboard the merchantship *Good Fortune* to make his fortune. Shipwrecked for 10 years on a deserted island, Enoch is finally rescued. Annie, meanwhile, has been reduced to poverty and Philip asks her to marry him, certain that Enoch is dead. Enoch is brokenheated when he returns and witnesses, unknown to them, Annie and Philip's happiness, but he vows never to let them know of his return until after his death, sacrificing his happiness for theirs. Such is the plot of Tennyson's long poem, which was suggested to him by the poet Thomas Woolner, and which was based on the true story of a sailor thought drowned at sea who returned home after several years to find that his wife had remarried. A similar case was reported after the *Arctic* went down in 1854; a New Orleans merchant named Fleury was believed drowned and his young widow remarried. The "widow" had three children by her new marriage and lived happily until a letter arrived from Fleury six years later. A whaler just setting out on a long voyage had rescued him, and when the whaler was also wrecked, Fleury was rescued by still another whaler starting out on a long voyage, which accounted for the many years he had spent at sea. An *Enoch Arden* has come to mean that rare person who truly loves someone better than himself.

Everyone has a favorite anticlimax, and one of the best is the last line of "Enoch Arden." As noted, Enoch Arden, thought dead at sea, returns home after some years to find his wife happily married, and resolves that she won't know of his return until his death. Tennyson ends the poem this way:

> So past the strong heroic soul away.
> And when they buried him, the little port
> Had seldom seen a costlier funeral.

The expression *Tennyson bindings* is used to indicate affectation of culture. According to Willard Espy, quoting Timothy Dickinson in Espy's *O Thou Improper, Thou Uncommon Noun*: "A nouveau-riche matron was showing a friend of similar stripe her library, which had been stocked by interior decorators. 'And here,' she said, 'is Tennyson.' 'No, no, darling,' corrected her friend. 'Those are green. Tennyson is *blue*.'"

Though a strikingly handsome man, Tennyson was often careless about his appearance. In 1855, dishevelled and unkempt, with unbrushed hair spilling over his shoulders and down his back, he appeared at Oxford to receive an honorary degree. As he came on stage someone in the gallery cried out, "Did you mother call you early, dear?"

Browning's difficult narrative poem *Sordello* (1840) always remained unintelligible to Tennyson, as it did to many, though it has since become widely regarded as one of the finest poems of its day. "There were only two lines in it that I understood," he once remarked, "and they are both lies: 'Who will may now hear Sordello's story told,' and 'Who would has heard Sordello's story told.'"

After reading an epigram on a poet's fate by Thomas Hood he wrote beside it:

> While I live, the Owls!
> When I die, the GHOULS!!!

∇ ∇ ∇

William Makepeace Thackeray (1811–1863)

English printers hated to set Thackeray's work in type, not because it wasn't neat but because it was minuscule. So tiny and perfect was the novelist's handwriting that he once told a friend that he would make a career of writing the Lord's Prayer on his thumbnail if he failed at literature.

While he entertained Dickens after dinner one evening, his little daughter interrupted the conversation with: "Papa, why do you not write books like *Nicholas Nickleby*?"

Thackeray confided that he couldn't start a novel until he knew every aspect of his characters. In fact, he claimed that he had to hear the sound of their voices before he began writing.

He suffered many indignities when a boy at Charterhouse, a private school, but, as Trollope pointed out, "his change of retrospective feeling about his schooldays was very characteristic. In his earlier books he always spoke of Charterhouse as Slaughterhouse…As he became famous and prosperous his memory suffered, and Slaughter House was changed into Grey Friars…"

Thackeray's American publisher, James T. Fields, took him out to eat some Massachusetts oysters, which were in fact one of the reasons the gourmet novelist had wanted to visit the United States. Fields demonstrated how to swallow the creatures alive and Thackeray quickly imitated him. Fields anxiously asked him how he felt after his initiation and Thackeray leaned back, drew a deep breath, and sadly replied, "As if I had swallowed a baby."

He called Victorian times "if not the most moral, certainly the most squeamish." But he could be as worried as the next person about what Mrs. Grundy might say. Once, as an editor, he rejected an Elizabeth Barrett Browning poem because it employed the word harlot.

An Irish woman begging for alms cried out ecstatically when Thackeray reached into his pocket: "May the blessing of God follow you all your life!"

But Thackeray had only been reaching for his snuff box.

"And never overtake you!" the woman added.

Thackeray had probably the most amusing assortment of pen names ever used by a writer. These included Dorothea Julia Ramsbottom; George Savage Fitzboodle; Michael Angelo Titmarsh; Théophile Wagstaff, Esq.; and C.J. Yellowplush, Esq. Other male authors who used women's names as pseudonyms are Prosper Mérimée and Benjamin Franklin.

Thackeray claimed to have heard George II yawning in church "so loud that the clergyman...burst out crying in his pulpit because the defender of the faith and dispenser of bishoprics would not listen to him."

One of the oddest stories about the Poet's Corner—part of the south transept of Westminster Abbey, where many of England's great authors are buried—concerns Thackeray's bust there. The novelist's daughter had always "deplored the length of whiskers on each side of the face of her father's bust," believing that the Italian sculptor Marachetti had made them far too long. Finally, as an old woman, she managed to persuade officials to let another sculptor move the bust into a secluded alcove and chip away at her father's stone sideburns until they were the right length. This accomplished, an appropriately bewhiskered Thackeray was restored to his proper niche in the nave.

▽ ▽ ▽

Thomas the Rhymer (Thomas of Erceldoune; fl. 1220–1297)

This border poet is also said to have been an oracle who predicted the death of Alexander III of Scotland, the battle of Bannockburn, and the union of England and Scotland under James I (James VI of Scotland) four centuries later.

Dylan Thomas (1914–1953)

When the Welsh poet wrote his radio play *Under Milk Wood*, everyone who read the script assumed that the fictional village therein, Llareggub, was authentically Welsh—until someone spelled it backward, after the play was already aired, and realized the poet's bawdy joke. For *bugger* in British English never means a child, as it does in American expressions like "he's just a little bugger." A *bugger* in England is a sodomite and *to bugger* is to sodomize—in fact, use of the word in print was actionable in England for many years. *Bugger* in this sense, which is American slang as well, derives, down a tortuous path, from the medieval Latin *Bulgarus*, meaning both a Bulgarian and a sodomite. The word first referred to a Bulgarian and then to the Bulgarian Albigenses or Bulgarian heretics, an 11th-century religious sect whose monks and nuns were believed, rightly or wrongly, to practice sodomy.

When the legendary drinker was well into his cups he could talk nonstop for long periods. One time, while on a BBC radio program, he halted suddenly in the middle of a drunken soliloquy. "Somebody's boring me," he said. "I think it's me."

In a letter to critic and novelist Pamela Hansford Johnson, he wrote:

> Few understand the work of cummings
> And few James Joyce's mental slummings
> And few young Ander's coded chatter
> But then it is the few that matter.

"I've had eighteen straight whiskies…I think that's the record …" Thomas said after a drinking spree, and he fell unconscious, never to speak another word before he died.

▽ ▽ ▽

Francis Thompson (1859–1907)

Addicted to opium and suffering from tuberculosis, the poet, author of "The Hound of Heaven," could not sleep at night and habitually stayed in bed all day long. All night he would pace round and round so that in one room where he lived he wore out the carpet in a perfect circle around a table. Always cold, he would stand with his back to the open fire, often setting his pants and coat afire. One time he badly burned his hands and set the curtains ablaze, the room "quite burned out," as he put it.

A lifetime of extreme poverty, ill-health and an addiction to opium unbalanced Thompson, even though he found success in his last years. The poet finally committed suicide because he believed that fellow poet Thomas Chatterton (*q.v.*), a suicide two centuries before, appeared to him and ordered him to take his life.

His tombstone in Kensal Green is inscribed with a line from his poem "To My Godchild": "Look for me in the nurseries of Heaven."

▽ ▽ ▽

James Thomson (1700–1748)
The author of "Rule Britannia" was set upon by robbers in 1730 as he walked from Scotland to London, which he had decided to make his home. Robbed of all his possessions and on the brink of starvation, he was forced to sell his long poem "Winter" (which later became part of his famous "The Seasons") for a pair of shoes.

When the Prince of Wales met the impoverished Thomson he inquired about the state of his affairs, which were not good when he last heard of them. "They are in a more poetical posture than formerly," Thomson replied, and the prince rewarded his quip with a £100 pension.

In his tragedy *Sophonisba* (1730) Thomson had one of his characters cry out to the heroine: "O! Sophonisba, Sophonisba, O!" His line did not move the audience—a wag in the pit cried out, "O! Jamey Thomson, Jamey Thomson, O!"

▽ ▽ ▽

Richard Tickell (fl. early 19th century)
Tickell was as adept at practical jokes as his friend and fellow playwright Richard Brinsley Sheridan. One time friends riding by in a carriage saw Sheridan lying in the road apparently in the agony of death as his conspirator Tickell, wringing his hands, stood over the body. But when they bent down to minister to him, both he and Tickell leaped up laughing. "On another occasion," a contemporary reported, "Sheridan having covered the floor of a dark passage, leading from the drawingroom, with all the plates and dishes of the house ranged closely together, provoked his unconscious playfellow to pursue him in the midst of them. Having left a path for his own escape, he passed through easily, but Tickell falling at full length into the ambuscade was very much cut in several places. The next day, Lord John Townshend, on paying a visit to the bedside of Tickell, found him covered over with patches, and indignantly vowing vengeance against Sheridan. But in the midst of his anger, he could not help exclaiming, 'But how amazingly well *done* it was !'"

John Horn Tooke (1736–1812)

The radical politician and philologist was asked by George III whether he played cards. "I cannot, Your Majesty," Tooke said, "tell a king from a knave."

∇ ∇ ∇

Thomas Traherne (1637?–1674)

Traherne's poems, which are said to foreshadow Whitman in their exuberant, unconventional style, did not come to light until almost the beginning of the 20th century, some 200 years after they were written. Left in manuscript by the author, who had published several religious works, a notebook of his poems was eventually discovered in a London street bookstall and purchased for a few pence by English critic W.T. Brooke. The poems were so good that they inspired a search for more of Traherne's work and other poems were found in a British Museum manuscript.

∇ ∇ ∇

Sir Herbert Beerbohm Tree (1853–1917)

The actor-manager, half-brother of critic and caricaturist Max Beerbohm, wrote this brief letter to an aspiring dramatist who had sent him a play:

> My dear Sir:
> I have read your play. Oh, my dear Sir!
> Yours faithfully.

The *London Morning Advertiser* asked the actor's wife for some autobiographical information and the self-effacing Lady Tree sent back just these four brief lines of verse:

> This is the life
> Of little me:
> I am the wife
> Of Beerbohm Tree.

∇ ∇ ∇

Violet Trefusis (1894–1972)

The daughter of Edward VII's mistress, Alice Keppel, novelist Violet Trefusis was more noted for her lesbian relationship with Victoria (Vita) Sackville-West than her fiction, though several of her cutting remarks are remembered. When, for example, someone told her that Gertrude Stein had said "A rose is a rose is a rose," she replied, "A pose is a pose is a pose."

G.M. (George Macaulay) Trevelyan (1876–1962)

Before he wrote of military campaigns the historian would walk every mile of the battlefields involved. Trevelyan once pointed out that Latin was a second language to cultivated Englishmen for over four centuries, from about 1400 to 1800, when it was a supreme insult to call someone a "Latinless dolt." He noted that grammar school boys were permitted to speak nothing but Latin even out of school and that "a spy aptly named *lupus* was sometimes paid to report whether they used English words while at play—if they did, they were flogged."

∇ ∇ ∇

Anthony Trollope (1815–1882)

A big, bluff, vociferous man, the novelist wore many hats. In addition to his prodigious output of composition—including over 50 novels—he was a fanatically devoted hunter and whist player and served as an important Post Office official for 33 years. Trollope rose every day at 5:30 and wrote steadily at the rate of 1,000 words an hour for 2 1/2 hours before going to work. Few are aware that he (not Smollett, as has been claimed) invented and introduced the streetcorner mailbox (or pillarbox) to England in the 1850s.

Trollope was a hard man to convert. Following another speaker at a Post Office meeting, he shouted, "I disagree with you entirely. What was it you said?"

Sir William Osler's controversial ideas on compulsory retirement at age 60 were suggested in part by Trollope's novel *The Fixed Period*, the plot of which "hinges upon the admirable scheme...into which at sixty men retired for a year of contemplation before a peaceful departure by chloroform."

Seven years after he married Rose Heseltine in Dublin, Trollope wrote to another Irish woman of his acquaintance:

My dearest Miss Dorothea Sankey:

   My affectionate and most excellent wife is, as you are aware, still living—and I am proud to say her health is good. Nevertheless, it is always well to take time by the forelock and be prepared for all events. Should anything happen to her, will you supply her place—as soon as a proper period of decent mourning is over?

Till then I am your devoted servant...

Poetic justice seemed served when Trollope's wife outlived him.

Frances Trollope (1780–1863)

The author and mother of Anthony Trollope was asked if she patterned her fictional characters on real people. "Of course I draw from life," she said, "but I always pulp my acquaintances before serving them up. You would never recognize a pig in a sausage."

Mrs. Trollope wrote her first book (*Domestic Manners of the Americans*) when she was 52, and she went on to write another 114 volumes over the rest of her life. Shortly before she died she was astonished to receive her son Anthony's first novel, which he had written at the age of 32. He himself would go on to write well over 50 books more.

∇ ∇ ∇

Martin Farquhar Tupper (1810–1889)

The prolific author of verse and prose was immensely popular in his day and well aware of it. One time he took the hand of a little girl he had just met and advised: "Now my child, you will always be able to say that you have shaken hands with the great Martin Tupper."

∇ ∇ ∇

Reggie Turner (1869–1938)

The drama critic, as witty as he was ugly, once commented that second editions of his books were so rare that they didn't exist. Another time his friend Oscar Wilde told him, "Last night I dreamed that I was at the banquet of the dead." "I'm sure you were the life and soul of the party," Turner replied.

∇ ∇ ∇

Thomas Turner (1729–1765)

The diarist was a grocer in Sussex and his daily diary from 1754 to 1765 offers much insight into the life of the English middle class at the time. He often bemoaned his wife's temper. One day he wrote: "Well might the wise man say, 'It were better to dwell in a corner of the house-top, than with a contentious woman in a wide house.'"

∇ ∇ ∇

Richard Twiss (1747–1821)

Perhaps the most insulting literary memorial on record is to the name of author Richard Twiss, who wrote an uncomplimentary travel book on Ireland. Some quick-witted Irishman promptly manufactured a chamber pot dubbed a Twiss, on the inside bottom of which was a portrait of the unlucky author, the picture captioned: *Let everyone piss/On lying Dick Twiss.*

∇ ∇ ∇

Kenneth Tynan (1927–1980)

The *Times Literary Supplement* received and printed this request for biographical material from a British man of letters busily at work on a book:

"Sir,—I am at present engaged in research for a book on the life and work of Kenneth Tynan, and I would be very grateful to hear from anyone who has letters, anecdotes, reminiscences, and other biographical information that might be helpful.

"Any material submitted will be safely guarded and promptly returned."

The letter was signed "Kenneth Tynan."

∇ ∇ ∇

William Tyndale (c. 1495–1536)

Tyndale, the first person to translate the New Testament from Greek to English, found himself opposed by the bishop of London, Cuthbert Tunstall, who wasn't at all pleased with his translation. Tunstall made an offer to London merchant Augustine Parkington to buy at any price all the copies Parkington could obtain of Tyndale's Bible so that he could burn them—and have them off the market. Parkington, however, relayed this proposal to Tyndale, who surprisingly agreed to the arrangement. "I am the gladder," he told Parkington, "for these two benefits shall come thereof: I shall get money of him for these books to get myself out of debt (and the whole world shall cry out upon the burning of God's word). And the overplus of the money that shall remain to me shall make me more studious to correct the said New Testament, and so newly to imprint the same once again, and I trust the second will much better like you than even did the first." The bargain was made. Soon "the Bishop had the books...and Tyndale had the money." Not long afterward, however, England was flooded with more, improved, New Testaments than ever, much to the bishop's chagrin.

∇ ∇ ∇ ∇ ∇ ∇ ∇ ∇ ∇

Nicholas Udall (c. 1505–1556)

Author of what is considered the first English comedy, *Ralph Roister Doister*, Udall was headmaster of Eton and Westminster and his pupils may well have provided him with actors for the play. He seems to have been a stern man for a comedy writer, however. One of his pupils complained of having been severely flogged by him "for fault but small, or none at all."

∇ ∇ ∇

Sir Thomas Urquhart (1611–1660)

Urquhart's translation of Rabelais is a masterpiece of the translator's art and he was one of the first to devise a universal language. A Royalist, the Scottish author escaped to the continent during the Commonwealth. He died there in 1660 when he heard that the monarchy had been restored. On hearing the news he smiled, began to laugh, laughed louder, laughed so intensely that he finally died of a fit of laughter, unable to stop even to save his life.

∇ ∇ ∇

Thomas Usk (d. 1388)

Usk's *Testament of Love* is so obscure, and dull, that it wasn't until 1897, almost five centuries after it had been written, that an English scholar discovered that "the leaves of the original manuscript had been shuffled and the body of the treatise misarranged." With the chapters in proper order it was found that the initial letters of the chapters formed an acrostic reading "Margaret of virtu, have merci on thin(e) Usk." Usk was tried for treason and executed by the so-called "Merciless Parliament" on March 4, 1388. He was hanged, then beheaded by what one contemporary writer described as "thirty blows" from a sword.

∇ ∇ ∇ ∇ ∇ ∇ ∇ ∇ ∇

Sir John Vanbrugh (1664–1726)

Vanbrugh's immensely successful play *The Relapse*, he admitted, "was got, conceived and born in six weeks space" after he saw Cibber's *Love's Last Shift* and thought he would like to develop the situation upon which Cibber had ended his play. Vanbrugh later became an architect and designed Blenheim Palace, among many massive structures. If Blenheim's rooms were only as wide as its walls were thick, Voltaire said, the chateau would have been convenient enough. It was probably Abel Evans who wrote the famous mock epitaph on Vanbrugh that goes, "Lie heavy on him, earth, for he/Laid many heavy loads on thee."

∇ ∇ ∇

Henry Vaughan (1622–1695); and Thomas Vaughan (1622–1666)

The Vaughans are among the few twins known as distinguished authors in world literature. Henry, born first, was by far the greater, known today as the Swan of Usk for his mystic religious poetry, while Thomas, who often wrote under the pseudonym Eugenius Philalethes, enjoyed a considerable reputation as a writer on magic and mysticism. Both men were imprisoned as Royalists in their youth and they jointly authored the volume of poems *Thalia Rediviva: the Pastimes and Diversions of a Country Muse* (1678).

∇ ∇ ∇

George Villiers (Second Duke of Buckingham; 1628–1687)

The handsome duke of Buckingham's brilliant comedy *The Rehearsal* (1672) made money and his father left him a rich estate, but this member of the Cabal lost everything through high living and died in poverty, "in the worst inn's worst room," as Pope put it. Among his many affairs, the most notorious was with the countess of Shrewsbury. Wanting her, he challenged her husband to a duel and killed him. The countess, holding Buckingham's horse during the duel, embraced the victor, still covered with her husband's blood, and went home with him.

∇ ∇ ∇ ∇ ∇ ∇ ∇ ∇ ∇

Thomas Griffiths Wainewright (1794–1852)

The journalist and art critic tried everything from forgery to murder to support his extravagant lifestyle. In 1830 he insured the life of his sister-in-law for £18,000. When she died in December of that same year he tried to collect on the policy, but the company refused to pay, suspecting foul play, and he fled to France. There he was arrested, detectives finding in his possession a large quantity of strychnine, with which, autopsies later revealed, he had killed not only his sister-in-law, but also his uncle, his mother-in-law, and a friend. Like the aesthete he was, Wainewright claimed at his trial that he had poisoned his sister-in-law because he found her ankles offensively thick. He was sentenced to life imprisonment and died in prison 15 years later. Dickens (in the story "Hunted Down"), Wilde and Bulwer-Lytton used him in their work.

∇ ∇ ∇

Wale (fl. 1100)

Before the title poet laureate was conferred upon any poet in England there were a number of court poets: King Henry I (1068–1135) had a Versificator Regis (King's Versifier) named Wale. Ben Jonson was granted a pension by James I in 1616 and was a poet laureate in the modern sense, and Chaucer, Skelton and Spenser had been called laureates before him; but it wasn't until John Dryden was appointed poet laureate by Charles II in 1668 that the position became official.

∇ ∇ ∇

Alfred Russel Wallace (1823–1913)

Wallace, who developed the theory of natural selection at the same time as Darwin in 1858, immediately wrote a letter to Darwin explaining his views, which resulted in their famous joint communication to the Linnean Society on the theory of evolution. Wallace, however, was a believer in the supernatural and took part in seances where he tried to contact the dead. In one paper the naturalist explained that humans had descended from the apes because the spirit world had intervened and made the transformation possible.

∇ ∇ ∇

Edgar Wallace (1875–1932)

The mystery author was incredibly quick and prolific. Wallace wrote his full-length novel *The Three Days' Mystery* in three days. He wrote his play *On The Spot* in just two and a half days and not a word of it was changed by the time it appeared on stage.

"Religion and immorality are the only things that sell books nowadays" the prolific mystery novelist wrote to his wife in 1905 before publishing his first thriller. "I am going to start a middle course and give them crime and blood and three murders to a chapter; such is the insanity of the age that I do not doubt the success of the venture."

Wallace, who wrote the first Hollywood screenplay for *King Kong*, decided to self-publish a longer version of his short story *The Four Just Men* after virtually every major British magazine had rejected the tale. Wallace sold 38,000 copies of the story but advertised it so widely in periodicals and on posters everywhere that he lost £400 on the venture. He later recalled: "There was, I discovered, such a thing as over-advertising."

∇ ∇ ∇

Edmund Waller (1606–1687)

The duchess of Newcastle showed the poet some verses on the death of a stag.

"Madam, I would give all my own poems to have written them," he told her.

Later a friend admonished him for this excessive praise.

"Nothing is too much to be given that a lady might be saved from the disgrace of such a vile performance," he replied.

A politician "nursed in the parliaments," Waller was a genius of political survival. When Cromwell came to power he wrote a poem praising the lord protector, and after Charles II's restoration he wrote another poem praising the king. When King Charles told him that he thought the poem he had written on Cromwell was much better than the panegyric on him, Waller even had an answer for that.

"Sir," he replied smartly, "we poets never succeed so well in writing truth as in writing fiction."

A friend repeated some sarcastic anonymous verses then circulating in London about a fellow poet:

Thy Brother murdered, and thy Sister whor'd,
Thy Mother too, and yet thy Penne's thy Sword...

Waller replied, "That men write ill things well, and good things ill; that Satyricall writing was downe-hill, most easie and naturall; that at Billingsgate one might hear great heights of such wit; that the cursed earth naturally produces briars and thornes and weeds, but roses and fine flowers require cultivation."

Waller was among the first to depart from the majority view that Milton's *Paradise Lost* was, in Dryden's words, "one of the greatest, most noble and sublime poems which either this age or nation has produced." He agreed rather with Dr. Johnson, who would later say that Milton used "English words with a foreign idiom," or Addison, who felt that "our language sunk under him," or T.S. Eliot, who declared that Milton wrote English "like a dead language." But Waller went further. "If its length be not considered a merit," he remarked of *Paradise Lost*, "it hath no other."

The poet fell in love with 18-year-old Lady Dorothy Sidney in 1635, but she jilted him and married Lord Spencer four years later, despite the fact that she was the "Sacharissa" of his romantic poems. Waller still harbored a resentment about this when he met her years later as an old lady.

"When, Mr. Waller, will you write such fine verses upon me again?" she asked.

"Oh, madam," he replied, "when Your Ladyship is as young again."

In 1643 he planned and took part in a "Waller's Plot" against Parliament in favor of the king, for which he was fined £10,000 and banished. When discovered, it is said, he showed cowardice and treachery, "confessing whatever he had said, heard, thought or seen, and all that he knew...or suspected of others." He survived in exile only by selling his wife's jewels.

∇ ∇ ∇

Horace Walpole (1717–1797)

Walpole achieved his first popular success in 1764 with the first English gothic novel, *The Castle of Otranto*. The novel was published pseudonymously (by "Onuphrio Muralto"), and some time passed before he was widely recognized as the book's author. He was about 48 when he commented, "It is charming to totter into vogue."

Walpole, whose *Castle of Otranto* (1764) is the prototype of the romantic novel, has also been called "the best letter writer in the English language." Once he quarreled with his uncle and went home to write him a letter concluding: "I am, sir, for the last time in my life, Your Humble Servant Horace Walpole."

In a 1772 letter to a friend, he wrote: "This world is a comedy to those who think, a tragedy to those who feel."

∇ ∇ ∇

Hugh Walpole (1884–1941)

Somerset Maugham's ridicule in *Cakes and Ale* (1930) of Walpole, easily recognizable as the model for Alroy Kear, is said to have blighted the last ten years of his life. Walpole began reading the novel, which he propped on the mantel, while dressing for dinner in his room at a friend's country house. His host found him there over an hour later, still in shirt-tails, his trousers bunched around his ankles. "I shan't forgive Willie easily," the author said of Maugham. "The beggar had drunk my claret."

Sir Robert Walpole (1676–1745)

The prime minister and father of author Horace Walpole, Sir Robert had been a great reader before he entered public life. One day, after he had retired from government, Walpole went into the library, "when, pulling down a book and holding it some minutes to his eyes, he suddenly and seemingly sullenly exchanged it for another. He held that about half as long, and looking at a third returned it instantly to its shelf and burst into tears. 'I have led a life of business so long,' said he, 'that I have lost my taste for reading, and now—what shall I do?'"

It was to Walpole that the title "prime minister" was first applied (though used as an abusive term that he rejected), and he was the first chief minister to reside at 10 Downing Street. A man of few morals in private or political life, he is said to have spent £50,000 annually in subsidizing newspapers and magazines that disseminated his political beliefs.

∇ ∇ ∇

John Warburton (1682–1759)

Antiquarian Warburton collected 50 or 60 rare Elizabethan and Jacobean plays, three of which now survive as the priceless Lansdowne manuscripts at the British Museum. Most of the often unique plays were destroyed when Warburton left them in the care of his cook, Betsy Baker, who burned them for fuel or used them to put under pie bottoms.

∇ ∇ ∇

William Warburton (1698–1779)

Oliver Goldsmith and Dr. Johnson were arguing about the merits of the quarrelsome author and scholar William Warburton, who later became bishop of Gloucester and was Pope's literary executor. Goldsmith contended that Warburton was a "weak" writer, but Johnson, who was grateful to him ("He praised me at a time when praise was of value to me"), defended the writer. "Warburton may be absurd," he said, "but he will never be weak; he flounders well."

Warburton was asked by the earl of Sandwich in a parliamentary debate to define "orthodoxy" and "heterodoxy." Replied Bishop Warburton: "Orthodoxy is my doxy; heterodoxy is another man's doxy."

∇ ∇ ∇

Dr. Barton Warren (fl. early 19th century)

When the witty Dr. Warren heard that a certain Dr. Vowel had died, the grammarian commented to a friend, "Thank heaven it was neither you nor I."

Charles Waterton (1782–1864)

Of all wildlife writers possibly the wildest was taxidermist Charles Waterton, author of the classic *Original Instructions for the Perfect Preservation of Birds, etc. for Cabinets of Natural History*. Waterton slept with a live sloth (after kissing his jealous pet chimp goodnight), kept a wildlife preserve devoted solely to scavengers such as vultures and gave an annual picnic for animals and lunatics only. The squire always went barefoot on his estate and frequently greeted guests by getting down on all fours, baring his teeth, growling fiercely, and finally sinking his teeth into their legs, all of which led someone to observe that he resembled a publisher more than an author.

∇ ∇ ∇

Alexander Pollock Watt (fl. c. 1900)

The first professional authors' agent appears to have been Alexander Pollock Watt, who had as his clients Thomas Hardy, Rudyard Kipling, Arthur Conan Doyle and Bret Harte, among other greats. Watt published a list of his clients, along with testimonials from them, in 1893. The firm he founded, A.P. Watt and Son, is still in business.

∇ ∇ ∇

Theodore Watts-Dunton (1832–1914)

Watts-Dunton did many things late in his long life, including his marriage to a woman much younger than himself when he was 73 (the two of them lived with Swinburne, whom Watts-Dunton kindly cared for in his declining years). When he was 64, the writer legally changed his name from Watts, adding his mother's maiden name, Dunton, because he thought Watts-Dunton sounded classier. His friend, James Whistler, however, sent him a biting three-word query about the name change: "Theodore, Watts Dunton?"

∇ ∇ ∇

Evelyn Waugh (1903–1966)

Dejected about life and his writing career, Waugh attempted suicide in 1925, three years before he published his first novel, the immensely successful *Decline and Fall*. Waugh thought about buying a revolver, but chose drowning instead. After burning an unpublished novel, he walked down to a deserted beach one night early in July and stripped naked. Leaving as a suicide note a quotation from Euripides that he had checked for accuracy, he walked out into the water and began swimming to his death. But even here he could not succeed at this point in his life. He swam smack into the midst of a huge school of jellyfish, and, as one biographer put it and anyone who has ever swam into a school of jellyfish can understand, "was stung back to reason."

His first name led many people who hadn't met Waugh to assume that he was a woman. When his first novel *Decline and Fall* was published in 1928 he had to write to *The Times Literary Supplement* to protest a review in which he was referred to throughout as "Miss Waugh."

"Send two hundred words upblown nurse," Waugh's editor cabled him regarding a rumor that an English nurse had been killed in an Italian air raid in Ethiopia. Finding that the story had no basis in fact, Waugh cabled back, "Nurse unupblown."

Author Nancy Mitford, angry at Waugh's treatment of a young French writer, asked the waspish novelist how he could behave so abominably and yet still consider himself a practicing Catholic. "You have no idea," replied Waugh, "how much nastier I would be if I was not a Catholic. Without supernatural aid I would hardly be a human being."

Cyril Connolly, who by his dishevelled, dirty appearance obviously had fallen on hard times, told Waugh that he was going to get a job as a waiter in a fashionable London restaurant to embarrass his rich friends for their failure to help him in his time of need. A worried look flashed across Waugh's face. "Ah, I see now I have touched even your cold heart," gloated Connolly. "Well, no, Cyril," Waugh replied, "it isn't quite that. I was thinking of your fingernails in the soup."

Waugh had a low opinion of literary collaboration. "I never could understand how two men can write a book together," he once said, "to me that's like three people getting together to have a baby."

∇ ∇ ∇

Beatrice Webb (1858–1943)

The British socialist chose her husband, Sidney, "for reason, not love," as she said, and when he sent her as an engagement present a full-length portrait of himself she sent it back. "Let me have your head only," she wrote, "it is only the head I am marrying."

Webb and her husband were the leading lights of the Fabian Society, a group of socialists whose thinking greatly influenced modern British life. But as progressive and free-thinking as she was, Beatrice Webb was among the most literal-minded of people. "Poetry means nothing to me," she once told Arnold Bennett. "It confuses me. I always want to translate it back into prose."

Beatrice Webb devoted her long life to Fabianism and the public interest; her marriage was devoid of sex and her earthly joys few. Toward the end of her life she dwelt upon her far more earthy "naughty" sister Rosie, who devoted her life to sex and good times. "You know," she concluded, "Rosie was right."

∇ ∇ ∇

John Webster (c. 1578–c. 1632)

Webster's tragedies *The White Devil* and *The Duchess of Malfi* have been reviewed in this century more than any play by any of Shakespeare's contemporaries. Webster based *The White Devil* on the story of Vittoria Accoramboni (1557–1585), a beautiful Italian noblewoman whose brother murdered her first husband so that she could marry the duke of Bracciano, who may have conspired with him in the murder. After they were married, Pope Sextus V, her first husband's uncle, vowed vengeance on the couple, and, warned in time, they fled from Rome to Venice, escaping the pope. The duke died a natural death that same year and left all his wealth to Vittoria, but one of his relatives had her assassinated by a band of *bravos* and claimed the fortune. He and his henchmen were later captured and put to death.

∇ ∇ ∇

Charles Jeremiah Wells (1798?–1879)

The poet's verse play *Joseph and his Brethren*, forgotten today, was much admired in its time by Swinburne, Rossetti and other prominent poets. Wells, however, couldn't make a living in England and moved to Brittany, later teaching at the university in Marseilles. He claimed that he had written about 10 volumes of poetry in his life and burned them all one night after his wife's death in 1874, having seen them rejected by all the major publishers in England.

∇ ∇ ∇

H.G. (Herbert George) Wells (1866–1946)

While leaving a party Wells found a hat that fit his unusually big head and walked away with it. He later wrote its owner, whose address he found on a label inside: "I stole your hat, I like your hat, I shall keep your hat. Whenever I look inside it I shall think of you. I take off your hat to you."

Wells had an affair with Elizabeth von Arnim, a cousin of Katherine Mansfield, during which, among many sexual hijinks, he claimed he made love to her under a tree in a park. A copy of *The Times* beneath them was opened to a rather prudish letter to the editor by the Victorian novelist Mrs. Humphry Ward.

He said he was attracted to Rebecca West, his lover for 10 years, by her "hard mind." She said he attracted her because he smelt of walnut.

The novelist invented a game called "Little Wars" that was inspired by a similar game Robert Louis Stevenson had invented and described in a magazine article. Complete with over 200 soldiers, hundreds of props, including little cannon that could fire wooden shells, the game was compulsory for anyone who arrived at the Wells's house while Wells was playing. "Sit down and keep your mouth shut," the novelist would order and assign the visitor to one side or another for a session that could last as long as 10 hours.

Wells first recorded, and perhaps invented, the word *extraterrestrial* as an adjective at the turn of the century. Meaning "outside the limits of the earth," the word was first used as a noun by American author L. Sprague de Camp in the May 1939 issue of *Astounding Science Fiction*, the author inventing the abbreviation *e.t.* in the same article. E.T. was used as the name of the extraterrestrial being in the popular film *E.T.* Wells may have patterned *extraterrestrial* on *extraterritorial*, which dates back to at least 1665.

Wells used the term "atomic bomb" in his science fiction story "The World Set Free," which he published in 1914—30 years before atomic bombs became a reality.

After Henry James published a patronizing piece about Wells in the *Times Literary Supplement*, Wells took the offensive. A novel by Henry James, he remarked, was like an empty church "with every light and line focused on the high altar. And on the altar, very reverently placed, intensely there, is a dead kitten, an eggshell, a bit of string."

He always carried two fountain pens in the pocket of his waistcoat. "The big one," he was once quoted as saying, "is for the long words, the little one for the short ones."

When a critic complained that his poetry lacked proper meter, Wells replied: "Meters are used for gas, not the outpourings of the human heart."

∇ ∇ ∇

John Wesley (1703–1791)
The prodigious Methodist preacher (he gave over 40,000 sermons) and hymn writer was as a baby saved from his father's burning office just before the roof caved in. He thought this a divine sign, and contemporary prints of him often

included the device of a house flaming, along with the biblical motto, "Is he not a brand plucked from the burning?"

"Once in seven years I burn all my sermons," he wrote in his *Journal*, "for it is a shame if I cannot write better sermons now than I did seven years ago."

∇ ∇ ∇

Rebecca West (Cecily Isabel Fairfield; 1892–1983)
"My legs have become very ugly," the novelist remarked in a late radio interview, "But then, what use would beautiful legs be to a woman of 85?" She went on writing with great vigor and panache until her death at over 90.

∇ ∇ ∇

William Whewell (1794–1866)
Queen Victoria was unaware that the River Cam in Cambridge was used as the town's sewer and on a visit there with Whewell asked about the large quantity of paper floating by. "All that paper, ma'am," the scientist and author explained diplomatically, "carries notices to inform visitors that the river is unfit for bathers."

∇ ∇ ∇

George Whitefield (1714–1770)
The popular evangelist, author and hymn writer was widely admired as a speaker, his voice so cultivated, it was said, "that he could make an audience either laugh or cry with his pronunciation of 'Mesopotamia.'" Dr. Johnson, however, said that he had "more familiarity and noise" than anything else.

∇ ∇ ∇

Samuel Wilberforce (1805–1873)
The first "Soapy Sam," Samuel Wilberforce, Bishop of Oxford and later Winchester, was a noncomforming and controversial clergyman and author if ever there was one. Wilberforce, son of the great antislavery leader William Wilberforce, tried to steer a middle course between High Church and Low Church factions in England. Although a devout man in his personal life, this position forced him to develop a suave, unctuous manner of speaking, persuasive but versatile and expedient almost to a fault. By 1860 he had earned the nickname Soapy Sam, which has since been applied to any slippery, unctuous speaker who can talk his way out of anything. The coining was perhaps given an assist by the initials "S.O.A.P." on the floral decorations above the stall where he preached—these standing for the names Sam Oxon and Alfred Port. Once

someone asked him about the nickname and he assured his questioner that he was called Soapy Sam "Because I am often in hot water and always come out with clean hands."

∇ ∇ ∇

Oscar Wilde (1854–1900)

In his student days Wilde attended a lecture by Walter Pater. The great scholar and man of letters was speaking in his usual whisper of a voice. "I hope you all heard me," Pater said to the group at lecture's end.

"We *over*heard you," Wilde responded.

When warden of New College, Reverend William A. Spooner reprimanded Oscar Wilde, then a student in his second year at Oxford, and as a punishment made him copy the 26th chapter of *Acts* in Greek. After he felt Wilde had worked long enough, Spooner told him to stop, but Wilde continued writing. "Did you hear me tell you, Mr. Wilde, that you needn't write anymore?" Spooner asked. "Oh, yes, I heard," Wilde replied, "but I was so interested in what I was copying that I could not leave off. It was all about a man named Paul, who went on a voyage and was caught in a terrible storm, and I was afraid that he would be drowned; but do you know, Mr. Spooner, he was saved; and when I found that he was saved, I thought of coming to tell you."

According to one acquaintance, Wilde looked "gigantic, smooth shaven and rosy, like a great priest of the moon." He scorned sport. One time he was asked if he ever took any exercise. "I am afraid I play no outdoor games at all," he replied. "Except dominoes. I have sometimes played dominoes outside French cafés."

Wilde was once asked to compile a list of the world's 100 best books. "I fear that would be impossible," he said, "I have written only five."

"Who am I to tamper with a masterpiece?" Wilde said when asked to make minor changes in one of his plays.

"A poet," he said, "can survive anything but a misprint."

Henry Arthur Jones was the most popular and one of the most prolific dramatists of the 1890s, but Wilde disliked his pamphleteering or perhaps considered this writer of comedies a too successful rival. In any case, he formulated these three rules of playwrighting: "The first rule for a young playwright to follow is not to write like Henry Arthur Jones...The second and third rules are the same."

Sir Lewis Morris, author of a volume of rather mediocre verse entitled *The Epic of Hades*, was complaining to Wilde about being ignored for the poet laureateship. "It is a complete conspiracy of silence against me—a conspiracy of silence!" he cried. "What ought I to do, Oscar?"

"Join it," Wilde replied.

Pshaw, an exclamation of impatience or contempt, is usually pronounced *shaw*. Oscar Wilde once asked George Bernard Shaw what title he'd give to a magazine he proposed starting. "I'd want to impress my own personality on the public," Shaw replied, banging his fist on the table. "I'd call it *Shaw's Magazine*. Shaw!—Shaw!—Shaw!"

"Yes," Wilde said, "*and how would you spell it?*"

Another time Wilde said of Shaw: "He hasn't an enemy in the world, and none of his friends like him!"

Wilde and a friend were discussing the work of Sir Thomas Hall Caine, Rossetti's great friend and the author of many sensational novels. "Mr. Hall Caine, it is true, aims at the grandiose," Wilde remarked, "but then he writes at the top of his voice. He is so loud that one cannot hear what he says."

James Payn, the English author and editor, had written 100 novels, all of which Wilde found obscure and inconsequential. "Mr. James Payn is an adept in the art of concealing what is not worth finding," he once observed.

In a letter to Robert Ross (1899), Wilde wrote, "Henry James is developing, but he will never arrive at passion, I fear."

Said Wilde of Henry James's extremely subtle, complex and sometimes almost obscure prose, "Mr. Henry James writes fiction as if it were a painful duty."

Wilde was asked if he knew the Irish novelist and poet George Moore. "Know him?" he replied, "I know him so well that I haven't spoken to him in ten years."

Sarah Bernhardt bested Wilde. Immediately after arguing with the actress about her intepretation of a role in one of his plays, Wilde took out a cigarette. "Do you mind if I smoke, madam?" he asked. "I don't care if you burn!" said the Divine Sarah.

Wilde so irritated the captain of the *Arizona*, on which he sailed to the United States for his lecture tour in 1881, that the captain later swore: "I wish I had had that man lashed to the bowsprit on the windward side."

A Chamber of Commerce type was giving Wilde a tour of Niagara Falls—the full treatment, complete with astounding statistics and breathless descriptions. When the man had finished, Wilde simply said, "It would be more impressive if it flowed the other way."

Someone in the audience got the better of Wilde when he spoke in Boston. "You're Philistines who have invaded the sacred sanctum of Art," Wilde told the audience.

"And you're driving us forth with the jawbone of an ass," that someone shouted back.

Members of Wilde's London club knew that his latest play had flopped, but tried to appear ignorant of the fact when the writer arrived late that evening.

"Oscar, how did your play go tonight?" asked one member.

"Oh," Wilde replied loftily, "the play was a great success but I'm afraid the audience was a failure."

"The difference between journalism and literature," he observed, "is that journalism is unreadable and literature is not read."

Wilde once confessed that he spent an entire morning pondering a line from which he finally took out a comma. However, he added, he put it back in by the end of the afternoon.

In order to ingratiate oneself with high society, he said, "one has either to feed people, amuse people, or shock people."

Summing up his impression of fox hunting, Wilde quipped. "It is the unspeakable in full pursuit of the uneatable."

The worst of Wilde is seen in his treatment of his loving wife, Constance. Wilde grew disgusted with her as she changed from a slim pretty girl to a heavy, "blotched" matron. One time he reportedly said that after kissing her, "I used to wash my mouth and open the window to cleanse my lips in the pure air."

Ironically, Wilde's accuser in his famous trial was the formulator of boxing's Queensberry rules, which are a synonym for fair play in sport or elsewhere. John

Sholto Douglas, or "Old Q." as the eighth marquis of Queensberry was known, was a patron of the turf notorious for his romantic escapades and dissolute life. John Douglas had served in the British army and navy before formulating his famous rules and sat in the House of Lords from 1872 to 1880. When he wrote his famous insulting letter to Oscar Wilde objecting to Wilde's homosexual relationship with his son, Lord Alfred Douglas, Wilde sued him for libel but, although he dropped the suit, the letter revealed information that led to the poet's conviction for "immoral conduct" later in 1895.

During the trial of the marquis of Queensberry for libel, Wilde denied that he had written the allegedly obscene story "The Priest and the Acolyte." "Was that story immoral?" he was asked by the court. "It was much worse than that," Wilde replied. "It was badly written."

At another point in Wilde's celebrated libel suit, the author made an irrelevant remark about his physician.

"Never mind your physician," said the lawyer cross-examining him.

"I never do," said Wilde archly.

"Oscar, do you think Marie Corelli is a great writer?" asked a friend visiting Wilde in jail.

"From the way she writes," Wilde replied, according to one version of the story, "she ought to be in here."

William Butler Yeats told a story of Wilde's visit to a Dieppe brothel with poet Ernest Dowson after Wilde's release from prison:

> Dowson impressed upon him the necessity of acquiring a more wholesome taste. They emptied their pockets onto the café table, and though there was not much, there was enough, if both heaps were put into one. Meanwhile the news had spread, and they set out accompanied by a cheering crowd. Arrived at their destination, Dowson and the crowd remained outside, and presently Wilde returned. He said in a low voice to Dowson, "The first in ten years, and it will be the last. It was like cold mutton..." and then aloud, so that the crowd might hear him, "But tell it in England, for it will entirely restore my character."

When one is surrounded by disciples, Wilde remarked toward the end, there is always a "Judas who writes the biography."

One of Wilde's last and best bon mots came while he lay dying in his seedy Paris hotel room, where he had registered as Sebastian Melmoth (the name of a wanderer in a gothic novel by his great-uncle Charles Maturin). His friend Robert

Ross was at his bedside when Wilde pointed at the garish walls surrounding him. "My wallpaper and I are fighting a duel to the death," he said. "One or another of us has to go."

Wilde's wit prevailed right to the end. In his final days, when a huge fee for an operation was mentioned, he said: "Ah, well, then I suppose I shall have to die beyond my means." It is said that as he lay dying, he called for champagne, saying in his last breath, "I am dying as I have lived, beyond my means."

∇ ∇ ∇

David Wilkens (fl. early 17th century)
Wilkens is said to be the author of the world's slowest selling book. Published in 1716 by the Oxford University Press, his translation of the New Testament from Coptic into Latin sold 500 copies in the 191 years it remained in print (until 1907), for an average of about two copies a year.

∇ ∇ ∇

John Wilkes (1727–1797)
The politician and author launched his career with an expedient marriage. Wrote the "merry, cockeyed, curious looking sprite" (as Byron described him) the morning after his wedding night: "I have made a sacrifice to Plutus, not to Venus."

John Montague, the fourth earl of Sandwich, for whom the sandwich was named—because he ate only sandwiches when he gambled for days on end—was Wilkes's mortal enemy. Under a *nom de débauche* Sandwich became a member of the notorious Hell-Fire Club, infamous for its wild orgies and black masses, but soon fell out with his friend, one of the club's founders. Wilkes had dressed a black baboon with horns and hoops and let him loose while Sandwich was invoking the devil during a black mass. The earl's embarrassment exceeded even his initial fright when he ran out of the chapel shouting, "Spare me, gracious Devil, I am as yet but half a sinner. I have never been as wicked as I intended!" The two became bitter enemies, but when Sandwich sought revenge before the House of Lords by reading Wilkes's indecent "Essay on Woman," a parody (now lost) on Pope's "Essay on Man," the strategy backfired. On that same day John Gay's *Beggar's Opera* happened to be playing in London and Sandwich became identified in the public's mind with the play's villain, the "despicable cad" who betrays the hero, and Sandwich's nickname became Jemmy Twitcher ever after.

When Wilkes was campaigning for a seat in Parliament, the opposition imported a boatload of voters from another district. Wilkes promptly bribed the ship's captain to deliver his cargo to Norway. Persistent he was. "I'd sooner vote for the devil than John Wilkes," a constituent once told him. "And what if your friend is not running?" Wilkes replied. But his most famous witticism, probably the most celebrated political putdown in history, made his onetime friend Lord Sandwich its victim. It appears that the earl had verbally attacked Wilkes, shouting, "You, Wilkes, will either die on the gallows or from syphilis!" Wilkes simply turned, tapped his snuffbox, and looked Sandwich full in the eye. "That depends, My Lord," he said, matter-of-factly, "on whether I embrace your principles or your mistress."

The reason Dr. Johnson made his famous remark "I'd rather dine with Jack Ketch [the public hangman] than John Wilkes" is seldom told. Wilkes had written a comic review of Johnson's *Dictionary* in which he addressed the great man's pronouncement that "The letter 'h' seldom, perhaps never, begins any but the first syllable." Wilkes wrote: "The author of this observation must be a man of quick apprehension and of most comprehensive genius," going on in the same fashion for several paragraphs. Johnson never forgave him.

Wilkes waited a long time to take revenge on the prince of Wales, who had taunted him at a party one evening by reciting Sheridan's verse "Johnny Wilkes, Johnny Wilkes, / You greatest of bilkes ..." His moment came at a Carlton House gathering, after Wilkes gave the toast, "The king; long life to him!" "Since when," the prince inquired, "have you been so anxious about my father's health?" Wilkes bowed graciously. "Since I have had the pleasure of Your Royal Highness's acquaintance," he replied.

The author's portrait adorned many signs hanging over London taverns, in honor of his support of the common man. On sighting several of these signs on a walk through London, an enemy of his remarked, "Wilkes swings everywhere but where he ought."

Poet Robert Southey credited him with remarking that in life "the chapter of accidents is the longest in the book."

Wilkes grew more cynical with each passing year, his philosophy perhaps best summed up in a couplet he wrote and circulated among his friends:

Life can little else supply
But a few good fucks and then we die.

Thomas Wirgman (fl. early 19th century)
There are a number of writers who have actually lost money writing books. Perhaps the biggest loser was author Thomas Wirgman, who spent the equivalent of more than $200,000 publishing a number of books in which each page was printed on paper of a different color. The books, including his *Grammar of Six Senses*, were all "complete gibberish," according to one critic, but then Wirgman cared only about the sequence of colors. Six copies of his many books were all that ever sold.

∇ ∇ ∇

George Wither (1588–1667)
When in 1622 the poet and pamphleteer published his tribute to his mistress, *Faire-Virtue, the mistress of Phil'arte* (Wither called himself Phil'arte), he dedicated the book of poems with the sentiment "To himselfe G.W. wisheth all happiness" and then proceeded to list seven reasons why he should have dedicated the book to himself instead of a patron.

∇ ∇ ∇

Sir P.G. (Pelham Grenville) Wodehouse (1881–1975)
A peppery old woman seated next to the novelist at a dinner raved about his books all evening, telling him that her sons never missed a book of his and that their rooms were filled with his novels. "And when I tell them" she finally said, "that I have actually been sitting at dinner, with Edgar Wallace, I don't know what they will say."

Though he became a naturalized American late in his life, Wodehouse is included in the volume because his work, and his butler Jeeves, are so quintessentially British. The humorist's *The Heart of a Goof* contains the most humorous dedication of his more than 120 books. It is dedicated to his daughter "without whose never-failing sympathy and encouragement this book would have been finished in half the time."

After he left William Randolph Hearst's estate San Simeon, where he had spent a week as a guest, Wodehouse wrote to a friend: "I sat on [Hearst's mistress Marion Davies's] right the first night, then found myself being edged further and further away till I got to the extreme end…Another day, and I should have been feeding on the floor."

After he and fellow guests at a party listened to an earnest young man's interminable discourse about the likelihood of nuclear warfare destroying the entire human race, Wodehouse was heard to murmur, "I can't wait."

Mary Wollstonecraft (1759–1797)

The author and mother of Mary Godwin, who wrote *Frankenstein* and became Shelley's second wife, did not believe in legal, state-sanctioned marriage and married William Godwin only for the sake of their expected child. Both were so ashamed of their legal marriage that they concealed it from their radical friends, pretending that they were still living as common-law partners. Mary died of septicemia 10 days after giving birth to her daughter.

∇ ∇ ∇

Virginia Woolf (1882–1941)

When he was the American ambassador to England, James Russell Lowell wrote verses welcoming his "Dear Little God-Daughter," Sir Leslie Stephen's daughter Virginia, hoping that she would prove "a sample of heredity." She became better known to the world as Virginia Woolf after her marriage to author Leonard Woolf in 1912.

She once wrote after rereading her previous year's diary: "I...am much struck by the rapid haphazard gallop at which it swings along, sometimes indeed jerking almost intolerably over the cobbles. Still, if it were not written rather faster than the fastest typewriting, if I stopped and took thought, it would never be written at all. The advantage of the method is that it sweeps up accidentally several stray matters which I should exclude if I hesitated, but which are the diamonds of the dustheap."

In 1910 Woolf and her wealthy friend Horace de Vere Cole perpetrated what came to be known as the *Dreadnought Hoax* when they donned the disguises of Abyssinian royalty in order to get aboard the famed warship *Dreadnought*. They were received with great honors by the captain of the vessel and given a grand tour of the ship.

On the publication of her *To the Lighthouse*, Lytton Strachey wrote to a mutual friend: "It is really most unfortunate that she rules out copulation—not the ghost of it visible—so that her presentation of things becomes little more...than an arabesque—an exquisite arabesque, of course."

She sent a copy of *To the Lighthouse* to Vita Sackville-West shortly after it was published in 1927. On reading the inscription "Vita from Virginia (In my opinion the best novel I have ever written)," Vita was surprised at her friend's immodesty, but later that night on opening the book, she found it was a dummy with blank pages.

The night that she heard of Arnold Bennett's death of typhoid in 1931 (*q.v.*), she wrote in her diary: "Queer how one regrets the dispersal of anybody...who had direct contact with life—for he abused me; and yet I rather wished him to go on abusing me, and me abusing him."

Author Alan Bennett made the following deadpan comment about Woolf: "Of all the honours that fell upon Virginia's head, none, I think, pleased her more than the *Evening Standard* award for the Tallest Woman Writer of 1927, an award she took by a neck from Elizabeth Bowen. And rightly, I think, for she was in a very real sense the tallest writer I have ever known. Which is not to say that her stories were tall. They were not. They were short. But she did stand head and shoulders over her contemporaries, and sometimes of course, much more so."

One afternoon Virginia Woolf called through the sitting room window to her husband Leonard, who was planting iris beneath an apple tree, to come quickly as Hitler was making a speech on the radio. "I shan't come," he shouted back. I'm planting iris, and they will be flowering long after he is dead."

When she committed suicide by walking into the River Ouse, she left the following note for her husband: "I have a feeling I shall go mad. I cannot go on longer in these terrible times. I hear voices and cannot concentrate on my work. I have fought against it but cannot fight any longer. I owe all my happiness to you but cannot go on and spoil your life."

▽ ▽ ▽

William Wordsworth (1770–1850)

"Wordsworth," recalled his friend Henry Crabb Robinson, an indefatigable reporter, "said he would shed his blood, if necessary, to defend the Established Church. Nor was he disconcerted by a laugh raised against him on account of his having before confessed that he knew not when he had been in a church in his own country."

He was not a witty man and usually knew it. In fact, he had some difficulty recognizing what was wit and what wasn't. One time he confided to company that he had made only one witty remark in his entire life. What was that, he was asked. "Well, I will tell you," he replied. "I was standing some time ago at the entrance of my cottage at Rydal Mount. A man accosted me with a question—'Pray, sir, have you seen my wife pass by?'; whereupon I said, 'Why, my good friend, I didn't know till this moment that you had a wife!'" While he roared with laughter the company stood in puzzled silence.

Sometimes when he was writing a poem, Wordsworth would let his dog criticize his work. Walking in the garden, reciting lines as he composed them, the poet carefully watched his canine-critic. He felt that if the rhythm was wrong, if he'd chosen a cacophonous word, the dog-critic's hackles would rise and he'd voice his disapproval by barking.

Said his friend Coleridge to him: "Since Milton, I know of no poet with so many *felicities* and unforgettable lines and stanzas as you."

When his *The Excursion, Being a Portion of the Recluse, a Poem* (1814) was published at two guineas a copy, he refused to lend it to a rich woman who complained to him that he was charging too much for "part of a work."

In a letter to Lady Beaumont he asserted: "Every great and original writer, in proportion as he is great and original, must himself create the taste by which he is to be relished."

Writing to a young De Quincy, who had solicited his friendship, he explained: "My friendship is not in my power to give; this is a gift which no man can make...A sound and healthy friendship is the growth of time and circumstance; it will spring up like a wildflower when these favour and when they do not it is in vain to look for it."

The painter Benjamin Haydon recalled in a letter Wordsworth's visit to Christie's and the poet's reaction to statues he saw there that depicted Cupid and Psyche kissing: "Cupid is taking her [Psyche's] lovely chin, and turning her pouting mouth to meet his while he archly bends his own down, as if saying, 'Pretty dear!'...Catching sight of the Cupid, as he and I were coming out, Wordsworth's face reddened, he showed his teeth and then said in a loud voice, 'THE DEV-V-V-VILS!'"

He and his wife, Mary, cared for his beloved sister Dorothy for the last 20 years of life. Dorothy had lost her mind as a result of physical ailments and could do nothing but sit, helpless, by the fire. Almost all her memory was destroyed, but she could still recite her brother's poems.

The philosopher Bertrand Russell summed up the poet's career: "In his youth Wordsworth sympathized with the French Revolution, went to France, wrote good poetry, and had a natural daughter. At this period he was called a 'bad' man. Then he became 'good,' abandoned his daughter, adopted correct principles, and wrote bad poetry."

Sir Henry Wotton (1568–1639)

The poet was knighted by James I after he advised the monarch of a plot to assassinate him, intelligence he had gathered while working as a spy in Italy for the earl of Essex. In 1604 James appointed him ambassador to Venice, where he spent most of the next 20 years. It was while visiting his friend Christopher Flecamore in Augsburg that Wotton wrote in his host's album his famous definition of an ambassador, which translates from the Latin as: "An ambassador is an honest man sent to lie abroad for the good of his country." When James learned of his witticism he was not amused, but Wotton managed to wheedle his way back into the king's favor.

∇ ∇ ∇

William Wycherley (1641–1716)

The prologue of Wycherley's *The Country Wife* (1673), which was attacked for obscenity in its time but is actually a satiric attack on sexual hypocrisy, invites anyone in the audience who dislikes the play to come at the end to the actors' dressing room where they would "patiently...give up to you/Our poets, virgins, nay, our mistresses too."

While in a Bath bookshop, Wycherley was pleased to hear a woman ask for a copy of his play *The Plain Dealer*. "Here's the plain dealer, madam, if you want him," a friend said, pushing him into her arms, and after Wycherley apologized, the woman assured him, "I love plain dealing best." She turned out to be the wealthy countess of Drogheda, and Wycherley courted and married her, as a result losing all King Charles's patronage. His wife proved pathologically jealous and followed the playwright everywhere. When she did allow him to meet alone with his friends it was in a tavern next to their house, where summer or winter he was made to sit with the window open and the blinds up so that she could see that no women were present. When his wife suddenly died a year or so after their marriage, Wycherley thought his problems were over, that he had inherited her fortune, and he ran up huge debts which he could not repay when he found that creditors would take all of the countess's money. He spent a full seven years in jail before James II, pleased with a manly character he thought to resemble him in *The Plain Dealer*, paid off his debts and settled a pension on him.

The beautiful Barbara Villiers, the duchess of Cleveland and Charles II's mistress, saw Wycherley driving by in a coach. Knowing he had in his play *Love in a Wood* written that great wits always have whores for mothers ("When parents are slaves/Their brats cannot be any other./Great wits and great lovers/Have always a punk to their mother."), the celebrated beauty shouted out, laughing,

"You, Wycherley, you are a son of a whore!" Wycherley, much pleased, overtook her carriage, and asked her if she would attend his play that night, vowing that he'd like to meet her there, even though, "I disappoint a very fine woman who has made me an assignation." "You would disappoint a woman who has favored you for one who has not?" the duchess asked. "Yes," replied Wycherley, "if she who has not favored me is the finer woman of the two. But he who will be constant to your ladyship till he can find a finer woman is sure to die your captive." The blushing duchess came to meet him, commencing one of the most famous affairs of the day.

It is said that Wycherley continued "chasing women beyond his capacity into a bad old age." His last amorous adventure may have been undertaken out of spite, in order to thwart his nephew, the next in line to his family property. In any case, at the age of 75 he married a 20-year-old girl. All the excitement proved too much for him and he died 10 days later.

∇ ∇ ∇

John Wyclif (1320?–1384)
The great religious reformer and author of the Wyclif Bible died of a stroke he suffered while attending mass and was buried in Lutterworth. But some 30 years later, in 1415, the council of Constance decreed that his bones be cast up and throw into a nearby stream and all of his writings burned.

∇ ∇ ∇ ∇ ∇ ∇ ∇ ∇

X.Y.Z.
Back in the late 19th century a writer using the pseudonym X.Y.Z. frequently advertised in the *Times* of London offering to do any kind of literary work for low wages. As a result his pen name became synonymous for "a hack of all work."

∇ ∇ ∇ ∇ ∇ ∇ ∇ ∇

William Butler Yeats (1865–1939)

The Irish poet departed the everyday world when he was working. While staying at Stone Cottage in Sussex in late December 1913, he took a walk one morning to the village post office. Finding it closed, he returned home in a rage. "But, Mr. Yeats," his housekeeper told him, "don't you know it's Christmas Day!"

His son Michael Yeats says that the poet drifted to another world while working on a poem: "He'd make a low, tuneless hum and his hand would start beating time. We knew then to creep away and leave him alone. He was oblivious to everything else. Once he was on the bus from Dublin and my sister, Anne, got on. She saw he was busy, so she sat by herself. When they got out at our gate, he looked at her vaguely and said, 'Oh, who is it you wish to see?'"

Though an eminently sane bard, Yeats was considered balmy by some as he strode alone the streets of Dublin "mouthing poetry…swinging his arms like a flail, unconscious of the alarm and bewilderment of the passersby." But, as Irish poet Katherine Tynan wrote, even the Dublin policemen eventually go used to him, saying "Shure, 'tisn't mad he is, nor yet drink taken. 'Tis the poethry that's disturbing his head," and left him alone.

"Poets should never marry," Maud Gonne wrote to him early in his career. "The world should thank me for not marrying you."

After living at Oxford in the early 1920s, Yeats let his house "in the Broad…to some American girl students." Writing to a friend he told the following story: "In the middle of the night Alan Porter [later the editor or sub-editor of the *Spectator*] climbed through the window. He was welcomed but found to be impotent. He explained [to the girl] that he had a great friend and when that friend had tired of a girl [he, Porter] had always taken her for himself. If he found a girl for himself he was impotent. The student said fetch your friend. He did. And after that all went well…"

"How are you?" he was asked one morning.
"Not very well," he replied. "I can only write prose today."
Another time he confided that he had done an excellent morning's work. He had written four lines of poetry and destroyed them.

Mrs. Pat Campbell, playing in Yeats's *Deirdre,* was throwing one of her usual tantrums at rehearsal when she spied Yeats pacing back and forth in an aisle of the Abbey Threatre. "I'd give anything to know what you're thinking!" she shouted at him.

"I'm thinking," Yeats replied, "of the master of a wayside Indian railway-station who sent a message to his company's headquarters saying, 'Tigress on the line: wire instructions.'"

While discussing the poetry of James Reed, he observed: "Too true, too sincere. The muse prefers the liars, the gay and warty lads."

When almost 69, Yeats found himself impotent sexually and believed that his condition had prevented him from writing anything new for several years. He decided to have an operation developed by Austrian physiologist Eugen Steinach which was in reality what we now call a vasectomy but was then believed to increase the production of the male hormone and restore potency. Though the operation failed to make any physical difference—Yeats would never have an erection again—the poet felt that he was mentally rejuvenated. He resumed writing poetry and, despite his limitations, was sexually intimate with several women during the last five years of his life.

"Sometimes he'd tear up things [poems]," his son recalled, "and throw them in the wastebasket. But my mother would rescue them and tape them and put them in files so they could be read nowadays by scholars."

Yeats came from a line of long-lived people (his father lived till 83 and his brother till 86). According to the poet's son, when the doctors advised Yeats that he had only about three more years to live, the poet told his wife, "I am disgracing the family by dying so young."

∇ ∇ ∇

Thomas Young (1773–1829)
Young was a scientist, physician and historian of medicine. Called "one of the most clearsighted men who ever lived," he gave the first descriptions of blood pressure, astigmatism and tides, and helped to decipher the Rosetta Stone. A child prodigy who had read the Bible twice by the time he was four, he knew 14 languages by the time he was 14.

∇ ∇ ∇

William Young (1702–1757)
Reverend Young, who collaborated with Henry Fielding in translating Aristophanes, was so absentminded that as an army chaplain he crossed over the enemy lines and had to be pointed back to his own forces. Another story has him writing a letter to himself. Fielding later based Parson Adams in *Joseph Andrews* (1742) upon him, though Young vehemently denied this.

Israel Zangwill (1864–1926)

America humorist Harry Golden told this story of Zangwill, who coined the expression "melting pot." It seems that the novelist once had to address an audience of influential Jews at London's Albert Hall, and many of them were furious because he had married a Gentile, Edith Ayrton. But Zangwill rose to the occasion. "Gentlemen," he began, "I know some of you are displeased because I married a Gentile. Yet I trust you will treat my new wife with ultimate courtesy. She deserves your respect, for she married a Jew."

"Mind your Jewish manners, I thought you were going to swallow me," said a woman sitting next to Zangwill at dinner when he yawned loudly. "Have no fear," replied the novelist. "My religion prohibits my doing that."

INDEX

Boldface type indicates main entry.

A

Abercrombie, Lascelles 1
Absentmindedness: of Bowles 27; of Campbell 44; of Disraeli 91; of Newton 199; of Smith, Adam 256; of Smith, Sydney 259; of Swinburne 275; of Tennyson 276; of Young 311-312
Accoramboni, Vittoria 295
According to Cocker (proverb) 60
Account of the Greatest English Poets (book) 234
Account of the Growth of Popery and Arbitrary Government in England, An (book) 182
Actors & Acting: Betterton on 22; Coward and 70; Hughes and 135; Shaw and 239; Sheridan on 248; Yeats and 310-311
Adams, Maude 13
Addison, Joseph 1, 34, 234, 266, 290
Admirable Crichton, The (play) 72
Adultery 48, 185, 222, 231—*See also Mistresses*
AE.—*See Russell, George William*
Afterlife—*See Heaven & Hell*
Agents, Literary 293
Ainsworth, Robert 2
Alaska (ship) 24
Albert, Prince (Great Britain) 92
Alchemy 199
Alcibiades (play) 201
Alcohol & Alcoholism: of Boyse 27; of Crabbe 71; Croll and 73; of Denham 83; Disraeli and 91; of Foote 103; of Hobbes 129; Hulme and 135; Johnson on 147; of Lowry 176; Mitford and 189; O'Carolan on 200; Porson and 211; of Rochester 219; Russell on 1; Shakespeare and 236; of Sheridan 251; of Smart 255; of Swinburne 275; of Thomas 281
Aldington, Richard 2
Aldrich, Robert 69
Alexander III, King (Scotland) 280
Alfred the Great, King (England) 2-3, 102
Alice in Wonderland (book) 48
Alligators 70
All the Year Round (magazine) 86
Ambassadors, The (book) 140
Ambient, Mark 275
Amelia (book) 185

American Revolution 3
Amner, Richard 269
Amnesia 52
Amours of Philander and Sylvia, The (book) 18
Anatomical Treatise on the Movement of the Heart and Blood in Animals, An (book) 124-125
Anatomy of Melancholy, The (book) 38
Ancient of Days (poem) 24
Andre, John 3
Anecdotes and Adventures of Fifteen Gentlemen, The (book) 171
Angry Penguins (journal) 179
Animals—*See specific animal*
Annals of Agriculture (book) 109
Anna Tellwright (book) 19
Anne I, Queen (Great Britain) 82
Annie Laurie (song) 93
Anonymous 3-4
Anstey, Christopher 5
Apolonius and Silla (book) 216
Appeal to the Parliament, An: or Sion's Plea Against the Prelacie (pamphlet) 172
Appius and Virginia (play) 84
Appleton's Cyclopedia of American Biography (encyclopedia) 17
Arabian Nights (book) 37, 61
Aram, Eugene 5
Arbuthnot, John 75
Arcadia (poem) 127, 254
Archer, William 5
Archives—*See Libraries*
Arctic (ship) 278
Arden, Eden (fictional character) 278
Areopagitica (pamphlet) 188
Ariel (schooner) 245
Aristophanes 311
Aristotle 227
Arithmetica integra (book) 216
Arithmetical Books (book) 60
Arizona (ship) 300
Armadillo 222
Armour, Jean 37
Arnold, Benedict 3
Arnold, Matthew 5-6, 32, 91, 269
Art of Cooking Made Plain and Easy, The (book) 112
Art of Seeing, The (book) 138
Asche, Oscar 6
Ash, John 6
Ashford, Daisy 6
Asquith, Margot (Countess of Oxford and Asquith) 7
Astor, Nancy Witcher (Viscountess of Astor) 7, 240
Astounding Science Fiction (magazine) 296
Atheism 116, 184
Attlee, Clement 56

Aubrey, John: on Beaumont/Fletcher 16; on Colet 65; on Digby 88; on Herbert 128; on Hobbes 130; on Marvell 182; on Milton 188-189; on More 194; on Oxford 203; on Petty 206; on Prynne 213; on Raleigh 214; on Rochester 219; on Shakespeare 231; on Sidney 254-255
Auden, W(ystan) H(ugh) 7, 184
Austen, Anna 8
Austen, J. Edward 8
Austen, Jane 7-9
Austin, Alfred 9
Author Hunting (book) 216
Author of Beltraffo, The (book) 275
Autobiography and Journals (book) 199
Autograph of William Shakespeare...together with 4000 ways of spelling the name (book) 231
Ayer, Sir Alfred 184
Ayrton, Edith 312

B

Babbage, Charles 277
Backgammon 144
Bacon, Francis 9-11, 125, 231
Bagnold, Enid 11
Bailey, Benjamin 160
Baillie, Joanna 11
Baillie, Matthew 11
Baker, Betsy 292
Balboa, Vasco Nunez de 160
Balder (poem) 92
Baldwin, Stanley 76
Baldwin, William 12
Bales, Peter 12
Balfour, Arthur James 7
Ballads Founded on Anecdotes of Animals (book) 23
Balzac, Honore de 146, 196
Banting, William 12
Bantingism (book) 12
Baring, Maurice 15
Barker, Robert 12-13
Barnacle, Nora 158, 160
Barnacles 78
Barnes, Barnabe 13
Barrie, J(ames) M(atthew) 6, 13-15, 52, 72, 133
Barrington, George 15
Barrow, Isaac 15
Barry, Elizabeth 218
Barton, Bernard 168
Bates, Dr. William 138
Battle of Abu Klea, The (poem) 184
Beach, Sylvia 159, 241
Beagle (ship) 77
Beaton, Cecil 271
Beattie, James 165
Beaumont, Francis 16, 161
Beaumont, Lady 307
Beaux' Strategem, The (play) 100